THE EUROPEAN SPORTS HISTORY REVIEW

Volume 3

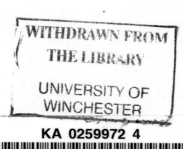

Editors and Advisers

Executive Academic Editor

J.A. Mangan
University of Strathclyde

EDITORIAL BOARD

Pieces appearing in this collection are abstracted and indexed in *Political Science Abstracts*, *Historical Abstracts and America: History and Life* and *Physical Education Index*

THE EUROPEAN SPORTS HISTORY REVIEW

Volume 3

EUROPE, SPORT, WORLD
Shaping Global Societies

Editor

J.A. Mangan
University of Strathclyde

FRANK CASS
LONDON • PORTLAND, OR

First published in 2001 in Great Britain by
FRANK CASS PUBLISHERS
Crown House, 47 Chase Side
London N14 5BP

and in the United States of America by
FRANK CASS PUBLISHERS
c/o ISBS, 5824 N.E. Hassalo Street
Portland, Oregon 97213-3644

Website: www.frankcass.com

British Library Cataloguing in Publication Data

Europe, sport, world : shaping global societies. –
(European sports history review ; v. 3)
1.Sports – Sociological aspects
I.Mangan, J. A. (James Anthony), 1939– II.The European
Sports History Review
306.4'83

ISBN 0-7146-5147 8 (cloth)
ISBN 0-7146-8171 7 (paper)
ISSN 1462-1495

Library of Congress Cataloging-in-Publication Data

Applied for.

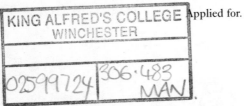
Printed in Great Britain by
Antony Rowe Ltd, Chippenham, Wilts

Contents

Prologue: Imperialism, Sport, Globalization

J.A. MANGAN

In *Mozart and the Enlightenment*, Nicholas Till writes of the interpretative problems raised by Mozart's operas – the result of apparent contradictions between content and style, ambiguities of tone and uncertainties of emphasis. The creative interpreter learns to prospect for meanings.[1] They do not lie on the surface. Mozart's contradictions exist beyond the operas in the contradictions of the real world of historical action, intellectual theory and biographical inspiration.

In this world there was one *overriding* contradiction. The Enlightenment mind might have been in no doubt as to where the spectre of chaos came from, namely medievalism, but in reality, it was the consequence of its own times: 'capitalism, and the demand for individualism and freedom it brought in its wake, were, ... inimical to social order. In order to survive and flourish a successful capitalist society needed to establish alternative sources of social authority that would guarantee stability without threatening the liberties upon which it depended.'[2] The Enlightenment found itself 'forced to confront the problem of how to ensure that the progress it espoused did not outrun the social cohesion it longed for'.[3] Enlightenment attempts to resolve this problem were painful and led to political polarization with confrontation between bourgeois individualism and the monarchal state.[4]

Till then makes the most interesting of observations: '*Around this essential dilemma turns much of modern history.*'[5]

This confrontation between individualism and authoritarianism too, of course, has been a dilemma of modern sport – and is to no little degree, if at some remove, the outcome of the Enlightenment experimentation with early capitalism.[6]

Europe in the period of nineteenth-century imperial expansion, experienced, if it did not adequately confront, the same problem: the reconciliation of progress and cohesion. The nineteenth century was the European century. Europe exported its politics, goods, ideas, customs –

and not least, its sports, to the rest of the world. Its sports, sometimes hugely disruptive,[7] were variously received: assimilated, to a lesser or greater degree, imitated likewise, occasionally resisted and certainly adapted to local talents, preferences, needs and possibilities. With Britain as the foremost European imperial nation, and England as the birthplace of several significant modern sports, the British Empire led the way in this hugely significant export of modern sport.

Within the Empire 'Anglo-Saxon' sport served as a cultural bond, moral metaphor and political symbol. At the same time in colony and dominion, it also served as a stimulus to independent assertion, the promotion of alternative sports, the striving for separate identity and the elevation of national status.

The export of European sport in this *first phase* of globalization is an extraordinary story of cultural diffusion with obvious and massive consequences for the twenty-first century that need no explanation here, but it is not, of course, the whole story. In the late nineteenth century the Orient accepted the sport of both Europe *and* the United States. This is true, too, of Latin America. And as the twentieth century progressed this became increasingly true also of the rest of the world.

The sports of Europe and the United States became the 'property' of newly enthusiastic nations who, having hitched themselves to the globalization wagon,[8] cherished and polished them, on occasion made better use of them and certainly made them their own. The result was that European sports became one part of the culture of a global society embracing nations as disparate as Afghanistan and Australia, while spin-off derivatives and new creations, mostly from the United States, became another part of the global culture.

In many places, as a result some local sports expired while some survived.

To add intricacy to intricacy, within Europe needless to say, shared enthusiasm for, and general appreciation of, Anglo-Saxon initiatives and influences were never to be taken for granted. Europe is hardly renowned for its internal harmony – in politics, culture or in sport. Nor was there always harmony among its mainland nations. Continental Europeans can be as exasperated by each other as by the English, and as much on the sports field and in the sports arena as elsewhere. For many years the Soviet Union and some of its satrapes peddled globally their own political brand of sport. Furthermore, European and American sports served to advance political antagonism between nations on other continents who took them for themselves. The globalization of sport as a result initially of Occidental initiatives and global responses had, and has, therefore, its advantages *and* disadvantages.

Globalization, of course, has been a process of considerable complexity. Its origins, arguably, were the least complex part of the process but this is not to say they too were not complex. Sports from other parts of the world entered Europe as soon as the world beyond Europe became known to Europeans. The global society witnessed 'to and fro' cultural diffusion. In consequence, the post-millennium global sports culture is neither narrowly monolithic nor is it exclusively the property of East or West. It is also no longer largely the protected preserve of the privileged.

Globalization, too, stimulated the resuscitation, even the recreation, of folk sports in national efforts to be both ostentatiously cosmopolitan *and* idiosyncratically individual. In a sentence, the urge to be different was stimulated by the prospect of uniformity. In terms of idiosyncrasy, there is also the matter of extremism in sport in the wake of the rebirth of Islamic fundamentalism.

However, the possibilities of diversity should not be exaggerated. There is an inexorable momentum towards a global monoculture driven by modern manifestations – among them advanced technology, sophisticated marketing, the mass media and even international sports studies. What is important is to recognize that this momentum began with European imperialism. In the thoughtful words of Edward Said, the globalization process was set in motion by modern imperialism:[9] 'partly because of empire, all cultures are involved in one another',[10] not least, in modern forms of entrepreneurial standardization 'under the sign of King Money'[11] with all its contemporary consequences for sport. It is not necessary to resort to convoluted expressions like 'non-isomorphic patterns', or 'national habitus codes' to appreciate this.[12] In fact, it may well be easier to appreciate it by avoiding such pretentious and polysyllabic extravagances![13]

What will be fascinating in future decades will be specific sectional, national and regional cultural adaptations to a *second phase* of globalization in the manner of the response to the *first phase* innovations of Europe and America. Possibly this could be among the most interesting responses to global sport in the global society of the third millennium.

The penultimate 'word' should be Nicholas Till's:

> People living in societies undergoing the fundamental transition from closed, customary and religious patterns of organisation to more open, individualistic, relativistic and secular systems experience with special intensity humankind's ... universal ... sense of a lost past in which order, wholeness and certainty prevailed. It is in these periods that the characteristic modern experiences of

deracination, alienation and doubt arise, and in which people seek new certainties of truth, virtue and beauty.

Global sport, successful and secular, and, in many ways, a replacement for religion, has a long way to go before it fully meets humankind's poignant needs! Despite this, its influence is now self-evidently enormous. Today, across the world, in the emerging global society even with its manifest and multiple differences, to adapt the words of two contemporary historians, sport (they wrote 'history'):

> saturates our lives; it informs our understanding of the world – not just in school or college textbooks, but in newspapers, magazines, films, radio and television; it colours our understanding of the built environment, and of the natural landscape too; it shapes our opinions about people – and peoples – about nations, societies, communities, individuals; it gives us ways of thinking about politics and about religion, about war and about culture.[14]

This is the measure of its importance. For this reason, its consideration in academia can only grow. Small wonder in some countries that it is now an expanding part of secondary school studies. In academia it has come a long way in a short time; it will go much further yet. The mote has been removed from many academic eyes!

In *Europe, Sport, World* only a small part of the saga of shaping the global sports society is recounted but in all cases, the stories here have not been told before in this form nor in a single collection. Here is its originality.

NOTES

1. Nicholas Till, *Mozart and the Enlightenment* (London: Faber and Faber), pp.ix–x.
2. Ibid., pp.2–3.
3. Ibid.
4. Ibid.
5. Ibid.
6. This is nowhere better discussed than in Dong Jinxia, 'Holding Up More than Half the Sky: Elite Sport, Women and Society in New China' (unpublished Ph.D. thesis, International Research Centre for Sport, Socialisation and Society, University of Strathclyde, 2001).
7. See, for example, J. A. Mangan, *The Games Ethic and Imperialism: Aspects of the Diffusion of an Ideal* (London and Portland, OR: Frank Cass, 1999), *passim*.
8. Marc Ferro, *Colonisation: A Global History* (London: Routledge, 1997), p.349 (emphasis added).
9. Edward W. Said, *Culture and Imperialism* (London: Knopf, 1993).
10. Ibid.
11. Ferro, *Colonisation*, p.360.
12. This ungainly and unhelpful jargon is used too frequently by the sports sociologist. It is a case of the more simple the idea the more obscure the language.
13. Till, *Mozart and the Enlightenment*, p.6.
14. Juliet Gardiner and Neil Wenborn, *The History Today Companion to British History* (London: Edlins and Brown, 1995), p.i.

Reconstructing the Fatherland: German *Turnen* in Southern Brazil

LEOMAR TESCHE and ARTUR BLASIO RAMBO

GERMAN EXPANSION AND IDENTITY CONSTRUCTION IN BRAZIL

This chapter deals with the local adaptation of the German *Turnen* Movement in southern Brazil from the mid-nineteenth century until the Second World War. The cultural migration of *Turnen* is prefaced by a short description of German immigration into southern Brazil[1] – one of the most important land movements in nineteenth-century South America – and involves a detailed analysis of documents associated with sample institutions of the period.

When the German immigrants established themselves in the southern states of Brazil in 1824, they began in the area, the development of a cultural, social, economic and religious community model that was absolutely new to the country. The imperial government allocated them large areas covered by rain forests in the states of Rio Grande do Sul, Santa Catarina and Paraná. The delay in demarcating the plots, the failure to meet government promises to the immigrants, the lack of support, the administrative authorities' inadequacies, the alien social environment, the hostility of the wilderness, the lack of knowledge of how to deal with the forest, and consequent difficulties in mastering the arable soil, made their first two decades of development very hard. They were left to their own devices and the success or failure of the migrants' enterprise depended entirely on themselves. They had emigrated with a firm determination not to go back to Germany, but they did not turn their backs fully on the past. They had to draw on their own cultural Germanic traditions to avoid disaster.

After the first shelters had been built, the first section of forest had been cleared and the first sowing completed, they set about establishing the basics of social organization. In time they created well-organized communities. Their priorities were the maintenance of their religion and the provision of a basic education for their children. The typical Brazilian German community lived around church, school, commerce and craftsmanship. It represented the model of a community structure that would become the pattern for all German communities in this southern part of Brazil. There it reproduced, sensibly adapted to local circumstances, the communities of the fatherland. Church (or chapel) and school were at the heart of community life. Churches or chapels representing diverse Christian sects were built in the community. In the church school religious principles, reading, writing, arithmetic, history, geography, nature studies and singing were taught. The school had the responsibility of ensuring that any deculturation of the first generations of German descendants born in Brazil did not occur. Generally speaking, the immigrant did not invent anything new for living and surviving in this novel situation, merely transplanting the lifestyle of his native Germany to the south of Brazil, without incorporating any major alterations. This state of affairs is widely recognized in studies of German existence in southern Brazil. With regard to sport a similar state of affairs characterized its evolution in this new land. By the 1850s the consolidation of the colonization process had begun among the German immigrants of Rio Grande do Sul. Businessmen, workers and craftsmen now made up the urban German communities in the state capital and in the emerging urban centres in the interior. It was high time to put into practice the means of preserving an unequivocal German identity. Many societies, clubs and associations with the aim of promoting Germanic culture were founded, and newspapers, almanacs and periodicals began to circulate. Initially these newspapers, almanacs and periodicals were their main instruments of ensuring the continuation of a German identity.

The major purpose of this cultural apparatus was to maintain the immigrants' and their descendants' teutonic identity in the new country and at the same time adapt it successfully to the new circumstances. Community schools throughout the colonies were largely responsible for the success of this enterprise in partnership with religious groups and related organizations involved in intense cultural activity.

If the preservation of German identity motivated the immigrants and their descendants, there was also a deep interest on the part of the German government, disseminators of German nationalism, to turn pan-German identity into a social, cultural and political reality worldwide when pan-Germanism[2] began to win supporters at the end of the nineteenth and the beginning of the early twentieth centuries. The dream was of a greater Germany inhabited by 100 million people including the Diaspora Germans. Preservation of German identity, at least in its essence then, was the joint motivation of the German state and the 'Brazilian' Germany in order to make them one with some 100 million Germans.

Among the plethora of pedagogical instruments at the service of this enterprise, mostly in the urban communities and their schools, *Turnen* – gymnastics and physical exercises – as it had been created and developed by Ludwig Friedrich Jahn and C.F. GutsMuths[3] would take priority, since it allowed the body to transcend its mere physical existence by conferring on it a social, cultural and political meaning.

EDUCATION AND GERMAN IDENTITY

Historical, social and pedagogical events in Germany in the nineteenth century, of course, determined the nature of *Turnen*. The ideas of Jahn, GutsMuths and Adolf Spiess[4] that linked the body, discipline, military training, nationalism and Germanism, represented by *Turnen* became an important source of German national identity.

In Brazil, specifically in Rio Grande do Sul, the isolation of the German immigrants and their descendants kept alive *Turnen* pedagogical principles through religious practice, cultural and linguistic habits, and social and pedagogical emphases. According to F. Altmann,[5] a student of this manifestation of cultural diasporic identity, hard though their lives were, the settlers did not fail to find time for leisure.[6] Singing, target shooting and gymnastics societies were early creations. The immigrants had a free hand to organize their own lives – and they organized them along the lines of past European practice. One migrant wrote to her relatives in Germany and the United States, 'We have lived in the Brazilian forest as little kings, freely and independently. The government neither helps us or hinders us.' In these conditions of indifference, in German-Brazilian schools *Turnen* became a deliberate means of ethnic identity preservation. Gymnastic Societies adopted the same approach thus reinforcing the schools in their efforts. The German immigrants were greatly concerned that their schools and clubs recreated, and thus maintained, the cultural customs of their former homeland in order that their descendants received an education that bridged the old and new worlds and maintained the security of cultural continuity.

In the pages that follow, the earliest leading schools associated with different groups that used sport, and in particular *Turnen*, to preserve a German identity in Rio Grande do Sul will receive close consideration. In addition, a typical Gymnastics Society of the Rio Grande do Sul area will also be considered – the Porto Alegre Gymnastics Society, founded in 1867 – in order to compare and constrast school and club in their respective approaches to *Turnen* as a mechanism of identity preservation. The period of analysis is from 1852 to 1942. These institutions were identified with distinct religious sects – the Brummers, Lutherans and Catholics. There was not always complete agreement between the various cultural groups (especially the religious ones) seeking to maintain a German identity despite widespread agreement concerning the importance of *Turnen*, physical education and education. The Brummers[7] were agnostics and there were disagreements, sometimes explicit, between these liberals, who arrived in 1852 and the conservative Lutherans and Catholics. The Brummers applied the ideas of GutsMuths and Jahn only to the gymnastics societies (*Turnverein*), while the Lutherans utilized them, with some of Spiess's ideas, in their schools. The Catholics, however, chose to follow the guidelines of Colégio Pedro II, Rio de Janeiro, and although they included gymnastics in their curricula, their emphasis on it was less pronounced.

THE DEUTSCHER HILFSVEREIN – COLÉGIO FARROUPILHA

As mentioned previously, the Germans brought with them their culture, practices, language, love for the distant homeland and nationalistic sentiments. They attempted to make the new environment a pleasant and familiar place to live in, pass on their Germanic culture to their descendants and share these attributes with fellow immigrants in a novel situation and novel circumstances. The Deutscher Hilfsverein represents one such attempt.

The Deutscher Hilfsverein – German Mutual Society – was established in 1853.[8] Its first educational classes were held in the buildings of the Porto Alegre Protestant Community. This location was called Knabenschule des Deutschen Hilfsverein – the German Mutual

Society Boys' School. It was the basis for the future Colégio Farroupilha founded in March 1886.

The foundation of the nationalist society, Germânia,[9] in 1855, which aimed at 'cultivating the memories of the old country, preserving the language, the way of being and German habits, through art and sociability', was of major importance to the Hilfsverein. The Hilfsverein, as mentioned earlier, was a mutual society, created to offer support to those Germans whose enterprises had failed. It had among its founders ten Brummers, who were called 'Sauerteig der deutschen Kolonie' (the yeast of the German colony). Most of the founding partners, however, were Lutherans who belonged to the Masonic Temple.[10] The Hilfsverein was thus the outcome of the efforts of different sections of the German community.

According to Leandro Telles,[11] 'Rationalism[12] predominated in the Protestant communities, influenced mainly by the Brummers, who constituted their "thinking heads".' Their church style and interior decoration were strongly influenced by Rationalism (*Auflärung*). Several Protestant churches in the hinterland of the state (in Nova Petrópolis, for example) and also one in Rio de Janeiro, still maintain the '*Aufklärung*' heritage, brought from Europe by the German immigrants in the nineteenth century, to Porto Alegre, and maintained energetically and proudly by the Brummers.[13]

In 1876, the board of directors, both of the Protestant community[14] and the Hilfsverein, belonging to the Masonic Temple,[15] decided to found a 'Liberal school'.[16] They were determined that the Hilfsverein and its school should be forward-looking in its philosophical and spiritual emphases. They also wanted to create a hospital and a nursing home so the Germans would have their own welfare services. In 1883, however, with only limited resources available, they chose firstly to found a school, financed from their own pockets, where the teachers would be selected, hired and paid by the society.

> The school whose creation we have recommended should give a young man such an education so that, from the basics to a given grade, when he finishes the third or fourth year, he will be prepared to face life's struggles, either if he wants to work with his hands or if he wants a commercial activity. The following disciplines should be in the curriculum: Reading, Arithmetic, Writing, Practical Teaching, Singing, Drawing, Geography,

Universal History, German, Portuguese, French, English, Physics, Literature, Gymnastics.[17]

The German School of the Mutual Society or as the Koseritz's almanac called it in 1886, the 'Schule des Hilfsvereins' (Knabenschule) was then founded. According to Telles,[18] 'it did not yet include gymnastics classes in the curriculum'. It is only around 1900 that this subject receives any mention. In the beginning the gymnastics classes taught by Professor Herrmann Englert[19] were not compulsory. Most boys did not attend them. The board of directors of the Turnerbund[20] in consequence asked the school council to make participation obligatory. It seems that this complaint yielded results. In an article of the *Deutsche Turnblätter*[21] of the time, the participation in gymnastics of all 201 male students and 79 female students from the Hilfsverein is reported. However, it noted also the girls' low attendance level and their parents' unconcern about their daughters' physical education. Again the demand was made that physical education classes should be made compulsory. The school was clearly keen to have *Turnen* in the compulsory curriculum. The school used Jahn's system. The Turnerbund by-laws stated clearly that all physical activities should be developed according to Jahn's principles.[22] Thus the Hilfsverein provides the first evidence of the firm intention of the German population to utilize *Turnen* as a symbol of Germanic identity. It was, however, far from being the only school to adopt this reassuring symbol.

THE COLÉGIO MAUÁ

Colégio Mauá,[23] the former Real Schule of Santa Cruz do Sul, Rio Grande do Sul, founded in 1870 to teach the sons of German immigrants and of their descendants, was eventually a boarding school, a day school and a teacher training college. Initially it faced the same financial problems, lack of teachers and shortage of space typical of the other early schools but it slowly grew in size. In the Colégio Mauá physical education classes were not held in the school, but at the Gymnastics Society, which hired teachers from Germany. The concept of 'body education' (*der körperlichen Erziehung*)[24] had a special importance for both the school and the Gymnastics Society, which made available to the school its sports gymnasium with all its equipment. Gymnastics, games and folk dances were practised there. Gymnastics, as in other gymnastics societies, was taught according to Jahn's ideas. In short, pupils received an efficient German training of the body, in keeping with the school's motto – 'mens sana in corpore sano'.

THE PROTESTANT SEMINARY FOR TEACHERS

In 1908, in the Pella and Bethânia Nursing Homes and Orphanage,[25] in the municipality of Taquari, the proposal for the establishment of a Lutheran seminary for the training of teachers was approved. At these nursing homes and orphanage, the general assembly of the Association, an institution which itself represents a cornerstone of the edifice of German Protestant life in Rio Grande do Sul, agreed to start, in early March 1909, a teachers' seminary so to provide an education to local youngsters, orphans from the Orphanage and others sent by their communities. In April 1909 the school opened with four students. The seminary was then transferred to Santa Cruz do Sul in 1910 and was later named Escola Sinodal. Later on it became part of Colégio Mauá and on 11 July 1926, it was transferred to São Leopoldo, creating 'a centre in which the cultural and spiritual heritage of our forefathers is cultivated' according to the *Deutsche Post*.[26] In this new seminary new disciplines were established such as *Turnen* for girls and *Turnspiel*[27] for both sexes.

The 1936–1938 Seminary Report (*Jahresbericht*)[28] provides details of the role of physical education in the seminary at that time. Exercises and games aimed at ensuring the student's physical development, while at the same time promoting psychological well-being, developing sound moral attitudes, technical skills, character formation and civic responsibility, and providing personal pleasure. In the 1935 *Jahresbericht*[29] there are details of the number of classes and hours per week for each discipline. For instance, *Turnen* for girls and *Turnspiele* for both sexes had two weekly one hour classes each respectively. Games involving balls and running were also taught, together with handball[30] and football. Altmann,[31] an alumnus of this seminary, has described life during his time there. The schedule was demanding: an early rise, twenty minutes of physical exercises in the school courtyard directed by one of the older students. Then a cold bath and then classes. The teachers on duty, and sometimes the principal himself joined in the courtyard exercises. The seminary teachers were carefully selected for their commitment. It was important that they were able to inculcate a

Germanic point of view in their pupils, while at the same time ensure
that they were fit and knowledgeable.

Soirees or arts evenings were held by the schools. At the seminary it
was no different. These evenings were very important to the community
and Altmann describes one of them: in the programme there was a play
by Hans Sachs[32] and choral and musical ensemble presentations.
Gymnastics exercises, (*Turnen*) always brought the programme to a
close.[33] The evening ended with a ball.

PRE-THEOLOGICAL INSTITUTE (IPT)

The IPT was established in 1921 in Cachoeira do Sul, as a 'preparatory
school' for the parsons of the Brazilian Lutheran Confession Church
(IECLB). It offered an education in the humanities and prepared the
students for studies in theology. The curriculum did not include
physical education, which may seem strange since one of the IPT's
objectives was the preservation of German identity, and that this was
partly attained by *Turnen* practices. This omission might have been due
to the limited number of students. Whatever the cause, it is clear from
the memories of P. Atkinson, one of its earliest students, that physical
activity was not a high priority: '... Our outings, excursions and walks in
these surroundings were neither quite frequent nor varied ...'[34] However,
as the Gymnastics Society Concordia was nearby, once a week the IPT's
few students participated in gymnastics classes, as well as playing
voluntary handball in the school courtyard.

In 1927 the school was transferred to São Leopoldo, together with
the Colégio Mauá Teachers' Seminary. Both remained there for four
years. Students now had physical education classes, involving '100
metres, resistance and relay races, high and long jumps, weight, discus
and javelin throwing, parallel bars, horse, hoops'.[35] On cold or rainy days,
there were long runs and handball games. The IPT prepared students
for the Diaspora Seminary in Kückenmüle in Germany and the students
had the further possibility of attending a German university. Thus the
IPT provided a bridge between Germans in Brazil and in Germany.

Rolf Droste has described other seminary activities: 'Frühsport
(dawn) exercises were practised three times a week. They included
jumping briskly out of bed, getting dressed, swiftly running a thousand
metres, callisthenics on dry and wet surfaces, a cold shower ...'[36] As
mentioned earlier, handball was also played. It had been part of the

programme from the beginning. Handball competitions, incidentally, took place not only in schools but in gymnastics societies. It is clear from the above that the school and its staff were clearly concerned with their students' physical fitness and offered them physical activities that would promote their healthy development. *Turnen* played its part in this.

JESUIT SCHOOLS

The former Gymnasio Anchieta, Porto Alegre, and the Gymnasio Nª. Sª Conceição, São Leopoldo were the area Jesuit schools, and both had been founded by German Jesuits and up to a point followed German teaching practices. However, pupils in these schools received both military training and gymnastic instruction. Cantarino Filho has stated that 'after 1894 these schools adopted the programme of the Pedro II School[37] with gymnastics and fencing as compulsory disciplines. Games were also common.'[38] Filho unfortunately does not describe the type of gymnastics, but in the 1893 programme there is a note on the banning of acrobatic exercises, that is, Jahn's gymnastics. It appears that programmes were thereafter more directed toward Spiess's system, which was aimed at schools and the army and more militaristic in emphasis. According to Filho, Jahn's gymnastics, practised at the time, 'had many opponents who praised other systems of physical education in schools because they believed that German Gymnastics was responsible for encouraging excessive muscular development'.[39]

At Gymnasio Anchieta gymnastics and military exercises were taught to all grades once a week. As the Gymnasio Nª Sª da Conceição July report of 1911 states that '... compulsory gymnastics has now begun, with a modern character and based on the most vigorous acrobatic exercises'.[40] Here is the first evidence of this activity in a Jesuit institution. The 1913 Conceicão school report states that 'we have established this year, under the efficient direction of the well-known Professor Ramon Rovira, an optional Gymnastics course, in which many students have participated with good results for their physical development'.[41]

It is clear then that there were differences between the combined programmes of Catholic schools and the gymnastics programmes of the Protestant schools. The Jesuits had a military component, due to the fact that their founder, Ignatius de Loyola, had been a soldier. The institutions' activities, therefore, reflected Jesuit tradition. They were also keener to be in the mainstream of Brazilian Catholic educational practice. In view of the developments discussed below it could be argued that this was a sensible attitude.

The distinctive characteristics of Protestant and Catholic institutions constituted differences that were to be of great importance following the creation of the New State (a dictorial regime established in Brazil from 1937 to 1945). Protestant schools, which still had on their staff German teachers and possessed school programmes aimed at specifically German needs, experienced far more repression than Catholic ones which were already more completely integrated into the Brazilian educational system. Furthermore, Protestant schools did not have a Military Battalion although their older students took part in military training.

In hinterland schools in the colonies, the Germanistic emphasis was particularly strong. It was part and parcel of life. German was the language spoken, whereas in urban centres this was not the case, not even in the schools that recruited German teachers to work in them. However, in the hinterland 'Physical Education suffered from a lack of methodology, was crude and its teachers were not adequately prepared', claims Mario Cantarino.[42] Yet, once the rural schools in Rio Grande do Sul made an agreement with the Sociedades Ginasticas the problems stopped.[43] The societies trained men to teach gymnastics and formed study groups to discuss gymnastics practice. Furthermore, these schools now had 'universal' teachers, from Germany, such as Professor Georg Black, assisting them.[44] For thirty-two years Black was responsible for the gymnastics of Sociedade Ginástica Porto Alegre (SOGIPA), and taught at several schools of the Porto Alegre area, such as Júlio de Castilhos, Bom Conselho, Rosário, Seminário Evangélico, São José, and at the Instituto Pré-Teológico. Black, besides being a pioneer in physical education, was an innovative teacher and significant cultural influence in Rio Grande do Sul.

Incidentally, it should be made quite clear that Ferreira Neto[45] is not accurate in his assertion that the creation of physical education programmes in Brazil was due to the state, the army and to intellectuals like Rui Barbosa, Fernando de Azevedo and Inezil Penna Marinho who are all considered to be the pioneers of this form of education. In Rio Grande do Sul physical education in schools had already been in existence for a long time prior to the action of these agencies and agents. It was a reality closely linked to the cultural needs of the German immigrants and their descendants. It provided cultural identity and security.

The schools' adoption of, and stress on, the practice of *Turnen* demonstrates that Jahn's system in schools was in tune with the idea of Germanic cultural preservation, with a desire for a separate ethnic identity and the need to sustain homeland cultural customs, especially the German language. The presence of Spiess's system, popular in Germany in the second half of the nineteenth century, was not greatly apparent in Brazil, probably because it did not accord with the interests of the German-Brazilians. The Spiess system did not offer support for Germanism (*Volksthum*) nor for ethnicity preservation. Its major objective was preparation for military service.

Turnen, it is reiterated yet again, in schools, in teacher training colleges and in the Sociedades de Ginástica, was concerned with issue of ethnic, cultural and social identity. Confusion about this certainly arose when teachers had to resort to other methodologies to control the students, often using 'pseudo military systems', with student marches, commands and a military dress code to ensure discipline. Consequently, those with insufficient knowledge on the subject, have argued that methods utilized in schools were essentially militarist, including Jahn's system. This, however, is far from the reality.

THE GYMNASTICS SOCIETY – TURNVEREIN

Documents of the early period of the twentieth century clearly reveal the significance of *Turnen* for the community and the members of the Turnerbund. After 1913, members received the monthly newspaper, the *Deutsche Turnblätter* direct to their homes and in this way were regularly and systematically kept informed of the Turnerbund activities. It constituted a vehicle that helped sustain the separate identity of their ethnic group. According to Giralda Seyferth '... it is replete with the idealization of German activity, the coverage of cultural and leisure societies considered perpetuators of German cultural values abroad, and the details of education in a 'German school'".[46]

The *Turnblatter* also published articles more directly linked to *Turnen* activities – including details of meetings, balance sheets and notes related to them. Its first edition in May 1915 made it clear, in an article entitled 'Gut Heil' (Good Happiness), that its main purposes were to help its members, strengthen the spirit of Germanism and promote the cultivation of German gymnastics and songs. Its existence, of course, was promoted through its wide circulation, and contact with other Sociedades de Ginástica.[47]

Some of its articles presented details of *Turnen* activities and included discussions as to how these activities could best preserve *Jahnian* German identity. There is, for instance, one entitled 'In memory of Friederich Ludwig Jahn', signed by HLF in August 1915, in which its author analyses Jahn's importance and the meaning of his work. At the end of the article, HLF remarked of Jahn and his historical period: 'knowing what was happening at that time, Germans here in Brazil can ... be sure that all German people brought up in this spirit will fight their enemy, and the founder of eternal peace will be the guardian angel of humanity'.[48]

In the December 1915 edition, there was an article dealing with 'the Meaning of the Gymnastics Societies for the Training of Our Youth'. Progress and prosperity, it argued, depended on healthy children, and that for this reason it was necessary to systematically both exercise them and introduce them to nature, and that the first countries to adopt gymnastics recognized the special importance of getting youngsters in touch with nature. It regretted that simple, free and direct activities, which ensured contact with nature, had been abandoned and replaced by practices involving equipment, with the excuse that natural free movement was anti-German! Gymnastics societies, it observed, regrettably favoured popular gymnastics as well as exercises for the body, such as swimming, fencing and scouting – that had recently come from Germany. The article pointed out that those responsible for the survival of Jahn's gymnastics had to work on *Turnen* members and, through them, provide the motivation to fight against everything that might hinder traditional Germanism, physically and morally.[49]

In the August 1939 issue of the *Deutsche Turnnblätter*, the article 'A Tribute to Jahn', written by August Spier, began with reflections on Jahn, and stressed that the founders of Brazilian gymnastics societies had learned to know and love the gymnastics and the ideals of German gymnastics societies, and had tried to apply their practices and ideals to Brazil. It concluded: 'we render tribute to Jahn as our old master'.[50] Spier appreciated the fact that Jahn's gymnastics had spread all over the world and had been widely adopted, even where its origins were not known. Spiers talked admiringly about the forty-seven years of the Turnerbund, its progress, ambitions, programmes and the increasing number of its members. He made it clear that it was not only club members who practised gymnastics, but also students from German–Brazilian schools who were allowed to use the equipment and the facilities of the Societies, which offered gymnastics to all ages. *All* were free to practice gymnastics and to enjoy it. Spier ended his article by stating 'we are legitimate sons and followers of Jahn, and we stand here to pass on his legacy to our successors'.[51]

Pastor Vath's speech, published in the same issue number, raised the question, 'Can the gymnast celebrate Jahn beyond the German frontiers?' Vath pointed out that there was an ocean between Brazilian and the land of the father of gymnastics, and that, besides, in Brazil there was a different language, and still different customs and neighbours, and that even nature there was alien. Furthermore, political goals were different. The New World had become home for the German–Brazilians, and this meant getting used to this world, finding new ways of earning a living and becoming its good citizens. Nevertheless, a German gymnast, argued Vath, had the right to celebrate German gymnastics. Accordingly, the gymnastics societies had maintained their loyalty to the fatherland across land and sea. Jahn's legacy – the gymnastics societies whose members are not Germans by law but by blood – had thus been protected. These members had accepted the responsibility of making their descendants healthy in body and in mind. Jahn's spirit was kept alive, pure in its essence, since the gymnastics societies, inspired by his ideals, made every effort to take his gymnastics system to the most distant places where Germans resided. It was this obligation to work towards Jahn's objectives without deviating a single step from the paths he had established, Vath contended, that ensured that the Gymnastics League had as its great mission to co-operate in building a bridge between the old country and the new land, and it would be capable of doing this only if Jahn's spirit was kept alive. Finally, Vath argued that Jahn's spirit had to be kept alive. The celebration of Jahn's memory was a perpetual responsibility.[52] Clearly as late as the end of the 1930s the influence of Germany on German–Brazilian culture was still strong.

CONCLUSION

In southern Brazil German immigrants had the opportunity to construct their own schools in their own image without interference. Indeed, they were determined to create for their children good quality schools that produced healthy students by using homeland practices and schools far from the fatherland that passed, without limitations, Germanic culture on to future generations.

The Brazilian state took no responsibility for the German immigrants' education, transferring its responsibility to the immigrant society. This liberalism was two-edged. It led to different interpretations of, and to disagreements on, the appropriate system of physical education mostly among Lutherans, Brummers and Catholics.

On arrival in Brazil, German immigrants were, in essence, abandoned by the government and forced to manage their lives according the customs, mores and beliefs they had brought with them from their country of origin. Thus cultural autonomy was unavoidable and as a result, an awakening to a 'New World' identity came late for some of these immigrants. Their cultural adaptation to this new environment was slow because survival demanded that they had to draw on their past culture to ensure their needs were met successfully.

In the effort to survive, the school was crucial to the creation and promotion of a necessary Germanic culture, and hence community security, in an alien environment, as well as playing a major role in ethnic preservation in a strange world. Much has been written about a variety of cultural activities of these 'New World' Germans and their role in the preservation of a German identity, but the role of *Turnen* has been neglected. *Turnen* education and physical education were, in fact, a *major* part of this preservation. This is very clear from the earlier analysis of a sample of schools. However, as has been made clear there was variation of emphasis. Protestant schools and the Brummers school (Colégio Farroupilha) resorted to approaches that had produced good results in Germany. Catholic schools, on the other hand, adapted more smoothly to the Brazilian setting, in part because their catholicity ensured that they were not strongly ethnic schools. Because of this, they decided to emulate Colégio Pedro II, the model for Brazilian education – a Catholic education – at that time. In general, in the German communities in Brazil, within *Turnen* itself there was a blending of ideas about methods, involving Jahn's *Turnen*, GutsMuths' gymnastics and some aspects of Spiess's method. Although the German-Brazilian population did not know a great deal about Spiess, in fact many aspects of his system were used. Therefore, *Turnen* was linked, as a curricular component, to other parts of the school system, especially to the strict discipline in schools.

Matters were rather different, however, in the regional community schools in Rio Grande do Sul, where the students practised *Turnen* in gymnastics societies and used the German language. Students there also engaged in musical events, parties and songs connected with their homeland. It was from those schools that emanated most completely the culture brought to Brazil by their forefathers and renewed through the Brummers who, with their arguments and actions, led the German–Brazilians to value themselves for themselves as a distinct community. They fought to survive in one piece and they fought for a large measure of freedom from other groups. And in the process they created a new culture adapted to their new country without shedding their original culture, as many other ethnic groups did. They combined old and new in a distinctive Brazilian–Germanic culture in which *Turnen* played a large part.

Turnen, thus had as its purpose the pursuit of a separate identity. In its original form it was not concerned essentially with schools but with the whole population. Then the Brummers came to believe that by applying Jahn's *Turnen* to schools, they would be assisting both the inculcation and the preservation of a German identity in Rio Grande do Sul. Therefore physical education in these German–Brazilian community schools strongly stressed *Turnen*. In time, it embraced both Jahn's ideas and GutsMuths's subsequent emendations.

The relevance of the seminary for the training of teachers as a major institution in the encouragement of German identity must also be recognized. It was there that *Turnen*, education and physical education were fused. It was from there that Jahn's methods, together with Germanic cultural ideals were taken to the most distant German communities, not only in Rio Grande do Sul but throughout Brazil.

In summary, *Turnen* was one of the aspects that contributed greatly to the distinct culture of German–Brazilians in Rio Grande do Sul in the nineteenth and twenteith centuries. It represented more than a mere option in the education of this ethnic group. It was introduced deliberately by the Brummers and taken up and perpetuated by teachers, pastors, intellectuals, businessmen and industrialists for the simple reason that they wished to, and were determined to, value and preserve their Germanic culture in all circumstances. The preservation of this German ethnic identity through *Turnen* in major institutions such as school and club was strongly stressed. Both the immigrants and their descendants were knowledgeable about the ideological ideals of Jahn.

Turnen was practised purposefully by the community who preserved its separate Germanic cultural identity by means of a number of agencies – Turnerbund (Sogipa), clubs, schools and church. In other words, *Turnen* provides a fascinating illustration of the longevity of European influence in one part of Latin America.

NOTES

1. Southern Brazil is more than twice the size of France with a similar climate to western Europe. This region encompasses the states of Rio Grande do Sul, Santa Catarina and Parana stretching along the borders of three other South American countries: Uruguay, Argentina and Paraguay. During the nineteenth century these three states of the Brazilian Empire were colonized mostly by Italians and German immigrants instead of Portuguese or Spanish.
2. Pan-Germanism was a doctrine prevalent in the nineteenth century, promoted by German nationalists to unite all Germans and their descendants in one single nation.
3. F.L. Jahn was the charismatic leader of *Turnen* movement and GutsMuths the educator who advocated gymnastics in German schools.
4. Adolf Spiess reformed the *Turnen* movement by changing the German school system.
5. See F. Altmann, *A Roda. Memoria de um professor* (São Leopoldo, 1991).
6. Ibid., p.26.
7. Brummers: German legionnaires in the 1800s, who in 1851 fought for Brazil against Rosas in Argentina. Veterans of the war between Prussia and Denmark and the barricades of 1848, they contributed to the intellectual and economic development of Rio Grande do Sul. The term Brummer means 'irascible'.
8. L. Telles, *Do Deutscher Hilsverein ao Colégio Farroupilha- 1858/1974* (Porto Alegre, 1974).
9. Ibid., p.39.
10. Further reading on the subject: E.N. Coceicao, *Maconaria. Raizes Historicas e Filosoficas* (São Paulo: 1998) and E. L. Colussi, *A Maconaria Gaucha no Seculo XIX* (Passo Fundo, 1998).
11. L. Telles, *Deutscher Hilfsverein*, p.48.
12. Rationalism according to Telles is the Enlightment mode of thought promoted by Brazilian intellectuals from the nineteenth century and particularly adopted by the Brummers.
13. The Brummers in Brazil adhered to Freemasonry and often to the Liberal Party in order to strengthen their political power.
14. L. Telles, *Deutscher Hilfsverein*, p.57.
15. Masonic temples in the Brazilian Empire during the nineteenth century were closely connected to community and local initiatives, and with political activities. Unsurprisingly, before the Empire era Freemasonry in Brazil became a focus for those conspiring for national independence, finally declared in 1822.
16. In nineteenth-century Brazil the 'Liberal school' was independent of the imperial government.
17. Telles, *Deutscher Hilfsverein*, p.74.
18. Ibid., p.70.
19. Ibid., p.73.
20. *Turnerbund* was the denomination used by German immigrants to identify local associations in Brazil dedicated to gymnastics as well as to cultural preservation of traditions.
21. Quoted in the newspaper *Deutsche Turnblätter, Monaliche Mitteilungen des Turner-Bundes in Porto Alegre*, Porto Alegre, agosto de 1915, Heft 4, pp.49–50.
22. These principles circulated among adherents in form of recommendations usually concerned with German nationalism and the exercise system invented by Jahn. For further reading on this

theme see C. Eisenberg, 'Friedrich Ludwig Jahn – der 'Erfinder' des Turnen', *Sportwissenschaft*, 2 (2000), 125–40.

23. The name Colegio Maua was assumed in 1941 during the nationalization of former German immigrants' associations and companies developed in Southern Brazil.

24. See the document issued by Realschule with the title 'Jahresbericht Realschule in Santa Cruz do Sul, Rio Grande do Sul, 1870. Brasilien 1930' in pp.3–4, the following prescription: '... Der körperliche Erziehung wurde besondere Aufmerksamkeit gewidmet. Der Turnverein stellte, wie bisher, in dankenswerter Weise die Turnhalle mit ihren Geräter zur Verfügung. Doch wurde auch das Turnspiel und der Volkstanz eifrig gepflegt'.

25. See in A. Hoppen, *Formacao de Professores Evangelicos no Rio Grande do Sul – 1909 a 1939* (São Leopoldo: date not available), pp.22–38.

26. Ibid., p.38.

27. The participation of women in Turnen activities had generally ocurred during the nineteenth-century through games (Turnspiel) or gymnastics festivals (Turnfest) as depicted by G. Pfister, 'Frauen bei Deutschen Turnfesten. Zum Wandel der Geschlechterordnung in der Turnbewegung', *Sportwissenschaft*, 2 (2000), pp.156–179.

28. See document 'Jahresbericht Deutsches Evangelisches Lehrer – Seminar, São Leopoldo, Rio Grande do Sul, Brasilien. 1936–1938', pp.41–3.

29. See document 'Jahresbericht. Deutsches Evangelisches Lehrer – Seminar. São Leopoldo, Rio Grande do Sul, Brasilien. 1935 . Dr. Alberich Franzmeyer. São Leopoldo- Rotermund', pp.12–34.

30. For further details see P.G. Oliveira, 'A Imigracao Alema e a Introducao do Punhobol no Rio Grande do Sul' (Masters Dissertation, University of Santa Maria, 1987).

31. Altmann, *A Roda*, *passim*.

32. Ibid., p.52.

33. See description of Turnen exhibition in R. Grossbrohmer und J. Winkelmann, 'Das Stabturnenzwischen Reduktion und Kompensation der Leibesübungen im Turnunterricht', in R. Naul (Hrgs), *Körperlichkeit und Schulturnen im Kaiserreich* (Wuppertal, 1985).

34. O.L. Witt, 'Breve História do Instituto Pré-Teológico', in R. Drost (org.), *Uma Escola Singular* (São Leopoldo, date not available), p.109.

35. Ibid., p.111.

36. R. Drost, *Uma Escola Singular*, p.76.

37. Pedro II School was a model for the whole educational system in the Empire of Brazil. This institution was located in Rio de Janeiro, capital of the country and had established standards for primary and secondary levels of teaching during the second half of the nineteenth century.

38. M.R. Cantarino, 'A Educacao Fisica no Brasil', in H. Ueberhorst (ed.), *Geschichte der Leibesübungen* (Berlin: 1989), pp.889 – 911.

39. Cantarino, *Educacao Fisica*, p.898.

40. See report *Chronica do Anno Lectivo de 1911* in the archives of Gymnasio N. S. da Conceicao em São Leopoldo, Estado do Rio Grande do Sul, 1911, p.51.

41. See report *Relatório do Gymnasio Anchieta – Porto Alegre – RS- Anno Lectivo 1913*, printed by Typographia do Centro, p.8.

42. Cantarino, *Educacao Fisica*, p.900.

43. For further description of these *Turnen* associations see Lamartine P. DaCosta, 'Bodies from Brazil: Fascist Aesthetics in a South American Setting', in J. Mangan (ed.), *Superman Supreme* (London: 2000), pp.163–80.

44. L. Tesche, 'A Pratica do Turnen entre os Imigrantes Alemaes e seus Descendentes no Rio Grande do Sul: 1867–1942' (Masters dissertation, University of Ijui, Rio Grande do Sul, 1996), 67.

45. A F. Ferreira Neto, 'A Pedagogia no Exercito e na Escola: a Educacao Fisica Brasileira, 1880–1950' (Doctoral Thesis, Unimep University, Piracicaba – São Paulo, 1999), 243.

46. G. Seyferth, *Nacionalismo e Identidade Etnica* (Florianopolis, 1982), p.172.

47. Quoted in the newspaper *Deutsche Turnblätter*. Porto Alegre: maio de 1915. No.1, p.1.

48. *Deutsche Turnblätter*, Porto Alegre: maio de 1915. No.4, pp.1–2.

49. *Deutsche Turnblätter*, Porto Alegre: dezembro de 1915. No.8, pp.81–4.
50. *Deutsche Turnblätter*, Porto Alegre: agosto de 1939.
51. *Deutsche Turnblätter*, Porto Alegre: setembro de 1935. No.22, p.3.
52. Ibid., p.5.

Educators, Imitators, Modernizers:
The Arrival and Spread of Modern Sport
in Japan

ALLEN GUTTMANN and LEE THOMPSON

CLOSURE

Franciscan and Jesuit missionaries from Portugal and Spain had arrived in Japan in the sixteenth century, decades before Tokugawa Ieyasu (1543–1606) defeated his rivals and consolidated his control over a more or less unified nation. The European missionaries actively propagated their religion among the 'heathen', many of which were eager to embrace Roman Catholicism. The missionaries proved to be too successful for their own good. The large number of converts to Christianity, especially in the area around Nagasaki, led to a viciously xenophobic reaction. The shogunate banned Christianity, murdered thousands of Japanese who refused to renounce their new religion, ordered the expulsion of the European priests, executed those who defied the order to leave, and sought to seal the country off from foreign influence.

The closure was never total. Some intercourse was permitted through a small Dutch settlement on the island of Dejima in Nagasaki harbour. (Protestants were thought to be less dangerous than Catholics.) The *Tokugawa Jikki* records that the eighth shogun, Tokugawa Yoshimune (1684–1751), watched what may have been the first Western sport introduced to Japan: an exhibition of fencing by the Dutch.[1] Of course, European and American sports had not yet developed into the forms familiar to us today.

The rare Japanese whom the ever-suspicious government permitted to visit the Dutch settlement were able to observe the long-nosed foreigners at their amusements, which included a precursor of badminton. The game was described in 1787 by Morishima Chûryô in *Kômôzatsuwa* (Tales of the Red Hairs), along with illustrations of the racket and shuttlecock.[2] Other examples include a woodblock print of the Tokugawa period showing the Dutch at a game of billiards. Such interest was unusual. While a number of eighteenth-century Japanese were eager students of Western medical science and military technology, which they studied in Dutch texts, few of them left evidence of much curiosity about Western sports.[3]

OPENING

On 8 July 1853, Commodore Matthew Perry arrived at the port of Uraga with a letter to the Tokugawa shogun from President Franklin Pierce, informing the Japanese that the United States (US) expected them to open their islands to trade and provide humane treatment for shipwrecked American seamen. Perry returned the following February with a larger naval force, and a treaty was signed on 31 March 1854.[4] Eight months later, Sir John Stirling successfully negotiated a similar treaty between Japan and Great Britain.

Mercantile motives brought Perry to Japanese shores, but sport played a small part in his initial interactions with his reluctant hosts. In addition to a minstrel show, Perry's sailors put on a display of manly fisticuffs. The Japanese responded with an exhibition by a score of beefy sumo wrestlers. Neither party seemed properly impressed by the other. The Americans were disgusted by the massive wrestlers and a contemporary Japanese woodblock print shows 'bulky ... wrestlers delivering the shogun's gift of bales of rice to the scrawny American sailors'.[5] During Stirling's negotiations, the British were allowed to land and indulge in 'athletic sports'.[6]

Townsend Harris, the first American consul, arrived in August 1856 and was met with 'consternation'.[7] Additional treaties with France and other European powers brought more diplomats, more merchants, and more dismay. For a dozen years, the shogunate was riven with internal disagreement and was undecided about what to do with the largely increasing number of foreigners with increasingly inconvenient demands. Inconclusive debates within the government led to ambiguous policies and general confusion. The resolution came in 1868 in the form of the 'Meiji Restoration'.

The term 'restoration' suggests that the revolution of 1868 that ended centuries of Tokugawa rule returned Japan to imperial rule, but the emperor enthroned in Tokyo was more or less the same figurehead he had been in Kyoto. In fact, real power was in the hands of clan activists whose 'restoration' was actually part of a bold venture in what might be termed instrumental modernisation. The new rulers were plagued by power struggles among the leading clans, but there was a consensus about foreign policy. Japan should acquire from the West the modern science and technology necessary to defend Japan against the very real threat of foreign domination. (China's helplessness in the face of European military might was an ominous indication of the danger to Japan.) In addition to the Western experts who were invited to Japan, over 11,000 Japanese went abroad for study between 1868 and 1902. Among them was Itô Hirobumi, the nation's first prime minister.[8]

The modernizers' emulation of the West's scientific and technological achievements was often constrained by the desire to preserve what began to be identified as Japanese culture. The five-volume published report of the Iwakura Tomomi mission's two-year sojourn in Europe and the US advocated modernization (human knowledge rushes toward enlightenment), but the authors cautioned against the hasty abandonment of 'old institutions and practices'.[9] There were, however, some intellectuals whose admiration of the West (and denigration of their own culture) was uncritical and extreme. Mori Arinori suggested in 1872 that the country adopt English as the national language and Takahashi Yoshio, writing in 1884, urged that Japanese husbands divorce their wives and marry Western women of robust physique and superior intellect.[10]

Inevitably, uncritical enthusiasm for Europe and the US aroused nationalistic opposition. Motoda Nagazane, for instance, condemned what he saw as the effort 'to convert Japanese into facsimiles of Europeans and Americans'.[11] Criticism of the modernizers often took the form of verbal or pictorial satire. The nineteenth-century novelist Kanagaki Robun ridiculed his countrymen for aping the 'barbarians' by wearing top hats, carrying umbrellas, eating beef, and ostentatiously consulting their pocket watches.[12] Cartoons in conservative journals lampooned sandal-shod students with thick-lensed spectacles and armloads of foreign books. Hostility was also expressed through the murder of foreigners resident in Japan. Townsend Harris's secretary, Hendrik Heusken, was killed in January 1861 and British diplomats were attacked that July. Xenophobia also accounted for the 1889 assassination of the minister of education, Mori Arinori, who was thought to have betrayed Japan's traditional culture.[13]

The 'Imperial Rescript on Education' of 1890, promulgated after two decades of modernization, was a positive assertion of Japanese culture. Calling upon all Japanese to venerate the emperor, the Rescript was a powerful statement of 'invented tradition'.[14] Its goal was to transform the deified emperor into the focal point of patriotic sentiment.[15] To 'revere the emperor' was not, however, necessarily to 'expel the barbarians'. The men behind the 'Imperial Rescript' – men like Motoda Nagazane and Nishimura Shigeki – wanted to slow but not reverse the drive to bring Japan into the modern world.[16] S.N. Eisenstadt's shrewd comment about the recent past applies as well to the crosscurrents of change in the Meiji period: 'Tradition or traditionalism ... tended to become a crucial ... symbol of legitimation for new patterns of behavior, organisation, cultural creativity, and discourse.'[17]

Steamships, telegraph lines and modern weaponry were very much on the modernizers' minds, not cricket bats and rowing shells. On their extended missions to Europe and America, Japanese officials investigated mines and factories, not baseball diamonds and tennis courts. Japanese children's songs, which were certainly composed for and not by children, listed lightning rods and gas lamps, not sports equipment, among 'worthy objects'.[18] The enthusiasm for modern sports – like the vogue among the Meiji elite of Western dress and cuisine – was an unintended consequence of the desire for locomotives and coastal artillery. To put it in the language of the businessmen, who arrived in Japan along with the foreign diplomats, advisors and teachers, the modernizers got more than they bargained for.

In the course of the Meiji period (1868–1912), a series of modern sports popular in the West was introduced to Japan.[19] Government attempts to modernize the military led to the introduction of gymnastics, fencing, rifle shooting, riding, and skiing. European and American residents in the trading communities of Yokohama or Kobe introduced football, rowing, athletics, tennis, baseball, cricket and golf. The Meiji government invited many scholars from Europe and America to teach in the newly established school system, and they introduced their students to baseball, association football, rowing, athletics, rugby, tennis and skating.[20] Foreign missionaries, especially those associated with the Young Men's Christian Association (YMCA), propagated basketball, volleyball, hockey and badminton. Students and other Japanese, who had lived abroad, brought back with them table tennis, handball, basketball and volleyball. Participation in the Olympics and other international sports events introduced wrestling, weightlifting and canoeing. In addition, voluntary sports clubs took up activities such as yachting and climbing.[21]

Although some scholars have seen the global diffusion of these sports as proof of 'cultural imperialism',[22] coercion played a very small part in their adoption by the Japanese. On the contrary, the modernizing elite seemed as eager to emulate Westerners at play as they were to learn from Westerners at work.[23] It should be emphasized, however, that enthusiasm for British and American sports was for the most part limited to this modernizing elite. This was especially true in the early years of the Meiji period. Farmers, who still constituted the vast majority of the population, remained for the most part content with the physical contests traditionally associated with their seasonal festivals.

In most societies en route to modernity, the military have played an important role and Japan was certainly no exception. The Meiji leaders imported the weaponry of modern warfare and passed legislation to reconstitute the nation's ineffective military. A conscript army replaced the samurai who had been Japan's traditional warriors.[24] (The samurai, deprived of their principal function, also lost their right to wear the swords that had distinguished them from lesser mortals.) Between 1867 and 1880, French officers supervised the new army's training. Reorganisation included the adoption of Western notions of physical fitness and the proper ways to attain it. At the newly established Toyama Military School (1875), the French instructed their Japanese counterparts in the gymnastic principles they had learned from Francisco Amoros at their military academy in Joinville. They also taught the Japanese officers how to ride and to fence in the European manner.[25] In the dissemination of modern sports, however, French officers were soon supplanted by British businessmen and diplomatic officials and by American educators and advisors to the Japanese government.

Despite the fact that Japanese terrain was seldom suitable for cricket, a sport requiring an extensive and well-tended field of play, British bowlers and batsmen refused to deny themselves the pleasures of that pastoral game. On 16 October 1869, 11 Britons resident in the port city of Kobe met a team from HMS *Ocean*. A cricket club was promptly organized three days later, thanks largely to the initiative of Arthur Hesketh Groom.[26] Shortly thereafter, the British founded the Yokohama Cricket and Athletic Club in Kobe, where occasional matches between the garrison and visiting naval personnel had actually taken place as early as 1864.[27] Although a few Japanese tried their hand at cricket, the sport never became popular. 'Today cricket is almost the only major foreign sport that does not interest Japanese at all.'[28] Readers consulting the *Kodansha Encyclopedia of Japan* will find an entry under 'cricket'; it provides information on insects of the order Orthoptera.

As early as 1862, the British organized horse races in Yokohama, gala spectacles attended by the entire foreign community. In 1868, the British residents of Kobe followed suit and celebrated Christmas Day with a horse race. It was not unqualified success. The Japanese mounts bolted when the race went by their stables. Three of the jockeys were thrown.[29] However, this mishap was not enough to extinguish the ardour of the Victorian upper class. The Kobe Jockey Club was organized in 1870, and within a few years, the turf became a theme for woodblock prints by Hasegawa and other artists. Prints from the 1880s show the emperor and his entourage in the grandstand at Ueno.[30]

Both forms of another British passion – football – were played at Japan's private universities during the Meiji period. Soccer, which was introduced at the School of Engineering around 1873 by 'an Englishman named Jones',[31] failed to gain much of a foothold. According to Kinoshita Hideaki, it was not until 1907 that two Japanese teams met on the soccer pitch.[32] The sport was not organized nationally until 1921. Rugby, then the more popular of the two football 'codes', was played at private universities like Keiô and Waseda. In 1890, only a year after a Cambridge graduate introduced the game to Keiô, the students played against the British members of the Yokohama Athletic Club.[33] In the Kansai area, which includes Kobe, Osaka, and Kyoto, Dôshisha University emerged as a hotbed of rugby enthusiasm. In 1927, these private schools joined with the nation's most prestigious public universities (Tokyo and Kyoto) to form a national federation for rugby.[34] Some sanguine British observers believed that 'the day is not far distant when [rugby] will eclipse baseball in popular esteem',[35] but that has not yet happened – despite the excitement that accompanied Kobe Steel's unprecedented string of seven consecutive national titles from 1989 to 1995.[36]

Athletics (track and field) events were introduced as part of the *undôkai* (sports days) at various schools. The earliest of these may have been the 'Student Competitive Games' held in 1874 at the Naval Academy in the Tsukiji section of Tokyo. The initiative apparently came from the thirty-four British naval officers who had assumed posts at the academy the previous year.[37] Prizes were awarded to the top placers.

Four years later, an American educator, William Clark, introduced athletics to the students of Sapporo Agricultural College. Educated Japanese learned to quote Dr Clark, in English: 'Boys, be ambitious', but interest in 'athletics' remained minimal until the initiatives taken in 1883 by Frederick W. Strange, an Englishman who arrived in Japan in 1875 to teach at Ichikô, which became the nation's most prestigious academy.[38]

Imbued with the Victorian conviction that sport was the proper antidote for an excess of intellectual endeavour, Strange summoned the students 'to come out and play games'. This historic athletics meeting took place on 16 June 1883. The participants were students from Ichikô and the college that eventually became Tokyo University. A 300-yard bamboo-fenced track was laid out on the college grounds. All of the customary running, jumping, vaulting and throwing events were included, along with the running of a three-legged race and hurling a cricket ball. For the shot put and the hammer throw, Strange made do with whatever equipment was available. For example, 'Instead of a pistol shot, the start was signalled by swinging down a folded Western-style umbrella.'[39] There was also 'a story that he brought out the school benches for use as hurdles'.[40] Thanks to the prestige of Tokyo University, this particular undôkai greatly influenced the development of athletics on other campuses where students were also keenly interested in foreign sports.[41]

To spread the gospel of manly sports, Strange wrote a short book entitled *Outdoor Games* (1883), which Shimomura Yasuhiro translated in 1885. In 1900 Shiki Shuji published *Rikujô kyôgi* (Track-and-Field Contests), the first book on the subject in Japanese. The term 'rikujô kyôgi' is still employed for athletics events.[42]

At the turn of the century, distance races became popular. When Yamaguchi Higher School staged an 11-mile race in 1899, other schools were stimulated to hold their own distance races, each one longer than the one before. In November 1901 the newspaper *Jiji Shimpô* sponsored a 12-hour race around the perimetre (1478 metres) of Tokyo's Lake Shinobazu. A 25-year-old rickshaw-puller, Andô Shotarô, won the event, circling the lake 71 times. In March 1909 a newspaper, Osaka's *Mainichi Shimbun*, sponsored what was publicized as the 'Kobe to Osaka Marathon Race'. (The distance was actually 19.56 miles.) A reservist from Okayama Prefecture, Kenko Chônosuke, won in 2 hours, 10 minutes, and 54 seconds.[43]

In the fall of 1902, Tokyo University's law department sponsored an undôkai at which one of the students, Fujii Minoru, was clocked in the 100 metres at 10.24 seconds, an astonishing time. The president of the university, Hamao Arita, proudly announced the time as a world record and was listed as such by *Spalding's Athletic Almanac*.[44]

According to Fujii Minoru's memoirs, reproduced in the 1997 bulletin of the Tokyo University Track and Field Club, his time was measured by an electric device developed by Tanakadate Aikitsu, a professor of physics who was also apparently the head judge at the meeting. The start and finish of the race activated an electric current in a machine that wound a tape at a speed of three centimetres per second. The current was cut when Fujii crossed the finish line, and the length of the tape was then measured to determine the elapsed time to one-hundredth of a second.[45] Noting that Fujii never again approached his sensational time of 10.24, sports historians have been sceptical about the alleged world record. In 1906, Fujii was said to have pole-vaulted 3.9 metres, which was 12 centimetres higher than the world record, but this remarkable achievement was not recognized outside of Japan.[46]

Japanese men have never done very well in athletics competition with European and American sprinters. In 1912, for instance, when the world record for 100 metres was 10.6 seconds, Mishima Yahiko held the Japanese title with the unimpressive time of 12 seconds. The 200-metre record set in 1911 by Akashi Kazue was a very slow 25.8 seconds.[47] Japanese runners were destined to do better in long-distance races than in the sprints. In fact, long-distance relay races have become a Japanese specialty.[48] In 1917, Tokyo's *Yomiuri Shimbun* celebrated the fiftieth anniversary of the 1867 transfer of the capital from Kyoto to Tokyo by sponsoring a 508-kilometre relay race from Kyoto's Sanjô Bridge to Tokyo's Ueno Park. Still another newspaper, the *Hôchi Shimbun*, invited students from Keiô, Waseda and other universities to participate in an *ekiden* (long-distance relay race) from Tokyo to the resort town of Hakone and back, a distance of over 200 kilometres. Ten thousand spectators watched the first race on 11 February 1920.[49]

Although very few girls were encouraged to participate in athletics, the most successful Japanese athlete of the early Shôwa period (1925–30), was Hitomi Kinue. After her graduation from what is now Tokyo Women's College of Physical Education, the *Mainichi Shimbun* hired her in April 1926 as a journalist. A month later, at the national athletics championships, she competed so impressively in the 100-metre dash, the long jump, the shot put and the baseball throw that she was chosen to be Japan's lone representative at the second quadrennial International Women's Games, which the Fédération Sportive Féminine Internationale had scheduled for Gothenburg, Sweden. Travelling by the Trans-Siberian Railway, the nineteen-year-old journeyed alone to Moscow and was then escorted to Sweden by a Moscow-based *Mainichi* reporter. Competing in six events, she won the standing and the running long jump, was second in the discus and third in the 100-yard dash. Her 5.5 metres in the running long jump set a world record. She was officially honoured as the outstanding athlete of the games. Four years later, when the International Women's Games were held in Prague, she competed in several events and won the long jump with a leap of 5.9 metres – despite the fact she was suffering from a sore throat and a fever. After the games, the Japanese team went on to dual meetings in Warsaw, Berlin, Paris and Brussels. Although Hitomi was exhausted and required almost daily injections, she competed in all these meetings. Returning by ship from Marseilles to Kobe, she arrived in such wretched health that her horrified father begged her to rest. She was determined, however, to fulfil all her obligations to her employer and to the national sports federation. She fulfilled these obligations, but she never recovered her health. By the spring of 1931, she had begun to cough blood and on 2 August, she died of respiratory failure.[50]

Fishermen and others who rowed and sailed on Japan's lakes, rivers and coastal waters must have had informal boat races, but Western-style aquatic sports seem to have only begun on 26 September 1861, when a regatta was held in Nagasaki. The participating vessels included four-oared gigs, Japanese sampans and houseboats.[51] However, rowing in the European and American style wasn't inaugurated until foreigners residing in Yokohama imported a boat in 1866.[52] The British in Kobe founded a Regatta and Athletics Club on 23 September 1870, and constructed a boathouse and a gymnasium.[53] In 1883, the Navy held rowing races that were attended by the emperor.

A major step was taken at Tokyo University in 1884 when Frederick W. Strange, who had played a major role in introducing athletics to young Japanese students, founded a boat club, modelled on those at Oxford and Cambridge. The club members constructed three boats and managed to borrow a technologically advanced four-seat racing shell equipped with sliding seats. In 1885, the club's team raced against the foreigners of the Yokohama Athletic Club. In 1887, the club organized intercollegiate races on the Sumida River, which flows through Tokyo. Providing Japanese students with an equivalent to the Henley Regatta was among Strange's last contributions to Japanese sports; he died of a heart attack in 1889.[54]

Rowing fever also spread to the Kansai area. In 1895, the governor of Shiga Prefecture sponsored the All-Japan Joint Rowing Meeting on Lake Biwa, the biggest lake in Japan. The meeting was well attended by middle-school and company crews. Although many universities and colleges in both the Kantô and the Kansai regions had crews, no regional organisations were formed before 1906.[55]

Competition was held in the water as well as on it. Swimming was considered a useful skill for a warrior, and, like the other martial arts, was taught by various schools at the end of the Tokugawa period. These native swimming styles survived into the Meiji period, for unlike practitioners of the other martial arts, swimmers were not immediately challenged by imported styles that threatened to render native ones obsolete.

In addition to its military function, swimming had a recreational aspect that came into its own in the Meiji period. From 1871 until their prohibition in 1917, various schools taught traditional swimming techniques at training facilities on the Sumida River. In 1898, Tokyo University established a swimming facility in Toda in Shizuoka Prefecture. Both Keiô University and Tokyo Higher Normal School accomplished the same in Kanagawa and Chiba Prefectures, in 1902.

The first modern swimming meeting was held on 13 August 1898 in the waters of Yokohama Bay. Swimmers from the foreign settlement raced the students of a Japanese swimming school over distances of 100, 400 and 800 yards. On 20 August 1905, the *Mainichi Shimbun* and the Nankai Railroad jointly sponsored a ten-mile swimming race in the waters of Osaka Bay. Only seven of the 28 starters finished the race. Sugimura Yôtarô, a student in Tokyo University's law department, won the race, finishing in six hours and ten minutes. The arduous feat earned Sugimura 300 yen, a barrel of sake and various other prizes. The first timed swimming competition, which was sponsored by the *Jiji Shimpô* newspaper, occurred six years later, on 28 August 1911, at Shibaura in Tokyo. Ugai Yasaburô won the 220-yard race in 2.32 minutes. Although Ugai swam then in a native style, he became known in the Taishô period (1912–25), as the first Japanese to adopt the crawl stroke. (Both Sugimura and Ugai swam in native styles; the crawl and other Western strokes were introduced after 1912.)[56]

Although it was impossible to have predicted it in the Meiji period, golf, which was obviously even less well suited than cricket to Japanese terrain, was destined to become the preferred sport of the Japanese corporate elite. Arthur Hesketh Groom, the same English merchant who had led the way to the formation of Kobe's cricket club, planted the Scottish game in Japanese soil. In 1903, a four-hole course was constructed at Mount Rokkô, near the port city, and in turn the Kobe Golf Club was founded. Its Yokohama counterpart followed in 1914. The first national championship was held in 1918, while the Nihon Gorufu Kyôkai (Japanese Golf Association) was formed six years later. By 1937, there were some 70 courses, but it was not until the 1960s that golf became a prerequisite for managerial success in the corporate world.[57]

Japanese pilgrims have for centuries climbed mountains in order to communicate with the gods whose home was amid the peaks, but what Kinoshita calls *shûkyôtozan* (religious ascent) was very different in purpose and technique from the activities of the Alpine Club (organized in London a year before the Meiji Restoration).[58] British sportsmen were the first to climb mountains in Japan simply because there were mountains to climb. The Rokkô Mountains, which loom behind Kobe, provided some initial adventures. Eventually, the more challenging peaks of central Japan became a favourite venue. In time, the central range became known as – in the Japanese pronunciation of the English word – the Nihon Arupusu (Japanese Alps).

Although the men and women of Kobe's British colony skied and skated,[59] geography dictated that winter sports were to be more popular in the snowy central mountains and on the northern island of Hokkaido than in the Kansai area. In January 1911, on snowy slopes near the town of Takeda in Niigata Prefecture, Theodor von Lerch, an Austrian military officer who had learned to ski from the famed Mathias Zdarsky, introduced the techniques of the sport to the men of the 58th Infantry Regiment. The following year, students at the national university in Sapporo founded an Alpine club to promote their favourite activity, mountain climbing, only to discover that it was more fun to glide swiftly down a slope than to clamber labouriously up one. Furthermore, they also seem to have been tutored by an Austrian called Egon von Kratzer. In 1916, one of the teachers at Sapporo's national university returned to Japan from a study period abroad and introduced the students to cross-country skiing. The university's club flourished and played a leading role in the formation, in 1925, of the Zen Nihon Ski Renmei (All-Japan Ski Federation).[60]

Basketball and volleyball came to Japan via the Young Men's Christian Association (YMCA), which was appropriate in that both games had been invented by YMCA members (basketball by James Naismith in 1891 and volleyball by William Morgan in 1896). Both sports emerged out of 'muscular Christianity'. The term, of course, refers to the efforts of Charles Kingsley and other nineteenth-century Englishmen to overcome the suspicion that had for centuries characterized Christian attitudes toward the human body. In the place of monastic asceticism, the proponents of 'muscular Christianity' advocated a robust, physically active engagement with the world. Sport was central to this engagement, with the YMCA institutionalizing and disseminating their ideals.[61] At the turn of the century, the YMCA was probably the West's most active exporter of modern sports to China, Korea and Japan.[62]

Despite their origin in an atmosphere of fervent faith, both basketball and volleyball were exemplary products of instrumental rationality. In a 1914 article published in the *American Physical Education Review* and in a short book entitled simply *Basketball* (1941), the game's inventor described his reaction to the challenge posed for him by his superiors when they asked him to create a ball game complicated enough to interest adults and spatially confined enough to be played indoors when New England winters daunted faint-hearted Christians. In his article and his book, Naismith reconstructed the sequence of logical steps he had taken as he reasoned his way to the solution of the problem. Perhaps the best indication of his instrumental approach was the placement of the basket. Fearful of potential injury from balls hurled forcefully at a ground-level vertical goal (as in soccer), Naismith elevated the goal above the players' heads and designed it so that its aperture was horizontal and narrow. Without envisaging playing a team of six to seven-foot tall slamdunkers, Naismith reasoned that the ball had to be thrown softly if its arc was to pass through the centre of the basket.[63] Although the origin of volleyball was less carefully documented, the game's invention was a similar triumph of rational design.

Ômori Heizô played YMCA basketball in the US in the 1890s. After returning to Japan, he introduced the game at the Tokyo Women's University, where he taught. Prospects for diffusion of the game diminished somewhat when Omori died, in the US, on his way home from the 1912 Olympics in Stockholm. However, progress resumed in 1913 when Franklin Brown fostered the sport at the Tokyo YMCA and when Elwood Brown included basketball in the first YMCA-sponsored Far Eastern Games, held in Manila that same year.[64] (The trials for the Far Eastern Games were subsidised, in part, by the *Mainichi Shimbun*, which seems to have had a hand in every other sporting event of the Taishô period.) At the first Japanese championships, which took place in 1921, the Tokyo YMCA was the easy winner.

The Tokyo YMCA was also the birthplace of Japanese volleyball, which Omori had observed at the Springfield YMCA in 1896. There was a volleyball tournament at the third Far Eastern Games, which were contested in Osaka in 1917. The game was yet to be widely played in Japan, and so a Japanese team was put together with mostly runners and basketball players who had had the rules explained to them only the day before their first game. Needless to say, they came in last among the three teams, losing by a wide margin to both China and the Philippines. Their losing streak at the Asian games continued until 1934 and they never managed to finish higher than last place.

Volleyball was more popular as a women's sport. At the sixth Asian Games in 1923, women's volleyball was an exhibition event, and the team from Himeji Women's Higher School won the championship, beating China.[65] A national volleyball federation was formed in 1927 and a basketball federation in 1930.[66] Despite the labours of Omori and his friends at the YMCA, neither basketball nor volleyball was widely played before the American 're-education' of Japan during the post-war Occupation. General MacArthur's influence seems to have been stronger than Franklin Brown's.[67]

Lawn tennis came to Japan in 1875 via the Yokohama Ladies Club.[68] Amherst College's George A. Leland introduced the game to Japanese students in 1878, a mere four years after England's Major Walter Wingfield patented it. Tennis was fashionable among the Western-oriented elite, but it was not widely played. Although students at Dôshisha Women's College took up the game in 1879,[69] the male undergraduates across the way at Dôshisha University seem not to have acquired the same enthusiasm. Perhaps young Japanese men scorned the sport as a 'girl's game'. At any rate, Kobe's socially exclusive lawn tennis club was not opened until 1900. The *Mainichi Shimbun*, always eager to promote the sporting events that increased its circulation, waited until 1910 to sponsor its first tennis tournament. Students and graduates of

Keiô University were prominent in the diffusion of tennis as they were in the spread of baseball and many other modern sports, but their tennis team was not organized until 1913.[70] Despite this rather hesitant acceptance of the game, Kumagai Kazuya took a silver medal in the men's singles at the Olympic Games in Antwerp in 1920. Partnered with Kashio Seiichirô, he won a second silver medal in the doubles competition. The following year, the Japanese team upset the US in the Davis Cup. In recent years, however, few Japanese players have reached the top ranks in tennis.

Participation in modern sports was not limited to college campuses and cities with a nucleus of foreign residents. Young people in smaller communities also organized clubs and built facilities to enable them to engage in modern sports. The Ryojô Youth Club, established in 1886 in the town of Yoshikimura in Yamaguchi Prefecture, serves as an example of a sports–centred voluntary association. Most of the original members seem to have been interested in debate, but verbal dexterity soon gave way to physical prowess. A sports festival was celebrated in May 1899 after a merger with the Sunday Club, which had been founded in 1895 by young men interested in literature and the martial arts. The sports festival included footraces over 220, 330, 440 and 880 yards, a three-legged race, and a marathon. There were also baseball and soccer games. In all, 126 young people participated in the festival. Over time, the use of the club's library declined, formal debates became sporadic and sports completely dominated the calendar. Tennis was especially popular. In 1926, a tournament was held to celebrate the club's fortieth anniversary. The matches were played on the grounds of Yoshikimura's school, where tennis courts had been constructed in 1920, but the Ryojô Club built its own courts in 1931 and was able, in 1934, to host Yamaguchi Prefecture's tennis tournament. Three years later, stifled by the militaristic and anti-Western atmosphere of the late 1930s, the club ceased to exist.[71]

In 1886 the Ministry of Education established a small number of highly selective 'Higher Middle Schools', which were renamed 'Higher Schools' in 1894. They served as preparatory schools for the Imperial Universities, and their headmasters were inspired by the example of Eton, Harrow, Rugby and other English 'public schools' (private schools for the wealthy).[72] One of the most important of these administrators was Kinoshita Hiroji, who served from 1889 to 1897 as headmaster of Tokyo's 'First Higher School' (usually referred to as simply Ichikô).[73]

After graduating from Tokyo University, Kinoshita spent several years studying law in Paris, but what most impressed him during his European sojourn was the annual Oxford v. Cambridge Boat Race on the Thames. He was particularly struck by the high-minded ethos of fair play, which reminded him of the Japanese claims for their own tradition of *bushidô* (the warrior's path). This ethos, Kinoshita attributed to the pupils' education at Eton and other 'public schools', where dedication to sport and the humanities (in that order) seemed to produce a lifelong devotion to public service.[74] If Ichikô was to produce a similar class of active young men eager to serve their country, sport had to be a central part of their school experience. And they were. 'From sunup to sundown – before, between, or after classes – the crack of bamboo swords and baseball bats filled the air...'[75]

There was no need for the masters to force sport upon recalcitrant pupils (which was then the case in India, where Hindu and Muslim boys initially resisted the efforts of English educators to bring them the joys of cricket and rowing).[76] When the pupils of Ichikô founded a Kôyûkai (Society of Friends) in October 1890, seven of the society's nine clubs devoted itself to sports. British influence was obvious in the clubs for rowing and for athletics, but indigenous traditions were strongly represented in the Japanese fencing club, and there was also American influence in terms of there being a baseball team.

BASEBALL AND MODERNITY

In the world of sport, American influence was eventually dominant. In a statistical analysis of sports participation in the 1980s and 1990s, the Dutch sociologist Maarten van Bottenburg observed that the percentage of the population participating in sports of American origin (42 per cent) is higher in Japan than in any European country, while the percentage participating in sports of British origin is lower than in any European country (23 per cent). The reason is clear. 'The British may have been dominant in commerce [in the Meiji period], but the Americans were more influential in the educational and cultural spheres.'[77]

By the end of the Meiji period, at the very latest, baseball became Japan's most popular modern participant sport. (One indication of this is the fact that 44 books on baseball, and only seven on soccer, were published during the Meiji period.)[78] British observers were not happy about this. Speaking to the Japan Society of London in 1933, N.K.

Roscoe revealed more than a trace of discomfort at the thought that the American game had outstripped its British rivals: 'As far as popularity goes I suppose there is no sport in Japan to equal baseball ... If the errand-boy is late in delivering the mid-day vegetables, the probability is that he has been briefly seduced from rectitude by an impromptu baseball game on a vacant lot.'[79]

Horace Wilson, a teacher at Kaisei Gakkô (later to become part of Tokyo University) introduced the game of baseball in 1873. Okubo Toshikazu, Makino Nobuaki and Kido Takamasa learned the game when they studied in the US from 1871 to 1874. Returning in 1875, they entered the Kaisei and helped popularize the game among the students. The game was also played in Tokyo at what later became Sapporo Agricultural College and at Ichikô. In addition, a number of other schools had informal teams of baseball enthusiasts who enjoyed the game despite a lack of proper facilities and equipment, and sometimes without a firm grasp of the rules.[80] 'Informal and unskilled players,' writes Kusaka Yuko, 'sought only sporadically the ephemeral enjoyment of these unorganized games.'[81]

Railroad engineer Hiraoka Hiroshi contributed to the establishment of baseball outside the schools. He had also learned the game during his years in the US, between 1871 and 1877. During this period he became acquainted with A.G. Spalding, the American businessman who was an important promoter of the game. Spalding gave Hiraoka an official baseball rulebook and some equipment. After returning to Japan, Hiraoka established the Shimbashi Athletic Club at the Shimbashi Railway Bureau, in 1882, and started a baseball team.[82] The baseball diamond at the club's facility in Shibaura in Tokyo was one of the first to provide seats for spectators.[83] Among the avid players was Kabayama Aisuke, the railway's manager. Subsequently, it was no accident that men engaged in modern transportation were among the first to play the game that was then – contrary to what Americans now think – the very symbol of modernity.[84]

By the 1920s most agreed that the game *was* wildly popular at the nation's secondary schools and colleges. When Nels Norgren of the University of Chicago led a collegiate team to Japan in 1922, he reported in amazement that baseball 'is more the national sport of Japan than it is of America'.[85] Norgren, who spent more time with Japan's educated elite than with the nation's rice farmers and factory hands, probably overstated the popular appeal of the game, but it was definitely an important part of campus life and was soon to become a national passion. Beginning in 1927, it was possible for fans to hear play-by-play radio broadcasts of intercollegiate and interscholastic baseball games. By 1932, 37.5 per cent of those who had radios were tuning in to sports broadcasts. Baseball games drew even more listeners than sumo tournaments.[86] In 1938, a German visitor, using almost exactly the same words as Norgren had in 1922, commented that baseball was more popular in Japan than in the US.[87] And twenty years after that, an American sportswriter repeated the claim: 'The Japanese like baseball better than we do.'[88]

Donald Roden, whose account of the Ichikô–Yokohama Athletic Club series is a classic of sports history, believes that baseball 'caught on' in Japan because 'it seemed to emphasize precisely those values that were celebrated in the civic rituals of the state: order, harmony, perseverance, and self-restraint'. That is, the Japanese adopted the game because such perceived values were familiar ones. This is also the interpretation of Tada Michitarô in *Asobi to Nihonjin* (Play and the Japanese).[89] It is certainly true that the Japanese have often described baseball as if it were, indeed, the inculcator of harmony, perseverance and self-restraint, but there was no need in the Meiji period to find these values solely in baseball when Japanese archery and the other martial arts were readily available. While it is certainly possible that the Japanese sought harmony in baseball, it seems more likely that the Japanese seized upon the game because it embodied values that were not traditionally Japanese. 'The myth of modernization,' writes William R. May, 'underlines baseball's continuing popularity.'[90] The American game, which Roden sees almost as a stately ceremony, had Mark Twain characterizing it as 'the outward and visible expression of the drive and push and rush and struggle of the raging, tearing, booming nineteenth century'. Twain was surely right. Baseball symbolized – for both the Japanese and their American contemporaries – not tradition but modernity. Like the telegraph, the telephone and many other technological marvels of that era, the import bore the magical stamp: Made in America.[91]

THE ROLE OF SPORT IN PHYSICAL EDUCATION

Sport and physical education are closely related phenomena, especially in Japan, where sport is widely considered a subcategory of physical education. To understand Japanese sport, it is also necessary to attend, briefly, to the development of physical education in Japan.

During the Edo period, most domains had schools to educate the children of the samurai. Most of these schools were established towards the end of the eighteenth century.[92] The arrival of Admiral Perry's armada of 'black ships' intensified the domains' previously rather desultory interest in modern methods of warfare and military training. Accordingly, many domain schools adopted gymnastics as a form of paramilitary training. Turning to European physical educators for guidance, the shogunate first adopted the Dutch version of gymnastics, then switched to the French system devised by Francisco Amoros. Different domains acquired and adapted their gymnastics from a number of different European countries: from Germany and the Scandinavian countries as well as from the Netherlands and France. Since many of these domain schools survived into the Meiji period as primary and middle schools, physical education in the late nineteenth and early twentieth centuries can best be understood as an extension of this paramilitary training.[93]

If Japan was to become a modern nation, the patchwork of local schools needed to be replaced with an educational system modelled on the systems developed in the US and Western Europe. Promulgating its first major Education Ordinance (*Gakusei*) in 1872, the Meiji government institutionalized physical education in the schools.[94] Meiji-period physical education was generally referred to as *taisô* (gymnastics).[95]

Implementing the Education Ordinance, the Tokyo Normal School was established in 1872 to train teachers for all subjects, including physical education. Just what activities were taught in the gymnastics classes of the day can be inferred from the response that the principal of the Osaka English School made in 1878 to a query from the Ministry of Education. According to the principal's eclectic list, the children marched, did calisthenics and gymnastic exercises, used Indian clubs, and played on the seesaw and the swings. They also practised the high jump and competed in soccer games.[96]

In 1879, the National Institute of Gymnastics (Taisô Denshûjo) was established to develop methods of physical education and train instructors for the schools.[97] The minister of education, Tanaka Fujimaro, travelled to the US and hired an American advisor, George A. Leland, to teach at the institute. Although German immigrants to the US had propagated the ideas of *Turnvater* Friedrich Ludwig Jahn, Leland favoured the American gymnastic system that he had learned at

Amherst College. Since this system, devised by Diocletian Lewis, required a good deal of equipment, Leland stocked the school's gymnasium with barbells, dumbbells, Indian clubs, beanbags and wooden rings.[98]

The main programme developed at the Institute under Leland's guidance came to be known as 'normal gymnastics' (*futsû taisô*) or 'light gymnastics' (*kei taisô*). But other forms of gymnastics were developed and taught as well. They included 'heavy gymnastics' (*jû taisô*) and 'outdoor activities' (*kogai undô*). Included among the latter were football, cricket, croquet, baseball and rowing.[99]

In the published collection of his translated lectures, *Taiikuron*, Leland stated that the ultimate goal of physical education was not a strong body, but a well-developed *kokoro* (translated as the English word 'mind'). Imamura remarks that Leland was rational in his methodology, but spiritual (*seishinshugiteki*) in his goals.[100] This is an interesting remark because many commentators assert that *seishinshugi* is what makes Japanese sport uniquely Japanese.

The Institute of Gymnastics was abolished in 1886 and a special course for 'gymnastic' training was offered at Tokyo Normal School (Tôkyô Shihan Gakkô). Admission to the course was restricted to army veterans of officer rank who applied within a year of their discharge from active service.[101] Many continental European educational systems, of course, also looked to the military to staff 'gymnastics' programmes that were, after all, essentially paramilitary.[102]

The 1887 Course of Study for Primary Schools (*Shogakkô Kyôsoku Taikô*) specified the programme for 'gymnastics' classes in primary schools. In the early years of the programme, classes were supposed to consist of appropriate 'play and games' (*yûgi*) and 'outdoor activities'. 'Normal gymnastics' were to be introduced gradually, after which the boys were to be taught some of the simpler 'military gymnastics'. The guidelines did not specify as to what was meant by 'appropriate games and outdoor activities'. Tsuboi Gendô's widely read book, *Kogai Yûgihô* (*Outdoor Games*; 1886, revised 1889), was probably used as a reference. It includes various noncompetitive games and a small number of sports (football, croquet, lawn tennis, baseball, and rowing. Baseball and rowing, however, were dropped from the revised edition.).[103]

After the first sports festivals (*undôkai*) at the Naval Academy in 1874, 'sports days' spread to schools throughout the country and became a mandatory extracurricular activity. The leading journal of education of the day, *Dai Nihon Kyôikukai Zasshi*, mentioned 32 separate *undôkai* held between 1884 and 1892, mainly at the nation's primary schools. Four-fifths of these sports festivals were interscholastic in the sense that more than a single school participated. Imamura groups the events held at these *undôkai* into four categories. The largest category is *yûgi kyôgi*, which covers sports and noncompetitive games. Nearly 70 per cent of the events fall in to this category. Of the events in this category, foot races are the most popular, accounting for 32.4 per cent of all events. Also included in this category are ball games (8.3 per cent), of which soccer is the most popular (4.8 per cent) and thereby clearly outstripping baseball (1.3 per cent). A second large category, various kinds of gymnastics, comprises 25 per cent of all events. Considering the important role assigned to the military at the Tokyo Normal School, one is surprised to discover that military gymnastics, the third category, accounted for only 3.9 per cent of the *undôkai* events. The smallest of Imamura's four categories is *bujutsu*, the martial arts, which constituted a mere 1.3 per cent of all events. Imamura concludes, quite plausibly, that although modern sport may have played a small part in the formal curriculum, it was a major part of the children's actual physical activities (*undô seikatsu*).[104]

In 1885, at the beginning of the period studied by Imamura, only four per cent of middle-school pupils were girls.[105] Legislation passed in 1889 did require that every prefecture should have at least one high school for girls, but the notion of using sport to prepare women for political and economic leadership remained (and to some degree still does) foreign. Physical education was considered to be a necessary part of the girls' curriculum, if for no other reason than to prepare them for their future role as healthy mothers of the boys destined to become the nation's defenders. However, this eugenic motivation ran counter to traditional notions about female modesty and beauty.

Sportswear was a knotty problem. It was difficult to do calisthenics in an obi (the tight sash worn with kimono) and nearly impossible to run in *geta* (Japanese sandals). The long sleeves of traditional Japanese kimono also hindered many sports activities.[106] The reform-minded Inokuchi Akuri, who had studied at Smith College in Northampton, Massachusetts, and at Boston's Normal School of Gymnastics, returned to Japan in 1903 and prescribed blouses, bloomers and skirts for her physical-education classes. In 1915, Nikaidô Tokuyo experimented with the simple tunics that she had seen while studying in England. Neither effort at dress reform was very successful. 'The transition was too drastic',[107] and so, it was not until the 1920s that Western sports clothes became standard for female physical education.

There was still another obstacle to the progress of physical education and sports at Japanese girls' schools and women's colleges. Male teachers competent to lead the girls in their exercises were in scarce supply and female teachers were even fewer. In 1912, there were 286 physical education teachers at the nation's 299 Women's Higher Schools – less than one per school. Of these 286 teachers, 150 were male and 136 female, but 128 of the men and only 22 of the women had proper credentials. The Ferris School, founded in 1884, supplied a few reasonably qualified female teachers who – in the words of Dean Matsuda Michi of Dôshisha Women's College – learned 'ethics and gymnastics', but it was not until 1918 that Tokyo's Normal School for Female Teachers instituted a two-year physical-education course for prospective teachers.[108]

The annual 'sports day' (*undôkai*) that the Normal School inaugurated for the girls at its affiliated middle school on 28 May 1891, was a good indication of prevalent attitudes. The programme for 1904 had four footraces and two tug-of -war contests, but there were six dances and ten displays of marching and doing calisthenics. The same day, the boys at the middle school affiliated with the Normal School for Male Teachers, played football, wrestled and competed in ten footraces. And they, too, had tug-of-war contests.[109]

Reporting on the Normal School's third annual celebration, journalists mentioned basketball and tennis, but the 'expressive games' and the 'technical games' were apparently the focus of most attention. The girls mounted bicycles, not in order to race, but rather to ride in formation 'like butterflies'. In time, however, the Normal School added classes in baseball to its physical-education curriculum, and the students petitioned for hockey. If they hoped to find an advocate in Inokuchi Akuri, they were disappointed. Although she was definitely an innovator when it came to dress reform, she was hardly a strong supporter of athletic competition for young women. She preferred Swedish gymnastics and the 'showpiece' of the programmes she devised was a 'Faust Dance' to the music of Charles Gounod.[110]

At schools founded by or under their influence of Protestant missionaries, in female physical-education programmes were generally more ambitious. At Dôshisha Women's College, for instance, lawn tennis was played as early as 1879. Tennis was considered, as it is today, an appropriately 'feminine' sport, but what does one make of the appearance of kendô in the diary kept in the 1890s by a student at Meiji Girls' School? 'Every day early in the morning I go to the kendô hall to practice kendô, and then attend morning service. Getting in a sweat and bracing up my spirits, I feel very refreshed. Then I find myself ready to meet my God within.'[111]

In April 1901, the Ministry of Education issued detailed instructions for the schedule to be followed in boys' and girls' physical-education classes during each year of primary school. The instructions indicated the exact amount of time to be devoted to each of several categories of activity: gymnastics, military gymnastics and games (*yûgi*). The instructions did not, however, specify what activities constituted games.[112]

The ministry's lack of specificity was remedied by a 'Detailed Plan for Primary School Instruction' (*Shôgakkô Kyôjuhô Saimoku*) published by the Tokyo Higher Normal School in April 1903. The plan listed no fewer than 64 different games, of which 44 involved competition.[113] This was in stark contrast to a book on games (*Yûgihô*) published only nine years earlier, in which 25 of the 48 listed activities involved singing and marching.[114]

In October 1904, the Ministry of Education returned to the question of an appropriate physical-education curriculum and appointed a Committee to Investigate Gymnastics and Games (Taisô Yûgi Torishirabe Iinkai). They met 37 times and submitted their report in October 1905. Most of the report concerned gymnastics, but the members of the committee did list games that should be included in the curriculum for primary schools. These were divided into competitive games, marching games and movement games. Under the first rubric, the committee recommended a broad spectrum of extra-curricular sports: running and jumping; a number of Western ballgames, including baseball and lawn tennis; sumo; and several of the Japanese martial arts (archery, fencing, jûjutsu). The report specifically stated, however, that there was no reason to include martial arts in the formal primary-school curriculum.[115]

During this period, games were not a part of the middle-school curriculum, but they were played as extra-curricular activities. The Ministry of Education's Committee to Investigate Gymnastics and Play recommended that games become a part of the regular curriculum and that more than one-third of class time be devoted to them.[116] As these various recommendations were implemented in the decade before the First World War, ordinary Japanese schoolchildren began to participate in the modern sports that had been introduced a generation earlier to the sons and daughters of the modernizing elite.

NOTES

This chapter is an adapted and abbreviated version of the chapter entitled 'The Arrival and Diffusion of Western Sports' in Allen Guttmann and Lee Thompson, *Tradition and Modernity in Japanese Sports* (forthcoming). Thanks are extended to Professor J.A. Mangan for editing this version.

1. Imamura Yoshio, *Nihon taiikushi* (Tokyo: Jumaidó, 1970), p.329.
2. Tanaka Tokuhisa and Yoshikawa Kumiko, *Supôtsu* (Tokyo: Kintô, 1990), pp.72–3; Imamura, *Nihon taiikushi*, p.330.
3. Donald Keene, *The Japanese Discovery of Europe, 1720-1830* (Stanford: Stanford University Press, 1969); W.G. Beasley, *Japan Encounters the Barbarian* (New Haven: Yale University Press, 1995).
4. George B. Sansom, *The Western World and Japan* (New York: Knopf, 1950), pp.277–80.
5. P.L. Cuyler, *Sumo* (New York: Weatherhill, 1979), p.11.
6. Hugh Cortazzi, *Victorians in Japan* (London: Athlone Press, 1987), p.7.
7. Sansom, *The Western World and Japan*, p.285.
8. Marius B. Jansen, *Japan and Its World* (Princeton: Princeton University Press, 1980), p.64. Between 1862 and 1868, i.e., even before the Meiji Restoration, more than 100 Japanese students were sent abroad to study; see Beasley, *Japan Encounters the Barbarian*, p.119.
9. Eugene Soviak, 'On the Nature of Western Progress: The Journal of the Iwakura Embassy', in Donald H. Shively (ed.), *Tradition and Modernization in Japanese Culture* (Princeton: Princeton University Press, 1971), pp.7–34.
10. Donald Keene, 'The Sino-Japanese War of 1894-95 and Its Cultural Effects in Japan', in Donald H. Shively (ed.), *Tradition and Modernization in Japanese Culture* (Princeton: Princeton University Press, 1971), p.170; Sansom, *The Western World and Japan*, p.371.
11. Motoda: quoted by Donald H. Shively, 'The Japanization of the Middle Meiji', in Donald H. Shively (ed.), *Tradition and Modernization in Japanese Culture* (Princeton: Princeton University Press, 1971), p.87.
12. H. Paul Varley, *Japanese Culture*, 3rd ed. (Honolulu: University of Hawaii Press, 1984), p.208.
13. Beasley, *Japan Encounters the Barbarians*, p.73; Shively, 'The Japanization of the Middle Meiji', p.88.
14. Eric Hobsbawm and Terence Ranger, *The Invention of Tradition* (Cambridge: Cambridge University Press, 1983). By the term 'invented tradition', Hobsbawm and Ranger mean consciously invented tradition, of which the Imperial Rescript was certainly an example. In the sense that all traditions are socially constructed, they could be said to be invented, whether consciously or not, but it is useful to make a distinction. See also Marilyn Ivy, who observes in her study of Japanese modernity, 'To say that all tradition is invented is still to rely on a *choice* between invention and authenticity, between fiction and reality, between discourse and history,' in *Discourses of the Vanishing* (Chicago: University of Chicago Press, 1995), p.21.
15. Herschel Webb, 'The Development of an Orthodox Attitude toward the Imperial Institution in the Nineteenth Century', in Marius B. Jansen (ed.), *Changing Japanese Attitudes toward Modernization* (Princeton: Princeton University Press, 1965), pp.167–91.
16. Donald H. Shively, 'Nishimura Shigeki', in Marius B. Jansen (ed.), *Changing Japanese Attitudes toward Modernization* (Princeton: Princeton University Press, 1965), pp.193–241.
17. S.N. Eisenstadt, *Japanese Civilization* (Chicago: University of Chicago Press, 1996), p.78.
18. Sansom, *The Western World and Japan*, p.383.
19. Toshio Saeki, 'Sport in Japan', in Eric A. Wagner (ed.), *Sport in Asia and Africa* (Westport: Greenwood Press, 1989), p.54.
20. Sociological research suggests that Japanese schools continue to play a larger role in the

socialization into sports than schools in the West; Yasuo Yamaguchi, 'A Comparative Study of Adolescent Socialization into Sport', *International Review of Sport Sociology*, 19, 1 (1984), 63–82.

21. Ikuo Abe, Yasuharu Kiyohara, and Ken Nakajima, 'Fascism, Sport and Society in Japan', *International Journal of the History of Sport*, 9, 1 (April 1992), 6.
22. On this, see Allen Guttmann, *Games and Empires* (New York: Columbia University Press, 1994).
23. Adoption of the *shûkyûsei* (weekly holiday system) facilitated regular participation in weekend sports. See David W. Plath, 'Land of the Rising Sunday', *Japan Quarterly*, 7, 3 (1960), 357–61.
24. Roger F. Hakett, 'The Meiji Leaders and Modernization', in Marius B. Jansen (ed.), *Changing Japanese Attitudes toward Modernization* (Princeton: Princeton University Press, 1965), pp.243–73.
25. Kinoshita Hideaki, *Supôtsu no Kindai Nihonshi* (Tokyo: Kyôrin Shoin, 1970), pp.3–7.
26. Shinsuke Tanada, 'Diffusion into the Orient: The Introduction of Western Sports in Kobe, Japan', *International Journal of the History of Sport*, 5, 3 (December 1988), 372–76.
27. Cortazzi, *Victorians in Japan*, p.293.
28. Edward Seidensticker, *Low City, High City* (New York: Alfred Knopf, 1983), p.167.
29. Cortazzi, *Victorians in Japan*, p.293.
30. Tanada, 'Diffusion into the Orient', pp.372–76; Kinoshita, *Supôtsu no Kindai Nihonshi*, p.9.
31. *Nihon taiikushi*, p.331.
32. Imamura Kinoshita, *Supôtsu no Kindai Nihonshi*, p.85.
33. Gareth Williams, 'Rugby Union', in Tony Mason (ed.), *Sport in Britain* (Cambridge: Cambridge University Press, 1989), p.338.
34. Tanaka Tokuhisa and Yoshikawa Kumiko, Spôtsu (Tokyo: Kintô, 1990), pp.42–7; Kinoshita, *Supôtsu no Kindai Nihonshi*, p.87.
35. N.K. Roscoe, 'The Development of Sport in Japan', *Transactions and Proceedings of the Japan Society*, 30 (1933), 65.
36. On Kobe's string of championships, see Hayase Keiichi, *Hirao Seiji, Hengen Jizai ni* (Osaka: Mainichi Shimbunsha, 1997). Many members of the championship team had played for Dôshisha, which is still a rugby power.
37. Imamura, *Nihon taiikushi*, p.332.
38. Ichikô is simply the abbreviation of the Japanese for 'First Higher Middle School'.
39. Teijirô Muramatsu, *Westerners in the Modernization of Japan* (Tokyo: Hitachi, 1995), p.224.
40. Roscoe, 'The Development of Sport in Japan', p.54.
41. Imamura, *Nihon taiikushi*, p.334.
42. Ibid., p.337, 424.
43. *Asahi Shimbun*, 28 January 1999; Imamura, *Nihon taiikushi*, p.424.
44. Imamura, *Nihon taiikushi*, p.423.
45. *Asahi Shimbun*, 20 January 1999.
46. William R. May, 'Sports', in Richard Gid Powers and Hidetoshi Kato (ed.), *The Handbook of Japanese Popular Culture* (Westport: Greenwood Press, 1989), p.173. Gordon Daniels gives Fujii's height as 3.424 metres and the world record as 3.427 metres, but vaulting records were not ordinarily measured to the millimetre; see 'Japanese Sport', in J.C. Binfield and John Stevenson (eds.), *Sport, Culture, and Politics* (Sheffield: Sheffield Academic Press, 1993), p.178. Imamura gives Fujii's record as 3.66 metres; *Nihon taiikushi*, p.423.
47. Tanaka and Yoshikawa, *Supôtsu*, pp.144–5.
48. The fondness for relay races supports Joy Hendry's comment about a predilection for cooperative sports; see *Understanding Japanese Society* (London: Croom Helm, 1987), p.47. On the other hand, sumo, kendô, kyûdô and the other sports that developed from the martial arts are all individual.
49. Kinoshita, *Supôtus no Kindai Nihonshi*, p.60; Tanaka and Yoshikawa, *Supôtsu*, p.168; *Miru Supôtsu no Shinkô* (Tokyo: Baseball Magazine, 1996), pp.174–80.
50. Ohara Toshihiko, *Hitomi Kinue Monogatari* (Tokyo: Asahi Shimbunsha, 1990).
51. Cortazzi, *Victorians in Japan*, p.19.
52. Imamura, *Nihon taiikushi*, p.331.
53. Cortazzi, *Victorians in Japan*, p.164..
54. Muramatsu, *Westerners in the Modernization of Japan*, pp.219–25; Kinoshita, *Supôtsu no Kindai Nihonshi*, pp.21–2, 122–3. Imamura, *Nihon taiikushi*, pp.425–6.
55. Ibid.

56. Sugimura later became deputy secretary-general of the League of Nations and a member of the International Olympic Committee. Imamura, *Nihon taiikushi*, p.434; Kinoshita, *Supôtsu no Kindai Nihonshi*, p.66; Ikeda Ikuo, *Miru Supôtsu no Shinkô*, p.33; *Asahi Shimbun*, 26 January 1999.
57. Tanaka and Yoshikawa, *Supôtsu*, pp.80–1.
58. Kinoshita, *Supôtsu no Kindai Nihonshi*, p.40.
59. Shinsuke Tanada, 'Introduction of European Sport in Kobe...', *Civilization in Sport History*, ed. Shigeo Shimizu (Kobe: Kobe University, 1987) pp.68–76.
60. Franz Klaus, 'Gedenken an Generalmajor Theodor von Lerch', *Zdarksy-Blätter*, 35 (March 1986), 11–13; Sasase Masashi, 'Hokkaidô Teikoku Daigaku Ski-bu ni okeru Tôzan to Kyôgi...', *Taiikushi Kenkyû*, 11 (1994), 41–54.
61. Bruce Haley, *The Healthy Body and Victorian Culture* (Cambridge: Harvard University Press, 1978); Elmer L. Johnson, *The History of YMCA Physical Education* (Chicago: Follett, 1979).
62. Guttmann, *Games and Empires*, pp.100–3.
63. James Naismith, 'Basketball', *American Physical Education Review*, 19, 5 (May 1914), 339–51; James Naismith, *Basketball* (New York: Association Press, 1941).
64. Ibid., pp.153–4; Kinoshita, *Supôtsu no Kindai Nihonshi*, pp.87–8.
65. *Asahi Shimbun*, 19 February 1999.
66. Tanaka and Yoshikawa, *Supôtsu*, pp.64–5; Kinoshita, *Supôtsu no Kindai Nihonshi*, pp.184–5.
67. Kinoshita, p.184.
68. Cortazzi, *Victorians in Japan*, p.292.
69. Yoshie Hata, 'The Influence of Protestantism of [*sic*] Modern Physical Education in Japan', *Civilization in Sport History*, pp.77–86.
70. Tanaka and Yoshikawa, *Supôtsu*, pp.66–7.
71. Matsumoto Junko, 'Yamaguchi Ken Yoshikimura no Ryojô Seinenkai "Undôbu" (1886–1937) ni Kan suru shiteki Kôsatsu...', *Taiikushi Kenkyû*, 10 (1993), 29–42.
72. For a detailed description and analysis of the games cult (athleticism) of the schools which greatly influenced schools in many parts of the world, see J.A. Mangan, *Athleticism in the Victorian and Edwardian Public School* (London and Portland, OR: Frank Cass, 2000).
73. Donald Roden, *Schooldays in Imperial Japan* (Berkeley: University of California Press, 1980).
74. For extensive consideration of the relationship between the English public schools, sport and militarism and for evidence of public school martial indoctrination, for which there are now a number of sources, see especially J.A. Mangan, 'Play up and Play the Game: the Rhetoric of Cohesion, Identity, Patriotism and Morality', in Mangan, *Athleticism*, pp.179–203; J.A. Mangan 'Duty unto Death: English Masculinity and Militarism in the Age of the New Imperialism', in J.A. Mangan (ed.), *Tribal Identities: Nationalism, Sport, Europe* (London and Portland, OR: Frank Cass, 1996), pp.10–38; J.A. Mangan 'Gamesfield and Battlefield: A Romantic Alliance in Verse and the Creation of Militaristic Masculinity', in John Nauright and Timothy J.L. Chandler (eds.), *Making Men: Ruby and Masculine Identity* (London and Portland, OR: Frank Cass, 1998), pp.141–57.
75. Roden, *Schooldays in Imperial Japan*, p.113.
76. Guttmann, *Games and Empires*, pp.34–6, but see Mangan, *The Games Ethic and Imperialism* for a further and sometimes hilarious description of the strenuous and successful efforts of the English public school missionary and educator to bring the games' cult to the Indian subcontinent.
77. Maarten van Bottenburg, *Verborgen Competitie: Over de Uiteenlopende Populariteit van Sporten* (Amsterdam: Bert Bakker, 1994), pp.132–3.
78. Ikuo Abe and J.A. Mangan, 'The British Impact on Boys' Sports and Games in Japan', *International Journal of the History of Sport*, 14, 2 (August 1997), 189.
79. Roscoe, 'Development of Sport in Japan', p.63.
80. Kiku Kôichi, *Kindai puro Supôtsu no rekishi shakaigaku* (Tokyo: Fumaidô shuppan, 1993), p.57.
81. Yuko Kusaka, 'The Development of Baseball Organizations in Japan', *International Review of Sport Sociology*, 22, 4 (1987), 266.
82. Imamura, *Nihon taiikushi*, pp.331–2.
83. Kiku, *Kindai puro Supôtsu no rekishi shakaigaku*, p.238.
84. Roscoe, 'Development of Sport in Japan', p.63; Watanabe Tohru, 'The Why of the Japanese Choice of Baseball', *Civilization in Sport History*, ed. Shigeo Shimizu (Kobe: Kobe University, 1987) pp.113–28. Details of the earliest period of Japanese baseball differ from account to account.

85. Norgren Nels quoted in Robert J. Sinclair, 'Baseball's Rising Sun: American Interwar Baseball Diplomacy and Japan', *Canadian Journal of the History of Sport*, 16, 2 (December 1985), 48.
86. Kôzu Masaru, *Nihon Kindai Supôtsushi no Teiryû* (Tokyo: Sôbun Kikaku, 1994), pp.241–50.
87. Arthur S. Grix, *Japan's Sport* (Berlin: Limpert, 1938), p.63.
88. Herbert Warren Wind, 'The Bouncing Ball', *Sports Illustrated*, 8 (24 February 1958), 57.
89. Tada Michitarô, *Asobi to Nihonjin* (Tokyo: Chikuma Shobô, 1974), p.76.
90. May, 'Sports', p.181.
91. Donald Roden, 'Baseball and the Quest for National Dignity', p.519; Mark Twain: quoted in Harry C. Palmer, 'The "Around the World" Tour', in Harry Clay Palmer (ed.), *Athletic Sports in America, England, and Australia* (Philadelphia: Hubbard Bros., 1889), p.447.
92. Imamura, *Nihon taiikushi*, p.204.
93. Ibid., p.216.
94. Ibid., p.306.
95. Ikuo Abe, Yasuharu Kiyohara and Ken Nakajima, 'Fascism, Sport and Society in Japan', *International Journal of the History of Sport*, 9, 1 (April 1992), 4. 'Taisô' referred both to gymnastic exercises and to physical education in general, which could include other forms of exercise such as sports.
96. Imamura, *Nihon taiikushi*, pp.327–9.
97. Ibid., pp.341–3.
98. Ikuo Abe and J.A. Mangan, 'The British Impact on Boys' Sports and Games in Japan', *International Journal of the History of Sport*, 14, 2 (August 1997), 198; Norbert Mosch, 'Die politische Funktion des Sports in Japan und Korea' (Ph.D. dissertation, University of Vienna, 1987), 93.
99. Imamura, *Nihon taiikushi*, pp.343–5.
100. Ibid., p.375.
101. Ibid., p.349.
102. Pierre Arnaud, *Le Militaire, l'écolier, le gymnaste* (Lyon: Presses universitaires de Lyon, 1991).
103. Imamura, *Nihon taiikushi*, pp.399–401.
104. Ibid., pp.410–16.
105. Hiroko Seiwa and Chieko Onishi, 'Women and Athletic Meetings in Japan' (unpublished paper, 1997).
106. Imamura, *Nihon taiikushi*, pp.416–17.
107. Miyoko Hagiwara, 'Japanese Women's Sports and Physical Education under the Influence of Their Traditional Costumes', p.266.
108. Nishimura Ayako, 'Zenkoku Kôtô Jôgakkô Chô Kaigi ni mirareru Kôtô Jôgakko no Taiiku Mondai', *Taiikushi Kenkyû*, 5 (March 1988), 7–21; Yoshie Hata, 'The Influence of Protestantism of [*sic*] Modern Physical Education in Japan', *Civilization in Sport History*, p.82.
109. Seiwa and Onishi, 'Women and Athletic Meetings in Japan'.
110. Ibid.
111. Hata, 'The Influence of Protestantism of [*sic*] Modern Physical Education in Japan', p.79.
112. Imamura, *Nihon taiikushi*, pp.475–77.
113. Only one ballgame was listed: football.
114. Imamura, *Nihon taiikushi*, p.478.
115. Ibid., pp.455–66.
116. Ibid., p.482.

Confucianism, Imperialism, Nationalism: Modern Sport, Ideology and Korean Culture

J.A. MANGAN and HA NAM-GIL

Perhaps there is little need for this reminder but sometimes we fail to see what is under our nose and fail equally to appreciate its significance. Thus,

> We live in a nationalized world. The concept of the nation is central to the dominant understandings both of political community and of personal identity ... Notions of national distinctiveness and of international competition or comparison have become intrinsic to the ways in which we think and speak about matters as varied as economics and topography, art and climate, sport and literature, diet and human character. We are equipped, as one ethnologist has put it with a 'nationalizing eye': when we wish to describe or explain difference, we think of it in terms of nations.[1]

Self-evidently, also, all nations possess cultural traditions. Sport is part of this cultural heritage. Prior to the nineteenth-century South-East Asian nations such as China, Japan and Korea developed very different traditions from those found in European nations. However, in the wake of European imperialism during the second half of the nineteenth century and the associated diffusion of its culture, including its newly fashionable sports, throughout the world, these new sports were transplanted in South-East Asia. Korea was not immune.

Sports from countries such as England (and the United States) were introduced to, and took root in Korea during the period 1876 to 1945. However, these sports became established in Korea only after an involved political process due to the fact that during the period in which they spread throughout South-East Asia, Korea endured dramatic political circumstances. Hence another necessary reminder:

> Nationalism is not the mental lubricant of a neatly describable transition from one inherently coherent cultural system to another. It is a conceptual language whose urges have been staged in complex ways by the conflicts and tensions ... generated in particular historical contexts: it has proved adaptable to the needs of imperial aggression and *of anti-imperial resistance* [emphasis added], both of economic traditionalism and of capitalist 'progress', both of the political right and of the political left, both of the expansionist state and its critics.[2]

This chapter explains the recent history of Korean sport by approaching its development from 1880 to 1945 from an ideological perspective. This approach is taken for two main reasons: firstly, because the dominant ideologies of the period, Confucianism, Imperialism and Nationalism, greatly influenced not only Korean culture of this time, but also the development of sport within it, and secondly, because to the present studies which have attempted to explain Korean sport history from an ideological perspective have been rare but insightful and furthermore, have never before been presented in the English language to an international forum.[3]

This chapter will briefly describe the introduction of modern sport into Korea, and then attempt to explain the subsequent evolution of Korean sport in terms of three distinct influences: Confucianism circa 1880; Japanese imperialism during the Japanese colonial period between 1910 and 1945; and finally, resistance to Japanese imperialism and the assertion of Korean nationalism in the same period. The reason for highlighting these three different influences is a simple one. During the period 1880 to 1945, the situation in Korea was such that politically, socially and culturally very little can be explained without them being addressed. Confucianism dominated Korean society during the 500 years of the Yi Dynasty (1392–1910) and though slowly diminishing in influence at the time thus exerted an influence on late nineteenth-century European cultural importations. Then from 1910 to 1945, Korea was under direct Japanese imperial rule. Japanese imperialism in turn stimulated national resistance. The clash of the respective forces of imperialism and nationalism could not but greatly influence modern Korean sport. As will be explained shortly, it became a political instrument. An appreciation of this fact allows an understanding of the relatively rapid process by which occidental sport was able to spread throughout Korea, a country with its own strong oriental traditions.

ARRIVAL

The arrival of modern sport was part of a global process of modernization. The term 'modern' in East Asia refers to a period of time in which Western culture began to be accepted, and entails 'Occidentalism' – the importation and imitation of things European and American. Korea began to accept Western culture from 1876 onwards, when its ocean ports were opened. Korea was now introduced to a wide range of new cultural 'forms and experiences'. Consequently, the period from 1876 until 1910, when Korea was formally annexed by Japan, is regarded as the Enlightenment Period in Korean history.

The formal acceptance of Western culture began with the Kapo Reforms of 1894,[4] initiated in an attempt to modernize Korea to ensure its independent survival. The assimilation of modern sport followed in their wake. The countries of South-East Asia, with national adaptations, had a more or less common sports tradition. The consequence of this was that by the end of the nineteenth century such Asian activities as archery, swinging, wrestling (Korean style), hockey, football (Korean style), darts and hawking, as well as martial arts which utilized the lance and sword, were popular on the Korean peninsula.[5] However, with the arrival of Occidental educational systems in Korea, and an increasing appreciation of their importance for autonomous survival, a variety of modern forms of sports were introduced. In turn, the history of Korean sport entered a transitional period, which proved to be a turning point in the associated evolving culture, and in which both Europeans and Americans had a part to play.

Christian missionaries were the ones who brought and put into practice their forms and methods of education, and so it can be said they played an especially large part in the introduction of Occidental culture, including sport. One area where missionaries had a marked influence was in the introduction and implementation of the concept of 'education for the whole man', an education that included sport and art.[6] In this way, and others, missionary teachers in mission schools played a significant role in the introduction of modern sport to Korea.

The first mission schools established in Korea included Paejae

School (1885), Ewha School (1886)[7] and Kyongsin School (1886). By
1910 numerous mission schools could be found throughout Korea.[8]
Unsurprisingly, the transplanting of Western sport closely followed the
establishment of these schools. Around 1890 sports such as baseball,
soccer, basketball and tennis were introduced.[9] In the school history of
Paejae there are descriptions of the introduction of gymnastics, tennis
and soccer,[10] while in Kyongsin Middle School/High School references
are to be found not only on the introduction of a variety of sports, but
also that from 1891 physical education was a part of the formal
curriculum.[11] Finally, the history of Ewha School records that from 1892
an American teacher by the name of Paine taught physical education.[12] It
is therefore evident from such school records that the role of
missionaries in the spread of modern sport in Korea was fundamental.

Teachers in government-established language institutions also had a
pivotal role in the introduction of modern sport in Korea. In 1894,
nation-wide institutional reforms were carried out in order to implement
modern forms of education. In 'A Policy Statement on Education for the
Nation's Future', King Kojong recommended the introduction of
practical Occidental learning. The establishment, or where they existed,
the re-organization of government or state schools was now officially
encouraged. One type of school at which reforms were implemented was
the government-sponsored language schools set up to promote the
knowledge of English. As the foreign teachers in these institutions were
allowed to introduce the sports they enjoyed, these schools became
centres in which new forms of sport were observed and played. The men
who transmitted these new sports included: the Englishmen W.D.F.
Hutchison, T.E. Halifax and A.B. Turner; the American P.L. Gillet; and
the Frenchman L. Martel.[13] From 1896, these men introduced
gymnastics, soccer and athletics to their students. In fact, it was foreign
language teachers who introduced soccer to Korea.[14] They were also the
first to sponsor an athletics meeting, a moment of some significance in
the history of Korean sport. At the time of this meeting, the
Independence Newspaper commented that 'not only was knowledge
important, but the training of both the mind and body was also
important'.[15] This was a crucial public recognition of the need for new
practices for new times. Both pupils *and* local residents participated in
this athletics meeting, which suggests a marked change in the attitude to
physical activity among at least some Koreans. Clearly this event was of

some historic importance to the cultural transformation of Korean society, but also, as will be seen later, to its political future. Under Japanese imperialism athletics meetings became major locations of resistance.

There was yet another agent of change. In the development of Korean sport, the missionary in the YMCA was of special importance. The Korean YMCA was established in 1903 under the name Whangsung YMCA. From that moment on, the Sports Club of the YMCA was crucial to the popularization of modern sport in Korea. People who played leading parts in this popularization included the Anglican clergyman A.B. Turner, and the American missionaries P.L. Gillet and B.P. Barnhart. Gillet was the first to coach baseball (1905) and basketball (1907),[16] and was also the first, in 1908, to introduce skating.[17] Barnhart, on the other hand, was the first to introduce volleyball and was also instrumental in the training of sports coaches. Through the introduction of these and other sports, for example, weight lifting, there can be no doubt that the YMCA was central to the development of modern Korean sport.

If the Christian missionaries in various schools and the YMCA were an important means by which modern sport took root in Korea, the influence of the Japanese, too, cannot be overlooked. From 1910 until 1945, as mentioned earlier, Korea was one of Japan's colonies. Japan itself, of course, had earlier been greatly influenced by the West and so some of the modern sports introduced into Korea by the Japanese included tennis, rugby, handball, table tennis and ice hockey. Tennis was first played in Korea in its capital, Seoul, in 1884, by American and British diplomats,[18] but the Japanese seem to have been responsible for its later more widespread appeal. Handball was a late arrival and was introduced only on 29 June 1936, when the Korean branch of the Japanese Handball Association was formed.[19] Sports such as rugby and ice hockey also appear to have been introduced by visiting Japanese teams. In short, since Korea was under Japanese control for 36 years it was inevitable that some modern sports spread to Korea via Japan.

In the last quarter of the nineteenth century a number of new sports in countries such as Britain, Germany and the United States (US) were already well organized and widespread. However, in Korean society dominated by Confucianism, even traditional folk sports, though extensive, were not well organized. Under such circumstances, along with the confrontation of the confident imperialisms of the British, the

US and Japanese and a concomitant process of modernization in which Korea had to accept Occidental enculturation, Korea came face-to-face, directly or indirectly, with an enforced cultural revolution. It accepted it but only in the belief that there was no alternative. Modern sport in a sense imposed itself on Korea by virtue of two imperialisms – Western and Eastern.

Undoubtedly, the special characteristics of any particular country are not only reflected in its indigenous culture but in the fact that behind that culture there is a dominant belief system. Accordingly, more often than not, in the course of a new ideology taking root in a new land, some sensibilities, customs and habits will work against its acceptance. Even though modern sport made advances throughout Korea towards the end of the nineteenth century, there were several elements working against its smooth acceptance: the lack of an industrial base that could produce the required equipment and an unsuitable natural environment – a lack of grass fields – were certainly barriers, but the biggest obstacles were Korean practices and Korean traditions grounded in Confucian philosophy.

Because the Kingdom of Choson, established by Yi Song-gye, was influenced by China and adopted Confucianism as its official political philosophy, the Yi Dynasty would have found it difficult, even if it so wished, to shake off the fetters of Confucianism.[20] During the Yi Dynasty, the Neo-Confucianism of Chu Hsi held sway. This new form of Confucianism functioned as the ideological core of Korean thought and influenced every facet of politics, society and culture. Confucianism is centred on the 'Three Cardinal Principles' and the 'Five Ethical Norms'.[21] However, Confucianism is not static. On the other hand, Korean forms of behaviour founded in Confucianism are complex. They are both flexible and inflexible, and include elements that must be inherited and preserved, but also elements which must, to ensure the evolution of Korea, be either changed or abandoned. Here lays one strength of Confucianism – adaptability – up to a point, and here resided the power of the Neo-Confucianism of Chu Hsi. Nevertheless, at the time of encroaching Occidental influence, Confucian elements that worked against the spread of sport include an emphasis on formalism, an appreciation of the literary arts and a respect for scholarship. Also included was a concomitant disdain for the military arts and the belief in the natural dominance of men over women.

Confucian formalism in Korea was highly structured and lacking in pragmatism. Confucianism emphasized rituals, rites and ceremonials thus binding Koreans to rigid formality in their everyday lives. A complicated system of honorifics, beautiful but impractical clothing that restricted energetic body movements, and the languid attitude of the ruling class (*Yangban*) all reflected this formalism. Consequently, the culture of the Korea's Confucian period was based more on passivity than activity and on collectivity rather than on the individual. As a result, Korea was initially a difficult place for dynamic, aggressive, competitive modern sport to make progress.

Among the more fundamental elements of Confucianism that blocked the growth of modern sport in Korean society, as mentioned earlier, were the cultivation of the arts, an emphasis on scholarship and contempt for militarism. During the 500 years of the Yi Dynasty, classic Chinese education was emphasized in Korea. Here, the ruling class respected and rejected, among other things, the arts and natural sciences, respectively. These inclinations resulted in a dislike for physical activity. The aristocrats (*Yangban*) eschewed any strenuous activity, as this was the proper burden of the common people. In such social circumstances, imported sport based on muscularity inevitably faced problems of acceptance.

In the traditional society of Korea, steeped as it was in Confucian custom, a further element of the cultural heritage that inhibited the development of modern sport, as noted previously, was the belief in the natural dominance of men over women. The Choson Kingdom lasted a total of 519 years – from 1392 to 1910. During this time some twenty-seven kings, but not one queen, ruled Korea, which provides ample evidence that Choson Korea was a male-controlled and dominated society. Originally, Confucian thought did not include the belief that men were superior to women but when the theory of *Yin* and *Yang* was incorporated into Confucianism, man was equated with the *Yang*, Spring and Heaven, and women with the *Yin*, Autumn and the Earth. As a corollary, men were associated with superior activities outside the house and women with inferior activities inside the house. Accordingly, women were restricted to essentially passive roles with severely limited outside access. Consequently, participation by women in energetic, strenuous, outdoor exercise was forbidden. Women were thus denied involvement in modern sport in principle and in practice.[22]

The fact that the Confucian heritage was a stumbling block to the acceptance of modern sport is well illustrated by a 1890s description of a soccer match, in which the traditional Confucian-style Korean clothing and the hair style of the period, are totally inappropriate for participation in such an activity. Furthermore, involvement was characterized by an attitude to the rules that verged on anarchy:

> When the athletes entered the field they all removed their hats (traditional Korean *Yangban* style hats).[23] It would have been good if they had taken off the horse hair headbands tying down their topknot hair styles, but then their long hair would have been flying freely, so nobody did that ... Most of them rolled up their baggy pants and ran around in their straw shoes, though a few participants who were wearing athletic shoes they had gotten from foreigners, could be seen ... There was no limit on the number of participants, but the number of members on each team had to be the same ... There were no goal posts, and it was considered a goal when the ball went over the head of the goal keeper.[24]

The extract illustrates the practical psychological and physical problems of modern sport for the Koreans of the time. During the Choson Period, young people, in keeping with Confucian practice grew their hair, tied it with a horse hair headband and on top of it placed a traditional Korean hat. They also wore long and loose traditional clothing appropriate to inactive lifestyles. Clearly then, the Choson Period's Confucian hairstyles and clothing were quite unsuitable for modern sport. Furthermore, it was not simply a matter of customary clothing but customary concepts. The concept of a goal was difficult to appreciate and the scoring of a goal had its own special difficulties. Unsurprisingly, therefore, it took some time before this sport was seen by the masses as an attractive form of leisure. For the innovator Korea was a society steeped in 'inappropriate' tradition.

The ruling *Yangban*'s attitude to modern sport was one of contempt. By 1884 foreign diplomats in Korea were enjoying tennis. Kim Ok-gyun, one of the period reformers keen to see the adoption of Western institutions and practices, built a tennis court near his house to play with American and British diplomats.[25] He was a rarity. Most *Yangban* considered sport beneath them and a manifestation of those physical activities associated with the inferior habits of the lower classes. This is abundantly clear from the following illustration:

> In order to entertain King Sunjong (1907–1910), foreign diplomats

in Seoul organized a tennis match. When playing they sweated much. After watching the tennis match, King Sunjong remarked in a rather exacerbated way, 'To personally do such hard work is really vexing. Why not just call your servants and have them do it?'[26]

In marked contrast, Europe, for example England from the Tudor period onwards, had kings who played tennis. Henry VIII (1509–47), in particular, revelled in such sports as tennis, fencing, wrestling and jousting. He also had a royal cockpit built, and in Whitehall, a bowling alley.[27] Essentially, in Western Europe from the second half of the nineteenth century onwards, sport as an activity of kings and commoners was the order of the day. But Korea was very different. As the passage above reveals, even at the beginning of the twentieth century the last king of the Choson Period, Sunjong, still regarded modern sport as a part of despised lower class culture. Confucian tradition therefore cast a long shadow.

In the Korean society of the 1900s, for reasons already rehearsed, women's participation in sports was more than difficult – it was almost impossible. They stood deep in the shadow of Confucianism. In 1886 there was an attempt to introduce gymnastics into Ewha Girls School, the first girls' school in Korea. It demonstrates all too vividly that Confucian tradition stood between these girls and modernity.

A big disturbance broke out when Pine, after taking office as the new principal, added a class in gymnastics to the curriculum. Traditionally, Korean women had been taught that, when walking, they should not move their arms, and that their stride should not exceed one foot length. They were also taught that when turning their heads, they should turn their whole body also, and when sitting that their feet and legs should be held tightly together. In other words, strenuous and open movements by women were considered immoral, and movements were to be limited to only those absolutely necessary for any activity. In such a period, public opinion was strongly against any gymnastic course in which women had to wave their arms, spread their legs, or run. Parents and elders visited the school and said that they would take their daughters home if they were made to exercise, and the government sent an official demand to Ewha Girl's School telling it to abandon the course in gymnastics. This was done because the women who studied at Ewha Girl's School were not accepted as wives by many of the noble families in Korea – physical training was thought to make a woman immoral...[28]

Unquestionably, women were victims in Confucian Korea. In such a society, participation in sport signified the 'immorality' of self-assertion. Accordingly, women were restricted to passivity. Vigorous activities were strictly forbidden. Confucian tradition functioned to suppress women. They lacked freedom and independence; they were inhibited in order to be controlled.

During the 500 years of the Choson Period, as mentioned earlier, rites, rituals and ceremonials of an over-emphasized formalism characterized Korean society. In particular, a strong contempt for physical activity typified the ruling class. This disdain had a great influence on the 'character' of the people. J. Strutt once famously remarked with some justification, 'In order to form a just estimation of the character of any particular people, it is absolutely necessary to investigate the sports and pastimes most generally prevalent among them.'[29] This is an apposite comment of direct relevance to Choson Korea. During the Choson Period, it should now be clear that the ideology dominating the politics, society and culture of Korea was Confucianism. Without question Confucianism impeded both the assimilation and dissemination of modern sport in Korea. In short, the speed at which modern sport infiltrated Korea at the end of the nineteenth century was strongly determined by its Confucian past.

In spite of the potency of Confucian tradition, in the 1880s Western sport slowly began to impinge on Korean society due to the influence of mission schools, foreign language schools and the YMCA, all of which operated under the aegis of a forward looking monarchy. Then from 29 August 1910 to 15 August 1945, Korea came under Japanese direct rule with the result that its sport was unable to escape from an intimidating Japanese influence. Here was a further obstructive ideology that made an impact on the progress of modern sport in Korean society.

John M. Mackenzie has asserted that in the era of European world supremacy, British imperialism was as much a dominant intellectual, cultural and technical idea as it was a set of economic, political and military imperatives.[30] In other words, imperialism was maintained by moral convictions, cultural certainties and technological innovations backed by military supremacy. This statement neatly fits the nature of

Japanese imperialism in Korea. Japanese rule over Korea from 1910 to 1945 shared precisely the same characteristics.

It would be quite wrong, of course, to take the view that after the Christian intrusion into Japan in the sixteenth century 'Japan shuts the door on foreigners *(sakoku)* until, in the middle of the nineteenth century, it is subjected to a new invasion by Westerners; it modernizes itself, then displays the power of its conversion by emulating the West to the point of becoming, in its turn, an imperial power.'[31]

This is a Eurocentric view. At the same time as Japan attempted to brutally rebut Christianity – a form of occidental religious imperialism in the sixteenth century – Japan simultaneously established around itself a sort of colonial system.[32] This included casting its covetous eyes on Korea and in the second half of the sixteenth century its attempt to place Korea under Japanese rule.[33] Japan, therefore, embarked on a policy of territorial expansion involving Korea well before the nineteenth century. Nevertheless, it was not until the late nineteenth century and the first half of the twentieth century that Japanese imperial ambitions over Korea came to full fruition.

Politically, technologically, economically and militarily in control of Korea, Japan now attempted a complete policy of cultural imperialism. By compelling Koreans to speak Japanese, censuring and controlling media organizations and enforcing the 'Japanization' of Korean names, the Japanese attempted the eradication of the Korean language and the elimination of Korean culture, including the latter's replacement with Japanese culture.

It is a truism, of course, to state that sport is part of a nation's culture. As such, it is reasonable to expect the Japanese, as part of their comprehensive policy of cultural (as well as political and economic) imperialism to assimilate Korea into the Japanese cultural mainstream by, among other things, introducing Japanese sports into Korea. But during the course of Japanese colonial rule sport was not used as a part and parcel of a positive imperial strategy. In the case of Britain, the leading imperialist nation in the nineteenth century, the introduction of sport into its colonies had a hegemonic purpose in the form of a 'moral metaphor, political symbol, and cultural bond'.[34] Britain purposefully introduced sports as instruments of imperialism. The Japanese did not use sport in the same way. In Korea, Japan, on the contrary, regulated and even suppressed sport as an actual or potential form of political subversion. The interesting fact is that it was the new Occidental sports, as much as old Korean sports that were subjected to this treatment. For a good reason – those Western cultural pastimes were now to be used by Koreans to subvert Eastern political purposes.

There are numerous examples of the regulation and suppression of Korean sport during the thirty-six years during which Japan ruled Korea. The most representative examples include the banning of the Combined Athletics Games and Folk Culture Competitions, but there was also the dissolution of sports organizations and the regulation of all team sport activities.

The suppression of the Combined Athletics Games is probably the outstanding example of political suppression. After missionaries had introduced their sports, pupils from various schools, along with local citizens, came together from time to time to hold athletics meetings. Such events, of course, gave impetus to the spread of this innovation in Korean society. In 1896, following an initial English Language School athletics meeting, several other local meetings were held in Korea. The sport prospered. And in 1907 the Combined Athletics Games, a large event involving the participation of citizens and pupils from 72 government, public and private schools, was held.[35] In 1910, however, the Japanese governor-general of Korea banned the event insisting on its permanent abolition. The reason was a political one. Meetings and assemblies of any kind were a threat to political stability and social order.[36] Sports meetings of various kinds provided excellent opportunities for displaying nationalist feelings and offering symbolic defiance to the colonialist.

The suppression of traditional Korean folk competitions was obviously part of the overall attempt to eliminate Korean culture. Like any other nation, Korea had its own traditional sports and the Japanese were determined to 'bury' them in pursuit of the 'Japanization' of the Korean people. Reports in *The Oriental Daily*[37] of the 1920s, for example, clearly demonstrate the truth of this. On 16 February 1926, *yut*-throwing[38] was banned by the Japanese police.[39] In June 1926, the Kanghwa Island Dano Festival[40] was banned.[41] And in 1927 the Korean-style Wrestling Competition sponsored by the Hoeryong Young Men's Association was banned.[42]

In addition to the proscription of the Combined Athletics Meeting, the prohibition of folk competitions and the suppression of other sports activities,[43] the Japanese, as part of their imperialistic policy, monitored and controlled team sports such as soccer and baseball which might stimulate feelings and demonstrations of nationalism. In 1932 the Baseball Regulation Law, and in 1934 the Soccer Regulation Law, were passed. These laws required Koreans to get permission to take part in any baseball or soccer game.[44] The Japanese also reorganized the control of sports organizations putting them directly under the administration of the governor-general and thus allowing the closest monitoring and controlling of these activities. By way of example, in 1920 Korean sportsmen had organized a civilian organization, the Choson Sports Association, to promote athletics events nationally. In February 1933, this Association was taken over by the governor-general, with its administrative office relocated and its activities brought under, the office and aegis of the governor-general, respectively. Eventually, even this was considered insufficient and in 1938 the Association was disbanded.

One reason why the Japanese leaned so heavily on the modern sports of the Koreans was that they were of occidental origin. They were alien to South-East Asia but more importantly were cultural possessions of the Western imperialist. On both grounds they were uncomfortable forms of colonial Japanese culture. However, there is an additional and even more significant reason why the Japanese viewed them with open hostility, suspicion and resentment. They were symbols of the democratic West and as such were embraced by the Koreans as symbols of hope and tokens of political resistance and national defiance. They represented, in effect, manifestations of the Korean independence movement. There is certainly irony in the fact that the Koreans utilized components of Occidental Imperialist culture as forms of protest against Oriental Imperialism! Japanese opposition to the modern sports of the West had one further source. Their priority was militarism. Sport was, in this regard, merely one part of training for war – and a lesser part. One influence of Japanese imperialism on Korean sport that cannot be overlooked or underestimated is the change in schools' physical education to resemble military training. In order to carry out their militaristic objectives, the Japanese reorganized school sport along military lines. This included adapting the playing areas into parade grounds for marching and drill.[45] Western sport lost out to this militaristic priority.

Despite their reservations about modern sport the Japanese did not adopt a policy of total prohibition. In a way sport was a form of training for Japan's wars. Furthermore, if it was adequately supervised, in theory, it was a harmless distraction for Koreans in their unpalatable political situation. Then again the Japanese saw sport as offering occasional opportunities for the bonding of Asian 'brothers' – however, remote that possibility might seem to the Korean 'brother'.

When all is said and done, however, the Japanese period of colonial rule and the brutal, repressive and inhibiting nature of Japanese imperialism, like the earlier but more gentle Confucianism, proved to be an obstacle to the evolution of modern sport in modern Korea. Without any doubt the ideologies of imperialism and Confucianism impeded the growth of modern sport in Korean culture – and yet it should not be overlooked that imperialism was, in fact, the medium by which modern sport reached Korea, was introduced into Korea and was absorbed throughout Korea. In short, while Oriental Imperialism was a negative force, Occidental Imperialism proved to be a positive force with regard to the assimilation of modern sport in modern Korea. There was also a further dimension to Occidental Imperialism's positive impact, namely the boost it gave as one means of resistance for a people bent under the yoke of Japanese totalitarianism.

As has been shrewdly noted:

> Sport is, and always has been, inextricably linked to the forces of nationalism and identity. It should be noted at the outset that, although nationalism is a political force, it is quite distinct from politics. Politics is a discourse concerned with the practice of forming, directing and administrating the state and other political units. Politics will use or adapt nationalism and a variety of other ideological forms, but has no intrinsic ideological basis in itself. All politics and political systems, be they democratic or totalitarian, will function within the nationalist sphere. Nationalism represents the values, beliefs and self-image, amongst other things, of people who declare themselves as a common group.[46]

RESISTANCE

Confucianism and Oriental Imperialism were, indeed, clear–cut ideological obstacles to the development of modern sport in Korea. However, in spite of a Confucian climate detrimental to its growth and its partial suppression under Japanese imperialism, modern sport did take root. In part, and quite considerably so, this was due to the influence of yet another ideology – the ideology of democratic nationalism, a concept 'now envisaged less as an essentially political body of ideas, and more as a mode of sensibility, projected and elaborated across a wide range of cultural fields [including sport]'.[47]

The unprovoked invasion of a nation and a policy of the most ruthless colonial oppression must produce in the victims the deepest resentment and among the more courageous victims a fierce urge to meet force with force. The relationship between sport and militarism and the utilization of sport as preparation for war is well known. It has received the close attention of military historians,[48] cultural historians[49] and those cultural historians with a strong interest of the relationship between sport, war and militarism.[50] The desire to ensure that the nation is fit and strong in body and mind not only in those nations bent on the domination of others but also in those nations determined to resist the domination of others, is a historical fact. It has a special relevance for South-East Asia in the nineteenth and twentieth centuries with nations caught cruelly in the vice of an imperialist military superiority of both Western and Eastern nations.

The indirect imperial intrusion of firstly European nations and then the direct imperial invasion of Japan forced the Koreans to review all of their cultural aspects. Their conclusion was inescapable. Sensible adaptation was required involving the incorporation of those elements of modernity that made nations strong. These included scientific education, technological training, military reform – and new forms of fitness training for the basic physical and psychological qualities for survival in a new age of modernity imposed by both East and West. The body was to be re-evaluated, body attitudes were to be reappraised and institutions to improve body fitness were to be approved. Prior to 1910 Western missionaries and educationalists may have had their ethnocentric convictions regarding the appropriate education for their charges. Yet, these convictions would have had a small impact in Korea if the Koreans themselves had not become convinced however optimistically in the short but not the long term, that in this education and in the face of the threat of subjugation from the world imperial powers lay the opportunity for eventual national self-assertion. In this Korean actions mirrored those of other Asian nations in the same predicament, notably China.

There is an interesting parallel with China in the pursuit of a Social Darwinian physicality to ensure national liberty and self-esteem. In 1915 when Yuan Shikai, the leader of the post-Qing China, was handed a

Japanese ultimatum – the so-called 'Twenty-One Demands' – claiming for the Mikado's government mutual protectorate over China,[51] no less a figure than the young Mao Zedong wrote an article on physical education for *New Youth* (*Xin guingnian*), the leading progressive magazine in China. Its opening lines read: 'Our nation is wanting in strength; the military spirit has not been encouraged. The physical condition of our people deteriorates daily ... If our bodies are not strong, we will tremble at the sight of [enemy] soldiers. How then can we attain our goals, or exercise far-reaching influence?'[52]

China, of course, had attempted to introduce Western physical education into its schools for some time[53] but like Korea, reception was mixed and for the same reasons: 'Tradition ... rejected the idea of physical exertion.'[54]

Mao was well aware of this. He wrote: 'Students feel that exercise is shameful ... Flowing garments, a slow gait, a grave, calm gaze – these constitute a fine deportment, respected by society. Why should one suddenly extend an arm or expose a leg, stretch and bend down? ...' [55]

He proposed the brutal transformation of this element of long established custom in the interest of national survival:

> Exercise should be savage and rude. To charge on horseback amidst the clash of arms and to be ever-victorious; to shake the mountains by one's cries and the colours of the sky by one's roars of anger ... All this is savage and rude and has nothing to do with delicacy. In order to progress in exercise one must be savage ... [Then] one will have great vigour and strong muscles and bones.[56]

In view of Japanese attitudes to both China and Korea, there is certainly a double irony in the fact that from the 1880s many Chinese like many Koreans 'made their way to Tokyo to soak up the new Western learning'. Among them were Kang Youwei and Liang Qichao, the influential leaders of the Emperor Guangxu's failed reformed movement:

> Kang's great contribution to the modernization debate had been to redefine Confucianism to make it forward-looking and therefore compatible with reform, instead of perpetually harking back to a supposed golden age in the remote past. Liang, a Hunanese, took Charles Darwin's thesis, 'the survival of the fittest', and applied it to China's nationals struggle against the encircling Powers. He argued that China had to modernise in order to survive.[57]

Again the similarities to Korean responses were remarkable. A huge slice of the mainland of South-East Asia was looking to the same solution in relation to the rise of Japan. China and Korea faced the same imperial challenge from the East and sought and identical answer to the problem: sport as preparation for war, and this sport was essentially Western in origin and in practice. The traumatic occupation by the Japanese brought home the fact, with a razor sharpness, that modernity – political, technological, economic and cultural – was emphatically no longer an option but an urgent necessity. It is this fact that determined the process by which modern sport became a crucial element in the self-modernization of Korea both before and after 1910.

Modern sport was increasingly welcomed in the later nineteenth century – a period of relative political independence but considerable external political threat. Resistance to modern sport gradually diminished, if not wholly overcome. At every level of society it was more and more appreciated that there were values of various kinds in the forms of sport that had evolved only recently in the Western nations. They ensured a necessary individual and collective competitiveness for a new era; they provided a new and necessary physical fitness; and they were an additional means of collective 'bonding'. Understandably, there was also a desire to emulate the beliefs and practices of clearly successful nations – recreational, philosophical, technological, entrepreneurial and political.

Thus, in a nutshell, to construct a rich, strong, independent country Korean leaders, prior to 1910, advocated educational reform along the lines of Western education models thereby allowing the spread of modern sport throughout schools and society. In 1895, as mentioned earlier, King Kojong issued a 'Policy Statement on Education for the Nation's Future', the content of which strongly emphasized the importance of physical education and sport in schools.[58] With this endorsement, simulated among other things by an anxious nationalism, modern sport became an element of Korean culture. The fusion of modern sport and nationalism centred on the borrowed philosophy of Social Darwinism, which embraced the common interpretation that 'only the strong survive'.

Faced with a national tragedy in which they had lost their sovereignty as a result of Japanese expansionism, the awareness that only the strong survived honed an even finer appreciation of the fact that sport could produce strength of body and mind. Confucian custom was finally set aside. Occupation brought about a transformation in the political awareness of Koreans. To borrow a telling expression: 'the movement forward across the path of an ancient legacy is [now] matched by the backward reach of modern nationalist scholarship'.[59] There was an acute realization that to maintain a free and strong independence it was necessary to make every effort to improve physical strength for any future struggle for freedom. Articles and essays urging physical training were now published in the scholarly journals of the time, and scholars, who now abandoned their Confucian beliefs, urged a more pragmatic education, advocated healthier bodies and stronger minds in part through physical training. Lee Gi (1848–1909), for example, advanced his Theory of Three Forms of Education – physical, moral and mental – which emphasized the necessity of physical training and strengthening of the mind through physical exercise.[60] This was a novel theory and out of step with traditional Korean principles of education. Pak Un-sik (1859–1925), at one time chief editor of the *Hwangsong News* (1895) and then the *Korean Daily News* (1904), argued in the academic journal *Journal of Western Friends* the reason why Korea had lost its national sovereignty and became a slave to another nation was because traditionally Koreans had revered too much the literary arts, neglected the martial arts, and been disdainful of physical effort.[61]

In August 1908, an editorial titled 'The Effect of Physical Education on the Country' was printed in the *Northwest Academic Monthly*. It contained three main assertions. First, through physical training, the individual can become courageous. Second, that sport and indeed all kinds of physical activity can strengthen the solidarity of the people. Third, that physical training through sport is the basis for the creation of a strong country.[62] It was a credo for the times – exaggerated but understandable. All these statements made then clearly demonstrate that Korean sport had become part of a nationalist obsession – political freedom through physical strength. 'An Exhortation for Physical Education', an editorial printed in the December issue of *Taekuk Academic Journal* in 1906, underlines the truth of this point:

> A few straightforward words to my fellow countrymen. A Western philosopher said, 'A strong mind dwells in a strong body.' In this short phrase there is an unlimited truth. The twentieth century is a time in which the weak fall prey to the strong. Whether an individual or country, if one is weak it is difficult to avoid falling by

the wayside. During the last one hundred years our country emphasised literary education and disregarded physical education. As a result, the physical constitution of citizens gradually weakened and their generous spirit and strong character declined, so that today we move only backward, never forward, and we find ourselves in this present situation wherein we have lost our national sovereignty. Because of this I recommend physical education to our people as the foundation of independence for our country.[63]

In summary, modern sport, it should now be abundantly clear, was introduced essentially through the physical education programme in schools and from there it then steadily spread into the wider society. When physical exercise was initially introduced to schools it met with a strong but not completely successful resistance on the part of some parents. But following the invasion of the Japanese the urgent need for modern education was swiftly recognized. Influential educationalists and others argued forcefully for reform, for change and for innovation. Eastern political imperialism had given an extraordinary impetus to Western cultural imperialism!

The Japanese occupied Korea in the 1880s but formally annexed Korea in 1910. It was in this traumatic period for the Koreans that the nationalist movement grew in conviction and in intensity. In 1910 Korea entered a brutal thirty-six-year period of Japanese colonial rule. It stimulated resistance aimed at independence. Japanese harsh imperialism bruised the Korean people's pride and this bruised pride progressed to furious nationalism. The Korean people now concentrated all their efforts on freedom. All forms of culture, including literature, music and art, contained symbols, emblems and tokens of nationalistic resistance. The Korean people now experienced the 'sense of beleaguered imprisonment infused with a passion for community that grounds anti-imperial resistance in cultural effort'.[64] Sport was an integral part of this effort.

In consequence, in the early years of the twentieth century politically motivated sports organizations emerged in Korea: the Daehan Sports Club in March 1906, the Whangsung YMCA Sports Club in April 1906, the Daedong Sports Club in August 1908, are to name just a few. Club members attempted to promote national awareness and stimulate national patriotism through sport. From 1910, however, when Japanese colonial rule in Korea officially commenced, the operation of autonomous, organized activities became impossible due to Japanese regulation and interference. The only sports organization virtually free from Japanese control or interference was the YMCA[65] – being an American, not a Korean organization. Subsequently, within the YMCA Koreans were momentarily free from their Japanese overlords but more importantly, they were free to plot resistance and plan for independence.

For this reason the young flocked to the YMCA. The American organizers for their part were greatly sympathetic to the Koreans' predicament and assisted them in their efforts to preserve and sustain traditional Korean sports such as wrestling (Korean-style) and archery (Korean-style).[66] This was, of course, a political gesture and statement.

Japanese colonial heavy handedness produced a national protest on 1 March 1919 which became known as the March First Movement. It was a failure domestically in its initial gesture but it attracted widespread international attention and won concessions from the Japanese. Their control became less repressive. Freedom to assemble and associate was allowed, permission was granted to print newspapers in Korean script and nationalistic sports organizations were tolerated. The Choson Sports Association and the Kivanso Sports Association both established in February 1919, and nation-wide organizations which played a central role in the nationalist movement, were allowed to continue. Furthermore, on the back of less relentless supervision, from 1920 to 1934 some 90 sports organizations were formed throughout the country.[67] These included the Choson Tennis Association (May 1922), the Choson Baseball Association (21 June 1923), the Choson Basketball Association (July 1925), The Choson Korean Wrestling Association (27 November 1927), the Choson College Soccer Federation (October 1926), the Korean Track and Field Association (October 1928), the Choson Rugby Association (March 1929), the Choson Skiing Association (December 1932), and the Choson Table Tennis Association (June 1933).[68]

By means of these sports organizations, at least, Korean nationalism was sustained. They also kept alive a commitment to independence. They were centres of patriotic sentiment, they allowed young nationalists to gather together and last but not least, they were locations where the process of building strong bodies and minds could be carried forward in the Social Darwinian belief that victory (freedom) would be achieved by the strong in due course. In short, these organizations provided hope, solidarity and fitness. They were forms of resistance through sport, in Alan Klein's vivid expression 'nurtured in the cracks and crevices of a stifling colonial regime'.[69]

It is perfectly clear from documents from this period that the formation of sports organizations was closely connected to the nationalism movement. On 17 February 1919, for example, on the occasion of the establishment of the Choson Sports Association, an editorial titled 'About the Choson Sports Association' was printed in *The Oriental Daily*. The editorial, in expressing strong support for the establishment of the Association, pointed out yet again, that because they had neglected to maintain strong bodies and keen minds, Koreans had become an inferior race subjected to the Japanese. It expressed the hope that the establishment of the Choson Sports Association could serve as a crucial instrument for the invigoration of 'the life force' of the people:

> ... Superior races win and inferior races lose ... Human beings originally got the pulsating life force flowing through Heaven and Earth to maintain life, and their bodies must be as strong as the pine tree and as clear and vital as the sun and moon. But in Korea the present situation is one in which body and mind have weakened and declined. This is because Koreans have lived an idle life and not taken care of their health, and thus been unable to develop the life force of Heaven and Earth. Sport, ... is a fundamental ability ... is the foundation for the development of culture.
>
> We wholeheartedly applaud the establishment of the Choson Sports Association ... [70]

The Choson Sports Association sponsored a variety of athletic meetings, tournaments and competitions including those for soccer, tennis, athletics, baseball and skating. In 1936 it sponsored a nation-wide 12-sport games event. Each of these gatherings gave opportunities for Koreans to express their feelings of patriotism, nationalism and opposition. This became so transparent that in July 1938, the Japanese, by now only too well aware the sports activities of the Korean people were symbols of nationalist resistance, dissolved the Choson Sports Association. Using a sharp comment from C.L.R. James, a caustic but fair observer of Occidental Imperialism, on a great West Indian cricketer's skill with the bat and its symbolic importance for all the West Indian colonized, the Choson Sports Association was a manifestation 'that atoned for a pervading humiliation, and nourished pride and hope'.[71]

From the March First Movement in 1919 until the disbandment of the Choson Sports Association in 1938, national resistance through sport in Korea took two main forms. The first form was resistance to the Japanese suppression of sports. An outstanding example of this was the imposition of the Soccer Regulation Law and the Kwanso Sports Association's opposition to it. In January 1934, the Japanese Office of the Korean governor-general issued the Soccer Regulation edict. This was yet another attempt to control sports that incited nationalistic feelings. However, in April of the same year the Kwanso Sports Association held their annual general meeting in which their opposition to the governor-general's action was very much apparent. Subsequently, the Japanese gave ground and regulation of soccer was greatly lessened.

The second form was the intense competitive attitude the Korean athletes adopted towards the Japanese. Koreans approached any match with the Japanese in the belief that they had to win at all cost because they viewed these meetings as a form of nationalist assertion. In October 1925 when the Korean soccer team was sent to Tokyo to play a match, *The Oriental Daily* printed an editorial calling for the most strenuous effort from the Korean players. It argued that soccer was not to be seen as something involving the feet alone, but as something representing far more – national struggle.[72] Then in December 1928 when the Korean student soccer team went to Japan to play a match, a similar editorial line was used by *The Oriental Daily*: Korean students, with sombre resolution, saw their team representatives off, choking back tears and repeatedly exhorting them to 'bring back the winner's flag, even if entailed the bad luck of smashing one's body or breaking one's leg'.[73]

This do–or–die approach was a characteristic of all sports at this time and during which victory over the Japanese was always reported. In October 1928, for example, *The Oriental Daily* enthusiastically reported victories by Korean students over Japanese students in basketball and athletics. Evidently, whenever Korean and Japanese teams met, the oppressed Koreans tried passionately to make a point about their superiority and to humiliate their oppressors. Sport was one way through which the colonized could both express their resentment and sustain their pride.

In Korea, after the March First Movement of 1919, there were many instances of such symbolic demonstrations against Japanese rule. On one unforgotten occasion, at least to Koreans, there was a delirious moment of national success on the international stage – the 1936 Olympic Marathon and the associated 'Incident of the Omission of the

Japanese Flag' – in which the delirium was a mixture of rage and joy.

In the 1932 Olympics the Korean runners Eun-bae Kim and Tae-hwa Kwon finished sixth and ninth, respectively. However, in 1936, at the Berlin Olympics, Korean runners finished first and third: Kee-chung Sohn won the gold medal in the time of 2 hours, 29 minutes and 19.2 seconds; while Seong-yong Nam won the bronze in 2 hours, 31 minutes and 42 seconds. News that Korean runners had won the gold and bronze medals in the marathon was received in Korea with mixed feelings of joy, anger and shame. Since Korea was still a colony of Japan, Korean athletes had been forced to enter the games under the flag of Japan,[74] which included having to stand on the victory rostrum with their laurel wreaths and a Japanese flag patch on their uniforms. An *Oriental Daily* reporter, Kil-yong Lee and some colleagues obtained a picture of Sohn and Seoung on the victory rostrum, and proceeded to circulate it with the Japanese flag patch intentionally erased. The picture was printed in the *Choson Daily News* and the magazine *New East Asia*. It was the turn of the Japanese to express anger. Japanese suppression of the Korean press resulted. Publication of *The Oriental Daily* was suspended indefinitely and publication of both the *Choson Daily News* and *New East Asia* was banned.[75] The 'Omission of the Flag' may be said to be the high point of Korean resistance through the medium of sport to Japanese imperial domination.

It is clear then that from 1880 to 1945, nationalism was the driving force in the emergence of Korean sport. Between 1880 to 1910, nationalism grew in response to the economic expansion of the Western powers and the political expansion of the Japanese. Modern sport introduced into schools during the early part of this period was, as seen by the Koreans, the means by which individual physical strength was cultivated and national character strengthened in pursuit of national autonomy. In the later part of this period Japanese imperialism became the reason for an intense national awareness of the need to adopt modern sport as a means for both training for freedom and a gesture of nationalism. Traditional Confucian contempt for the physical was rejected. Nationalism, now inspired by political imperialism, became the ideological impetus for acceptance of modern sport throughout the society.

CONCLUSION

Examination of the history of modern sport in Korea clearly reveals that specific ideologies in specific historical moments determined the motives for its assimilation. It demonstrates that modern sport in Korea in the second half of the nineteenth century developed against a continuous nationalist backdrop.

Nationalist sentiment that turned its back on Confucian tradition in response to politically threatening and worrying circumstances between 1876 and 1945 exerted a considerable influence on the progress of modern sport in Korea. Confucian custom with its passive social conduct system in the emerging conditions of the second half of the nineteenth century became a liability. Nationalism, on the other hand, which leaned heavily on the active ideas and systems of the Western powers social conduct, appeared to be an asset. The role of imperialism in determining this innovative nationalism was interestingly paradoxical. Imperialism incorporated elements that worked both for and against successful modernization.

Japanese imperialism, like Korean Confucianism, may be seen as having hindered modernization – politically, economically and culturally. Sport as an element of Korean modern culture suffered in consequence. But the source of modern Korean sport should never be overlooked – Western imperialism, largely the result of the Western *middle-class* missionary effort.

Edward Said claims confidently that the 'Irish experience and other colonial histories in other parts of the contemporary world testify to a new phenomenon: a spiral away and extrapolation from Europe and the West.'[76] In fact, Korea is characterized by a pronounced spin in the *other* direction. In his statement Said seems strangely unaware of, or certainly ignores, Japanese imperialism. It provoked Korea to embrace elements of Western culture that offered the prospect of the unity of corporate resistance through instruments of Western invention – sports on the playing fields and other areas where people could pursue fitness for liberty, plan projects for freedom and make gestures of defiance.

Perhaps the most paradoxical element of all in the evolution of modern sport in twentieth century Korea is the fact that Occidental cultural imperialism in the form of modern sport became a Korean nationalist means of resisting Oriental political imperialism. In this way, imperialism as a malign phenomenon became a benign phenomenon! It is salutary to recall, therefore, the calm and reasonable words of Marc Ferro regarding anti-colonist retrospection: 'if they remember infamous crimes ... they also recall with gratitude their school teachers ...'[77]

Finally, few now find the political dimension to sport insignificant and tangential.[78] This is just as well for twentieth century Korea provides a vivid illustration of sport as a mechanism of political resistance.

NOTES

1. Geoffrey Cubitt (ed.), *Imagining Nations* (Manchester: Manchester University Press, 1998), p.1.
2. Ibid., pp.2–3.
3. Korean scholarship on the history of sports in Korea from 1876 until 1945 includes the following two representative works: Hyong-gi Kwak, 'Kundae hakkyocheyuk-ui palchon yangsang-gwa uimi' (Aspects of the Development of Modern Physical Education and its Significance in the History of Physical Education) (unpublished Ph.D. dissertation, Seoul National University, 1989); and 'Ilcheha-ui ch'eyukundong-e taehan koch'al' (Research on the Suppression of the Sports Movement under Japanese Rule), by Hyon-song Na, in *Huigap kinyom nonmunjib* (Collection of Papers in Commemoration of Na Hyon-song's Sixtieth Birthday) (Seoul: Seoul National University, 1976), pp.101–27.
4. The Kapo Reforms of 1894, which mark the beginning of modernization in Korea, involved administrative, economic and social reforms such as reorganisation of government organs and the abolition of class discrimination in the hiring of public officials. See Andrew C. Nahm, *Korea, Tradition & Transformation: A History of the Korean People* (Seoul: Hollym Publishing, 1988), pp.179–83.
5. Maeng-ryol Cho and Hui-dok No, *Cheyuksa* (History of Physical Education) (Seoul: Hyong-sol Publishing, 1998), pp.311–56.
6. Ch'on-sok Oh, *Hanguk-ui sinkyoyuksa* (A History of Korea's New Education) (Seoul: Hyunda Kyoukchongsu Co., 1964), p.54.
7. This school was established by Mary F. Scranton. It still exists today as Ewha Women's University.
8. For details of the establishment of these schools, see Ha Nam-gil and J.A. Mangan, 'A Curious Conjunction–Sport, Religion, and Nationalism: Christianity and the Modern History of Korea', *International Journal of the History of Sport*, 11, 3 (December 1994), 329–54.
9. In-su Son, *Hanguk kyoyuk sasangsa* (The History of Korean Educational Thought) (Seoul: Chaedong Culture, 1965), p.208.
10. *Paejae p'alsipnyonsa* (The Eighty-Year History of Paejae), compiled by the Committee for the Compilation of *The Eighty-Year History of Paejae* (Seoul: 1965), pp.218–99.
11. Ch'un-sop Ko, *Kyongsin p'alsipnyon yaksa* (The Brief Eighty-Year History of Kyongsin) (Seoul: Kyongsin Middle and High School, 1970), pp.33–4.
12. *Ewha p'alsipnyonsa* (The Eighty-Year History of Ewha), compiled by the Compilation Committee for *The Eighty-Year History of Ewha* (Seoul: Ewha University Publishing Division, 1987), pp.65–7.
13. Yang-un Hyon, *Curriculum Vitae*, 1945, p.1; Hyong-gi Kwak, 'Kundae hakkyocheyuk-ui palchon yangsang-gwa uimi', pp.142–5.
14. Hyon-song Na, *Hanguk undongkyonggisa* (The History of Athletic Competition in Korea)

(Seoul: Pomun, 1985), p.47.

15. *Toknip shinmun* (Independence Newspaper), 5 May 1896.
16. Hyon-song Na, *Hanguk sup'otchusa* (The History of Korean Sport) (Seoul: Munch'on, 1958), p.65.
17. *Hwangsong sinmun* (Hwangsong Newspaper), 17 May 1908.
18. Hyong-gi Kwak, 'Kundae hakkyocheyuk-ui palchon yangsang-gwa uimi', 73–4
19. Hyon-song Na, *The History of Korean Sports*, p.118.
20. See Nahm, *Korea, Tradition & Transformation*, p.94.
21. The cardinal principles were loyalty to the rule (*ch'ung*), filial piety to parents (*hyo*), and the feminine virtues such as chastity, obedience, and faithfulness (*yol*). The five ethical norms dealt with certain responsibilities and obligations governing the relationship between individuals, and included: the principle of righteousness and justice between the ruler and his subjects (*kunsinyuui*); cordiality or closeness between parents and sons (especially sons) (*pujayuch'in*); distinctions between husband and wife (*pubuyubyol*); and relationships between friends (*changyuyuso*). See Nahm, *Korea, Tradition & Transformation*, p.113.
22. *Cholmun yoksa yongu moim, yonghwa ch'orom ilknun Hanguksa* (Youth History Study Meetings, Korean History Read Like a Movie) (Seoul: Myongjin Publishing, 1999), pp.196–202.
23. The long hair was tied/braided and rolled up and then the *manggon* placed over the top. The aristocratic class of the Yi Dynasty wore their traditional hat (*kat*) over the *manggon*.
24. Kyu-t'ae Lee, 'Yunip'om-i toen kaehwa chokki' (The Blooming Vest that Became a Uniform), in *Kaehwa paekgyong* (One-Hundred Blooming Vistas) (Seoul: Sint'aeyang, 1969), pp.218–19.
25. Kyu-t'ae Lee, '*Esei Hangukhak*' (Essay of Korean Studies) *Choson Ilbo* (Choson Daily), issue 18623.
26. Kyu-t'ae Lee, *One-Hundred Blossoming Vistas* , pp.378–9.
27. P. McIntosh, *Sport in Society* (London: West London Press, 1987), p.41; D. Brailsford, *Sport and Society: Elizabeth to Ann* (London: Routledge & Kegan Paul, 1969), p.26.
28. Kyu-t'ae Lee, *One-Hundred Blossoming Vistas*, pp.260–1.
29. J. Strutt, *Sports and Pastimes of the People of England* (London: Thoamas Tegg, 1831), p.xvii.
30. Jeffrey Richards (ed.), *Imperialism and Juvenile Literature* (Manchester: Manchester University Press, 1989), p.52; J. A. Mangan, *The Cultural Bond: Sport, Empire, Society* (London: Frank Cass, 1992), p.1.
31. Marc Ferro, *Colonization: A Global History* (London: Routledge, 1997), p.50.
32. Ibid.
33. Ibid., p.51.
34. J.A. Mangan, *The Cultural Bond: Sport, Empire, Society*, pp.1–10.
35. Hyo-chu Sin, *Ch'eyuksa* (History of Sports) (Seoul: Myongji Publishing, 1998), pp.54–5.
36. See Hyon-hui Lee, *Hanguksa taekye: Ilbon kangchomgi* (An Outline of Korean History: The Period of Japanese Occupation) (Seoul: Samjin, 1973), p.46.
37. To be completed by Ha Nam-Gil (Brief description of the newspaper).
38. *ut* is a simple game played with four wooden sticks – each of which is bevelled on one side and flat on the other – that are thrown like dice. It is still one of Korea's most popular games.
39. *Donga Ilbo* (The Oriental Daily), issue 2002, 20 Feb. 1926, 4.
40. This festival is held on the fifth day of the fifth month. Swings are hung from every high tree, and people dressed in colourful traditional clothes ride on them. Offerings of cherries are also made to shrines of dead ancestors. See Richard Rutt, *History of the Korean People* (Seoul: RAS-KB, 1982), p.284.
41. *The Oriental Daily*, issue 2075, 17 June 1926, 4.
42. *The Oriental Daily*, issue 2420, 29 May 1927, 4.
43. On the historic day of 1 March 1919 a nationwide independence movement began against Japanese imperialism. In response the Japanese government ordered Korean assemblies to be put under close surveillance or to be prohibited. The Combined Athletics Meeting and Folk

Sports Festival suffered, as did football and baseball games. The Japanese viewed them with suspicion as venues for national bonding and expression. Henceforth they attempted to control such events tightly.

44. Hyon-song Na, Research on the Suppression of the Sport Movement under Japanese Rule, p.117.
45. For a recent discussion of Japanese militarism, imperialism and education, see J. A. Mangan and Takeshi Komagome, 'Militarism, Sacrifice and Emperor Worship: The Expendable Male Body in Fascist Japanese Martial Culture', in J.A. Mangan (ed.), *Superman Supreme: Fascist Body as Political Icon – Global Fascism* (London and Portland, OR: Frank Cass, 2000), pp.81–214.
46. Mike Cronin, *Sport and Nationalism in Ireland: Gaelic Games, Soccer and Irish Identity since 1884* (Dublin: Four Courts Press, 1999), p.52.
47. Cubitt, *Imagining Nations*, p.3.
48. Within a European context, for a recent discussion of these historians, see J.A. Mangan, 'Regression and Progression: Introduction to the Cass Edition', *Athleticism in the Victorian and Edwardian Public School* (London and Portland, OR: Frank Cass, 2000), pp.xl–xlvii.
49. In a British context, see, in particular, Geoffrey Best, 'Militarism and the Victorian Public School', in Ian Bradley, *The Victorian Public School* (Dublin: Gill and Macmillan, 1975), pp.
50. See, for example, Mangan, 'Regression and Progression', pp. , also 'Duty Unto Death: English Masculinity and Militarism in the Age of the New Imperialism', in J.A. Mangan (ed.), *Tribal Identities: Nationalism, Europe, Sport* (London and Portland, OR: Frank Cass, 1996), pp.10–38.
51. See Phillip Short, *Mao: A Life* (London: Hodder and Stoughton, 1999), p.58.
52. Ibid.
53. See Fan Hong, *Footbinding, Feminism and Freedom: The Liberation of Women's Bodies in Modern China* (London and Portland, OR: Frank Cass, 1997), pp.77–148.
54. Short, *Mao*, p.59.
55. Ibid.
56. Ibid.
57. Ibid., p.38.
58. See Ha Nam-gil and J.A. Mangan, 'A Curious Conjunction', pp.329–54.
59. Cubitt, Imagining Nations, p.9.
60. Ki-on Han, *Hanguk kyoyuksasang yongu* (Research on Korean Education Thought) (Seoul: Seoul University Publishing Division, 1969), p.120.
61. *Sou hakhoebo* (The Journal of Western Friends), p.10: 6; Hyong-gi Kwak, 'Kundae hakkyocheyuk-ui palchon yangsang-gwa uimi', 52.
62. Chong-man Lee, '*Ch'eyuk-i kukka-e taehan hyoryok*' (The Effect of Physical Training on the Country), *Sobuk hakhoe wolbo* (The Northwest Academic Monthly), 6 (1908), 11.
63. Ch'oe Ch'ang-yol, '*Ch'eyuk-ul kwongoham*' (An Exhortation for Physical Education), in *T'aekuk hakbo* (T'aekuk Academic Journal), 5 (1906), 12; Hak-rae Lee, *Hanguk kundae ch'eyuksa yongu* (Research on the History of Modern Korean Sport) (Seoul: Knowledge Industry, 1990), p.36.
64. Edward W. Said, *Culture and Imperialism* (London: Chatto and Windus, 1993), p.259.
65. For more details on the role of the YMCA in the history of Korean sport see Ha Nam-gil and J.A. Mangan, 'A Curious Conjunction', pp.345–51.
66. Ibid.
67. See *The Oriental Daily* coverage of all Korean sports organisations in a series printed in the 9–13 January 1934, issues of *The Oriental Daily*.
68. Ho-chu Sin, '*Ch'eyuksa*' (History of Sports) (Seoul: Myongji Publishing, 1998), pp.56–7.
69. Alan M. Klein, 'Sport and Colonialism in Latin America and the Caribbean', Studies in Latin American, *Popular Culture*, 10 (1991), 267.
70. *The Oriental Daily*, 16 July 1920.

71. C.L.R. James, Beyond a Boundary (New York: Pantheon, 1983), p.99.
72. *The Oriental Daily*, 30 December 1928.
73. *The Oriental Daily*, 27 December 1928.
74. Olympic records of that time listed Kee-chung Sohn as Kitei Son (JPN) and Seong-yong Nam as Shoryu Nan (JPN). See Stan Greenberg, *The Guinness Olympics Fact Book* (London: Guinness Publishing Ltd., 1991), p.196.
75. '*Inch'on Kim Song-su chon*' (The Complete Work of Kim Song-su), compiled by the Inch'on Commemoration Committee (Seoul: Py'onghwat'ang Printing, 1976), pp.387–8; Hak-rae Lee, *Hanguk kundae ch'eyuksa yongu*, p.192.
76. Said, *Culture and Imperialism*, p.288.
77. Ferro, *Colonization: A Global History*, p.vii.
78. Klein, 'Sport and Colonialism in Latin America', 257.

Complex Creolization: The Evolution of Modern Sport in Singapore

PETER A. HORTON

As Sir Charles Tennyson said, the Victorian British taught the world to play.[1] However, this phenomenon should not been viewed exclusively as the generous outpouring of a benevolent philanthropic culture. It was also as potent a weapon as any sword and as forceful a cultural imposition as any from the Roman Empire to the Third Reich. Sport was central to the hegemony of the British Empire. Sport was the bonding element of the concrete that held the Empire together. Anthony Kirk-Greene suggests that together with the English language, sport is one of the most enduring aspects of the cultural heritage of the British.[2] Today, in all former British imperial territories, sport remains as one of the most important cultural institutions and is still a viable basis upon which allegiances, both past and present, are expressed. This very successful 'Spiritual Export'[3] still provides a medium through which the members of 'family' can communicate, even if the clashes do at times become a little heated!

The dominant influence and cultural process at work in the establishment and later development of modern sport in Singapore was unquestionably that of British Imperialism. The notion of sport being a central and highly significant avenue for cultural imperialism over the past two decades has been well illustrated by historians.[4] Earlier analyses of the earliest days of sport in Singapore tend to reinforce all previous notions of the extent of British cultural imperialism.[5] However, closer and contextually based modern inquiry reveals the existence of a parallel force that powerfully influenced the emerging sport of Singapore. It was, in fact, a combination of environmental conditions working in concert with a host of social, cultural and ethnic influences that produced an interaction resulting in a set of social dynamics that shaped the development of the modern sport of Singapore. This combination of factors embraced the very nature of Singapore; its *raison d'être*, its strategic, economic and political role, and its geography and climate. All played significant roles in the emergence and later transformation of its sport. Culture rides on the bodies of the people just as it resides in their hearts and minds as an element of their collective history. In the initial stages of Singapore's evolution, the most influential groups associated with sport were unquestionably the British *and* the Chinese by virtue of a combination of power, influence and wealth. In addition to the initial overwhelming influence of the Imperial British and the wealthy Chinese, other social groups such as the Eurasians, the Malays and the Indians all contributed to sport in Singapore.[6] The resultant sports legacies, and indeed the culture itself, are a consequence of these varied situational factors and not simply the outcome of the dominant values, beliefs and imperatives of the British. Unquestionably the games remain, yet the culture moves on; today globalization, driven by mass media and information technology, is the master source and force of cultural imposition.

THE NASCENT SPORTS CULTURE

Singapore today reflects the dominant political, social and cultural influence of the foremost racial and cultural group – the ethnic Chinese. However, the government actively supports the cultures, religions and social structures of the minority ethnic groups – the Malay and the Indian.[7] The glib description 'ethnic Chinese' of course, in no way adequately characterizes this incredibly complex social grouping. The Chinese in Singapore are multi-dimensional people in terms of dialect spoken, ancestral heritage, religion, education and certainly class and status even though most are now Singapore-born.[8]

In modern Singapore today, the fundamental structures of sport, the games played and, to an extent, the motivating forces represent residual elements of the colonial British culture.[9] The sport of the masses is soccer, while rugby is the favoured football code at the leading independent boys' schools. Hockey, netball and tennis predominate at the leading girls' schools and all schools are to varying degrees, ensnared by the traditional athletics and swimming championship cultures. The structure and content of school physical education programmes are still fundamentally based on the British model.[10] Nevertheless, throughout the history of physical education in Singapore there has always been an on-going and very influential Chinese presence.[11] Furthermore, today the sport of Singapore is a manifestation of a highly materialistic, meritocratic and extremely prosperous young nation and the pragmatic policies of its government.

In short, it would be a mistake to allocate sole responsibility for the nature of the nation's sport to one cultural force. Indeed, the relationship between the dominant cultural forces, whether British, Chinese, or, as in recent times the pervasive cultural influences of Americanization or globalization, on recipient cultures such as Singapore, is a far more integrated and symbiotic alliance than previously believed. Initially, the cultural imperialism of the British and the Chinese, matched of course by the lesser but very pertinent cultural influence of the Malays, evolved in parallel and only gradually began to intertwine into a complex cultural helix. This process characterized the era of British rule, and after independence in 1965, continued as a direct outcome of the policies of the ruling People's Action Party (PAP).

Sport in Singapore initially mimicked the sporting pursuits of the various class groups of Britain. Yet, unlike other imperial territories such as the colonies of Australia, Singapore was always much more cosmopolitan with the influence of a considerable array of ethnic, cultural and other national groups constantly apparent.[12] The British, as the ruling group, initially established all predominant social institutions. Government, finance, commerce, religion, education and the military were all controlled, as were the people, by their imperial masters. The template of the future Singapore was very much shaped by the model established by the British following Stamford Raffles' arrival in 1819. However, it is suggested here that the influence of the clan organizations or Bangs of the Chinese clearly matched that of the British.[13]

When the British first colonized the small island of Singapura in 1819, it was nothing more than a rather shabby outpost of the declining empire of the Sultan of Johore.[14] It had very little going for it except its magnificent strategic position and outstanding off-shore harbour potential, both of which were immediately recognized by Stamford Raffles and the man who actually did much of the early establishment work for the East India Company, William Farquhar.[15] The island provided meagre farming for small bands of Malays (500 Orang Kallang and 200 Orang Seletar), while the village at the mouth of the Singapore river was home for the 150 or so Orang Gelam, and various Orang Laut (sea people) lived on their boats in the harbour. There were at this time only some 30 Chinese inhabitants.[16] By 1860 the population of the Straits

Settlement of Singapore had exploded to nearly 82,000![17]   The largest
single immigrant group was the Chinese, numbering over 50,000 and
made up of Hokkiens, Cantonese, Teo-Chews and Hakkas, nearly all of
whom came from the provinces of Kwangtung and Fukien in South East
China.[18] Most of the migrants were fleeing the political, social and
economic conditions of late Imperial China.[19] Thus, to the vast majority
of the various peoples that now lived in Singapore the concept of
Western competitive sport meant nothing. It had no place in their day-
to-day lives and was in no way part of their culture. Any recreational
'sporting' activity they participated in would have been their own
traditional recreational or ceremonial activities. Naturally, such games
and play would have involved an element of competition but obviously,
not that inspired by Western sports.[20] Long before the formal settlement
of the colony, the Malay people of early Singapore had their distinct play
culture.[21] Life in their kampongs[22] reverberated with the voices of play.
Children flew kites, spun tops and boys and men played several
traditional games such as sepak raga – a football game using a rattan ball
that involves kicking the ball in the air for as long as possible.[23] The
Orang Laut played in and under the sea: swimming, diving, boating and
sailing provided children with basic play and training. The enjoyment of
the early Malays derived from play is still retained by the Malays of
today; of all the ethnic groups in Singapore, the Malays have an obvious
love of play and this is encouraged and fostered by the government.[24]

EARLY EDUCATION: A CHINESE EXEMPLAR

The educational institutions of Singapore were, and obviously still
remain, the major conduits of cultural imposition. The establishment of
the sports systems in the various schools of the Singapore colony has had
an enduring impact on the development of the sports of the island-
nation.[25] Most children who attended schools such as Raffles Institution,
the various mission schools and the English vernacular schools were the
children of either the wealthy Chinese or the emerging Chinese middle
class. A minority of pupils came from the families of wealthy Eurasians
and other minority groups such as the Indians with only a rare
smattering of expatriate children as most were sent home to boarding
schools. A private education, incidentally, was not the sole preserve of
the expatriates: many prominent Chinese families preferred to have their

sons educated by personal tutors. The Raffles Institution soon assumed the mantle of the premier school of the colony.[26] The first, and many say the finest, Chinese scholar produced by the Raffles Institution during the nineteenth century was Dr Lim Boon Keng. He was the 'first Chinese lad'[27] to win the Higher Scholarship, which had been instituted by the governor, Sir Cecil Clementi Smith in 1885.[28] Lim Boon Keng's story is part of the folk-history of the Chinese Singaporeans. Despite adversity and near poverty he rose to become a graduate of the medical school at Edinburgh University. After his return to Singapore, Lim Boon Keng not only gained professional fame but also was later to become a major activist in the 'moral, social and educational' reforms within the Chinese population of the colony.[29] A product of a transposed English public school system it is ironic that he is widely viewed as one of the leading figures in the revival of the Chinese schools and Confucianism in Singapore at the turn of the century.[30] Lim Boon Keng later became one of the promoters and founders of the Singapore Chinese Girls' School, the administrative officer of the Chinese Volunteer Company and founder member of the Straits Chinese British Association.[31] Obviously, he was a highly respected member of the Chinese community in Singapore. Furthermore, the story of his life explicitly demonstrates the extent of the hegemonic power of British cultural and social imperialism at work. Lim Boon Keng's general lifestyle and charitable deeds would not have been out of place had he been an 'English' gentleman in Australia, New Zealand, or the Home Counties! In reality, he was very much an ethnic Chinese immersed, indeed born, into the culture of the British Empire. This is not a cause for regret among Singaporean Chinese. To this day the sons of Chinese families invoke his auspicious memory by naming their sons after him. Lim Boon Keng encapsulates the essence of the interface and intersection of the two major social influences that have been responsible for the cultural template of modern Singapore.

It would be fanciful to say that the British established a 'system' of education in Singapore in the first half of the nineteenth century. Considering the modern state of Singapore's preoccupation with education and qualifications it is rather ironic that Stamford Raffles, as early as 1819, embraced a passionate notion of making Singapore the educational centre of a region stretching from India to Australia.[32] Raffles' dream died with the lack of interest and funds from the East India Company, and in 1830, it even withdrew what funds it had previously given as education grants.[33] Gradually, via the agency of groups of private individuals (merchants) non-mission schools emerged. The Singapore Institution was established in 1823 (The London Missionary Society opened its first school in China a year earlier) and in 1868 it was renamed the Raffles Institution. Then in 1834, the American Board of Commissioners of Foreign Missions decided on Singapore as its base for its missions in China and within three years had nineteen missionaries working in the colony.[34] In 1842 the Anglican Mission of London founded St Margaret's School, the first English medium girls' school in Singapore. Raffles Girls' School in 1844, the Convent of the Holy Infant Jesus in 1854 and St Anna's School in 1879 followed suit. The American Methodist Church founded the Methodist Girls' School in 1887 and Fairfield Methodist Girls' School in 1889. All such English vernacular schools accepted students from all ethnic groups, though students were generally Chinese or Indians who aspired to careers in the civil service or the professions.[35]

The British instigated the Straits Settlements education policy in 1867 and its major thrusts were the promotion of the English language schools and paternalistic support of the schools for the Malays.[36] Each year from 1888 to 1918, the Government gave scholarships to ten Malay boys to attend the Raffles Institution.[37] The British merely tolerated the Chinese language schools; they neither assumed a financial nor an educational management role nor, because they were unable to, attempted to exert educational control.[38] It can be said, therefore, that the British literally divorced themselves from both control and support of the Chinese schools.

Until the end of the Ching dynasty in 1912, the ideology, as well as the actual curriculum of the Chinese schools in Singapore, came from China via an imperial edict.[39] Such Chinese influence then continued after the fall of the Ching Dynasty. While the British were trying to Christianize the Malays and create quasi English public schools founded upon Athleticism and Muscular Christianity,[40] the young Chinese who attended the Chinese schools were being as strongly directed to another set of idealistic goals. It was not until after the First World War that the British made any attempt to control or curb the extent of Chinese education in Singapore and this fundamentally was undertaken to repress political activism.[41] Although, the spirit of Athleticism and muscular Christianity was very apparent in such schools as the Raffles Institution and St Andrew's (established in 1871) it was not until well after 1920 that most of the English schools acquired adequate sports fields. The Department of Education reports from 1880 to 1920 lamented the fact that the sports facilities at the boys' schools were utterly inadequate.[42] Only the Raffles Institution possessed a sports field worthy of hosting a game of cricket or a sports day.[43]

The English-medium girls' schools were similarly bereft of sporting facilities. With many of the schools being housed in converted shop-houses, facilities for anything but formal classroom work were clearly non-existent. Even so, the major restraining factor against girls' participation in school sport and physical education were the entrenched social attitudes of the period. Towards the end of the nineteenth century, restrictive patriarchal ideas were slowly diminishing in Britain, but not so in Singapore. Furthermore, there existed the additional confounding factor of traditional Asian attitudes to the behaviour *per se* of girls and women.[44] For both the Chinese and the Malays, in general the litany of acceptable behaviour for a girl did not include unrestrained physical activity, and mostly certainly not in public; such behaviour was viewed as taboo![45] Raffles Girls' School, however, did have a playing field, though there is little evidence of its use for sport until the early twentieth century. In fact, the Department of Education's Annual Reports did not refer to physical education in any of their girls' schools until 1921. In contrast, the 1907 Imperial edict from China insisted that 'tichao'[46] had to be an integral part of the curriculum of all modern Chinese girls' schools,[47] although the manner in which it was undertaken in Singapore – 'fully dressed and in a stoic and orderly manner'[48] – did little to suggest that girls were involved in a high level of vigorous physical activity. However, as Teo suggests, 'it did initiate the transition to an acceptance of physical activity for girls'.[49]

The colonial government also off-loaded a considerable percentage of its educational responsibilities to the Missions. Many of Singapore's 'top' schools today, such as St Joseph's, Methodist Girls School, Fairfield Methodist School, St Andrew's School and the Anglo-Chinese School were founded and initially directed by specific church/mission groups. Such schools until well into the twentieth century received rather meagre levels of financial support from the colonial government of Singapore by way of government grant aids.[50] Thus, it can be seen that influences, other than British, were making an impact upon Singapore's premier schools and thus directly upon their sports. Indeed, the greatest influence, if the number of actual English language schools established by a single 'national' identity is considered, was undoubtedly American! By 1915, the American Methodists Mission had set up seven schools in Singapore.[51]

The educational institutions of Singapore were and, obviously, still are major conduits of cultural diffusion – from both West and East. The establishment of the sports systems in the various schools – British, Chinese, American – of the Singapore colony all had an enduring impact upon the gradual development of the sport of the island-nation. Yet it is possible to suggest degrees of influence. As the premier boys' school, the Raffles Institution played a pivotal role in the diffusion of sport in the colony. The Raffles Institution, or the Singapore Institution as it was known in the first 33 years of its existence, was founded on the lines of an English public school. Consequently, sport was a central feature of the educational philosophy of the school.[52] By 1839, the school had a gymnasium, and the playing field, crude as it was, was well used for cricket and football. The strength of its sporting tradition is generally attributed to the tenure of R.W. Hullet who was the headmaster from 1871 to 1906.[53] Hullet instilled the cult of Athleticism in this the leading school of the colony using the symbolic trappings he had himself revered during his public school days and at Cambridge. A cricket club was established and closely imitated the Singapore Cricket Club's structure and function in that it assumed the overall organizational responsibilities role for all sport at the school. Senior boys, presumably prefects, ran the club and levied its members in order to run its operation. Young expatriate teachers were not only prominent in the club's organization, but they in fact 'turned out' in both the football and cricket teams. The 'ribboned blazer', inappropriate as it was climatically, was in evidence in spirit at least, following the institution of the school's colours system in 1887. Sports days were held and success was much sought after, and invariably reported in the *Rafflesian*, a fortnightly school magazine.[54] By the turn of the century the Raffles Institution was, in essence, a transposed lesser English public school with a largely Straits Chinese student body. As the school from which the future leaders of commerce, government and law would emerge, Raffles became an effective and very powerful agent of British cultural imperialism. The other leading boys' schools, although founded by a variety of missions, also later assumed the then fashionable Athleticism and propagated this predominant element of Anglo-Saxon culture. There was a paradox in all this, touched upon earlier, in that these bastions of Western culture and others, spawned men such as Dr Lim Boon Keng and Sir Song Ong Siang, who were to become the leaders and promoters of Chinese culture and education.[55] At the same time, the British influence did not disappear! It remained, survived and prospered as elsewhere. Why? Because it was a caste-mark?

THE DIFFUSION OF SPORT

An earlier analysis of the diffusion of modern sport and the establishment of modern sport in Singapore largely stressed the centrality of the role of British cultural imperialism.[56] However, even though the residual British cultural heritage had a tremendous structural impact upon the development of sport, as mentioned above (and physical education), in Singapore, there was another effective form of cultural imperialism at work; that of the Chinese. As the Chinese diaspora spread, its cultural influence was greatly significant throughout Southeast Asia. In Singapore the parallel cultural imperialism of the Chinese was responsible for many institutional and attitudinal characteristics still in existence today. So much so that the ethnic Chinese now dominate, not only in numbers, but in terms of power. Their influence extends to all areas of social activity: industry, commerce, government, education, law and culture; in turn, sport, recreation and physical education have been particularly affected. The traditional attitude of the Chinese was to view sport as being of little merit. As J.D. Vaughan once suggested, 'the true Chinaman [*sic*] ridicules the idea of exercise in any shape'.[57] In the early years of independent Singapore government policy, accordingly the prevailing social perception of sport bestowed on it only a relatively lowly status. Its virtues, nonetheless, were recognized. Lee Kuan Yew, the political mastermind behind the establishment and development of modern Singapore viewed sport eugenically. He saw its function as being: 'to generate healthy, vigorous exercise for the whole population, enhancing the valuable qualities we have in our people – keen, bright, educated and more *productive* if they are more fit'.[58]

Among the Chinese the perception of sport had long been that it was not a *serious* activity.[59] Assets such as educational qualifications, a successful career, social status and wealth were all considered of major importance. In comparison, sport was regarded of minor importance.[60] Even today, Chinese Singaporeans are loath to take anything but a recreational or a health interest in physical activity: real seriousness involves qualifications, career and materialism. This is not to say that health is not, or never has been, important to the Chinese; obviously it is and has always been so. The point is that prior to the 1990s this preoccupation did not include the notion of achieving good health, and the associated prosperity, through strenuous activity. It was to be achieved through consumption rather than 'production' via a holistic regime that included the use of potions, traditional medicines, food and rest. Quasi-meditative exercise regimes, such as Qi Gong and Tai-chi, in a sense are 'cop-outs' as far as heavy physical exertion is concerned. Such activities should not be viewed solely as exercise programmes. They are a means to restore the physiological (and psychological) balance through breathing and movement sequences. Today many, generally older, people engage daily in such activities. Yet, these activities do not emphasize the effort, or the related sweat, implicit in vigorous physical exertion that is endemic to manual labour and thus the lowest classes of society.

In the 1990s, a range of government initiatives embracing a major paradigm shift with regard to sport, recreation and health-related physical activity saw sport enlisted as a political-economic tool. Physical activity began to subsume the traditional methods used by the Chinese in the quest for health and wellbeing. Subsequently, today, health and personal fitness and the associated positive self-image remain the primary motivations for exercise for the vast majority of Singaporeans. The quest for fitness, so important for many young Singaporeans, is motivated by concerns of social status and an acceptable body image.

As the sport of Singapore emerged, the relationship between the development of sport and power was most apparent. For sport to become an acceptable cultural form, it had to be embraced by the dominant social classes.[61] Sport was adopted by the British bourgeoisie as a vehicle for proselytizing its credos of muscular Christianity, Athleticism, amateurism and the eugenics of Social Darwinism.[62] These features of bourgeois ideology were exported as the 'cultural baggage' of the British as they colonized Africa, the East, the Antipodes and elsewhere.[63] Once the basic social infrastructures became established in Singapore and other colonies as well as the dominions, the bourgeoisie began its effort to implant Britain's cultural artefacts. These efforts had varying degrees of success throughout the British Empire. The level of success in imperial territories such as Australia and New Zealand was far more complete than in Singapore where the complexity of the ethnic mix, as well as climatic and geographic factors, did not allow for a smooth uptake of the most robust aspects of British culture.[64]

The early British who arrived to colonize Singapore, initially for the East India Company and then the Crown, possessed no modern sports as such because these had yet to become popular in Britain.[65] However, leisure pursuits and recreations were, at this time, popular features of the cultural fabric of the upper echelons of society, particularly of those members who had arrived via tours of duty on the sub-continent. This upper-class establishment quickly entered into an ebullient round of social engagements, parties, promenading and horse riding activities.[66] Such recreations were undertaken to assuage the excesses of the dining table and for desirable social objectives.[67] As games became more acceptable, the affluent adopted activities such as cricket, as part of approved behaviour. Soon to follow, in what was to become a predictable pattern in British colonies, were horse racing, hunting, sailing, rowing and both football codes. The formation process of the British sporting ethos in Singapore is said to have crystallized with the founding of the Singapore Cricket Club (SCC) in 1852.[68] The history of the SCC with its now legendary clubhouse on the Padang[69] is in many ways the history of modern sport (English sport, that is) in Singapore. The club was to become a haven of social as well as sporting activity for the young expatriates of the colony. Following its establishment, the SCC rapidly assumed the hallmarks of Victorian middle-class chauvinism. Women had only token access to the activities of the club whilst a 'whites only' regulation existed.[70] Thus, to a large degree the club's culture directly reflected the social mores and ethos of the Victorian bourgeoisie of the time.[71] Women were very much for decoration, were given only limited access to the club's rooms and could not participate in any of the club's sporting activities.[72]

Further evidence of the nature of the racist and patriarchal control of sporting and recreational activities in colonial Singapore can be gleaned from a consideration of the history of the Singapore Swimming Club (SSC).[73] The SSC was formally established, at a beachside locale, in 1894, and turned out to be very much the preserve of young British (and some continental Europeans) male professionals, and in which membership was very much sought after by newcomers.[74] The club formed an integral element in the social hierarchy of the colony and its status can be gleaned from the comment made by George Creighton, assistant club secretary from 1948 to 1952: '... SSC was easier for the young men to join as you did not have to be Number One to be eligible, as was the case with Tanglin [Club]'.[75] He added, however, that membership was avidly sought after particularly because the club, unlike the Tanglin Club, had a swimming pool. The club also had a very attractive setting and an active tradition of 'social activity'! The class barriers were fiercely defended, with the club blocking any membership application from what was considered to be the 'rank and file'.[76] The rank of warrant officer was even contested as being worthy of acceptance. Stories of racial discrimination abounded:[77] a Mrs Hazel, who on her application form had put down her place of birth as 'KL' (Kuala Lumpur), was informed that she had to be to seen to confirm she was white![78] This kind of discrimination lasted until well after the Second World War. It was only in 1951 that Asian guests were allowed in the club but then only once a month after 7.00 p.m. In fact, it was another ten years before the club opened its doors to Asians[79] and 29 years before women were allowed to use the club on public holidays and a further eight years before they were granted the concession of being able to use the club on Sundays but only after 4.00 p.m. In 1946, women were given 'permission' to use the club's facilities all day on Sundays. Yet, even to this day, women still do not have the right to 'full' membership of the club, nor indeed of the SCC. Racism, male chauvinism and discriminatory class practices were not, of course, exclusive to the British. All racial interactions in colonial Singapore were very apparent, and at times were characterized by insurmountable social barriers.[80]

SPORT, RECREATION AND THE STRAITS CHINESE

From 1819 to 1867 Singapore was ruled from the India Office and throughout this time the Singapore-based government viewed the majority of Chinese as itinerant workers. Initially the wealthy Chinese middle class was tolerated, if not fully accepted by the British establishment. The Chinese middle class had assumed many of the cultural symbols of the British middle class, including language and religion, as well as recreational activities, among them sport.[81] In fact, as C.M. Turnbull suggests, governance at this time, 'scarcely impinged on the life of its Asian population'.[82] However, developments in the global transport and communications systems brought the British expatriates closer to Britain and thus to its class and social structures. 'The old free and easy, uniquely Singaporean, way of life changed to a more formal middle-class society, staid, honest, respectable, non-adventurous, narrow-minded, reflecting the values of mid-Victorian Britain.'[83] The previously convivial and integrated social life amongst the Europeans was also affected. It 'became more sophisticated, snobbish and exclusively Western'.[84] The atmosphere also changed for the wealthy middle-class Chinese businessmen. They were now not quite so 'socially acceptable' and although Britons had to do business with Chinese, a new apartheid-like environment emerged at the upper levels where previously it had not existed. The single critical symbolic incident in this process was the withdrawal of the Chinese members from the Singapore Chamber of Commerce in 1860.[85] It should not be inferred that the middle-class Chinese became Anglo-phobic at this stage. They did not. Elements such as the spiritual and social mores and attitudes of the British middle-class were still highly revered and eagerly assumed, albeit mimetically, by the wealthy Asians, as well as the Arabs, Indians and Armenians.[86, 87, 88] In fact, in the case of the Chinese population, for example, greater social distances existed between their upper and lower social groups than between the wealthier Chinese and the British![89] As the wealthy Chinese enthusiastically adopted modern sport, the majority of the Chinese males, who were the main labourers, had no liking for it; for them, the reality of life was continual labour and the quest for money. For recreation, these men sought comfort in opium, prostitutes and gambling.[90] Furthermore, to this day gambling is still the major 'social diversion' for many working-class Singaporeans, particularly the Chinese. Almost immediately after settling the colony one of Raffles first acts as administrator was to prohibit gaming by authorizing magistrates to 'flog and banish gamblers and confiscate their property'.[91] At various times from 1823 to 1888 gambling in the gaming houses and gambling farms of the Chinese was legalized, regulated and then finally abolished. The ban on the gaming houses came in 1888 with the passage of the Common Gaming Houses Ordinance Number V.[92] The preamble to the ordinance included the following comment:

> As a rule the Chinese have fully recognized the evils of the gambling habit, and before leaving the subject it deserves to be recorded that in the Federated Malay States the gambling farms, which for so many years had yielded a large revenue, have been

abolished at the express request of the Chinese themselves, the change having come with the foundation of the Chinese Republic.[93]

This paternalistic and patronizing comment provides further evidence of the direct influence of the Chinese government, in this case the Republican government, upon the social behaviour of the Chinese residents in the British territories in the region. It would appear that the authoritarian tentacles of an alien nation had reached out and effected a change to the law in territories under British rule.[94] Clearly, the British neither considered the Chinese living in the Straits Territories to be their responsibility nor their social activity the sole concern of British law. Even though few, if any, of the lowly Chinese workers would have actually been British citizens, it is still very surprising to see this insouciant attitude of the colonial government to laws governing residents in the colony of Singapore. The British, did, however, assume a highly paternalistic approach to governance over the Chinese and Malay populations in the Straits Settlements and this typified the attitude of the domestic British 'do–gooder' middle class in its attempt to control the social behaviour of the lower echelons of society.[95] The gambling houses of Singapore were viewed as pernicious dens of iniquity and the campaign for their prohibition continued throughout the nineteenth century and up to the Japanese occupation of the island in 1942, when the Japanese abolished all bans on opium smoking and prostitution. The reason behind this is not clear, but it may well be surmised that both practices would have had a destabilizing, as well as an opiating effect, on the largest section of the male population of the occupied territory.[96]

For the wealthy, the sport of horse racing in Singapore provided, as it still does throughout the world, a most respectable and very acceptable medium through which they could satisfy their gambling passion. By 1861, the rich Chinese had appropriated the 'sport of kings'. They donated trophies, were owners and indeed, became members of the sporting club. So complete was this process that, '... In 1898 "Vanitas", owned by Mr Tan Boo Liat, won the Viceroy's Cup in India – the only occasion on which a horse from the Straits or Federated Malay States has secured this handsome and coveted trophy.'[97] Whilst the opium smokers, gamblers and customers of the brothels were being leaned upon by the police and the agents of morality in Victorian Singapore, the Chinese middle class and the wealthier tradesmen had appropriated the trappings and social mores of the official dominant culture. In contrast, the vast majority of migrant Chinese workers, who had left China to find a haven from the political, social and economic turmoil endemic in late Imperial China, retained their traditional religious beliefs and proudly adhered to their Chinese cultural heritage.[98]

In short, as the Chinese middle-class gained power and access, its members readily adopted the trappings of Western 'civilization'. Sport was a very obvious trapping. Early in 1885, the Straits Chinese Recreation Club (SCRC) was established 'for the purpose of playing lawn tennis, cricket and practising English athletic sports'.[99] The SCRC was based at Hong Lim Green, which was named after a Singapore-born Chinese businessman, Cheang Hong Lim, who had donated $3,000 to convert a piece of open land into a public park and to provide for the construction of an enclosing iron-railing fence. In this action the ambiguity of life in the Straits Settlements during the late 1880s presents itself most graphically. Cheang Hong Lim's father, Cheang Sam Teo and his partner Tay Han Long, had amassed their wealth from their monopoly of the opium and betel vine sales in the region.[100] Cheang Hong Lim was the fortunate and respectable beneficiary!

The SCRC was initially set up in the closing months of 1884 as a tennis club at a particular venue that was, according to the club's honourary secretary in 1885, Liow Cheng Koon, to have been 'quite beyond the centre of town, [and] a place not worth mentioning'.[101] Two years after the establishment of the SCRC, the clubhouse, proudly situated behind its iron-railings, was officially opened on the 2 July by Tso Ping Lung, the Chinese Consul. The Consul was the Imperial Chinese government's representative of the Chinese in Singapore. His comments stress that all were viewed as being citizens of China. His rather prosaic speech offers an excellent insight into the perception of sport in late nineteenth-century China. Similarly, it demonstrates how the diffusion of modern sport to the colony of Singapore had begun to impact upon this enclave of Chinese culture.

> Whilst in China, I am sorry to say, no play whatever is allowed to students in the school. Those who study too hard very often suffer from consumption or other diseases merely on account of not having sufficient exercise. It is a pity that they do not understand what the proverb says: 'All work and no play makes Jack a dull boy.' I believe no member of this Club is likely to become a dull boy:

certainly not. Should any outsider feel dull, let him lose no time in joining the Club, and then he will, no doubt, feel much better.[102]

THE PARALELL PROCESS AT WORK

The Chinese suffered a humiliating defeat in the Sino-Japanese War in 1895 at the hands of the Prussian-trained Japanese army. This defeat, coupled with the subsequent acquisition of the title as the 'Sickman of Asia', forced the Chinese government to attempt to overcome the traditional loathing of the Chinese for physical exercise. From 1895, a huge paradigm shift occurred in Chinese education with regard to the place and value of physical education in the curriculum.[103] The potency of the Japanese military was attributed to their better physical condition which had emerged from the intense practice of a system of military drill, which ironically, the Japanese had themselves adopted from the Prussians.[104] Wealthy Chinese students returning from their studies in Japan brought back a belief in the need for structured physical education lessons and physical training drills. Some of the new teachers who returned to China established the 'Saving China with Tichao' movement.[105]

The expatriates involved in the European settlement and development of Western trade with the coastal cities and ports of China brought with them their established cultural practices. The demonstration of the sporting and recreational activity of the expatriates involved in commercial and diplomatic realms, brought the local Chinese into contact with the typically British pursuits of horse racing, cricket, football, yachting and swimming. The most direct and enduring impact upon physical education, sport and leisure in China during the second half of the nineteenth century, however, came from the Christian missionaries. The missionaries, who taught in the secular schools, as well as the Christian missionary schools, brought modern educational curricula to the Chinese.[106] It is one of the great ironies of the cultural history of the region that much of the sport that was promoted as a feature of mainland Chinese nationalism had been adopted from the teaching of the American missionaries-cum-physical educators of the Young Men's Christian Association (YMCA). With the result that the sports, which one axiomatically associates with the 'Y', basketball and volleyball, are considered, even to this day, 'traditional' sports at Chinese secondary schools in Singapore.[107]

For over a thousand years physical activity had played no significant role in Chinese educational practice, indeed, as can be inferred from comments of Tso Ping Lung, it was virtually neglected.[108] This attitude of the Chinese is reinforced by contemporary reflections of their attitude to vigorous physical activity.[109] However, although not being totally engrossed in the cult of games to the same extent as Western schools, the mainland Chinese schools in the late nineteenth century and throughout the turbulent early years of the twentieth century gradually embraced the concept of physical education. In 1901, an imperial edict regarding education from the court of the Ching dynasty was proclaimed; this is viewed to be the single most important event in the development of education in modern China, as it called for schools to be introduced by all local governments.[110] Significantly, it included an order to all secondary schools to include physical culture, in the form of military drill, in their programmes.[111] It must be remembered that all such edicts and Ministry of Education policy statements from the Ching and the later Republican governments were conveyed to the Chinese schools in Singapore via the Consul and all were dutifully obeyed.[112] Yen maintains that this, not so indirect, control by the Chinese Ministry of Education over Chinese schools in Singapore was very extensive and included the provision of the curriculum, the selection of texts, the training of teachers and even regular systematic inspections of the schools.[113] The relationship between the Chinese Ministry of Education and the Chinese schools in Singapore and Malaya amazingly continued until 1949.[114]

It is important to note that despite the modernization of physical education in both China and Singapore, considerable emphasis was placed upon military applications of physical drill and training and in the inculcation of nationalistic and patriotic sentiments.[115] The first two decades of the twentieth century represented a period of mountainous turmoil for the Chinese both in China and in Singapore. The leading Chinese boys' schools in Singapore, such as Tuan Mong, Yu Ying, Chung Cheng and Yuan Ching had a strongly emphasized military ethos.[116] Students participated daily in military drill, sang patriotic songs whilst the curriculum was replete with activities that stressed the patriotism and nationalism embraced in Chinese education.[117] The Chinese boys' schools in Singapore at this time were, apparently, nurseries for Chinese nationalism.

At the same time it should not be overlooked that in Singapore, the middle class and wealthy Chinese enthusiastically embraced modern sport, as they assumed the external trappings and the associated ethos of the manly games and athletic pursuits of the British. It should also be noted that they ensured their sons at these middle class English style schools developed the same enthusiasms for such activities.

'VIEWED WITH SUSPICION AND MISTRUST'[118]

The evolution of modern sport in colonial Singapore largely centred on the British and the Chinese. However, a third social group – the Eurasians – also played a major and often forgotten role in the successful diffusion of sport into the colony of Singapore. From the earliest days of the settlement, people of mixed race, from multifarious lines of parentage, were considered as a separate social group. Records dating back as far as 1821 and as recently as the 1980s, referred to them as a separate social grouping. In 1970 Eurasians were considered to 'number a little over 20,000...[they] tended to be middle-class, official, professional and commercial people, whose fluency in English and experience in administration and commerce gave them an advantage'.[119] In the earliest days of Singapore, the Eurasians were considered, just as the Armenians, Arabs and Jews were, to be an important social group, so much so that a cohort of Eurasians formed an influential part of the initial committee of the Chamber of Commerce, when it was founded in 1837.[120] At all times, the Eurasian population of early Singapore was accorded great respect by the British, who made commercial deals with them and included them in social activities. They were by far more highly regarded by the British than the rich Chinese, who were always viewed with suspicion and mistrust.[121] Eurasians and the 'prosperous Chinese' were, in the 1880s, the only social groups which showed any interest in the early efforts of the colonial secretary of the time, Sir Cecil Clementi Smith, to establish a system of tertiary education.[122] The Eurasians, who were educated, socially and culturally Westernized, and rich, were well accepted and as a group adopted the trappings of the dominant ideology. They were a small, highly respected minority group that enthusiastically embraced modern sport as a cultural form and as such, made a very significant contribution to the development of modern sport in the colony of Singapore. On the 23 June 1883, this contribution was practically realized with the founding of the Singapore Recreation Club (SRC). The SRC, initially established to provide a cricket club for Eurasian gentlemen, was to become 'recognized as the premier Eurasian club in Singapore'.[123] A very clear racially drawn line was most evident in the social activity of colonial Singapore, even between the groups who provided the commercial and financial leaders of the colony. The Cricket club was for 'whites', the Straits Chinese Recreation was for the Chinese whilst the 'mixed-races' were catered for by the Recreation Club.[124]

The institutionalized system of separate social activity and development that pervaded the British Empire was particularly apparent in the colony of Singapore, as is exemplified in the emergence of the original sports clubs. This pattern of separate development not only extended to the leading clubs but throughout all social strata with the soccer clubs of the Malays and the Chinese all being founded on strict ethnic lines. Both groups had their own unofficial football associations by the turn of the century. Malays and the Chinese continued to play in separate league competitions following the formal establishment of their own leagues. The Malay Football Association (MFA) was established in 1909, whilst The Straits Chinese Football Association (SCFA) officially came into being in 1911.[125] Association football (soccer) is to this day Singapore's national sport, and indeed it was unquestionably the most popular sport in Singapore during the era when sport itself was becoming popular with the masses and when the foundations of a nascent sports culture of the colony were being laid down. An analysis of soccer throughout the colonial days of Singapore could well be used to illustrate the same class trends during a similar period in England.[126] At this time, the working class stamped sports such as soccer with the characteristics and attitudes associated with their class. In Singapore, however, the lines drawn were not solely based on class, they were also most definitely founded along racial lines.[127] There did exist elements of interaction between the three main soccer fraternities – the British, the Chinese and the Malays – though the individual players from various factions were rarely to be found within a single club. However, in the 1920s Sino-Malay teams were selected to play against visiting representative teams: a famous 4–2 victory against an Australian team being achieved in 1928 at the Anson Road Stadium.[128] It is apparent that both the working class Chinese and the Malay communities had embraced soccer as their game. It is suggested that the major initial contribution the Malays made to the diffusion of sport in Singapore was the endowment of the love of play and the autotelic motivation that underpins such play. This enthusiasm for playing games and competing in physical contests proved to be fertile soil in which the seeds of rationalized sport could be sown. The current predominance of Malay athletes in many sports, particularly soccer, bears testimony to the success of the process.

However, just as the British dominated culturally and administratively in colonial times, it is the ethnic Chinese who presently dominate the Republic. The Malays are now the major ethnic minority and they are still playing enthusiastically. To this day the most famous national sporting hero is a Malay soccer player, Fandi Ahmad. Indeed, he is probably still the only 'sporting' millionaire in the Republic. In Singapore the routes to prosperity are well prescribed and defined, focussing largely upon access to academic success and the subsequent meritocracy. However, unlike other racial groups, working-class Malay Singaporeans still retain the belief that sport is a viable avenue to prosperity.

CONCLUSION

The communalism in Singaporean sport persisted in an officially sanctioned form throughout the whole of the colonial era. In 1965, as Singapore was gaining independence an aspect of the racial disharmony that surfaced was the intense and violent rivalry on the sports field. This was seen to be one of the major manifestations of the problem in achieving unity and racial harmony in this multi-racially structured state, which came to a head with the Race Riots of 1964. The communal based clubs were viewed to 'only lead to fragmentation of a migrant people into racial groups each falsely believing in racial superiority of its kind'.[129] To ameliorate the threat of further racial unrest, which had erupted during the early 1960s the Lee government virtually banned the racial exclusivity of the premier clubs and the communal nature of the ordinary sports clubs. Lau Teng Chuan remarks that this represented one of the first government incursions of the sovereign-state of Singapore into sport.

> Despite being placed low in priority among the Government's objectives in social reforms, sports were thus given a role in breaking down communalism and its dangers. Communal clubs were advised to open their doors to encourage a wider multiracial membership. Even the traditional and conservative Cricket Club

and the Tanglin Club responded. Sports are for everyone regardless of race, creed or religion. In schools equal opportunities are given to all children to play games which before tended to be the sports of Chinese schools, Malay schools and English schools.[130]

Lee Kuan Yew had at this time very little regard for elite sport, labelling it as a waste of time during a period when the nation had only to be concerned with the pressing concerns of survival.[131] Yet, being the shrewd politician he was, and undoubtedly still is, he immediately recognized the potential sport had to produce both good and bad influences in his country during those turbulent times. Throughout the short history of Singapore, the government has continually utilized sport in its many guises to address specific policy needs. The eugenics of the 1960s and 1970s has been partially replaced with a policy that embraces the projection of successful sporting individuals as national heroes and heroines. This policy has been vigorously pursued through the government's sports excellence programmes – SPEX 2000[132] and SPEX 21.[133] Such schemes involve elite athletes and administrative bodies covering a wide range of sports, from the Olympic sports to more traditional sporting activities, such as the local martial arts of Silat and Wushu and dragon boat racing. The schemes as yet are to have borne any significant 'sporting' success results, though socially and certainly politically they are making a real impact. Sport is now viewed as an acceptable means of expression and a valid arena for endeavour by the people, and with the government's continuing political and fiscal support sporting success will, undoubtedly, be achieved in some form or another. Success may not be gained in New Zealand-like proportions (a nation with a similar population to Singapore), nor might it be gained in terms of Olympic Gold medals; the point of the success hopefully will be that sport will have entered into the national psyche. At this stage sport in Singapore will have matured to the point where the status of sport will be enhanced to the extent that the people, in the glorification of the uniqueness of mankind, will embrace all aspects of physical activity as well as elite sport. It must be said, however, that if or when this status is reached the nature of the sport sub-culture will be unique, representing the idiosyncratic nature of this dynamic and pragmatic young nation. Superficially, it may well appear that sport in Singapore is a cloned construct of global forms yet, upon investigation, it will be found that the combination and outcome of the internal dynamics have produced a typically Singaporean social form.

As in most imperial territories and certainly those of the British Empire, sport was, and still is, a highly effective agent of cultural imperialism. The diffusion and establishment of sport in the territories of the British Empire have long been viewed as a singular process with the dominating value–system and the actual games absorbed by the recipient territories being easily portrayed as 'British'. The nature and extent of the contributions made by the colonial territories to this process, in terms of; the people, their cultures, the climate and the geography of the settlements, have been previously viewed to be rather minimal and generally passive in nature. The accepted position is that the cult of Athleticism coupled with the ideology of Muscular Christianity inexorably infused the British games culture into the cultures of its colonies.[134] Singapore was considered to have had taken part compliantly in this process with this dominant ideology manifest in the SCC and the military, providing the unopposed model for the island's future sport. A superficial analysis would tend to suggest that this process was emphatic and complete, but this was not the case. Britain's cultural impact unquestionably played a significant role in the structural and attitudinal aspects of the development of the Republic's sport. It was after all the colonizing power. However, the 'Anglo Saxon attitudes' were not the only cultural forces imposing themselves upon the colony of Singapore, nor were they the most influential. The Chinese, the numerically dominant ethnic group, sometimes as allies and sometimes as opponents, also exerted a tremendous and enduring influence upon the evolution of sport in Singapore. This influence was carried along by a powerful, oriental parallel cultural imperialism which proved to be an effective figurational force that facilitated the creolization of the occidental model of sport and the establishment of the template of Singapore's idiosyncratic sport.

As powerful as the ethnic Chinese influence was in this process, it was the combined effect of all the figurational dynamics at work during the formative years that in essence formed this model. It was the combination of all these associated factors that helped to create the social milieu that was to become the Republic of Singapore. Ethnic groups and various socio-cultural factors exerted their influence, whilst significant individuals, global trends and the island's climate and geography also played major roles in the establishment of the nation's cultural practices. The diffusion of modern sport to Singapore and the emergence of the nation's sport culture constituted a complex process, one that should not be simplistically defined or rationalized. The process was the product of disparate and associated and separate and fused influences, and of course, it continues to develop. The influences of the post-modern epoch now assume a dominant position in this developmental process; the uniqueness of nations such as Singapore, it is hoped, will avert the creation of a global mono-sports culture. This uniqueness will help to retain variety in sport and prevent it from becoming boringly uniform. Sport has a universality that is appealing to many men and women and this is best expressed through the kaleidoscope of different nations, cultures, ideologies and ethnic groups.

NOTES

1. C. Tennyson, 'They Taught the World to Play', *Victorian Studies* (March 1959).
2. A. Kirk-Greene, 'Badge of Office: Sport and His Excellency in the British Empire', in J.A. Mangan (ed.), *The Cultural Bond: Sport, Empire, Society* (London and Portland, OR: Frank Cass, 1992), pp.178–9; P.A. Horton, '"Padang or Paddock"? A Comparative View of Colonial Sport in Two Imperial Territories', *International Journal of the History of Sport*, 14, 1 (April 1997), 1.
3. J.A. Mangan, 'Prologue: Britain's Chief Spiritual Export: Imperial Sport as Moral Metaphor, Political Symbol and Cultural Bond', in Mangan (ed.), *The Cultural Bond*, p.1.
4. See: J.A. Mangan, *Athleticism in the Victorian and Edwardian Public Schools: the Emergence and Consolidation of an Educational Ideology* (Cambridge: Cambridge University Press, 1981); J.A. Mangan, *The Games Ethics and Imperialism* (Harmondsworth: Viking Press, 1986); J.A. Mangan (ed.), *Pleasure, Profit and Proselytism: British Culture and Sport at Home and Abroad, 1700–1914* (London: Frank Cass, 1988); J.A. Mangan, 'Duty unto Death: English Masculinity and Militarism in the Age of the New Imperialism', *International Journal of the History of Sport*, 12, 2 (August 1995); J.A. Mangan and W. Baker (eds.), *Sport in Africa: Essays in Social History* (New York: Africana, 1987); R.D. Mandell, *Sport A Cultural History* (New York: Columbia University Press, 1984); J.L. Arbena, *Sport and Society in Latin America: Diffusion, Dependency and the Rise of Mass Culture* (Westport: Greenwood Press, 1988). See also: R. Cashman, *'Ave a Go Yer Mug!' Australian Cricket Crowds from Larrikin to Ocker* (Sydney: Collins, 1984); R. Cashman, *Patrons, Players and the Crowd: The Phenomenon of Indian Cricket* (Bombay: Orient Longman 1988); R. Cashman, *Paradise of Sport: The Rise of Organised Sport in Australia* (Melbourne: Oxford University Press, 1995).
5. See: Horton, '"Padang or Paddock"? '; J.E. Saunders, 'From Reflections of Kampong Play Culture to Mirrors of Modern Sport: The Development of Physical Education in Singapore Schools', a paper presented at The Second International Congress of the International Society for the History of Physical Education and Sport, Berlin, 30 June– 4 July 1993; D. Oon, 'Government Involvement in Sport in Singapore, 1959-1982' (unpublished Ph.D. thesis, University of Queensland, 1984); T.C. Lau, 'Sports in Nation Building: The Singapore Story' (unpublished research paper, University of Oregon, 1973).
6. See Shahrom Ahmat, 'The Singapore Malay Community', *Journal of the Historical Society* (University of Singapore: December 1971), pp.39–46, and K.S. Sandhu, *Indians in Malaya: Aspects of their Immigration and Settlement, 1786-1957* (Cambridge: Cambridge University Press, 1969).
7. Ibid.
8. Chiew Seen-Kong, 'Ethnicity and National Integration: The Evolution of a Multi-ethnic

Society', in P. Chen (ed.), *Singapore: Development Policies and Trends*, (Singapore: Oxford University Press, 1983), pp.30–64.

9. Horton, '"Padang or Paddock"?, 1–20.
10. Saunders, 'From Reflections of Kampong Play Culture to Mirrors of Modern Sport', *passim*.
11. Lee T.H., 'Chinese Education in Malaya, 1894-1911: Nationalism in the First Chinese Schools', in Lee Lai To (ed.), *The 1911 Revolution: The Chinese in British and Dutch Southeast Asia* (Singapore: Heinemann, 1987), pp.48–62.
12. Chiew Seen-Kong, 'Ethnicity and National Integration'.
13. Traditionally, various Chinese dialect groups were structured along the lines of Bangs. The Bang structure of the Chinese community in Singapore is based on dialect (locality) and clan (surname) associations. In the nineteenth century and even in modern Singapore certain associations have a monopoly of certain trades or occupations. Although it has been said that these clans provided new immigrants with both work and a sense of belonging they often served to restrict and subjugate newly arrived immigrants. Their sphere of influence went far beyond trade as the clan, characterized by the surname, implied common ancestry and thus common religious ties, and the clan meeting places were invariably their temples. The earliest recorded Chinese clan association in Singapore is the Tsao Clan Association of the Tsao clansmen from the Taishan district of the Guandong Province of Southeast China. The Bangs were to become central to organized crime, prostitution, opium dens and extortion rackets in colonial Singapore. Later they became the basis for many of the infamous triad-gangs. Ironically, they were also responsible for the establishment of schools, temples, cultural groups and hospitals. See Lim How Seng *et al.* (eds.), *The History of the Chinese Clan Associations in Singapore* (Singapore: National Archives Publication, 1986), pp.15–77.
14. C.M. Turnbull, *A History of Singapore 1819-1988*, 2nd ed. (Singapore: Oxford University Press, 1988), pp.1–5.
15. E. Chew, 'The Foundation of a British Settlement', in E. Chew and E. Lee (eds.), *A History of Singapore* (Singapore: Oxford University Press, 1991), pp.36–40.
16. W. Bartley, 'Population in Singapore in 1819', *Journal of the Malaysian Branch, Royal Asiatic Society*, XI, 2 (1933), p.177.
17. See S.H. Cheng 'Demographic trends', in P. Chen (ed.), *Singapore: Development Policies and Trends* (Singapore: Oxford University Press, 1983), pp.65–86.
18. W.E. Makepeace, R. St.J. Braddell and G.S. Brookes (eds.), *One Hundred Years of Singapore* (London: Murray, 1921), in Horton, '"Padang or Paddock"?', 4–5.
19. See, C.H. Yen, *A Social History of the Chinese in Singapore and Malaya, 1800-1911* (Singapore: Oxford University Press, 1986).
20. Horton, '"Padang or Paddock"?', 3–4.
21. Saunders, 'From Reflections of Kampong Play Culture to Mirrors of Modern Sport'.
22. Kampong is the Malay word for 'village'.
23. Shahrom Ahmat, 'The Singapore Malay Community'.
24. This is very apparent when reading the official monthly bulletins of the Singapore Sports Council (the government's sport administration body), *Sports* from 1993 to 2000.
25. For an outstanding overview of the history of physical education and sport in Singapore's schools see Eikman Teo, 'A History of Physical Education in Singapore Since 1819' (an unpublished research study, School of Physical Education, Nanyang Technological University, Singapore, 1998).
26. See E. Wijeysingha, *A History of Raffles Institution 1823-1963* (Singapore: Pioneer Books 1963).
27. Song Ong Siang, *A Hundred Years of the Chinese in Singapore* (Singapore: Oxford University Press, 1923), p.234.
28. Turnbull, *A History of Singapore 1819-1988*, p.101.
29. Song, *A Hundred Years of the Chinese in Singapore*, p.235.
30. Ibid., p.246.
31. Ibid., pp.234–46.
32. Turnbull, *A History of Singapore 1819-1988*, pp.24–5.
33. Ibid., p.59.
34. Ibid., p.60.
35. D.D. Chelliah, *A History of the Educational Policy of the Straits Settlements, 1800-1925* (Kuala

Lumpur: The Government Press, 1940), p.89 and S. Arasaratnam, *Indians in Malaysia and Singapore* (Kuala Lumpur: Oxford University Press, 1979), p.180, in E. Teo, 'A History of Physical Education in Singapore Since 1819', 36. It should be pointed out that secondary education was not available in any Singapore school until after 1884, when in the same year Raffles Institution began post-primary classes. So, possibly the need for large sporting facilities in schools may not have existed.

36. See *The Report of the Committee appointed to enquire into the system of Vernacular Education in the Colony of Singapore* (Singapore: Government Printing Office, 1894), and P. Loh, *Seeds of Separation: Educational Policy in Malaya, 1874-1940* (Kuala Lumpur: Oxford University Press, 1975).

37. Chelliah, *A History of the Educational Policy of the Straits Settlements*, pp.66–7.

38. See, T.R. Doraisamy, *150 Years of Education in Singapore* (Singapore Teachers' Training College Publications, 1969), Chapter 5.

39. E. Lee, 'The Colonial Legacy', in, K. S. Sandhu and P. Wheatley, *Management of Success: The Moulding of Modern Singapore* (Singapore: Institute of Southeast Asian Studies, 1988), p.22.

40. For the definitive account of the emergence of the ideology of Athleticism in the English public schools, see the acclaimed analysis: J.A. Mangan, *Athleticism in the Victorian and Edwardian Public School, passim.*

41. K. Watson, 'Rulers and Ruled: Racial Perceptions, Curriculum and Schooling in Colonial Malaya and Singapore', in J.A. Mangan (ed.), *The Imperial Curriculum: Racial Images and Education in the British Colonial Experience* (London: Routledge, 1993), p.162.

42. See The Department of Education Annual Reports, 1880-1920, (Singapore: Government Printing Office)

43. E.Wijeysingha, *The Story of Raffles Institution, 1823-1985* (Singapore: Pioneer Books, 1989) pp.115–8.

44. J.N. Brownfoot, 'Emancipation, Exercise and Imperialism: Girls and the Games Ethic in Colonial Malaya', *International Journal of the History of Sport*, 7, 1 (1990), 61–84.

45. Ibid.

46. Tichao or gymnastics refers to the amalgam of drill, calisthenics and breathing exercises now viewed as 'traditional' Chinese exercises.

47. Fan Hong, *Footbinding, Feminism and Freedom: The Liberation of Women's Bodies in Modern China* (London and Portland, OR: Frank Cass, 1997), p.68.

48. Teo, 'A History of Physical Education in Singapore Since 1819', p.68.

49. Ibid.

50. Chelliah, *A History of the Educational Policy of the Straits Settlements*, pp.31–85.

51. See 'History of Sports Archives', *90 years of the Anglo-Chinese School, 1886-1976: Souvenir History* (Singapore: ACS publication, 1976) pp.33–45.

52. Wijeysingha (1963), pp.83–107.

53. Ibid.

54. Ibid.

55. See Song, *A Hundred Years of the Chinese in Singapore*, pp.234–46, and Turnbull, *A History of Singapore 1819-1988*, p.102.

56. Horton, '"Padang or Paddock"? '.

57. J.D. Vaughan, *The Manners and Customs of the Chinese of the Straits Settlements* (Kuala Lumpur: Oxford University Press, 1974), p.3.

58. Lee Kuan Yew (1973). The Opening Ceremony of the National Stadium, at which he launched the National 'Sport for All Campaign', June 1973.

59. More recently, the government has attempted to raise the profile of sport outside of the school and possibly the military by taking various initiatives and launching several of the 'famed' Singaporean national campaigns. These started in 1973 with the eugenically driven 'Sport for All Campaign' followed by 'The Next Lap', a policy statement in sport, in 1991. The major policy shift, however, was signalled with the sports excellence initiative, SPEX 2000, which was launched in 1993.

60. By the nineteenth century Chinese education almost exclusively concerned itself with the scholars knowledge of the Classics bringing about the 'cult of the frail scholar'. See, Song Luzeng, 'China and the Olympic Movement', *China Sports*, 24, 7 (1991), 44–7.

61. See John Hargreaves, *Sport, Power and Culture* (London: Polity Press, 1986), pp.1–109.
62. Mangan, *Athleticism in the Victorian and Edwardian Public Schools, passim.*
63. Mangan, *The Cultural Bond, passim.* This influence spread, of course, well beyond imperial Territories. See J.A. Mangan, for example, 'The *Early* Evolution of Modern Sport in Latin America: A Mainly English Middle Class Inspiration?', in J.A. Mangan and Lamartine DaCosta, *The Latin American World: Sport in Society* (London and Portland, OR: Frank Cass, forthcoming). An abbreviated version is available in The Proceedings of the Seventh Brazilian Congress of the History of Sport, Physical Education, Leisure and Dance (Universidad Federaldo Rio Grande Do Sul, Porto Alegre, Brazil, May 2000).
64. Horton, '"Padang or Paddock"?', 7–12.
65. For a view of the relationship between sport and popular culture prior to the Industrial Revolution see Hargreaves, *Sport, Power and Culture*, pp.16–37.
66. N. Edwards, *The Singapore House and Residential Life 1819-1939* (Singapore: Oxford University Press, 1990), pp.101–118.
67. I. Sharp, *The Singapore Cricket Club: Established 1852*, 2nd ed. (Singapore: Singapore Cricket Club, 1993), pp.13–17.
68. Ibid., *passim.*
69. 'Padang' is the Malay word for 'field'. The Padang in Singapore is the most hallowed of recreation areas situated in the centre of the city. It was the first and premier of common areas established by the British who named it 'The Esplanade'; the Malay name was soon adopted after settlement.
70. Sharp, *The Singapore Cricket Club*, p.38.
71. For a consideration of the 'Division and Accommodation among "Ladies and Gentlemen" at the end of the 19th century', see Hargreaves, *Sport, Power and Culture*, pp.73–5.
72. Horton, '"Padang or Paddock"?', 9.
73. See, Yeo Toon Joo (ed.), *The First 100 Years: Singapore Swimming Club* (Singapore: Total Communications, 1990).
74. Ibid., p.17.
75. G. Creighton, quoted in, ibid., pp.17–18. (George Creighton was assistant secretary of the Singapore Swimming Club from 1948 to 1952.)
76. Ibid., p.38.
77. Yeo, *The First 100 Years, passim.*
78. Ibid., p.39.
79. Ibid., p.115.
80. Edwards, *The Singapore House*, pp.105–8.
81. Turnbull, *A History of Singapore 1819-1988*, p.76.
82. See, Song, *A Hundred Years of the Chinese in Singapore*, Chapter VII.
83. Turnbull, *A History of Singapore 1819-1988*, p.64.
84. Ibid., p.65.
85. Ibid.
86. Ibid.
87. Edwards, *The Singapore House*, p.107.
88. See Song, *A Hundred Years of the Chinese in Singapore.*
89. Edwards, *The Singapore House, passim.*
90. Turnbull, *A History of Singapore 1819-1988*, pp.85–7.
91. Ibid., p.26.
92. Song, *A Hundred Years of the Chinese in Singapore*, pp.16–19.
93. Ibid., p.19.
94. This sense of control over migrant Chinese was formalized in 1909, when the government in Peking invoked the legal principle of *jus sanquinis*, by claiming all ethnic Chinese who had descended through the male line however far away they lived, were to be considered as Chinese nationals.
95. Hargreaves, *Sport, Power and Culture*, pp.58–68.
96. See ibid., Chapter 6, 'Syonan: Light of the South, 1942-1945', for a most thorough account of the years of Japanese occupation of Singapore.
97. Song, *A Hundred Years of the Chinese in Singapore*, pp.154–5.

98. See, Yen, *A Social History of the Chinese in Singapore*.

99. Song, *A Hundred Years of the Chinese in Singapore*, p.216.

100. Ibid., p.168.

101. Low Cheng Koon, ibid., p.227.

102. Song, *A Hundred Years of the Chinese in Singapore*, p.226.

103. See, Tsang C.S., *Nationalism in School Education in China* (Hong Kong: PEP, 1967), and Tien C.Y., *Chinese Military Theory: Ancient and Modern* (Stevenage: SPA Books, 1992).

104. D.B. Van Dalen and B.L. Bennett, *A World History of Physical Education* (Englewood Cliffs, NJ: Prentice Hall, 1972), pp.622–31.

105. Fan Hong, op. cit., p.84. For a discussion of the wider impact of the influence of Japanese militarism on the attitudes to physical fitness in the interest of national survival, see J.A. Mangan Ha Nam-Gil, 'Confucianism, Imperialism, Nationalism: Modern Sport, Ideology and Korean Culture', Chapter 6 of this volume.

106. J. Cleverly, *The Schooling of China: Tradition and Modernity in Chinese Education* (Sydney: Allen and Unwin, 1991), pp.31–33.

107. See, *The Annual Report of the Education Department/Ministry, 1955-57 (Survey)*, (Singapore: Government Printers), pp.34–62.

108. Cited above, Song, *A Hundred Years of the Chinese in Singapore*.

109. See Vaughan, *The Manners and Customs of the Chinese* and Yen, *A Social History of the Chinese in Singapore*.

110. Ibid., p. 300.

111. Tien, *Chinese Military Theory*, p.125.

112. P. Loh, *Seeds of Separatism: Educational Policy in Malaya, 1874–1940* (Kuala Lumpur: Oxford University Press, 1975), p.43.

113. Yen, *A Social History of the Chinese in Singapore*, *passim*.

114. Ibid., p.302.

115. See, Annual Report of the Department of Education (1917), p.235.

116. See the Annual Reports of the Department of Education, 1905–10 (Singapore).

117. Lee Ting Hui, 'Policies and Politics in Chinese Schools in the Straits Settlements and the Federated Malay States' (unpublished MA thesis, University of Malaya, 1957), pp.25–7.

118. R.N. Jackson, *Pickering: Protector of the Chinese* (Kuala Lumpur, 1965), in Turnbull, *A History of Singapore 1819-1988*, p.86.

119. Turnbull, *A History of Singapore 1819-1988*, p.325.

120. Ibid., p.68.

121. Jackson, *Pickering*, p.86.

122. Turnbull, *A History of Singapore 1819-1988*, p.116.

123. Makepeace, *et al.*, op. cit., pp.365–367.

124. Sharp, *The Singapore Cricket Club*, p.34.

125. Oon, 'Government Involvement in Sport in Singapore', 59, suggested, that a Straits Chinese National Football Association was formed as early as 1881. However, this must have been a 'loose organization' informally constituted as official records from the SAF clearly cite 1911 as the year the Straits Chinese Football Association (SCFA) was formally established. Oon does, however, cite the Registrar of Societies as his source and if substantiated this means that the SCFA were the first soccer body in Singapore proceeding the Football Association of Singapore (British dominated) by some 11 years!

126. Hargreaves, *Sport, Power and Culture*, pp.65–72.

127. Edwards, *The Singapore House*, pp.101–30.

128. Sim (ed.), *The Singapore Asian Football Companion* (SAFA Publication, 1928).

129. Lau Teng Chuan, 'Origin and Development of Sports For All in Singapore' a paper presented at the International Conference on the History of Sports and Physical Education, 20-24 November 1974, at the University of Otago, Dunedin, New Zealand, p.3.

130. Ibid.

131. This point can be educed from the text of Lee Kuan Yew's speech at the opening of the National Stadium 21 July 1973. Sport, at this time, was not considered to be about elitism and success on the international stage, it was about the creation of a healthy and productive community:

With a population of just over 2 million, let us not waste time to go out of our way to produce gold medallists, whether for Olympic, Asian or SEAP games. There are no national benefits from gold medallists for small countries. For the super powers, with large populations, winning in sports become (*sic*) national propaganda to persuade people of the superiority of the competing political system. But it is foolish and wasteful for the smaller countries to copy this ... Our purpose is to generate healthy, vigorous exercise for the whole population, enhancing the valuable qualities we have in our people – keen, bright, educated and more productive if they are fit.

132. See *Sports*, the Official Publication of the Singapore Sports Council, 22, 1 (January 1994), for a complete overview of the government's policy statement and planning for the 'Sports Excellence 2000: Winning for Singapore' programme (SPEX 2000).
133. SPEX 2000 was renamed SPEX 21 in February 2000.
134. For a rather more subtle perspective on this, see J.A. Mangan, 'Prologue: Britain's Chief Spiritual Export: Imperial Sport as Moral Metaphor, Political Symbol and Cultural Bond', in Mangan, *The Cultural Bond*, pp.1–10.

Globalization, the Games Ethic and Imperialism: Further Aspects of the Diffusion of an Ideal

J.A. MANGAN and COLM HICKEY

SETTING THE SCENE

The late nineteenth century essentially English ideology of Athleticism (also referred to at times as The Games Cult or Games Ethic) greatly influenced the famous English public schools,[1] the less famous grammar schools,[2] certainly the distinguished universities of Oxford and Cambridge[3] and eventually the wider society in the late Victorian and Edwardian eras.[4] Recently it has been further revealed that the ideology had a substantial, if hitherto largely unrecognized, impact on some English teacher training colleges[5] and elementary schools[6] in the same period. It is also clear that the ideology spread, virtually simultaneously, throughout the British Empire, to both private and state secondary schools,[7] and indeed that it spread even further afield.[8]

This chapter adds additional colour to an already colourful historical canvas. It 'sketches in' fresh details of a fundamentally British moral crusade in the guise of the promotion of educational principle and practice, which directly and indirectly, had a quite extraordinary global influence in the late nineteenth and early twentieth centuries, and later an extensive, if sometimes serendipitous, impact on all the inhabited continents in the modern global sport age. The dissemination of 'Anglo-Saxon' sport can be considered, retrospectively, of course, from a number of perspectives – but many period proselytizers saw themselves as moral crusaders.

It scarcely needs to be repeated that the participants of the extraordinary games-playing educational revolution that occurred initially in British public (private schools for the privileged) schools were responsible, far from exclusively, but to a remarkable degree, *both directly and indirectly*, for a twentieth century 'global sports culture' of extraordinary enthusiasm, commitment and importance involving countless millions across the world. This is the measure of, and significance of, the cultural diorama in which below yet another small part of the canvas is painted in for the first time.

The international cultural changes, consequent cultural patterns and extensive cultural manifestations, not to mention the political, social, economic and emotional ramifications of the emergence of Athleticism in Britain's middle and upper-middle class schools in the second half of the nineteenth century are nothing short of astounding. Calculatedly and accidentally, committedly and casually, English ideologues and enthusiasts and simultaneous and later British, imperial and international neophytes in their time made an initial and influential contribution to a modern global sports culture of quite remarkable power and impact. Can this British supremacy, in its early days of influence, be matched anywhere else in the world?

IMPERIAL PROSELYTISM

After 1850 with the image of the English public schoolboy steadily and satisfactorily reinstated in the eyes of the schools' middle and upper-middle class clientele due to innovatory reforms substantially associated with newly developed gamesfields,[9] the public schools increasingly prepared their pupils for imperial roles in the Neo-imperial expansion of the late nineteenth century.[10] It has been suggested, without too much exaggeration, that: 'The Victorians were determined to civilize the rest of the world, and an integral feature of that process as they understood it was to disseminate the gospel of athleticism which had triumphed so spectacularly at home in the third quarter of the nineteenth century.'[11]

One by-product was the emergence of a coterie of public school headmasters whose proselytising efforts inspired and influenced public schoolboys to both establish and promote Athleticism in various capacities throughout Britain's empire.[12] This proselytism was endorsed and encouraged by school staff throughout the British Isles, who effectively, via the medium of emotional doggerel and prose 'interpreted the moral world for their pupils, framed moral laws for their use and were, in fact, the metaphysicians of a Victorian and Edwardian sub-culture'.[13] Subsequently, this morality closely associated with gamesfields was spread with zeal and conviction throughout the empire by public school educated men who carried with them the ethnocentric conviction that games, as a moral imperative, were crucial to the maintenance of the imperial ideal. All this is well documented.[14]

However, what has been far less well documented is the fact that there were those who had received an *elementary school and teacher training college education* impregnated with the period values of Athleticism, who also journeyed confidently to the furthest corners of the empire. Teachers who carried with them the same late Victorian and Edwardian certainty that team games were a desirable educational instrument. In some cases these men left Britain either to build and run colonial training colleges or to take over the running of existing colleges. Three excellent examples are A.J. Newman at Mico Teacher Training College in Jamaica, H.A.E. Milnes at Auckland Teacher Training College in New Zealand and J.E. Adamson at Pretoria Normal College in South Africa. An examination of aspects of their background, beliefs and careers will allow a further understanding of the impact of Athleticism in three very different colonies, and in hitherto non–debated (in these terms) colonial educational institutions. The importance that these men placed upon games and their associated moral significance will also allow an understanding of attempted imperial educational emphases in these countries up until the First World War, but also, to an extent, the nature of an ideal middle–class masculinity promoted in these imperial societies. For as Harold Perkin reminds us: 'The history of societies is reflected more vividly in the way they spend their leisure than in their politics or work. Sport ... is much more than a pastime or recreation. It is ... an expression of ... ideal man (and woman) hood.'[15]

AN IMPERIAL MATRIX

The training of teachers was a major concern of the British and Foreign School Society.[16] From its inception in 1811 it had vigorously promoted its overseas missions and a number of freed black slaves were trained at its teacher training establishment at Borough Road in London before returning to work in Africa.[17] G.F. Bartle,[18] the historian of the college, states that the last years of the eighteenth century witnessed a great increase in missionary zeal and points to a number of missionary societies such as the London Missionary Society, the Wesleyan Missionary Society and the British and Foreign Bible Society, who all sought to spread Christianity abroad.[19] J.A. Mangan makes the same point and draws particular attention to the Church Missionary Society and its wooing of middle-class public schoolboys for missionary work.[20] The aristocratic supporters of these societies became increasingly concerned with the education of the poor but when, in 1808, the influential Quaker philanthropist, William Allen, joined the committee of the Royal Lancastrian Institution (the forerunner of the British and Foreign School Society) 'the conversion of the heathen population overseas became as important an objective of the Lancastrian movement as the instruction of poorer children in the cities of the mother country'.[21] One of the earliest and strongest footholds of the respective society was in the Caribbean.

BOROUGH ROAD TO THE CARIBBEAN

The Emancipation Act of 1833, which freed Negro slaves among others, created in Britain a wave of enthusiasm for both their religious and secular education. In 1835, two years after providing £20,000 in grants to assist in the building of elementary schools in the West Indies, the Whig government established a Negro Education Grant of £25,000 per annum for ten years. As there were already a number of Baptist and Wesleyan missionaries in the West Indies who had originally trained as teachers at Borough Road, a mechanism was in place for the introduction of a system based upon lines established and promoted by the British and Foreign School Society. These will be discussed later.

Education in the West Indies was further strengthened by the Mico bequest. This had arisen from a legacy left by Lady Micault, a wealthy aristocrat who initially had made funds available for the redemption of Christian slaves in Algiers. The scheme was unsuccessful, however, and a residual sum of £115,000 was made available. English abolitionists successfully persuaded the Court of Chancery to make what now had become known as the Mico funds, available for Negro education in the West Indies. It was originally envisaged that there would be four teacher training colleges of a Christian, though non-denominational character, on four islands: Jamaica, Demerara, Antigua and Trinidad. The British and Foreign School Society became heavily involved with the plans for the colleges on Jamaica and Demerara and sent two men – Edwin Wallbridge and James McSwiney – to assume responsibility for these institutions. The enterprise in Demerara ran into financial difficulties, however, following the withdrawal of the Negro Education Grant in

1833[22] and so with the closing of the college, Wallbridge returned to England while McSwiney took over as principal at the college in Kingston, Jamaica.

The aims of the Mico trust for the training of teachers were set out in a letter to the secretary of state in 1843. They were 'the selection of efficient Superintendents for a service needing not only an aptitude for imparting knowledge to others, but especially an agency animated with an anxious desire to reform their hearts, watch over their conduct, preserve them from the demoralising influence of corrupt society and both by precept and example to inculcate the paramount obligation of Christian truth'.[23] For the next half century the Mico training college in Kingston was run by a Board of Visitors on the island and its ties with mainstream educational developments in Britain were consequently weakened. The principal for much of that period was Dr John Martin who had been on the staff as a master since 1845. In 1863 he was appointed superintendent of the college and became its first principal when the post was created in 1882. In 1884 he retired and it was decided to appoint someone with experience of elementary education in Britain. The Board appointed as co-principals L.G. Gruchy, a former student of St John's Teacher Training College (1871–72) and Dr W. Gillies, a Presbyterian churchman. Gillies retired in 1898 when A.A.B. Macfarlane, another former student of St John's, joined Gruchy.

Education in Jamaica presented a fundamental problem to the authorities. Whilst there was general agreement that the indigenous population needed to be educated, there was disagreement concerning the nature of education to be provided. By 1858, the educational curriculum at the college was impressively varied and included history, geography, astronomy, etymology, science, grammar, composition, arithmetic and moral science. Furthermore, the Annual Report of 1858 commented that 'every effort is directed to open and draw out the minds of the students, the object being to train them to teach themselves more than to impart to them any given amount of knowledge'.[24] This liberal curriculum enjoyed at Mico was met with criticism. Jamaica was a peasant agricultural community. Accordingly, it was argued in some quarters, that the training of teachers should reflect this and more practical instruction should be given. This view was not held by many of the agricultural labourers, however, who wished for a greater degree of personal independence and had no desire to work on the estates of the wealthy. They were not alone in their antagonism. 'The Baptists, with their strong following in Jamaica, effectively supported this critical attitude and attacked schemes for "industrial education" as a ruse for returning the people to conditions of slavery.'[25]

In essence, teacher education in Jamaica went through four phases in the century after the Negro Education Grant of 1835. The first phase involved the creation of some form of rudimentary Christian education of an either denominational or, as in the case of Mico College, non-denominational nature. The second phase, lasting from the 1850s to the 1870s, saw 'the triumph of the literary curriculum'[26] with the training colleges' curriculum having little relevance to practical education:

> Since the aim of popular education did not appear to be practical, its increase was not encouraged ... In these circumstances, one suspects that the training colleges were regarded as no more than a preparation in whatever may be considered necessary to qualify the students for their office. They were in themselves the apex of education for the handful of brighter and more ambitious pupils who emerged from the depressed elementary schools. If little could be done for the generality, much should be done for the few.[27]

The third phase was from 1870 to 1900 when an explicit attempt was made to ensure the training college curriculum was more in touch with the views of those who wanted elementary schools to reflect the fact that the island was primarily agricultural, and in turn for schools and colleges to have more agricultural training.

The upshot of a long-running dispute about the appropriate curriculum for colleges and schools was that the government set up its own training college in 1870: 'The Inspector of Schools made it clear that it was more important that a teacher be of good honest principles than of high intellectual culture.'[28] The findings, conclusions and recommendations of the later Lumb Commission[29] set up in 1898 to examine into all aspects of education including teacher training can be viewed against this background. The Commission was highly critical of the wide range of subjects taught at Mico. It recommended that the college course be reduced from three to two years and called for the withdrawal, among other things, from the curriculum of elocution, Latin, French and algebra.

Subsequently there were to be further curricula reforms but those of which involving playing fields rather than classrooms. They constituted the fourth phase of the training college's development – the assimilation of Athleticism. This assimilation should not be a matter of surprise in view of the nature of the colleges in England at the time,[30] and the fact that: 'The vast majority of those responsible for teacher training have, throughout its history in the [West Indian] region, been English ... trained in the English nineteenth century training colleges ... Men of goodwill they conceived of their duty as giving to the promising West Indian student as near as possible what his English counterpart might receive.'[31]

What the English counterparts were receiving at this time, among other things, was a solid induction into the values of Athleticism. Thus new 'men of goodwill' in the West Indies saw themselves as having something new, valuable and worthwhile to offer. Even more importantly, the education that these British trainers of teachers offered was, as mentioned earlier, one that many Jamaicans, rightly or wrongly, desired. The trainers were not out of step with their trainees: 'The prestige accorded to the English system by its own products when they come out here seems to have been little questioned by the West Indians to whom it has been offered. This is a characteristic feature of people who are insecure but ambitious to improve themselves and their society. They take the pattern of the dominant group and endeavour to emulate it uncritically.'[32]

Macfarlane retired in 1919 and was succeeded by two short-term appointments from within the staff: C.B. Ferguson and J. Hartley Duff, until a permanent principal, Arthur James Newman, was appointed in 1924 who radically altered the nature of the college and completed the process of the assimilation of Athleticism.

Newman was four months short of his thirtieth birthday when he was appointed principal of Mico Training College in 1924. He had been educated at Acton County School and Westminster Training College (1911–14) where he obtained a degree in Latin, French, mathematics and education. He taught at Helston County School until the outbreak of the First World War during which he was awarded the Military Cross. After the war he returned to teaching at Mercer's School, Holborn. Later, he assumed a lecturer position in English and education at Westminster Teacher Training College.

Newman had the necessary qualifications and experience to help ensure the smooth diffusion of imperial athleticism into Mico Training College. He had been a student at Westminster when the principal, Herbert Workman, was galvanizing the athletic life of the college and reconstructing the college in the image of a fashionable public school.[33] Newman now threw himself enthusiastically into the task of fully restructuring and reorientating Mico College using as a principle means the encouragement and promotion of Athleticism. As the official college history noted, 'He re-organized and improved college games and introduced the house system whereby college activities were stimulated by friendly rivalry.'[34] Cricket was a foremost means of implementing educational reform.

For the Victorians (and Edwardians) cricket 'was elevated by the middle classes to the status of a moral discipline ... [it] became the symbol *par excellence* of imperial solidarity and superiority epitomizing a set of consolidatory moral imperatives that both exemplified and explained imperial ambition and achievements.'[35] Thus, cricket was more than just a game to the Victorians – it was a great deal more:

> They glorified it as a perfect system of ethics and morals which embodied all that was most noble in the Anglo–Saxon character. They prized it as a national symbol, perhaps because ... it was an exclusively English creation unsullied by oriental or European influences. In an extremely xenophobic age, the Victorians came to regard cricket as ... proof of their moral and cultural supremacy.[36]

In the West Indies the transmission of this belief in the moral value of cricket can be seen clearly in the autobiography of C.L.R. James, *Beyond a Boundary*. The son of an elementary schoolmaster, James won a scholarship to Queen's Royal College, one of Trinidad's two secondary schools: 'James ... had no doubt that cricket in the English-speaking Caribbean was a major bulwark against social and political change. *At the same time* he viewed it as a reflection on the pitch of a wider manifestation – the stylized epitome of a moral order and the metaphoric essence of a cultured civilization.'[37] He certainly stated caustically with specific reference to his Caribbean school modelled on British public school lines: 'It was only long years after that I understood the limitation on spirit, vision and self-respect which was imposed on us by the fact that our masters, our curriculum, our core of morals, everything began from the basis that Britain was the source of all light and leading, and our business was to admire ...'[38]

If he was sardonic in this passage, in at least one other he was complimentary. He saw virtue in Englishmen passing on successfully the public school code:

In the playing fields, especially the cricket field, it triumphed. Very rapidly we learnt to 'play with the team', which meant subordinating your personal inclinations and even interests. We kept a 'stiff upper lip' in that we did not complain about ill fortune. We did not denounce failures, but 'well tried' or 'hard luck' came easily to our lips. We were generous to opponents and congratulated them on victories, even when we knew they did not deserve them ... Generation after generation of boys of the middle class went through this training and experience ...[39]

One link between West Indian cricket, colonialism and moral hegemony has been noted by Brian Stoddart who maintains that at least until 1914 'the colonial elites established and maintained a cultural primacy through cricket as much through economic power and political position'.[40] Furthermore, he argues that through cricket 'these elites established and maintained their position by determining that their values, traditions and standards be accepted by the populace at large as the cultural programme most appropriate to the community, even though the bulk of that community had no access to the institutions through which the programme was inculcated'.[41] Cricket was crucial in the Caribbean, according to Stoddart, because Britain gave it ethical significance. This associated ethical code was seen by the Caribbean elite both as a means of forging a close imperial bond and as a mechanism for asserting its own cultural dominance. As a consequence, he concludes:

> ... agencies such as the church and the elite schools became as important in the Caribbean as they had been at home in fostering the skills and social traditions which carried in them the imperial message of cricket. The consistent recruitment of religious and educational personnel from Great Britain ... was ... the most obvious indicator of this cultural reproduction until the eve of the First World War.[42]

However, Aviston Downes takes a rather more subtle view of West Indian events: 'while British imperial cricket culture did provide a site for the fortification of planter-merchant power, this hegemony was far from coherent ... while it is fashionable for Gramscians to focus on "the contradictory consciousness" of the proletariat, not near enough attention is concentrated on the ambivalence of the ruling classes'.[43] He adds that it was precisely this ambivalence, as well as internal contradictions within the middle class cricket culture, that helped ensure colonial confrontation. He adds an even more telling point that 'the trail of literary commentaries on West Indian cricket culture reflected planter-merchant perspectives and interests',[44] and these were contradicted 'beyond the boundary'[45] thus weakening further any hegemonic intention. No doubt this is true enough and shrewdly noted. Nevertheless, to add more subtlety to some subtlety, it was not simply the planter-mercantile community who represented the white middle classes in the West Indies. The educationalists did also, and they too had influence, at least to some extent benign, as C.L.R. James bears witness.

> ... the expatriate Englishmen and the local white aristocracy, with some few coloured men who had won acceptance in these circles, were not the decisive forces in the inculcation of the cricket [games] ethic which so shaped and permeated West Indian social life. This was done by English university men, chiefly from Oxford and Cambridge, during the last third of the 19th and the first third of the 20th [centuries]. Many of these were masters at the secondary schools in the larger territories, and their social influence went far beyond their actual numbers ... These Oxford and Cambridge men taught us Latin and Greek, mathematics and English literature. But they also taught, rather diffused, what I can only call the British public school code.[46]

This was the code that James quietly praised in the earlier extract. To these men, even though few in number and influence, should be added the staff of Mico College.

Keith Sandiford has picked up James's point and asserted strongly, if perhaps a little extravagantly, in a statement specifically about Barbados, but which has a more general West Indies applicability, that:

> ... English cultural leaders exalted cricket as the sport least tainted by human foibles and recommended participation in it as a virtual panacea for all social ills. That attitude was exported to Barbados by a long and imposing list of British educators, chief among whom perhaps were Horace Deighton, the famous headmaster of Harrison College from 1872 to 1905; Arthur Somers-Cocks, a teacher in Harrison College at the turn of the century; Edward B. Knapp, who taught classics at Harrison College from 1913 to 1938; and Graham Wilkes who served as Games Master at the Lodge

School during the 1950s. One of Deighton's products, G.B.R. Burton who served as Comermere's headmaster from 1897 to 1925, was convinced that cricketing ability had much to do with the results of World War I. He passionately argued, while that contest was still raging, that 'the boy who has played football and cricket for the honour of his team or school, forgetful of self, but ready to act on his own initiative if necessary, has shown himself superior in every way in this War to his opponent'.[47]

That sport promoted superior qualities, whether or not it was 'a virtual panacea for all social ills', was, of course, a widely held view throughout the empire[48] and while rhetoric does not invariably capture reality, it can capture an element of reality. Sandiford also argues categorically that cricket was 'an instrument of social control and a medium of socialization'.[49] Educators, politicians and priests considered cricket could keep the wayward out of mischief and the well-behaved on the straight and narrow, and no doubt as C.L.R. James would maintain, there was an element of truth in this.

Sandiford, however, recognizes the fact that not only West Indies of middle class, but also working class commitment to cricket, but *not* the college as one source. 'The working class,' he asserts, 'bought into the cult of cricket from the earliest moments of its appearance.'[50] One good reason was that for many lower class parents, 'cricket ... ranked with formal education as among the two safest escape routes from poverty and oblivion'.[51] The greatest of the West Indian cricketers, Sir Garfield Sobers, has frequently stated 'that the one vital motivating impulse behind his dedication to cricket was the determination to escape from poverty after his father's tragic and untimely death'.[52] The result was that Sobers became 'the champion of the poor and the downtrodden ... as a member of the working classes. He ... had sprung from the grass roots. Hence the basis of his phenomenal appeal.'[53]

Both Stoddart's and Sandiford's analyses of the role of cricket in Caribbean society are at one and the same time then persuasive and incomplete. They are not sufficiently alert to the ways in which cricket was received and perceived in their schools by the less wealthy and less well educated of Caribbean society. However, James was. For a time in the 1920s he was a lecturer in a teacher training college in Trinidad and recalls playing cricket against the elementary school attached to it. Lecturer and pupils were enthusiastic participants. The significant point is that the diffusion of Athleticism into the imperial Caribbean was more comprehensive than Stoddart, with his concentration on Gramscian elite influence, or Sandiford with his emphasis on emulatory elite education, suggest. To make this point is not to over-egg the pudding. The point is, simply, that in empire the role and influence of the lesser status *teacher training colleges* as agents in the diffusion of Athleticism among the community's less privileged – those who attended elementary schools, some of whom eventually made the game as much theirs as others – should not be overlooked. If Downes is to be believed, some, even many of the working class, may not have been impressed by the hegemonists, although Sandiford suggests otherwise, but some, as James would agree, certainly were.

As Alan Klein has noted of the writings of C.L.R. James:

> What is clear from the outset of James' work is the inordinate [but not complete] degree of hegemonic control exerted by cricket in Trinidad. British rule and Victorian customs are funnelled through a variety of British institutions on the island, first and foremost in the Black middle class, but ultimately even to the *working class*. Cricket is central to this process.[54]

Klein is preoccupied, incidentally, by cricket as a medium of social, cultural and political resistance. James, from a more secure insider's perspective, provides balance to Klein's imbalance. There was far more to cricket than a capacity for general resistance. 'In a society,' remarks James, 'very conscious of class and social differentiation, a heritage of slavery, it provided a common meeting ground of all classes without coercion or exhortation from above.'[55] Disinterest, as well as self-interest, can be part of history – and completeness of coverage requires its recognition. James and Klein both touch the truth. James also brings invaluable experience to bear when he again adds a missing dimension to Klein – the propensity for cricket to act as means of integration, rather than polarization beyond West Indian boundaries: '... the West Indies, clearing their way with bat and ball ... made a public entry into the community of nations',[56] and he added fairly, 'it had been done under the aegis of the men who more than all others created the British public school tradition ... They would recognize Frank Worrell as a representative of all they were and stood for.'[57] The inglorious and ignored principles of the teacher training colleges in their small way and at quite a distance in terms of status, could be added to those 'Oxbridge' public schoolboys who made their more 'public' contribution in the more prestigious secondary schools!

The educators of Mico College played their part in the socialization process, obviously, both before and after the coming of cricket. But in terms of the concern of this chapter Mico College is significant in a number of ways. Firstly, it was eventually a Muscular Christian enclave. Secondly, it was an institution for the less affluent of the indigenous population and previous studies of imperial athleticism have greatly concentrated on the elite of colonial societies. Thirdly, it was an institution to which three out of the five London teacher training colleges made a significant contribution: Borough Road, St John's and Westminster. Finally, as was the case elsewhere in the West Indies, it used cricket as a means of socialization and social control as well as simple enjoyment. In short, members of teacher training colleges in Britain, *as well as* members of public schools and universities, transmitted ideological priorities from Britain to empire, and, incidentally, not only in the West Indies! These training college men clearly demonstrate the commitment of the staff of the imperial teacher training college to the ideology of Athleticism. While this commitment was not as influential as that of others it was nevertheless real and part of the imperial purpose.

J.E.C. Welldon, headmaster of Harrow from 1881 to 1895, himself an ardent imperialist, once asserted that 'The pluck, the energy, the perseverance, the good temper, the self-control, the discipline, the co-operation, the esprit de corps, which merit success in cricket or football, are the very qualities which will win the day in peace or war ... In the history of the British Empire it is written that England has owed her sovereignty to her sports.'[58] Welldon, without a shred of doubt, would have endorsed the following ringing declamation:

> The strength and stability of any organization, ... must rest on the physical, intellectual and moral vigour of its members, and the history of evolution shows that the vigour is maintained by struggle, rivalry and competition. This is as true of a school as any other social organization. On the fields and in the classrooms healthy and honourable rivalry is to be encouraged in every way. Tennyson's 'Ulysses' is as fine a character as can be put before a schoolboy and there is no need to water down this element.
>
> 'Much have I seen and known

and drunk delight of battle with my peers.'
For the poet supports the psychologist when he says that Ulysses
and his men were 'One equal temper of heroic hearts' ... A school
must find play for the instinct of pugnacity in field and form if it
is to be "One equal temper of heroic hearts", and that way
happiness lies.[59]

The author continued:

> ... a clean and vigorous physical life is the safest foundation for a
> moral life, though we may not succeed in satisfying ourselves why
> the latter should grow out of the former. We can, however, discern
> the dim outlines of a bridge. Continuous almost with physical
> vigour, to which such things as air, food, bath, games and physical
> exercises are the avenues, is athletic alertness.[60]

It is not hard to guess that these words were written in the heyday of
Athleticism. The man who penned them was Sir John Ernest Adamson.
In a distinguished career in imperial education, he was at one time
director of education for the Transvaal and subsequently the first
principal of Rhodes University College and was later knighted in 1925 for
his services to education. What is both interesting and illuminating is not
so much what Adamson wrote but how and why he came to write it. For
Adamson was not a product of the ancient universities, nor of a major,
nor indeed a minor public school, nor even of a grammar school, he was
educated at an elementary school and then a teacher training college!

Adamson's involvement in South African education is to be traced
back to the aftermath of the Boer War when, in the Transvaal, a teacher
training college was established in 1902 to introduce reluctant Boers to
the 'benefits' of an English education. This was in the hope that they
would absorb at least some of the beliefs and behaviour of their
conquerors. The creation of the college was therefore quite a deliberate
action. It arose out of a specific policy:

> During and after the Boer War, the ... authorities intent upon a
> policy of anglicizing the Boers introduced men and women
> teachers from all quarters of the British Empire. Education in the
> Transvaal had to be orientated 'to win over the young generation
> of Dutch Africaners to English ways of thought and speech and to
> get them to understand the great news of the English imperial
> idea'.[61]

The aim was to establish 'a strong and well trained force with which to inculcate the English language and ideals into the younger generation whose fathers had ... been subdued by force of arms'.[62] Exactly the same policy and approach was followed in India after 1857.[63] Sensibly from their point of view, as Martin Conroy, in *Education as Cultural Imperialism*, argues trenchantly, 'the European powers used education to affect change, but only those changes that solidified their influence'.[64]

The Transvaal scheme was expensive, which created problems: ' ... men teachers in particular, were dissatisfied with their conditions of service and demanded higher salaries than it was possible for the colony to pay and this served to deter others from coming to the Transvaal'.[65] As a result of the reluctance of such teachers to come to South Africa in the numbers hoped for, the then director of education, Edmund Beale Sargant,[66] an English public schoolboy (Rugby) and Cambridge graduate 'was compelled to employ Dutch teachers', but he did this with reluctance. He felt that his work was being hampered 'through having to use as instruments of education persons of whose loyalty [he] was not fully persuaded'.[67] Faced with the problem that the colony could not afford the salaries demanded by metropolitan teachers, and in light of the lack of confidence in the loyalty of the Dutch teachers, the decision was taken to open a state training college that would provide a local flow of schoolteachers imbued with 'Anglo-Saxon' period educational ideals and beliefs. The matter was first discussed at an Inspectors' Conference in November 1901 and the decision was taken to appoint John Adamson, a lecturer in teaching methods at Carmarthen Training College, Wales as principal from November 1902 with H.S. Scott,[68] a lecturer at Borough Road College, as caretaker principal from September 1902. On Adamson's appointment, Scott would then become an inspector in the education department.

Scott's career can be dealt with briefly. He was educated first at St Paul's and then Eton where he was a King's Scholar from 1887 to 1892 and as a capable and keen sportsman, he participated in the college wall game of 1891. On leaving Eton he went to Hertford College, Oxford and graduated in 1895. He was appointed to the staff of Borough Road College as one in a long line of 'Oxbridge' tutors brought in on the recommendation of the Cross Commission[69] to inject something of an Oxbridge ethos which was considerably games orientated by this time.[70] These men spent a brief time in the college before taking up other posts elsewhere. Scott was heavily involved in the games of the college, playing for both the cricket and rugby teams. In January 1902 he left Borough Road for South Africa. Later, after almost a quarter of a century as an inspector of education, he was briefly director of education for the Transvaal before finishing his career as director of education for Kenya. In the context of his time Scott had impeccable credentials for imperial educational work. With an Eton and Oxford education and his athletic ability, enthusiasm and commitment, he was firmly in the mould of the colonial administrator. In his consideration of the 'athletic imperative' in imperial administration, Anthony Kirk-Greene argues that the link between athleticism and acceptability was very strong:

> ... the reasoning seems to have run thus. The success of the district officer in Africa depends on his possessing 'character'; character is tested, developed and improved by participation in team games; team games are an important and integral part of the British public school system. Therefore, the best type of colonial administrator will be found among those with a recognized record of above-average athletic success at school or university.[71]

After Scott's departure to the inspectorate, Adamson, the man chosen, as mentioned earlier, as his replacement at the training college in Pretoria, in terms of inculcating desirable period values, proved to be an inspired choice. He could not have been more different in his upbringing in relation to Scott. Nevertheless, he was to become one of the foremost educationalists in South African history.[72] Adamson was born in 1867 in Wakefield, Yorkshire. He was educated at St Michael's Primary School, Wakefield and he entered St Mark's Teacher Training College, Cheltenham in 1889. After completing his college training, as noted previously, he took up an appointment at Carmarthen Teacher Training College in 1891. He completed his Master of Arts in 1901, and on the recommendation of the influential educationalist Sir Michael Sadler, became principal of the training college in Pretoria in 1902. His stay as principal was brief for in 1905 he was made director of education for the Transvaal, a post he held until his knighthood in 1924. The following year he became the first principal of Rhodes University College where he remained until his retirement in 1930.

Adamson's period at St Mark's in the early 1890s was consonant with the blossoming of Athleticism there.[73] His arrival was therefore timely. He was an advocate of the ideology in life and in empire. As the earlier quotation suggests, he fully subscribed to the then common view that games was an important factor in the physical *and* moral development of the young. However, he was not simply a period 'clone'. As befitted a man, whose origins were in a small terraced house of an industrial Victorian town, Adamson also wanted others from similar backgrounds to have the chances he had had. He was a meritocrat and wished to broaden access to education to all the talented. Consequently, it has been written of him that his 'most important contribution to education in the Transvaal lay, without doubt, in his efforts to create equality of opportunity between the more and the less privileged communities – a principle that was by no means generally acceptable in 1907'.[74]

Adamson's extraordinary career merits a moment of reflection. It demonstrates that it was possible for at least some educationalists generally on the bottom rung to climb the social ladder and become part of, and accepted by the Establishment. His professional success to an extent challenges the widely held view that the teacher training colleges of the late Victorian and Edwardian age were mediocre institutions providing an inferior education for inferior students in an inadequate section of the education system. In reality, after the Cross Commission, the colleges had an intimate relationship with the public schools and the ancient universities via staff selections, and it is a point of some significance that this relationship was assisted, promoted and sustained through subscription to the dominant educational ideology of the age – Athleticism. For at least some of those in the colleges who embraced the ideology, personified its values, disseminated its principles and implemented its practices there were, it seems, professional opportunities at every level.

Yet another example of an elementary school and training college educated man who became principal of a colonial teacher training college is provided by Herbert Albert Edwin Milnes. Milnes was born in Beeston near Leeds in 1876, and educated at Beeston Hill Higher Board School, Dewsbury Road School and finally, the Central Higher Grade School. He trained at Borough Road College from 1893 to 1895. After qualifying as a teacher he returned to Beeston Hill School where he quickly established himself as an outstanding teacher. One of his first actions was to set up a school football club and it then won the soccer shield open to all Leeds schools. Unsurprisingly, in view of such Yorkshire successes, in 1900 he returned to Borough Road College as a lecturer and it was there that he honed his interest in games and the morality of games at a time when Athleticism was arguably at its zenith.[75]

The principal of the college was Arthur Burrell. He had been appointed in 1899 when the previous principal, Herbert Withers, took up the position of professor of education at Manchester University. Burrell was a graduate of Wadham College, Oxford and he had taught for twenty years at Bradford Grammar School, a school wholly in the ideological mainstream period.[76]

Burrell, like the earlier great Borough Road reforming principal, P.A. Barnett,[77] was a physical fitness fanatic and under Burrell's principalship the ethos of the college at this time was strikingly similar to the college under Barnett. Furthermore, as in Barnett's time it was strikingly similar in turn to Hely Hutchinson Almond's Loretto.[78] Almond, as is now well known, was profoundly influenced by the writings of Herbert Spencer, Archibald MacLaren and John Ruskin and blended their ideas 'into a conceptual and practical whole which went under the name of "Lorettonianism"'. It constituted 'an elaborate and systematic programme of health education covering food, clothes, physical exercise, sleep, fresh air and cold baths'.[79] That was not all. Significantly for Almond, the essential qualities that Loretto tried to inculcate were 'First – Character. Second – Physique. Third – Intelligence. Fourth – Manners. Fifth – Information' *in that order*![80] In developing character, games were of the first importance to Almond. For his part, Burrell was probably the only principal who:

> personally supervised a weekly remedial gymnastics class for physically underdeveloped students. He formed a special gymnastics squad, engaged a boxing instructor, founded an annual boxing championship and pressed the college committee to provide funds so that every student had an opportunity of learning to swim at Brentford baths. He encouraged early morning runs and afternoon paper chases, whatever the weather. 'We shall not do our duty by the students', he wrote in one of his Reports 'until we see every single member of the college taking daily exercise.'[81]

Borough Road, as will become clear later, was undoubtedly a model for Milnes when it came to creating his own college in New Zealand. Burrell, too, it seems, had a model to inspire him. In all probability, he took full advantage of the experience of Allan Ramsay Smith whom he appointed as a house tutor in 1902. Smith was a former head boy of Loretto, a graduate of Trinity College, Oxford, an Oxford rugby blue, and a Scottish rugby international.[82] As noted earlier, there were powerful resonances of Loretto in Borough Road. Here was one source. Milnes also played representative rugby (for Yorkshire) and Smith and Milnes, with R.T. Gabe (a Welsh international centre), played in an extremely strong college XV. Even in such company Milnes was noted for his total dedication to the values and practices of Athleticism. Burrell, outlived Milnes, who was killed in the Great War at Passchendale, and wrote admiringly in his biography of his former student:

> He was clean, healthy, virile, he had the air of a person who was going to do what he thought right whether you liked it or no; ... There was not an ounce of superfluous flesh upon him and from the beginning he kept fit ... When he took to football he had found his métier, and he was never out of the rugby game. His cold baths in a day when the love of them in college was not universal, were proverbial, and the lightness of his bedclothes ('the fewer bedclothes the harder you get') made other people, who believed only in the theory, shiver.[83]

Later in the biography, Burrell provided one other sharply focused cameo of Milnes, the epitome of the neo-spartan masculinity of Athleticism:

> It is difficult to say what are the outstanding recollections round which all others group to make his memory. But this is what I seem to see. He swings, a burly close-knit figure, clad in a minimum of garments, on his way to the Fives court; or returns, past my study window, from the football field a mass of mud and health; or he trots heavily meeting or passing by me on my bicycle, on some foggy or drizzly morning at seven o'clock, when ... the grumblers are mooching in overcoats.[84]

In 1905, Milnes left Borough Road College to become the first principal of a teacher training college in Auckland, New Zealand.[85] On arrival in the North Island, he discovered that the college was only an idea. He was required to build it. He did. He relished the challenge. The college in every sense would be his personal creation.[86]

Once again, as with his arrival at Borough Road College, Milnes had timed his arrival in Auckland well. He was 'in the vanguard of a new games-playing movement at a time when there was a sea-change in attitudes concerning the value of games'[87] *at every level* in the educational system. At this time in Britain there was pressure for games in the elementary school at the highest administrative level[88] and New Zealand closely followed this form of British practice. There was also at the time a general tendency on the part of new teachers educated earlier in the secondary schools, modelled on the British public school in which games were commonplace, to pass on their skills, enthusiasms and beliefs associated with the games field to their elementary school pupils.[89]

It is important to reiterate that Milnes was not simply a fitness fanatic. As with Almond, it was the morality of games playing and its associated capacity, as he and many of the time believed, for developing 'character' that was his main conviction as an educationalist. As he wrote in the *Journal of Education* in May 1912:

> As character training is admitted to be our goal, it is interesting to see what effect the play of school games has upon it, and consequently comes the corollary, what are the most suitable games to produce this effect? Games undoubtedly have a great effect on character, summed up in one word 'sportsmanlike. They give it its true initiative, promptitude, courage, unselfishness and the power of leadership; they promote social growth and in many and other ways improve one's powers, but when all is said and done it is learning 'to play the game' and never to hit 'below the belt' that constitute the great values.[90]

He also appreciated the value to the teacher, as had the head teachers of the public schools some fifty years earlier, of playing with his pupils: 'A student unable to take part in a game is not, in my opinion, suited for school teaching. Playing with your children is the surest help to influencing them I know, and if the teacher is unable to do this he loses a help he cannot get in any other way.'[91]

On the outbreak of the Great War, Milnes volunteered and in October 1917, as mentioned earlier, he died at Passchendale. Professor Dettmann of University College, Auckland asked of him rhetorically at the memorial service: 'In our day and generation has there ever been a man in our city ... in whom nature has so perfectly mixed and combined the elements of manhood? – his wonderful physical endowment, an example among men of his standing, his mental equipment [and] to crown all his gift of character ...'[92]

This fragment of the ovation captures succinctly the admired virtues of imperial manhood in the late Victorian and Edwardian period. Two of the qualities Dettman singled out for special mention – physical endowment and character – were, as is now abundantly clear from many sources, considered at the time, the benefits of the games culture of school and college. From the comments of Burrell and Dettmann it is clear that Milnes practised what he preached. And the legacy of his example is still extant and appreciated in New Zealand.

In Newman, Adamson and Milnes Athleticism in Empire had three committed advocates of games as moral education. The practical consequences over time, however, were more cultural than moral. These three men were part of an imperial cadre who took modern games from Britain to the West Indies, to South Africa and to New Zealand and who helped create cultural priorities which produced in time a clear sense of national worth by virtue of international excellence on games fields. Such men made their contribution to the dissemination of modern sport as a moralistic educational necessity and as a practical means of ensuring physical health providing enjoyable recreational pastimes but ultimately, serendipitously as a source of national identity and pride.

Despite more developed considerations of the ideology and later global developments that have overshadowed it, it should not be overlooked that Newman, Adamson and Milnes made a quite specific contribution to the diffusion of the influential ideology of Athleticism. They took the ideology to imperial teacher training colleges and elementary schools. They are part of an imperial education that in this regard has been little explored and written about. Consequently, if the full extent of their influence is not easy to assess, the nature of their action nevertheless poses few problems. At the same time, much certainly remains to be revealed, more proselytizers certainly await discovery and their influence waits to be recorded. Imperial teacher training colleges did not 'glitter' in the imperial educational crown. Their lustre may have reflected setting rather than jewel but they were part of the structure of ideological purpose and are not to be ignored. They existed, they proselytized, and they influenced. They were part of the transmission of a fundamentally well meaning, if certainly ethnocentric, imperialism. They are not to be dismissed. The three men discussed in this chapter provide solid evidence of the fact that Athleticism not only infiltrated and influenced the teacher training colleges and elementary schools of Britain, but also those of its empire.

With this discovery and earlier ones, slowly and steadily, the imperial cultural 'canvas' is being covered – and one of the most significant cultural phenomena of late Victorian and Edwardian middle-class Britain – Athleticism – is being progressively better understood both in its imperial influence and its later contribution to the sport of the modern 'global village'.[93] The final word should be left to Marc Ferro: 'One of the leading features of colonization was to set in motion the process of the unification of the world ... Colonization was indeed a standardising process.'[94]

NOTES

1. See J.A. Mangan, *Athleticism in the Victorian and Edwardian Public School: the emergence and consolidation of an educational ideology* (Cambridge: Cambridge University Press, 1981). *Athleticism* is now published by Frank Cass in paperback with a substantial new Introduction by the author, and a foreword and introduction respectively by the distinguished cultural historians, Sheldon Rothblatt and Jeffrey Richards.
2. J.A. Mangan, 'Imitating their Betters and Disassociating from their Inferiors: Grammar Schools and the Games Ethic in the Late 19th and Early 20th Centuries', *The Fitness of the Nation: Physical and Health Education in the 19th and 20th Centuries*, Proceedings of the 1982 Annual Conference of the History of Education Society of Great Britain, History of Education Society, Leicester, 1983.
3. See J.A. Mangan, '"Oars and the Man": Pleasure and Purpose in Victorian and Edwardian Cambridge', *British Journal of Sports History*, 1, 1 (1984), 52–77, and J.A. Mangan, '"Lamentable Barbarians and Pitiful Sheep": Rhetoric of protest and pleasure in late Victorian and Edwardian Oxbridge', in Tom Winnifrith and Cyril Barnet (eds.), *Leisure in Art and Literature* (London: Macmillan, 1992), pp.130–154 in the Series: Warwick Studies in the European Humanities edited by Michael Mallett.
4. See J.A. Mangan and Colm Hickey, 'English Elementary Education Revisited and Revised: Drill and Athleticism in Tandem', in J.A. Mangan (ed.), *Sport in Europe: Politics, Class, Gender, The European Sports History Review*, Vol.1 (London and Portland, OR: Frank Cass, 1999), pp.63–89.
5. See Colm Hickey, 'Athleticism and the London Training Colleges' (unpublished Ph.D. thesis, University of Strathclyde), forthcoming.
6. J.A. Mangan and Colm Hickey, 'Athleticism in the Service of the Proletariat: Preparation for the English Elementary School and the Extension of Middle-Class Manliness', *Making European Masculinities, The European Sports History Review*, 2 (London and Portland, OR: Frank Cass, 2000).
7. See J.A. Mangan, *The Games Ethic and Imperialism: Aspects of the Diffusion of an Ideal* (London and Portland, OR: Frank Cass, 1999).
8. J.A. Mangan, 'The *Early* Evolution of Modern Sport in Latin America: A Mainly English Middle Class Inspiration?', in J.A. Mangan and Lamartine DaCosta (eds.), *The Latin American World: Sport in Society* (London and Portland, OR: Frank Cass, forthcoming).
9. Mangan, *Athleticism, passim.*
10. Mangan, *Games Ethic*, Chapters 1 and 2, pp.21–70.
11. Keith A.P. Sandiford, *Cricket and the Victorians* (Aldershot: Scholar Press, 1994), p.145.
12. For merely one illustration of this, see J.A. Mangan, 'Ethics and Ethnocentricity: Imperial

Education in British Tropical History', in William J. Baker and James A. Mangan (eds.), *Sport in Africa: Essays in Social History* (New York: Holmes and Meier, 1987), pp.138–71. For further illustrations in the same volume, see Anthony Kirk-Greene, 'Imperial Administration and the Athletic Imperative: The Case of the District Officer in Africa', pp.81–113, and Anthony Clayton, 'Sport and African Soldiers: The Military Diffusion of Sport throughout Sub-Saharan Africa', pp.114–37.

13. See J.A. Mangan, 'Moralists, Metaphysicians and Mythologists: The "Signifiers" of a Victorian and Edwardian Sub-culture', in Susan J. Bandy, *Coroebus Triumphs: The Alliance of Sport and the Arts* (San Diego: San Diego State University Press, 1988), pp.141–62.

14. A recent contribution to the documentation that is worth a mention is Martin Crotty, 'Making the Australian Male: The Construction of Manly Middle-Class Youth in Australia 1870-1920' (unpublished Ph.D. thesis, University of Melbourne, 1999).

15. H. Perkin, 'Teaching the Nations How to Play: Sport and Society in the British Empire and Commonwealth', *International Journal of the History of Sport*, 6, 2 (1985), 145–53.

16. The British and Foreign School Society was established in 1814. It grew out of a committee of trustees set up in 1808 to help Joseph Lancaster, the founder of the monitorial system of education, pay his debts and to run his institution (Borough Road) on a more secure footing. Lancaster, however, was hopelessly irresponsible and often acted without the knowledge or approval of the committee. He resigned in 1814 and the committee then named itself the British and Foreign School Society. The use of the term 'foreign' reflected the enthusiasms of William Allen, the well-known philanthropist and supporter of the anti-slavery movement who was an influential member of the committee. See G.F. Bartle, *A History of Borough Road College* (Kettering: Dalkeith Press, 1976), pp.1–7 and H.B. Binns, *A History of Education 1808-1908* (London, Longmans, 1908): *passim*.

17. For a fuller discussion of the early overseas work of the society, see G.F. Bartle 'The role of the British and Foreign School Society in the education of the emancipated Negro, 1814-1875', *Journal of Educational Administration and History*, XV, 1 (January 1983).

18. G.F. Bartle wrote voluminously on all aspects of the British and Foreign School Society. His collected papers have been privately published by the society.

19. Bartle, *A History of Borough Road College*, 1976, p.   .

20. Mangan, *The Games Ethic*, pp.168–78.

21. Bartle, *A History*, p.13.

22. Bartle, 'The Role', *passim*.

23. S.C. Gordon, *A Century of West Indian Education* (London: Longmans, 1963), p.173.

24. *Mico College Annual Report, 1858*, quoted in Gordon, *A Century*, p.185.

25. S. Walters, *Teacher Training Colleges in the West Indies* (Oxford: Oxford University Press, 1960), p.4.

26. Ibid., p.5.

27. Ibid., p.6.

28. Trevor Turner, 'The Socialisation Intent in Colonial Jamaican Education', *Caribbean Journal of Education*, 4, 1, and 2 (1977), 58.

29. The Lumb Commission was established in 1898 to examine teacher training on the island. It recommended a more restricted training college curriculum. Gordon, *A Century*, pp.107–66.

30. See J.A. Mangan and Colm Hickey, 'Athleticism in the Service of the Proletariat', *passim*.

31. Gordon, *A Century*, p.4.

32. Walters, *Teacher Training Colleges*, p.17.

33. See Colm Hickey, 'Athleticism and the London Training Colleges' (doctoral thesis, University of Strathclyde, forthcoming).

34. *Mico College 125th Anniversary 1836-1961* (The College, Kingston, Jamaica), p.15.

35. J.A. Mangan, 'Prologue: Britain's Chief Spiritual Export: Imperial Sport as Moral Metaphor, Political Symbol and Cultural Bond', *The Cultural Bond: Sport, Empire, Society* (London: Frank Cass, 1992), p.2.

36. Sandiford, *Cricket and the Victorians*, p.1.

37. Mangan, *The Cultural Bond*, p.7 (emphasis added).

38. C.L.R. James, *Beyond a Boundary* (London: Hutchinson, 1963), pp.25–6.
39. C.L.R. James, 'Cricket in West Indian Culture', *New Society*, 36 (6 June 1963), p.8.
40. B. Stoddart, 'Cricket and Colonialism in the English-Speaking Caribbean to 1914: Towards a Cultural Analysis', in J.A. Mangan (ed.), *Pleasure, Profit, Proselytism: British Culture and Sport at Home and Abroad 1700-1914* (London and Portland, OR: Frank Cass, 1988), p.251.
41. Ibid.
42. Ibid.
43. Aviston D. Downes, '"Flannelled Fools"? Cricket and the Political Economy of the British West Indies, 1895–1906', *International Journal of the History of Sport*, 17, 4 (2000).
44. Ibid.
45. Ibid.
46. James, 'Cricket in West Indian Culture', p.8.
47. Keith A.P. Sandiford, 'Cricket, Culture and the Barbadian Identity', *Culture, Sport, Society*, forthcoming.
48. It was expressed with particular force in the Dominions, see, for example, J.A. Mangan, 'Noble specimens of manhood: schoolboy literature and the creation of a colonial chivalric code', in Jeffrey Richards (ed.), *Imperialism and Juvenile Literature* (Manchester: Manchester University Press, 1989), pp.173–94.
49. Sandiford, 'Cricket, Culture and the Barbadian Identity', 354.
50. Ibid.
51. Keith A.P. Sandiford, 'Cricket and the Barbadian Society', *Canadian Journal of History*, XXI (December 1986), 368.
52. Ibid.
53. Ibid.
54. Alan M. Klein, 'Sport and Colonialism in Latin America and the Caribbean', *Studies in Latin American Popular Culture*, 10 (1991), 266 (emphasis added).
55. James, 'Cricket in West Indian Culture', p.8.
56. Ibid., p.9.
57. Ibid., p.9.
58. From the introduction by J.E.C. Welldon to Arthur Stanley, *Patriotic Song* (Pearson, 1891), p. viii, quoted in Mangan, *The Games Ethic*, pp.35–6.
59. J.E. Adamson, *The Individual and the Environment: Some Aspects of the Theory of Education as Adjustment* (London: Longmans, 1921), p.353.
60. Sandiford, 'Cricket, Culture and the Barbadian Identity', 361.
61. A.L. Behr, *Education in South Africa* (Pretoria: J.L. Van Schaik, 1966), p.245.
62. Ernst G. Malherbe, *Education in South Africa 1652-1975*, 2 vols., 2, 1652-1922, *A Critical Survey of the Development of Educational Administration in the Cape, Natal Transvaal and the Orange Free State* (Johaanesburg: Juta and Co., 1925), p.279.
63. See Mangan, *Games Ethic*, pp.122–141.
64. Martin Conroy, *Education as Cultural Imperialism* (New York: McKay, 1974), p.82.
65. Behr, *Education*, p.245.
66. Edmund Beale Sargant (1855–1938) was educated at Rugby, University College, London and Trinity College, Cambridge. He was seventh wrangler and graduated with a First degree in natural sciences. He joined the permanent civil service in 1881 and was made director of education in South Africa in 1897.
67. Behr, *Education*, p.246.
68. H.S. Scott was educated at St Paul's and Eton from 1887 to 1892. He graduated from Hertford College, Oxford in 1895 and joined the staff at Borough Road until 1902 when he went to South Africa. He spent 25 years in Africa and was Director of Education for the Transvaal and finally Director of Education for Kenya.
69. The Cross Commission 1886-1888 was set up under the chairmanship of Richard Asseshton Cross to inquire into the state of elementary education. After an exhaustive examination of all elements of elementary education, including the training colleges, it produced both a Majority and Minority *Report*. The significance for the colleges, however, was its almost unanimous

conclusion that they were in need of change and should become more open to period educational developments. The biggest change was that many colleges began to adopt a policy of appointing 'Oxbridge' graduates to vacant principalships and that some began a deliberate policy of recruiting young games playing (usually Oxbridge) graduates to their staffs. The consequence of this was that the colleges rapidly and enthusiastically adopted the prevailing ideology of athleticism. See Colm Hickey, 'Athleticism and the London Training Colleges', Chapter 3.

70. See, for example, Mangan, 'Oars and the Man ...' *passim* and 'Lamentable Barbarians and Pitiful Sheep', *passim*.

71. Kirk-Greene, 'Imperial Administration and the Athletic Imperative ...', in Baker and Mangan, *Sport in Africa*, p.85.

72. John Ernest Adamson was born in January 1867. He attended St Michael's Elementary School in Wakefield and later St Mark's Training College, Chelsea from 1889 to 1890. He became a lecturer in the theory and method of teaching at Carmarthen Training College in 1891. He took his MA in philosophy in 1901. The following year, on the recommendation of Sir Michael Sadler, he was appointed principal of Pretoria Normal College. He was director of education of the Transvaal from 1905 to 1924. He was knighted in 1924. He sat on the council of the University of the Cape of Good Hope from 1906 to 1917 and thereafter as the University of South Africa from 1918 to 1922. He was vice chancellor of the University of South Africa from 1922 to 1924. In 1925 he became the first principal of Rhodes University College, a post he held until he retired in 1930. He died in April 1950. He was the author of numerous works on education, including *Theory of Education in Plato's Republic* (1903), *The Teacher's Logic* (1904), *Poems from The South* (1915), *Externals and Essentials* (1933) and *The Individual and the Environment, Some Aspects of the Theory of Education as Adjustment* (1921).

73. Hickey, 'Athleticism and the London Training Colleges', Chapter 4.

74. *Transvaal Education Department 1876-1976 Centenary Publication* (Pretoria: Transvaal Education Department), 1976, p.58.

75. Bartle, *A History*, pp.57–9. See also Mangan and Hickey, 'Athleticism in the Service of the Proletariat', pp.114–35, and Colm Hickey, 'Athleticism and the London Training Colleges', Chapter 4.

76. Arthur Burrell was in charge of the junior department at Bradford Grammar School. He was a firm proponent of athleticism and at Borough Road took a personal interest in physical fitness, even supervising a weekly boxing class for the underdeveloped students.

77. P.S. Barnett was educated at the City of London School and Trinity College, Oxford, where he obtained a First in classical greats. He then became professor of English at Firth College, Sheffield and gained experience there of elementary education as he was a member of the local school board. He was principal of Borough Road from 1889 to 1893 when he left to take up a place on the inspectorate. He was the author of a number of books on education, including *The Little Book of Health and Courtesy* (1905) and *Common Sense in Education* (1899).

78. Mangan *Athleticism*, p.58.

79. Ibid., p.55.

80. Ibid.

81. Bartle, *A History*, p.58.

82. A.R. Smith (1875–1926). Smith was educated at Loretto from 1889 to 1894. He was a prefect, editor of the school magazine, *The Lorettonian*, and head boy. He represented the school at hockey, fives and rugby and, while at Trinity College, Oxford, from 1894 to 1900 played for Scotland, captaining them in 1898. After Oxford he travelled around the world. He joined the staff of Borough Road in 1900. In 1901 he was appointed H.M. junior inspector of schools. In 1903 he became an inspector, a post he held until his appointment as headmaster of Loretto in 1908. He died in 1926.

83. Burrell, *Bert Milnes*, pp.12–13.

84. Ibid., p.17.

85. Ibid.

86. E. Walker, 'An Interview with Mr Milnes in New Zealand', *B's Hum*, XVIII, 128 (May 1905), pp.5–6.

87. B. Sutton-Smith, *A History of Children's Play in New Zealand 1840–1950* (Philadelphia: University of Pennsylvania Press, 1981).

88. The Elemendary Education Code of 1906 allowed for the playing of games in school-time. See P.C. McIntosh, *A History of Physical Education in England from 1800*, 2nd ed. (London: Bell, 1968), pp.143–55.

89. Mangan and Hickey, 'English Elementary Education', *passim*.

90. *Journal of Education*, 1912, quoted in Sutton-Smith, *A History*, p.198.

91. D. Baird, 'History of Physical Education in New Zealand' (unpublished MA thesis, Wellington Victoria University, 1942), quoted in Sutton-Smith, *A History*, p.197.

92. Burrell, *Bert Milnes*, p.198.

93. It was, of course, only one influence in the globalization of sport, but it was certainly, in the early stages of the process, a major one.

94. Marc Ferro, *Colonization: A Global History* (London: Routledge, 1997), p.350. For an even more implicit statement along these lines, see Edward W. Said, *Culture and Imperialism* (London: Chatto and Windus, 1993), p.xxii, in which he asserts that the globalization process was set in motion by modern imperialism.

'Linesmen, Referees and Arbitrators': Politics, Modernization and Soccer in Palestine

AMIR BEN-PORAT

INTRODUCTION

The relationship between British colonialism and the dissemination of the most popular game in the world – soccer – is considered in this chapter. It is now well known that British Imperial 'missionaries', soldiers, educationalists, merchants, clerics and administrators, exported the game of soccer to almost every corner of the globe.[1] Here the concern is the influence of the British Mandate (1922–48) on the development of soccer in Palestine. The chapter deals with both the Jewish and the Arab communities. It should be noted at once, that football was neither imported into, nor established in Palestine by the British. However, they did have a definite impact on the modernization of the game in this area of the Middle East.

The first part of the chapter deals briefly with the major parameters that the Mandate authorities used in specifying their policy in Palestine. To a certain extent, this policy was contingent on the terms of reference of the Mandate system. The formation of Palestine included three competing and contradictory interests: those of the Jewish community; the Arab community; and the British government. The struggles between the Jews and the Arabs in Palestine over the future rule of the 'country' and British government policy, are highly important parameters associated with the specific issues of this chapter, as they determined the practical constraints on every act and process. However, these parameters are not covered here in any great detail as other works have considered this subject.[2] Instead, what is dealt with at some length is the fact that these major parameters, which both specified and limited the practices of the Mandate Government in Palestine, interestingly laid the groundwork for the specific association between football and Britain.

The second part describes the evolution of soccer in Palestine from 1917 to 1948, and considers the roles of the British in this evolution. Three metaphors referring to the roles of the British in football in Palestine are offered here: the British as a Linesman; the British as a Referee; and the British as an Arbitrator. By fulfilling the second role, the British participated in the game of football as a participant, and by fulfilling the third role, they assumed their political position; that is, as the mandated government of Palestine.

The third part re-evaluates the role played by the British in football in Palestine and also briefly considers their impact on the formation of soccer after 1948 in the Israeli state.

THE BRITISH IN PALESTINE: MAJOR PARAMETERS

'The Beginning of the Mandate: On December 1917, General Sir Edmund Allenby entered the city of Jerusalem on foot, ... followed by a parade of troops to receive the plaudits of the assembled notables of the city, and savour his triumph as liberator of the impoverished and war-devastated Turkish province'.[3] In September 1918, the British Army arrived in the north of the country and Palestine was thereafter ruled by the 'Occupied Enemy Territory Administration', an army-civilian body which governed Palestine until April 1920. A territory by the name of 'Palestine' was now recognized as a distinct 'political entity'.

A few years before, in November 1915, Britain and France had discussed the possibility of formulating an agreement concerning the partition of the Turkish territories in the Middle East. The British government had shown great interest in the territory of Palestine, which was considered necessary to the defence of the Suez Canal. The French government, on the other hand, was more interested in Syria and Lebanon. In May 1916, the two powers signed the 'Sykes–Picot Accord', the draft of which assigned to France, Lebanon and the northern part of Palestine, while to Britain, the southern part of Palestine, the south of Mesopotamia including Baghdad, and the Palestine coastline at Haifa. As for central Palestine and Jerusalem, these were to be governed by an international administration. The Accord-signing parties recognized the concept of an Arab state or of a Confederation of Arab states, in the 'empty' territory between the zones allotted to the British and the French, to be established after the War.[4] The Russian government was also a party to this agreement, but this was not revealed until after the

Russian Revolution of 1917. The Accord was implemented after the First World War only in part: Palestine including Jerusalem, was recognized as 'British' and a Mandate was granted at the San Remo conference of 1920 and later ratified by the League of Nations.

On the 2 November 1917, in the Balfour Declaration (in the form of a letter addressed to Lord Rothschild), the British government had enunciated a policy favouring the 'establishment in Palestine of a National Home for the Jewish people ... it being clearly understood that nothing shall be done which may prejudice the civil and religious rights of existing non-Jewish communities in Palestine.'[5] Thus, at the end of the First World War the British began their, for the time being, military rule over Palestine with two promises: a promise to establish an Arab state – which they kept by supporting the formulation of Saudi Arabia (1925) and the creation of Transjordan (1922) – and a promise to establish in Palestine a 'National-Home' for the Jewish people. In 1918, the number of Arabs in Palestine amounted to about 500,000, while there were some 56,000 Jews.[6]

Between December 1917 and July 1920, the British Army ran Palestine. The Great Powers, in their conference in San Remo (April–May 1920) granted the British a Mandate over Palestine and also over Iraq, which was ratified by the Permanent Mandate Commission of the League of Nations on 22 July 1922. The British government was recognized as a 'trustee', with no authority to initiate and change the 'Mandate Decree' without the consent of the League of Nations. In addition, the British high commissioner had to report annually to the Mandate Committee in Geneva. The operation of the Mandate began on 1 July 1920 with the arrival of Sir Herbert Samuel, who was nominated by the British government in London to assume the position of high commissioner of Palestine. Practically – though not formally – Palestine had become a British colony, a status that lasted until May 1948.

BRITISH POLICY IN PALESTINE

The Mandate's terms on Palestine imposed some constraints on the British rulers. However, the latter had considerable freedom to initiate and implement a policy in Palestine that suited their interests. The practices of the civil rule were based by the Foreign Jurisdiction Act, 1890 which specified the authority of legislation in countries not under direct British sovereignty.[7]

The government, which was established by the British in Palestine, was one of a 'pure Crown Colony'[8] under the authority of the Colonial Office, with a high commissioner. They set up a small executive council of high-ranking officers, a mixed advisory council without, however, executive authority, and a countrywide administration in which the British occupied the senior positions. Junior positions, however, were distributed to Palestinian Jews and Arabs. British Judges presided over all the courts higher than the magistrates' courts. The police force comprised Palestinians (Jews and Arabs) along with British officers. In the early years of the Mandate (1922), the military force in Palestine was small; only 6,300 military personnel and 100 police officers. At that time, the Mandate government employed 800 people in its various departments. Gradually, due to the intensifying conflict between the Jews and the Arabs, and also the revolts of both sides against the British, the size of the army increased –toward its end days in May 1948, it had swollen to 100,000 soldiers. The government employees amounted to 10,000, only 250 of whom were British.[9] This imposed onerous conditions on the British government in London over its practical policy in Palestine. The terms of the Mandate were specified in the 'Mandate Trusteeship'. However, British policy in Palestine was based on the economic and political interest of the government in London. Indeed, the major objective of the British government in Palestine was, according to N. Gross,[10] to promote the strategic interests of the British Empire. This policy was motivated by the British interest in Iraqi oil and the security of the imperial roads to India. In the 1930s, the British negotiated a retreat of their forces from Egypt and subsequently, Palestine was considered as an alternative base for the British army. This meant that the British took their rule in this country very seriously.

Gross, and also G. Shaffer,[11] suggest that the strategy mentioned above was translated into a pragmatic policy of minimum intervention in the economy and political-cultural life of the local communities of the Arabs and the Jews. The British 'made an effort to minimize as much as possible the offence to the local traditions, to the social tissue and particularity of the local leadership. In these domains the relation of Britain to Eretz-Israel was similar to the relation to its other colonies.'[12]

It is suggested here that basically, the British imported to Palestine the 'spirit of capitalism', and made an effort to introduce a laissez-faire economy and instil a liberal approach – in so far as a colonial regime can be considered sincerely liberal – to the domain of Palestine and its rival parties. This process, however, was interrupted more than a few times by 'incidents' between the Arabs and the Jews, and by the Second World War. In contrast to other colonialists at that time (for example, the French), British policy was to refrain from directly interfering in the lives of the local population and from imposing their culture upon them. However, it must be specified that this policy had its limits: everything concerning issues of security and 'state policy' was solely at British discretion. Also, the British determined the practical extent of the autonomy of the Jewish and the Arabs communities. They insisted on a certain kind of 'balanced policy' with regard to the Jews and the Arabs – though not, however, one of parity.[13]

Furthermore, by their presence in Palestine, the British constituted a 'reference model' for the local populations: some Jews and Arabs were impressed by the British culture and adopted its manners as a routine lifestyle.[14] Yet, even without such emulation, and with no explicit intention, the impact of the British culture was unavoidable. Football in Palestine constituted one of those things that was influenced and shaped by the British Mandate. Yet, because of the peculiarities of the Palestine situation, the depth of this influence and its extent were not the same as in other British colonies.

THREE MODELS

In one study of European football, it has been suggested that two British models – 'Aristocratic' and 'Technical-Commercial' – were involved in the penetration of football into different regions on the continent.[15]

The first of these models is class related, '... Where a local aristocracy was interested in sport, it quickly chose to promote a game to reproduce the myth of the English aristocracy ... It is clear that playing football contributed to the reproduction of English propensities so admired by the continental aristocracy.'[16] Thus, the upper classes on the continent 'imported' the English game of football, which, in the middle of the nineteenth century was extravagantly considered to be a game of the British aristocracy (and also, of the haute bourgeoisie). The adoption of football was taken to be an act of emulating and adopting the values of 'gentlemanly fair play'. However, this model can only partially explain a short period in the introduction and formulation of football in Europe, for any association between aristocracy and football, assumed or real, was short. By the second half of the nineteenth century this game had already been adopted by the working classes,[17] and the history of football in Britain and on the continent, took different directions.

The Technical-Commercial model suggests that football on the continent was taken there by engineers and merchants – some of the former were British who lived and worked in Europe, while some were students who had learned the game at university: '[They] were exporting a technology, a practical knowledge which they disseminated in its entirety and ... football was one of the elements'.[18] Traders supported the development of football clubs in different urban regions: 'It was a number of young bourgeois businessmen, entrepreneurs, mobile, highly qualified people seeking openings and new markets, who encouraged the development of football and created the first organized teams in Europe.'[19] To an extent this model was also relevant in some countries in South America, such as Argentina and Uruguay, where 'The first groups of men to play something like the modern game of football in nineteenth-century Latin America were British Sailors.'[20] However, it should be made quite clear that the model applied to South America especially Argentina, does not take account of a third influence: the Educational.[21]

These two models virtually subsume the establishment of European football, which quickly began to develop autonomously. Yet, football penetrated other parts of the globe in a different manner, via the British army, missionaries, educationalists and the colonial administration. Thus, there is room for a third – Imperialist or Colonialist – model.[22]

Generally, football in the 'British colonies' followed the same form as almost any other sphere of life manipulated by the British rulers. Although the British assumed a so-called liberal policy in their colonies, such as allowing the 'natives' cultural autonomy, they nevertheless considered themselves to be missionaries of enlightenment and modernization. The British administrators in the colonies and no less importantly, their mentors in public schools, believed strongly in the civilizing role of British Imperialism.[23] This belief was instilled into the members of the English public schools, which provided the British colonies with administrators, teachers, missionaries and officers.

The Imperialist model had two basic means of introducing the game to the natives: first, the British colonialists imported and disseminated the game to 'non footballing' areas of the empire as part of the 'civilizing process'. This was achieved by encouraging emulation in the interests of progress *and* political stability. The indigenous population watched the British playing football among themselves, and then started their own teams. Compulsion, however, was widely used in colonial schools as exemplified by a case in Kashmir, where the game of football was imposed upon the local school pupils by a British missionary – Cecil Earle Tyndale-Biscoe – in the interests of teaching them 'fair play' or, in other words, providing them with 'character training'.[24]

The second means was a similar form of political bonding used in specific situations in which football was already known and played by the indigenous people. A European power, which was offered a trusteeship over a territory (for example, a mandate), would often consider football, among other things, a matter worthy of attention and support as an instrument of control. It would establish its own clubs and sometimes play local teams; it would invite teams from the metropolis to play against local teams; it would join the local league and even impose some 'rationalization', 'bureaucratization' and 'equality of opportunity'[25] in relation to the participation of local ethnic groups.

It is possible to specify three non-exclusive models or metaphors specifying the colonialist and native behaviour (mainly that of the former): Linesmen – where the colonialists established their own clubs, organized their exclusive league and occasionally played against the native clubs. They encouraged 'fair play', following football rules that had been enacted in the metropolitan country. Referees – the colonialist clubs joined the local league, and also joined the specific management organizations, such as the Football Association (FA), or encouraged the establishment of such organizations. Some individuals even joined natives' clubs. Yet, while the colonialists took care to develop football into a modern game, they nonetheless maintained a distinction between this game and their participation in its events and other domains. Arbitrators – the colonialists insisted that football be organized and played under certain political parameters, such as not allowing politics in the stadiums, or by imposing co-operation between ethnic communities (a single league system, one 'national selection'). In essence, in this model the colonialists used direct political measures to control the mandated territory, including football and sport in general.

This chapter deals specifically with the link between football and the British (Mandate) in Palestine from 1920 to 1948. Based on their relatively liberal policy in Palestine, and given the on-going conflicts between the Jewish and Arab communities, it is suggested that Britain used two models interchangeably: the Referee and the Arbitrator. The selection of one model rather than the other was contingent on the situation. It is possible to observe clear distinctions of use in the 1920s, the 1930s and the 1940s – the roots of which were in the political, rather than the footballing realm.

FOOTBALL: JEWS, ARABS AND BRITISH. FOOTBALL BEFORE 1917

Football had already been played in Palestine before 1917 – the year that the British army entered Palestine in pursuit of the Ottoman battalions. In 1906, a football club Rishon Le-Zion was established in Jaffa. Other clubs were established in 1911 in Jerusalem (Maccabi) and in the Jewish colonies;[26] in 1912, the Ofer club was established in the Herzlia High School in Tel Aviv, as was Bnei-Yaacov, also in Tel Aviv. Football games were arranged during the town of Rehovot's Passover Festival in 1908 and thereafter, in almost every other Passover Festival before the First World War.[27] In 1913, Zvi Nesher, a gymnastics educator, published the first local guidebook of football. The Palestinian Arabs also played the game. A Jewish spectator reported that in 1910 he was present at a game arranged between the Jewish team from the Herzlia High School and Arab students from the American College in Beirut.[28]

It appears that Jewish immigrants from Europe, who had been introduced to the game in their countries of emigration, imported football to Palestine.[29] Arab merchants and students who studied in Beirut and Damascus, introduced the game to their communities in Palestine.[30] Thus, when the British army entered the country, both Jews and Arabs were already playing the game. However, the British impact on the development of football as a sport and as a modern system was impressive. It was part and parcel of a major British contribution to Palestine, that is 'the introduction of the spirit of capitalism' and British policy involving the triangular relationship of the Jewish and Arab communities and the Mandate government.

FOOTBALL AS POLITICS

In the Jewish community before and during the Mandate, football was regarded as a political (Zionist) project. Sports education – including and especially physical education, in the Jewish schools in Palestine –

was treated as an integral subject of nationalistic-Zionist socialization[31] and was integrated into dominant nationalistic ideology and political practice. The game of football was part of this process – political leaders, sports activists (functionaries) and even sportsmen, considered football in political terms; it was hailed as a 'missionary of the process of nation building'. In addition, because of the dominant position of working class organizations in the Jewish community (through the trade unions and political parties), it was also viewed as a 'missionary' of social class assertion. Sport, class and politics were tightly intertwined.

Hence, football clubs in the Jewish community were organized and assembled along political party lines. The Maccabi federation (established in 1912) was affiliated to the bourgeois political parties, while Hapoel was an organ of the Histadrut (The General Federation of Labour), Elizur was related to the religious–Zionist Party and the Beitar federation was associated with the right-wing Revisionists.[32] Nevertheless, all had a common denominator – they were primarily Zionist organizations. Football, therefore, was one of the elements that specified the boundary between the Arab and Jewish communities: clubs from different communities played each other occasionally but mixed clubs (teams), that is Jews who played in an Arab club or vice-versa, were extremely rare. On the other hand, British players did sign up with local Arab or Jewish clubs.

As noted above, Arabs in Palestine had already played football before the coming of the British, as students and traders had imported it first. However, the British made an effective contribution to the development of the game in the Arab community through the establishment of British government schools.[33] The schools played football. As for the Jewish community, the game was closely associated with Arab nationality and, as described below, Arab leaders used football to consolidate internal solidarity among their people and also made some effort to extend this solidarity to the Egyptians and the Syrians.

THE BRITISH ARE COMING

Football in the Mandate period has three protagonists: the British, the Jews and the Arabs. Football as an organized modern game and almost everything else at that time, were deeply influenced by the political situation. The Arabs and Jews were engaged in consolidating their communities' autonomy and power and football was included in this effort. The British attitude to the game's organization was an extension of their general policy in Palestine. This involved joining the local and also the countrywide league and cup competitions. They also made an effort to provide the basic conditions for co-operation between Jewish and Arab clubs, they did not force them to co-operate, except when Palestine was invited to take part in the World Cup games. In this case, the British then insisted that the 'Palestine select' include Arab, Jewish and British players.

The British were initially optimistic in their hopes for inter-ethnic co-operation. In 1921, the administrators of the 'Temporary Government' (as noted above, the British Mandate over Palestine was finally endorsed by the League of Nations in April 1922) established a Sports Club and invited Jews and Arabs to join it. In the same year, the British organized a soccer tournament for both army and civilian teams.[34] In the 1920s, clubs from both groups played in the same league. Moreover, the railway workers had a football team that included both Arab and Jewish players.[35] However, by the mid-1930s, football in Palestine had become segregated. Regular league games and cup competitions were now exclusive. Jews and Arabs had separate clubs and ran separate leagues. Clubs from now opposed communities met from time to time on the soccer field. However, co-operation between the two communities was rare and contingent the political situation. In 1928, both sides were involved in establishing the Palestine Football Association, but for political reasons, the Arabs broke-away in 1934 and established their own association.

THE PERIOD OF AN ELEMENT OF CO-OPERATION

After the four year long enforced break caused by the First World War, football recovered. 'This post-war period saw the resumption of football in Eretz-Israel (Palestine), in which British teams fulfilled an important role.'[36] The Jewish sports organization, Maccabi, resumed its activities in a variety of sports. Already by the summer of 1919, Maccabi Ness-Ziona played and won a game against Maccabi Jaffa (a club which was established that year). A week later, Maccabi Jerusalem was defeated by a British team, probably a British army team, 6–0. In a second meeting between these teams, the British won 4–0. In September 1919, the Arab National Club of Jerusalem played against Maccabi Jerusalem and won 1–0. However, football matches were mostly played between teams from the same locality.

In October 1919, while Palestine was run by the Military government, Maccabi organized a Sports Festival in Jerusalem, which included a football competition. The intention of the organizers, among them the Zionist leader, Ze'ev Zabotinski, who was deported by the British governor on political grounds a few years later, was that the festival propagate Zionism, but the governor of Jerusalem, General Stors, stopped this. It was observed that 'The assembly took place in a field behind the Tomb of Shimon Ha-Zaddik (the righteous). Contrary to the original planning, the procession from the Lemel School to the assembly ground was prohibited by the British Governor, General Stors ... The waving of the flag was also prohibited.'[37]

The Jewish newspaper *Doar-Hayom* (the *Daily Post*) was critical of what it regarded as the inept management of this event. The organizers concluded that 'From a sport's viewpoint this festival was a success, however it was a failure regarding order, punctuality and discipline.'[38] Four British officers (Raiter, Hudson, Hud and MacKenzie) were among the referees, and the festival schedule included athletic events, gymnastics and games. The participation of the British on this particular occasion signified the early co-operation of the military and later on, the civil administration with Jewish sport authorities. It is possible to offer certain reasons for this participation: one, the organizers of the festival simply needed some outsiders who were both objective and professional as referees; and two, for political reasons, the organizers had an interest in the participation of British army officers in a Jewish event. It had been the intention of the organizers, as noted above, to turn the event into a nationalistic demonstration. While the military governor prevented the expression of some nationalistic gestures, he allowed a kind of symbolic participation of British officers as referees and judges, possibly in the interest of good community relations.

The attitude of the military governor to the political-Zionist intentions of the festival's organizers was, in retrospect, a clear sign of the British policy in Palestine concerning the triangular relationship of British, Arabs and Jews. This policy allowed the parties to express their nationalistic ambitions in an orderly manner, but, the British government in Palestine tried to adopt a kind of 'balanced policy' and this was projected on certain sport events. Yet, it should be noted that at that time Palestine was ruled by military government and it is probable that General Stors was following a strict policy in order to prevent any possible reason for public political tension between the Jews and Arabs.

Nevertheless, in March 1932 and April 1935, Maccabi organized the 'Maccabiah', an international Sports Festival of Jewish athletes (men and women) from all over the world. This event was highly politicized, being overtly nationalistic-Zionist in character, with the British high commissioner failing to interfere in this 'Jews only' festival!

In order to consolidate their rule in Palestine, the British administration had to bring in some professional people and units from Britain: soldiers, police, engineers, and so forth. These people and units played football usually on the Sabbath or on Sunday. Almost immediately after their arrival, therefore, the British became involved in football: first, in its leagues and cup games, and then, in the basic conditions of its modernization.

The modest history of Jewish football in Palestine before the arrival of the British has been noted above. Yet, it is worth stating again that the importation and the development of football was a by-product of the Jewish immigration to Palestine and the immigrants continuing relationships with Jewish communities in Europe, mainly through the Zionist organization(s). In 1920, for example, Shimon Lumek, an ex-player of Ha-Koach Vienna (a well known Jewish football club), immigrated to Palestine and joined Maccabi Tel-Aviv (which was then called Maccabi Jaffa): 'His presence raised the level of the team's performance significantly' and also 'influenced other teams which looked up to Maccabi Tel-Aviv as "a role model"'.[39] A noticeable change in the quality of the team was noted in February 1921, when Maccabi Tel-Aviv won a game against a British military team, and defeated the Christian-Arab Sport Club of Jaffa.[40] The first Cup competition was organized by the British in 1922. Maccabi Tel-Aviv, which included a British player, Captain Harper, was drawn to play against a British military hospital in Sarafand (a military base in the centre of the country). The game took place in one of the British military camps and most of the crowd comprised British soldiers who, according to some sport writers, were hostile to Maccabi. The final score was a draw and a second leg was set for the following day at Maccabi's ground in Tel-Aviv. This game also ended in a draw. However, Maccabi claimed that the British referee was the twelfth player of the British team. In the third game, Maccabi lost heavily '... mainly because the players were tired and because of the "English terror" on the pitch'.[41] Eventually, the 'Royal Flyers', a British army team from the base in 'Ramle', won the Cup – as they were to continue to do for the next six years. In 1927, five Jewish teams took part in the Cup competition; Hapoel Haifa made it to the 'final four' but lost to the Royal Flyers. It so happened that in the same year, the high commissioner, Lord Plummer, decided (for economic and political reasons) to reduce the British forces in Palestine. As a result, the Royal Flyers left Palestine and took the Cup to Britain. However, the reduction of the British forces had a positive effect on Jewish and Arab football – far fewer British football teams stood between the indigenous people and the Cup.[42]

It should not be overlooked that a further major influence on Jewish football and, to a certain extent, on Arab football in Palestine, was continental. This was due to players who had been introduced to the game in their continental country of origin and to the tactics they brought with them. Among other things, this influence was reflected in the style adopted: while the British tended to base their play on the 'long ball', the Jewish teams inclined to dribbling and short passes.[43]

Continental 'role modelling' was reinforced by the visit of the famous football club 'Ha–Koach Vienna'. This team visited Palestine in the first week of January 1924, as the guest of the Maccabi Federation in Eretz-Israel. Ha–Koach Vienna was a Jewish football club in terms of its ownership, management and players, and played regularly in the Austrian League and cup competitions. In 1924, the team won the Austrian league championship and was regarded very highly: on the way to Palestine, Ha–Koach stopped off in London and heavily defeated the well-known British team, 'West Ham'.[44]

During their first visit to Palestine, Ha–Koach played three games. The report by *Doar Hayom* of the reception is indicative: 'a large crowd came to the train station in Tel Aviv to welcome the team. The district governor, Campbell, and the mayor of Tel-Aviv, Dizengoff, welcomed the guests.'[45] The first game was in Tel-Aviv against Maccabi, in which Ha–Koach won the game 5–1. The only goal for Maccabi was scored by Lumek, the ex Ha–Koach Vienna player. The second game was in Jerusalem against a selection of the British army – two British officers were flown from Baghdad in order to strengthen the British team.[46] Nevertheless, Ha–Koach Vienna won 3–0. The third game was played in Haifa against a mixed local team, comprising British policemen and Arab office workers from the railway station. Surprisingly, perhaps, this game ended in a draw. In January 1925, Ha–Koach Vienna again visited Palestine, and in the first game, which was played in Jerusalem, Ha–Koach defeated a selection of British players. The match was attended by a crowd of 10,000, which was an impressive turnout considering the size of the population in Jerusalem at that time. The second game was in Tel-Aviv, against a Maccabi Eretz-Israel select, which at that time represented the entire Jewish community. In the presence of about 7000 spectators, according to the newspaper *Ha-aretz*, or about 10,000 spectators according to *Doar Hayom*, Ha-Koach thrashed Maccabi 11–2.[47]

The initial visit of Ha-Koach Vienna left at least three significant imprints on football in Palestine. Firstly, it reinforced the influence of the central European system of football, particularly among the Jewish clubs. Secondly, the visit increased local interest in football, with the result that Maccabi in Jerusalem established a local football association with six Jewish teams. In the winter of 1924, the leadership of Maccabi in Palestine decided to create a countrywide Maccabi football federation, with its management located in Jerusalem. Thirdly, the Ha-Koach's visit inspired co-operation between Jewish and Arab clubs. In Haifa, a British officer organized a local league with nine Arab and Jewish teams. This league's life was short because violence broke out during matches and there were fierce disputes between clubs' management. In 1926, the deputy governor of the Haifa district, Kitrush, tried again and created a local league of twelve clubs. However, this again only lasted for a short period.[48]

It is worth re-emphasizing that in the mid-1920s, football in Palestine was organized locally and ethnically. Indeed, there was no country-wide league system and although both Jews and Arabs made some attempts to organize a kind of a league system for their own clubs, the British neither initiated nor imposed any special football policy. They became involved in local initiatives (such as in Haifa, as noted above), and were keen to take part in different events, including local leagues and cup tournaments. Thus, as long as football was organized and played locally or even when it was organized on a countrywide federation system (such as that of Maccabi), the Mandate government applied a laissez-faire policy. At certain football events, the Mandate administration intervened, mainly to prevent inter-community tension or, to encourage inter-community co-operation. However, when football became an international issue, for example, with the establishment of the Palestine Football Association, the British imposed certain conditions on the parties.

Whatever the Continental influence, the British influence was clearly evident through the footballing ambience that was imported and encouraged by them. This included major and minor elements. Major elements included the organization of cup tournaments and district leagues, which were directly set up or encouraged by local British officers with some support from the district governor. Minor matters included the introduction of a somewhat standardized football outfit – Jewish teams usually wore long trousers, a button-up shirt and 'working boots'[49] and the introduction of soccer 'lingo: words like 'off side', 'linesman', 'goal', 'back', 'penalty' and so forth, were adopted on the pitch and terraces. In this way, the presence of British football traditions in Palestine – had a real effect on the indigenous football, especially that of the Jews,[50] but probably also that of the Arabs.

In April 1924, a group of workers established a new club, Haifa (literally, 'the worker'). Some other workers' clubs were established in north of the country, in the kibbutzim, in the Workers' Labour Camps, in Tel-Aviv and in Jerusalem. In May 1926, these different workers' clubs founded the Hapoel Federation under the auspices of the Histadrut – the General Federation of Labour an inclusive Jewish organization, which had been started in December 1921 by the left-wing parties. The reason for Hapoel's formation was political: workers groups (which, it should be noted, already were members of the Histadrut) in various places came to the conclusion that they should establish their own class-based sport clubs because Maccabi was a bourgeois organization and the policy of its leadership clashed with the workers' interests: 'We could find social differences. Class differences ... The worker in this country creates his own separate life ...'[51] A staunch supporter of Hapoel argued in *Ozenu* (*Our Strength*, the Hapoel magazine) that, 'There are contradictions between the workers' sport and the civil sport in Eretz-Israel.'[52] Twelve Hapoel clubs were registered in the federation at the beginning of 1926.

Maccabi did not like the presence of another Jewish sports federation, which among other things undermined the assumed hegemony of Maccabi over the Jewish community in Palestine. Meetings between Maccabi and Hapoel teams turned into physical confrontation on the terraces and on the pitch.[53] Maccabi declared a boycott of Hapoel and forbade its teams to play against it. Maccabi also turned to Arab football clubs for support against Hapoel but the latter refused to take part in this intra-community dispute. An appeal to British football clubs not to play Hapoel teams failed. The British also refused to take sides in an intra-community dispute. In fact, at that time, the British played football with any available club; for example, on 4 April 1924, before Hapoel teams had formed a separate federation, the *Ha'aretz* newspaper reported that, 'Yesterday a football match between the Tel-Aviv Police selection and Hapoel Tel-Aviv ended 2:1 in favour of the former.'[54] So football in the mid-1920s was played by different Jewish teams from Maccabi, Hapoel and independent clubs (not associated to either of the above federations), as well as by Arab teams and British teams. Games were arranged within and between communities. The British played Jewish and Arab teams without explicit preference. In 1927, the British organized a cup tournament and invited five Jewish teams to participate. However, the cup games according to *Davar*, the official newspaper of the Histadrut, were disorganized and, one British team dominated the competition.[55]

In reality, at this time football was just a 'game', or in other words, it was not sufficiently institutionalized and was played sporadically, mainly locally. The situation changed with the establishment of the Palestinian Football Association.

ONE STEP FORWARD

The initiative to modernize the game by integrating the various teams into a countrywide federation was that of Maccabi, which in many ways constituted the biggest sports organization in Palestine. Josef Yekutiely, a prominent member of the Maccabi management, travelled to Egypt and met with Josef Mohammed, a football referee associated with the Fédération Internationale de Football Association (FIFA). Mohammed gave Yekutiely a copy of the structure of the Egyptian Football Association. This was the first step in a relatively short process of creating a football association in Palestine and of gaining membership of FIFA – the world organization of football.

FIFA policy at that time was that only the football federations of actual states could be considered for membership. Thus, in Palestine, the football association had to be that of the Mandatory state. This meant that the association had to represent every party in the country. Moreover, even before the formal application to FIFA, the British government in Palestine had insisted that the football association include both communities. Maccabi was the initiator of this project; Hapoel was invited first and thus the Jewish side already dominated the core of the anticipated organization. The Arab clubs were also invited, the invitation being arranged through a Mandate administrator who issued an invitation to 'all' the football clubs in Palestine to participate in the 'foundation meeting' of the Football Association of Palestine. This meeting took place on 14 August 1928, in Maccabi House in Jerusalem, where 15 representatives were present, 14 from the Jewish clubs (Maccabi and Hapoel) and one Arab representative, a gentleman from the Nusseibeh family who participated on behalf of the Islamic Sports Club. The fact that this particular representative does not appear in the minutes of the rest of the meetings that followed is of significance. The omission has been excused on two different grounds: it is argued that the participation of the Arab representative in the first meeting was imposed by the British in order to keep (or pretend to keep) the balance between the parties in Palestine, and thus the gentleman's presence was necessary at the foundation meeting only. Further, it is suggested that because all the meetings were conducted in Hebrew, the Arab representative just ignored them.[56] At all events, in 1929 the Palestine Football Association was accepted as a member of FIFA, with the application being recommended by the Egyptian Football Association.

At the very beginning, the Association ran league and cup competitions that included Arab, Jewish and British clubs. In a memo that was sent to FIFA in 1929, the structure of the league was as follows: the first division had ten teams, the second division had 20 teams, five of which were Arab teams, and the third division had 39 teams, six being Arab.[57] In the FIFA Year Book of 1931, the Palestine Football Association is noted under 'P', with 30 clubs and 32 teams.

Cup competitions were resumed in 1928, under the organization and supervision of the Palestine Football Association. The wine company, Carmel Mizrachi, contributed a Cup. Seven Jewish teams and five British teams took part in the 1928 Cup competition. One British team, 'The Gaza Flyers', made it to the 'final four' but lost to Hapoel Tel-Aviv. Eventually, Hapoel Tel-Aviv won the Cup that year. In 1929, due to the emigration of three of its players, Hapoel Tel-Aviv considered recruiting three British players from teams in Palestine, to its ranks, yet this idea was quashed by the Hapoel Federation Secretariat. In that same year, six teams, three of them British, took part in a district cup competition. It subsequently appears that British teams were willing to participate in almost any football event.

During the early years of the 1930s, British teams took part in the

Association's cup competitions. For example, in 1930, the 'Northhamptonshire-48' faced Maccabi Tel-Aviv in the final: 'The Ground was packed with about ten thousand people from all over the country, among them many from the Government administration. The Cup was placed on a table at the side of the ground, the members of the Cup-committee sat near it.'[58] Many British soldiers were also present. The referee was English and the Maccabi people were unhappy with this choice before the game. Inevitably, however, by the end of the game they had changed their minds as Maccabi won the Cup. In 1932 the 'British Police' team won the title by the decree of the Federation's management; in the thirtieth minute, the British referee awarded a penalty in favour of the British Police team. The Hapoel Haifa players disagreed with the referee's decision and refused to continue with the game. The end result was that the Association Management ruled that the Cup be given to the British Police team.[59]

Only the British Police football team took part in the cup competitions in the 1930s. The high commissioner, Lord Plummer,[60] it appears, prohibited league games because of the tense political situation in Palestine. In 1932, the policy was reconsidered by the new high commissioner, Sir Alan Waqcop, thereby allowing British teams to resume participation in the league and cup competitions. British army teams, however, did not rejoin the league and only the Police team remained. The cup competitions continued in the 1930s and also during the Second World War. In 1943, the team of the "Royal Artillery' played in the final of the 'War Cup' and routed Hapoel Jerusalem 7–1.

The Football Association made a serious effort to run the league and cup games on a regular basis. Usually, the management and the chairman were Jewish, except for a short period when the ex-general commissioner of the police served in this position. In 1930, the first division included eleven Jewish and five British teams; the latter being the British Police, the 49th Regiment, the Stoopdes-Regiment, The Ramle-Flyers and the Jerusalem Flyers. As noted previously, the league was interrupted due to the political situation in Palestine (and also because of a harsh dispute between Maccabi and Hapoel), but when it was resumed in 1932, only nine teams, including the British Police, took part. This team actually won the league championship that year, but this was to be the last time that a British team won the Palestine league championship.

In 1934, the Arabs, who were dissatisfied with the situation in the

Football Association in that it was practically dominated and run by the Jewish faction, established their own sports organization, The General Palestinian Sports Federation. Inspired by political motives, Arab teams' preferences subsequently moved from the Palestine Football Association in favour of the new Arab organization. However, in 1936, in response to the Arab revolt against the British Mandate government, their Sports Federation was abolished by the Mandate government. Hence, a few Arab teams applied to the Palestine Football Association in 1941, but in 1943 they left the Association for good.[61]

It has been made apparent that the active participation of the British in Palestinian football during the late 1920s and the early 1930s was rather impressive. For example, during 1929 a number of British teams played against Jewish teams several times. These teams included those from the warships *Eagle*, *Valiant* and *Oak*: The Flyers, a British team from Amman; an Army Select, a team of Officers stationed in Jaffa; the Air Force; the Police Selection; the Ramle Flyers; the Malta Battalion; the Army Wireless team; and yet another, unnamed British team.[62] It is worth stating again that in 1926, the high commissioner, Lord Plummer, decided to reduce the size of the army in Palestine, which also led to a reduction in British participation in football. However, different British units toured the country, so although the immediate involvement of British football teams was significantly reduced, the remaining army, police and visiting units were quite active; British teams also played against Arab teams. Matches between British and Jewish teams continued to reported in the newspapers. For instance, a match between a team of the 'King's Battalion' and Hapoel Tel-Aviv that took place in November 1931 was reported as follows: 'The English Battalion made a great impression because of the subtlety and awareness of its game; every one of the players controls the ball. The best part of this team is the defence.'[63] This particular game ended in a draw. In January 1932, the British Police team met Maccabi Tel-Aviv, with the game also ending in a draw.[64] The number of meetings between British and Jewish teams increased with the willingness of the army commander to allow army teams to play against civilian teams: 'After a request by the Eretz-Israel Football Association, the Army Chief of command allowed the army companies to play football with civilian teams ... .'[65] In April 1930, the Palestinian Select travelled to Egypt. Ironically, this 'select' team was very selective for, as a result of certain disagreements with Maccabi, Hapoel boycotted the team. Nor were Arabs included. Thus, the so-called Palestine select included six players from Maccabi clubs, while the rest of the players were English, from the best units of the British Army in Eretz-Israel.'[66] The Palestinian Select played three friendly games in Egypt and was beaten in all of them.

In 1934, Palestine took part in the preparatory round of the World Cup games, being drawn to play against Egypt. The Palestine Select included only Jewish players – Arabs refused to participate in the Football Association and were planning their own sports federation. The first leg was arranged in Cairo: 'This was Friday, 16 March 1934. A huge Egyptian crowd surrounded the pitch. The match was preceded by a ceremony: the national anthems of the two states were played ... the diplomatic corps and members of the Egyptian King's Court were present.'[67] The referee was English. The Egyptian team won the game easily, with a score of 7–1.

The second leg took place in Tel-Aviv, three weeks later and the referee again was British. The Egyptian selection won this game too. Four years later, in January 1938, and also in the World Cup games, the Palestinian select met the Greek Select. As in 1934 the Palestinian team included only Jewish players and as in 1934 lost in both the first and second legs.

During the second half of the 1930s and first half of the 1940s, the Football Association continued with the league and cup games. Also apparent was that various international teams visited Palestine to play against Jewish and Arab teams. In the late 1930s, the following teams visited the country: the Cairo Police Select; Bochkai from Hungary; Z.P.R Bucharest from Rumania; Admira from Austria; Aris from Greece; and Ha-Koach Vienna. A few Maccabi and Hapoel teams travelled to Europe, Australia, and the United States. In 1940, in Tel-Aviv, the Palestine Select (only Jewish players) played a friendly match with the select from Lebanon and won. In 1941, a British team 'The Wanderers' – a selection of British league stars touring the Middle East to entertain the British troops stationed there – played against the Palestine Select which, bowing to the demands by the British administration, was a mixed select, including seven Jewish players, two British, one Arab (the goal keeper) and one Greek. The Wanderers won by a score of 8–3. Between 1943 and 1944 the league and cup games were named 'War games'. Many British Army teams played against local teams. The Royal Artillery team won the Football Association War Cup in 1943.

The end of the Second World War brought to an end a 'historical period' in Palestine. In 1944, the Arabs had established the 'General Federation of Sports in Palestine' – an Arabs-only organization. An Arab National Football League was established and in 1947, this league included 65 clubs. Certain Jewish organizations declared the British rule over Palestine as 'illegal' and revolted. Nevertheless, football continued almost until the last moment before the British withdrew – the ending of the Mandate in May 1948; the last Association's Cup match was played in 1947.

On the 14 May 1948, the high commissioner, Sir Allan Cunningham sailed back home to Britain. The Jews and Arabs had other business to attend to between them, and consequently football was set aside until these issues were settled.

EPILOGUE

The Israeli football league was resumed at the end of 1949, with some help from the army. It took some time for the Football Association to organize a new system of leagues and cup competitions. Arab clubs set up by Arabs who remained in the country joined the league by means of membership of one of the major sport federations, a federation that continued to be effective after its establishment.

Despite the political incidents between the two governments, it seems that little animosity remained between the Israelis and the British after May 1948. In May 1950, for example, the British league team, Hull City, played the Hapoel Tel-Aviv and Hapoel Select teams in Israel and won both games. Dundee United, from Scotland, visited Israel in May 1951. The team played three games, winning two and losing one. Later that summer, Hapoel Tel-Aviv travelled to Britain and played against Arsenal and Manchester United. Hapoel lost both games. Evidently, and at least partly in terms of football, the relationship between Israel and Britain was normalized in a very short period after the termination of British rule over Palestine.

One may approach British colonialism in different places in the world in a variety of ways. It is certainly simplistic to think of colonialism as simply abominable. It is most important to differentiate between the colonialists and their policies (which were mostly decided in the metropolis) and to consider some of the contributions of the colonial system. The role that the British played both in encouraging the game of football and in creating the conditions for its modernization, should be listed in the positive column. As noted earlier in the chapter, the British did not bring football to Palestine, however, they were involved in the creation and consolidation of the conditions for the game to become a 'sport' – an organized system of (equal) competition administered and run under formal rules. Britain's practical attitude towards football was virtually a direct derivation and reflection of their Mandate policy in Palestine: sometimes they acted as referee and at other times as arbitrator. Most importantly, the British played football in Palestine because they loved and appreciated the game, and hence, became a collective 'role model' for the indigenous people.

NOTES

Throughout this chapter football refers to soccer. H = Hebrew

 1. See, for example, J.A. Mangan, *The Games Ethic and Imperialism* (London and Portland, OR: Frank Cass, 1999).
 2. R.H.S. Croosman, *Palestine Mission: A Personal Record* (London: Hamish Hamilton, 1946); B. Wasseratein, *The British in Palestine: The Mandatory* Government and the Jewish-Arab Conflict 1917–1929 (Oxford: Blackwell, 1991); H. Sidebotham, *Great Britain and Palestine* (London: Macmillan, 1937); J.M. Cohen, *Palestine: Retreat From the Mandate* (London, Paul Elk, 1978); C. Sykes, *Crossroad to Israel* (Bloomington, Indiana, 1973).
 3. A.J. Sherman, *Mandate Days* (London: Thames and Hudson, 1997), p.35.
 4. Sidebotham, *Great Britain and Palestine*, pp.209–10.
 5. Sherman, *Mandate Days*, p.13.
 6. B. Eliave (ed.), *The Jewish National Home* (Jerusalem: Keter Publishing House, 1976), p.13. (H)
 7. J. Shavit and G. Biger, 'The British Mandate in Eretz-Israel: Rule Administration and Legislation', in Y. Porat and J. Shavit (eds.), *The History of Eretz-Israel, The British Mandate and Jewish National Home* (Jerusalem: Keter Publishing House, 1990). (H)
 8. Sherman, *Mandate Days*, p.43. On the colonial system of the British vis-à-vis that of the French and others, see; S.C. Easton, *The Twilight of European Colonialism* (New York: Holt, Rinehart and Winston, 1960).
 9. Shavit and Biger, *The British Mandate*, p.92.
10. N. Gross, 'The Economic Policy of the British Mandate Government in Eretz-Israel', *Katedra*, 24 (1982) 153–80. Also, G. Sheffer, 'The British Pragmatic Principles', *Katedra*, 29 (1983), 113–45.
11. Gross, 'The Economic Policy'; Shaffer, 'The British Pragmatic Principles'.
12. Ibid.
13. Gross, 'The Economic Policy', 160.
14. H. Lazar, *In and Out of Palestine* (Jerusalem: Keter Publishing House, 1990).
15. P. Lanfranchi, 'Exposing Football: Notes on the Development of Football in Europe', in R. Guilannotti and J. Williams (eds.), *Games Without Frontiers* (Aldershot: Arena, 1994), pp. 23–45.
16. Ibid., p.25.
17. M. Bowden, 'Soccer', in K.B. Raitz (ed.), *The Theater of Sport* (Baltimore: John Hopkins University Press, 1995), pp.97–240; M. Polley, *Moving the Goalposts* (London: Routledge, 1998), *passim*.
18. Lanfranchi, 'Exposing Football', p.27.

19. Ibid., p.31.
20. T. Mason, *Passion of the People?* (London: Routledge, 1998), p.1.
21. See J.A. Mangan, 'The *Early* Evolution of Sport in Latin America: A Mainly English Middle Class Inspiration?' in J.A. Mangan and Lamartine Da Costa (eds.), *The Latin American World: Sport in Society – At the Edge* (London and Portland, OR: Frank Cass, 2001), forthcoming.
22. See J.A. Mangan, 'Prologue: Britain's Chief Spiritual Export: Imperial Sport as Moral Metaphor, Political Symbol and Cultural Bond', in J.A. Mangan (ed.), *The Cultural Bond: Sport, Empire, Society* (London and Portland, OR: Frank Cass, 1990) pp.1–10.
23. Mangan, *The Games Ethic and Imperialism, passim.*
24. Mangan, *The Games Ethic, and Imperialism*, pp.184–96; See also J.A. Mangan, 'Ethics and Ethnocentricity: Imperial Education in British Tropical Africa', in William J. Baker and J.A. Mangan, *Sport in Africa: Essays in Social History* (New York: Holmes Meier, 1987), pp.138–71.
25. A. Guttmann, *From Ritual to Record* (New York: Columbia University Press, 1978).
26. H. Kaufman, 'The Zionist Sports Association: From National Sport to Political Sport', *Zemanim*, 63 (1998), 81–90.
27. H. Kaufman, '"Hapoel" In the Mandate Period' (unpublished Ph.D. thesis, Haifa University, 1993); U. Zimry, *Physical Education and Sport in Eretz-Israel, 1917–1927* (Haifa: Wingate Institute, 1971).
28. *Et-Mol* (Yesterday) A periodical (1982), 22. (H).
29. Kaufman, '"Hapoel" in The Mandate', p.59.
30. S. Tamir, *Sport and Palestinian National Identity in the Mandate State* (Jerusalem: Department of Sociology, Hebrew University, 1999).
31. Kaufman, '"Hapoel" in the Mandate Period', p.37.
32. A. Ben-Porat, 'The Commodification of Football In Israel', *International Review of Sociology*, 33, 3 (1998), 269–76.
33. Tamir, *Sport and Palestinian National Identity*, p. .
34. Kaufman, '"Hapoel" in the Mandate', p. .
35. Kaufman, '"Hapoel In the Mandate', p. .
36. Zimry, *Physical Education and Sport*, p.110.
37. Ibid, p.14. Also, N. Beith Ha-Levi, *Seventy Years of Football* (Wingate Archives, N.D.).
38. Zimry, *Physical Education and Sport*, p.15.
39. Kaufman, '"Hapoel" in the Mandate Period', p.60.
40. Zimry, *Physical Education*, p.25.
41. I. Brenner, *Dyukan Sport [Sports Illustration]* (Tel Aviv, 1958), p.5.
42. H. Kaufman, 'Police State', *Shem HaMishak* [The Name of the Game], August 1997, pp. 26–27.
43. Beith Ha-Levi, *Seventy Years*, p.69.
44. Y. Guby, and Y. Paz, *70th Anniversary Israel Football Association* (Tel-Aviv: The Football Association, 1998).
45. Zimry, *Physical Education*, p.35.
46. N. Ben-Avraham, *Sport Israel* (Tel-Aviv: Persumay Sport Publishers, 1968).
47. Zimry, *Physical Education*, p.37.
48. Ibid., p.38.
49. Beith Ha-Levi, *Seventy Years of Football*, p.44.
50. H. Kaufman, 'Confrontation in the Mandate Period between Hapoel Federation and Macabi Federation Concerning Participation in The Maccabias', *Be-Tenu'a*, B, 3 (1994) p.58.
51. Zimry, *Physical Education*, p.56.
52. Kaufman, 'Confrontation in the Mandate', p.59.
53. Kaufman, '"Hapoel" In The Mandate Period', p.92.
54. Ibid, p.180.
55. *Davar*, 25 Jan. 1932 (An article about the participation of British teams)
56. Tamir, *Sport and Palestinian National Identity*, p.2.
57. Ibid.
58. *Ha'aretz*, 4 May 1930.
59. Kaufman, *Police State*, p.27.

60. Ibid.
61. Tamir, *Sport and Palestinian National Identity*, p.4.
62. *Ha'aretz*, 16 Oct. 1929.
63. *Ha'aretz*, 23 Nov. 1931.
64. *Davar*, 1 Feb. 1930.
65. *Ha'aretz*, 25 Jan. 1932.
66. *Ha'aretz*, 25 Jan. 1932.
67. Brenner, *Dyukan Sport*, p.32.

'Charging Amazons and Fair Invaders': The 1922 Dick, Kerr's Ladies' Soccer Tour of North America – Sowing Seed

ALETHEA MELLING

In September 1922, Dick, Kerr's Ladies' FC boarded the *SS Montclare* on her maiden voyage to North America and Canada. The tour was arranged between Alfred Frankland, the manager of Dick, Kerr's Ladies and two other men – David Brooks an ex-Irish International soccer football player and Mr Zelickman, a Jewish immigrant and manager of Brooklyn, one of the major soccer clubs in North America at the time. The tour was endorsed by the United States Soccer Football Association (USSFA) who were to eventually take control of the itinerary.[1] In terms of organization, achievement and impact upon American women's sports, the tour was of little significance. In retrospect however, it raised some very pertinent questions regarding the roles of women, national identity and the status of soccer football on both sides of the Atlantic. Although the tour failed to raise enthusiasm amongst American women for playing the game, the reasons behind this are instrumental in furthering understandings of transatlantic perspectives on gender and sport, particularly soccer.

The 1920s were characterized by diverse attitudes towards women and sport in America.[2] Despite having a well-established physical culture for women dating back to the eighteenth century, there was still a significant amount of medical and ideological opposition to women and vigorous sport in the decades before and after the First World War.[3] The more conservative element of the middle classes expressed concerns over women's sports threatening traditional modes of feminine behaviour. However, as working-class women became involved in sport after the First World War, the focus changed from emphasis on propriety to gender roles and sexuality.[4] These issues were highlighted by middle-class fears of a breakdown in social order through working-class unrest before the First World War, as well as a perceived radical feminist consciousness developing out of the suffragist movement during the post-war era.[5] Although the 1920s were comprehended as a period of revolutionary change and the rapid growth in youth and leisure cultures, the majority of Americans remained very conservative, clinging onto traditions and notions of a definitive social hierarchy and gender roles. Soccer for women would therefore have been regarded as too revolutionary within this context.[6]

Conservative attitudes to gender roles were not the only reasons why women's soccer failed to develop during the 1920s, a time regarded as being the 'golden era' for the sport.[7] The status of soccer in America was a major issue, as it was played by working-class immigrants of British, Scottish, Irish, Italian and Hispanic origin.[8] This fact immediately ensured the dismissal of soccer as a suitable collegiate sport for middle-class girls as it was considered masculine and moreover, un-American. Furthermore, working-class immigrant women would have been unlikely to adopt the game, as they were subject to rigorous patriarchal controls and less likely to have access to sport than their middle-class born American peers. Moreover, during a period when America was searching for a national identity, the adoption of a British sport would not have been popular. The ethno-cultural conflict and xenophobia that characterized the First World War would have rendered the sport unpatriotic due to its immigrant connections.[9] Finally, if there was a chance that the sport could have been successful, some entrepreneur would have developed it. In this period of growing consumerism, sport was like other aspects of leisure – a business.[10] Gail Newsham has expressed surprise at Zelickman charging a US$1,000 advance on match fixtures, with no reference to giving the money to a charity, as was customary for the British women's game.[11] However, Zelickman's action was the norm in America, as sport was inextricably linked to commercialism and consumerism. The Dick, Kerr's Tour of America in 1922 provides a microcosmic study of a fast growing, consumer driven, multi-cultural society, trying to hold on to traditions that had provided stability in the past, whilst looking forward to creating a new, all embracing, national identity.

SOCCER, GENDER AND NATIONAL IDENTITY

Women's soccer, or football as it is commonly known in Europe, has a long history in the Great Britain, with roots in the folk games of the

Caledonian region of Scotland during the eighteenth century.[12] However, the first serious attempts at organizing the sport took place in the late nineteenth century within the more progressive British girls' schools. The first official game was played at Crouch End Athletic in 1894, organized by Nettie Honeyball, captain of the British Ladies and Lady Florence Dixie, who ran a travelling Scottish team.[13] The game remained within the exclusive confines of upper and middle-class girls' schools until the First World War when it became the favoured sport of the munitions girls, spreading with a contagious diffusion, the length and breadth of the British Isles. The soccer played in the munitions factories was different to that played previously, in the sense that it became predominantly working class.[14] Munitions soccer teams were recorded in munitions factories at Renfrew in Scotland, Newport and Swansea in Wales and from Belfast in Northern Ireland, to Bath in the south of Britain.[15] The development of the women's teams was the result of a demand for a form of rational recreation that reflected the reordering of gender roles necessary for the war-effort.[16] The teams were organized by the workers and encouraged by middle-class welfare supervisors who looked after the moral and physical welfare of women working in the munitions factories.[17]

The objective of women's war time soccer, or to use their term, 'ladies' football', was to boost morale and foster patriotism by raising money for ex-servicemen and other war related charities.[18] The game continued into the immediate post-war era, driven by public enthusiasm and the wartime ideology of the plucky heroine, 'doing her bit for Britain'.[19] During 1920, in the post-war spirit of peace and reconciliation, international tours were organized between English and French teams. The French teams were made up from members of women's athletics clubs in the Paris region. The first of these international tours was organized by Alfred Frankland of Dick, Kerr's Ladies, the most successful British women's soccer club to come out of the war, and Madame Alice Milliat, the famous advocate of women's athletics in Europe.[20] This was to be the start of a long tradition in Anglo-French women's soccer. The money raised from these internationals was given to war related charities.

However, after 1920, public enthusiasm for fund-raising began to decline and following a short post-war boom in the economy, Britain slumped into depression. Concerns over the condition of ex-servicemen were replaced by the grim realities of industrial unrest.[21] The popularity of women's soccer was to be affected by these social and economic changes. Moreover, in an attempt to return society to traditional pre-war social forms, women were discouraged from maintaining the masculine roles they had assumed as part of the war-effort. Furthermore, post-war feminism in Britain was concerned with promoting motherhood as the ideal. The ideology of the plucky heroine was substituted for one of pro-natalism in a bid to replace the thousands of men killed during the war.[22] This drive to return to pre-war forms was Europe-wide and affected not only the employment of women, but also their physical culture.[23] In December 1921, the Football Association (FA) in Britain issued an edict banning women playing on the grounds of their member clubs. This had an immediate and devastating effect on the women's game, as no other venues could cope with the crowd capacity women's soccer attracted. The FA's reason for banning the game was supposedly on the grounds of the misappropriation of gate receipts meant for charity.[24] However, more realistically, it was part of a dominant agenda against certain aspects of women's physical culture, such as soccer and athletics. Developed during the war, these sports were now considered detrimental to the female reproductive process.[25] Although the pro-women's soccer lobby defended their position well, the FA ban was the start of an irreversible decline in the game, maximized by media criticism and popular ideology openly attacking vigorous physical exercise for women.[26] These changes were a source of considerable anxiety for the organizers of the game, as they were forced to play on farmer's fields and rugby football pitches. The number of teams began to decline, just leaving a hard core, led by Dick, Kerr's Ladies.[27] In this context of shifting popularity from plucky heroines to social pariahs, an invitation to cross the Atlantic to play women's collegiate teams in North America and Canada seemed an ideal opportunity to boost football's declining profile.

In 1922, Alfred Frankland was in negotiation with David Brooks, an ex-Irish International, and Mr Zelickman, the manager of Brooklyn, regarding a tour starting in Quebec, Canada, and continuing through North America. The proposed 24–match tour would last four months, with the team returning home in 1923.[28] After a very rough crossing, they arrived in Quebec on 22 September 1922.[29] In terms of organization and management, the tour was a total disaster. On arriving in Quebec the Dick, Kerr team discovered they had been booked to play on the 2 September, 20 days before their arrival. Moreover, Zelickman had been

demanding large advances to arrange a match and there was no evidence
to suggest any of this money went to charitable causes.[30] Also, upon their
arrival, the Dominion Football Association (DFA) issued a statement
that the games would not be allowed in Canada. The FA in Britain had
been opposed to the tour and Newsham suggests they used their
influence on the Dominion Football Association in Canada to prevent
the women playing there.[31] This hypothesis is strong, as the FA was
currently in dispute with the rest of Europe over Germany and was
thereby concentrating its efforts in promoting the game in the
Dominions.[32] Newsham notes that the extracts from the annual general
meeting of the DFA, held in Winnipeg on 5 September 1922, suggest
that the FA in London had approached the DFA, voicing concerns over
the ladies' tour. This resulted in a motion being carried forward that the
DFA '... did not approve of ladies' football [soccer]' and that they 'join
with the Football Association' regarding this matter. Newsham states
that although the FA in London had been unable to prevent this visit,
they could effectively use their influence over the DFA to prevent the
women actually playing soccer.[33]

The women's team was to face further problems on their arrival in
Canada. After the initial disappointment of the ban, rather than playing
women's collegiate teams as had been planned, the team learned they
had been booked to play men's teams across industrial districts of North
America. The reason given, as stated by Zelickman and Brooks, was that
they had been unable to find enough suitably experienced women's
teams to play Dick, Kerr's Ladies.[34] The truth is, however, there was
unlikely to have been any women's soccer teams due to the nature and
status of soccer in America and that of women's sport in general. The
only American women's competition the Dick, Kerr's team played
against was in the field of athletics, where four Dick, Kerr's players beat
the American women's Olympic team in a quarter-mile relay at
Philadelphia's baseball ground.[35] However, at this time mixed sex sport,
although frowned upon in Britain, was by no means unheard of in
America, which in turn raises another of the interesting points this
article seeks to develop later.

After the disappointment in Canada, Zelickman took the team to
New York to begin the tour of the Atlantic Coast. Yet, Zelickman had
mismanaged the tour to such an extent that engagements in Chicago,
Detroit and Cleveland had to be abandoned as well as fixtures for other
mid-western states. The problems were compounded to such a degree

that the USSFA were obliged to send a representative, Thomas Bagnall, to take over the management of the tour and from then on the situation improved.[36] Dick, Kerr's Ladies went on to complete their tour of North America, playing male immigrant teams from the largely working-class and industrial areas that formed the stronghold of soccer in the early 1920s.

The Dick, Kerr's Tour of America raises several important transatlantic social and cultural issues. The first and most fundamental centres upon of why was there no women's soccer in America when it had been so successful in Britain during the First World War; especially in the context of America being regarded as a leader in women's sport? Although some of the reasons are general to western societies' attitudes towards women and physical culture during this period, the answers to this question are multifarious and have a resonance beyond sport. They are concerned with race, class, gender, national identity and consumerism. With this in mind, the status and nature of soccer in America during the immediate post-war era must be explored.

Soccer, according to Nathan Abrams, had a long history in America, with its roots going back to colonial days.[37] Young men and occasionally young women played the kicking game or football as it was known in the United States. Apparently, it was played in a most riotous manner, not unlike British 'folk football', with many players chasing an improvised ball around the town, inevitably leading to public disturbances.[38] Abrams believes that soccer football, as it came to be known, never took off in America due to its association with the Old World in Europe. Abrams draws on Eric Hobsbawm's concept of 'invented tradition' to explain how football (subsequently referred to as soccer) was rejected in favour of baseball. Abrams states that the latter half of the nineteenth century was 'very fertile' for the invention of tradition, as it marked a period of immense change in both western Europe and the US.[39] He believed that these social changes demanded 'new constructions to ensure and express social identity'. The very diverse ethno-cultural nature of American society in the latter half of the nineteenth century was further augmented by an influx of immigrants. The state was faced with the problem of creating a homogeneous society with a common identity that was uniquely 'American'. The 'invented traditions' developed during this period were a means of achieving this. Baseball was chosen rather than soccer due to the fact that it developed during the very nationalistic era of the mid-nineteenth century.[40] The influx of immigrants during this period created something of a nationalistic fervour among native-born Americans and an 'anti-foreign sentiment'. For example, in 1882, the British historian, Edward A. Freeman, made the racist statement that America's social problems may be solved if only 'every Irishman [were to] kill a Negro and be hanged for it'. Furthermore, in 1907, Professor J.W. Burgess of Columbia said to the Kaiser in Berlin that, 'Uncle Sam does not want such rabble for citizens.'[41] Nativism and anti-foreign sentiment worked to reject soccer as a national sport as it had too many connections with Britain and Europe. Furthermore, soccer was already stigmatized as the sport of the 'rabble' element within working-class immigrant culture. Baseball, on the other hand, was developed into a vehicle for uniting born Americans from all cultures into a homogeneous mass. It was, like soccer in England, a common reference point for all, regardless of age, class, occupation or gender.[42] Abrams states the tradition of baseball was invented during the 1860s as a vehicle of national identity and in the process soccer was marginalized.[43] According to Abrams, Boston schoolboys played the folk version of the soccer game during the latter end of the nineteenth century in front of crowds of up to 45,000. Hybrids of this kicking game were developed in the universities of Harvard and Yale using rules adopted from Association and rugby football.[44] However, soccer in its Association form was generally confined to the north and played by immigrants; it became 'the exotic domain of amateur immigrant working men'.[45] In contrast, Andrei S. Markovits describes baseball as America's most popular sport until the 1950s, and one whose popularity 'depended on its identity as American'.[46]

Nevertheless, soccer continued within immigrant communities, forging a sense of identity distinct from 'Americanism'. Moreover, soccer clubs formed a place of contact for immigrant workers with a 'camaraderie of language and culture'.[47] Abrams states soccer was a powerful tool of self-help, providing a 'symbolic umbrella' that united a heterogeneous community.[48] Also, British and Scottish manufacturing entrepreneurs had encouraged soccer: 'No sooner did a mill go up than English or Scottish operatives organized an eleven.'[49] During the latter end of the nineteenth century, clubs developed in Fall River, Newark, Paterson and other textile areas. By 1890, there were about 25 clubs in Fall River and seven in Philadelphia with gates over 2000 during this period. In 1906, when the Corinthians, an elite upper-class amateur team from Britain, visited Fall River, they lost 3–0; the only defeat they suffered during their tour of America and Canada. The Corinthians visited Chicago, Cincinnati, Cleveland, Philadelphia, New York, New Jersey, Fall River and Fore River. The opposing teams were constructed largely from ex-professional immigrant players from Ireland, Britain and Scotland. Indeed, Irish, Scottish, British, Hispanic and Italian immigrants dominated soccer at this time.[50]

These points are extremely interesting when considering the reasons why there was no women's soccer in North America at the time of the Dick, Kerr's tour. Furthermore, they go a long way to explaining why Dick, Kerr's Ladies had no immediate impact on women's sport in North America, despite drawing crowds of up to 8,500 for each fixture.[51] Firstly, the Dick, Kerr team's itinerary almost matched that of the Corinthians' tour, in that the opposing teams were from almost exactly the same immigrant backgrounds and industrial areas. Their first game was against Paterson F.C., one of the textile area clubs referred to by Abrams. This was played on 24 September 1922 at the Olympic Park, Clifton, New Jersey, with the British team losing 6–3 in front of a crowd of 5,000. The second match was played on 30 September against J. and P. Coats F.C., Pawtucket, Rhode Island in front of a crowd of 8,500, where the girls managed a 4–4 draw. On 31 September, they played a Hispanic team, Centro-Hispano at the New York Oval in front of 7,000 spectators. On 8 October, the Dick, Kerr's team drew 4–4 to the Washington Stars at Washington, DC, and four days later they beat the New Bedford All Stars 5–4 at Sargent's Field in front of a gate of 6,000. At New York City on 14 October, they won 8–4 against New York F.C. On 15 October, they achieved a 4–4 draw to Fall River F.C., at St Mark's Stadium, Fall River in front of a crowd of 4,000; Fall River F.C. being the only club to beat the Corinthians elite squad 16 years earlier. On 22 October, the team beat Baltimore S.C., at Baltimore, Maryland. The last match was played on the 4 November at the Philadelphia Baseball Ground against a Philadelphia team, where the women lost 5–4 at the then largest baseball ground in America, with a crowd capacity of 45,000.[52] By taking on male immigrant teams, the girls had already firmly associated themselves and their game with what was at the time, a very stigmatized group in American society. Furthermore, women's soccer would never have had a chance during this period for exactly the same reasons that men's soccer was later rejected as a national sport; that is, it was un-American.

The First World War, rather than reducing ethno-cultural

differences, actually served to enhance them. According to the American historian, Ellis W. Hawley, the war 'spawned a repressive social apparatus that tended to fall into the hands of nativist groups or social traditionalists and be used in their actions against what they regarded as un-American elements'. Hawley saw the loyalty apparatus, set up as a result of the war, as a tool of the new nativist and anti-immigrant, anti-urban 'crusade'. He believed the result of these measures to develop America for 'one hundred per-cent Americans', was increased by ethno-cultural intolerance throughout the 1920s.[53] The Dick, Kerr's tour coincided with a period of extreme anti-foreign sentiment enhanced by the war. Therefore, it is no coincidence that the *New York Times* referred to the women's team as 'the fair invaders'.[54]

Although working-class women began to take part in sport after the First World War, the biggest developments took place in collegiate sports of middle-class youth. In her letter home to the *Lancashire Daily Post*, Alice Kell mentions that women's colleges in the Baltimore area were experimenting with soccer.[55] If this were the case, it would have been unique. The young, middle-class college women at this time embodied what was regarded as wholesome and 'all-American' femininity.[56] They were most unlikely to associate themselves with immigrant sporting activities. Susan Cahn in her study of sport in America makes no reference to soccer at this time and neither do Richard A. Swanson and Betty Spears in their work on the development of physical education.[57] The reason women's soccer was so popular in Britain during and immediately after the First World War was due to the fact it was the national sport and the state encouraged it among the women of the munitions factories for the duration of the war. In contrast, native born Americans would have regarded it as unpatriotic.[58] Soccer was rejected by the sporting middle classes and American-born women of the working classes. The only other remaining social group was immigrant women. However, they were less likely to play soccer football than the collegiate group as they came from ethno-cultural backgrounds that were extremely patriarchal, with clearly defined gender roles for men and women. Southern Italian, Hispanic and Jewish women would not have been allowed to play soccer for social, religious and cultural reasons. Evidence that women were socially excluded from the men's game is demonstrated when Dick, Kerr's visited Fall River, a centre for the sport. Here the local media reported that a special stand was made available for accompanied and single women to watch the match, indicating that this was not the norm. Furthermore, tickets were sold at other venues in advance of the game to save women the indignity of having to visit the box office:

> Special courtesy is to be shown to the ladies of this city who are interested in seeing the game. A half section of grandstand will be reserved for ladies and ladies accompanied by gentlemen only. A special price of twenty-five cents for ladies tickets. Men will pay full price.
>
> Advance sale of tickets is provided for the ladies who would not care to approach the box office at the field.[59]

SOCCER AND THE SEEDS OF SOCIO-PHYSICAL EMANCIPATION FOR WOMEN

Roberta Park has drawn attention to a growing physical culture for women in America during the period 1776 to 1865.[60] This predates the physical revolution that took place for middle-class women in Victorian and Edwardian England. Cahn states that by the turn of the century, 'Women across the nation shared a greater access to athletics, developments in elite sports, school athletics and public recreation,' thus bringing the concept of the 'athletic girl into sharper focus'.[61] Sport for women in America, as in England, tended to be a middle-class affair until the First World War. This is exemplified by the formation of the Chicago Women's Athletic Club in 1903, which boasted swimming pools, Turkish baths, and various 'sitting rooms'. Cahn believes this was as much an elite social club as a serious sporting institution. The Chicago venture was emulated in several other cities including New York and Illinois.[62] A number of women, however, did take their sport, particularly golf and tennis, very seriously. In contrast, sport for working-class women and girls was limited to efforts by middle-class philanthropists. Before the First World War the little sport that was available took the form of rational recreation run on a very similar line to that taking place in Britain through girls clubs and Sunday schools. This 'Progressive Era Activism' gave American working-class women their first taste of organized sport. In a situation paralleled in Britain, the Young Women's Christian Association organized activities for schoolgirls and city playgrounds were developed. Progressive employers also began to offer rational recreation for female employees.[63]

However, as in Britain, most of the late nineteenth- and early twentieth-century sporting developments for women took place on college campuses and were the preserve of the middle-classes, with the result that in 1904, the student newspaper of the University of Minnesota announced the 'athletic girl' as a new gender concept. Cahn states, 'With her exuberant physicality, disregard for Victorian notions of female restraint, and her intrepid incursion into male cultural domains, the athletic woman captured the spirit of modern womanhood.'[64] The athletic girl came to be symbolically associated with a new type of 'feminism' that developed in America immediately after the First World War[65] – a 'feminism' that developed out of the radical element of the pre-1919 suffrage movement. There were those who described themselves as suffragettes and those who called themselves 'feminists'; the latter being the more extreme. Feminists believed in a complete freedom to pursue the career of one's choice, total education and political independence – in short, 'emancipation from sexual stereotypes of any kind'.[66] Henrietta Rodman, leader of the Feminist Alliance, declared in 1913 that feminists demanded '... the removal of all social, political and economic and other discriminations which are based on sex, and the award of all rights and duties in all fields on the basis of individual capacity alone'.[67] Feminism was concerned with economic and social power, gender roles and sexuality. According to William Chafe, enfranchisement was only one of their objectives. Some more 'extreme' feminists proposed homosexuality as a lifestyle and a New York group, Heterodoxy, who championed unorthodox behaviour, described themselves as 'The most unruly individualistic females you ever fell among.'[68] However, these were very much a minority and not at all representative of the majority of American women. Cahn believed that 'with her physical daring and spirited temperament', the athletic girl took her place within a growing, but still minority, feminist consciousness. After 1919 sports women, together with political feminists and young working women, empowered by their war experience, formed what was perceived as 'a threatening centre of new women whose public presence prompted shrill calls for a return to more familiar patriarchal arrangements'.[69]

The young working-class women of the Dick, Kerr's team appeared to represent the physically emancipated 'new women' in both their style and sporting behaviour. In September 1922, the *New York Times* referred to the team as 'Jauntily togged out in light athletic suits familiar to the followers of soccer football, the women's bobbed hair held in restraint by outing caps ...'[70] A month later, in October, *The New York*

Times reported a crowd of '7,000 persons paying admission to watch the unusual sight of women players in full soccer regalia meeting a male team on even terms.' This apparently caused such a sensation that as soon as they came onto the field '... clad in black and white sweaters and blue running shorts ... they immediately became targets for a dozen cameramen and had to run for cover until the field was cleared of spectators ...'[71] The 'new woman' style of the team was mentioned again in the *Fall River Globe*, in which references were made to members of the team playing 'bare headed, allowing their bobbed hair to show'.[72] According to Frederick Lewis Allen's memoir of the 1920s, *Only Yesterday*, bobbed hair was a sign of radicalism. The bob became increasingly popular throughout the summer of 1922 and by 1924, hairdressers and barbers were in competition for what Allen described as '... the cream of this booming business'.[73] The Dick, Kerr team represented what Allen described as a 'first class revolt against the accepted American order ...'[74] Their bobbed hair, minimal sport attire and physical freedom was characteristic of what Allen recalled as a cultural revolution in manners and morals within the younger generation of society. In 1920 a fashion correspondent to the *New York Times* reported that, 'the American woman ... has lifted her skirts far beyond any modest limitation'.[75] The Dick, Kerr's team wore shorts far more revealing than the nine inches off the ground the fashion correspondent was referring to. They were more akin to the 'wilder young things who rolled their stockings below their knees, revealing to the shocked eyes of virtue a fleeting glance of shin – bones and knee cap'.[76] When E. Gerber stated Babe Didrikson and the Golden Cyclones, 'shattered tradition by appearing in blue shorts and a snappy white jersey'[77] in 1928, tradition had already been 'shattered' six years earlier by a team of women soccer players from Britain. Cahn believed that the dominant conservative element in American society were 'disturbed' by what they regarded as challenges to the traditional gender order, such as that represented by the Dick, Kerr's team, and pushed for a return to pre-war social forms.[78]

Despite some developments in feminist consciousness and Cahn's view of the athletic girl as symbolic of America's new woman, the 'new women' were in fact very much an exception. Furthermore, although the jazz age of the 1920s was looked upon as revolutionary at the time, the historian Arthur Schlesinger Jr, has argued that this era, 'far from being a decade of of flaming non-conformity [was] in fact a period so grey that men would have gone out and made a New Deal, even without the stimulus of a depression, out of sheer boredom'.[79] The historian of the 1920s, Paul Carter has stated that America's lack of a 'past' included 'the lack of a revolutionary tradition to draw on, and without it the attempt to bring about a great liberation during the twenties was inevitably crippled and impoverished'. Carter believed the concept of a 'great liberation' was 'played out on a stage before an audience, much of which was frightened, anti-intellectual and reactionary'.[80] Moreover, this also applied to the women's movement that fell far short of what the nineteenth amendment had promised. So much so that the formidable Belle Moskowitz, a major figure in Al Smith's administration at Albany, declared to a Columbia University forum in 1926 that women by nature were intellectually inferior to men.[81] This was the context in which sport for women was developing in America at the time Dick, Kerr's Ladies made their tour.

Although, as in Britain, opportunities for sport were increasing, the 'revolutionary' nature of women's physical culture remained under the intense scrutiny of the dominant conservative majority. All other issues apart, this was not the time for American women of any class to adopt a game that was associated with the rougher spectrum of male working class immigrants. In both Britain and America, the medical profession had questioned the suitability of 'masculine sports' for women.[82] In 1901, at the very beginning of women's 'sporting revolution' in America, Dr George Engelmann, president of the American Gynaecological Society, warned of the negative consequences of female muscular development and its capacity to lessen inhibitions, resulting in the loss of emotional and sexual control. Medical critics in America used the same nineteenth century Social Darwinist arguments as those in Britain regarding sport and its effects on women's capacity to reproduce.[83] Cahn believes that these theories of women's physical culture were partially the result of pre-war social and economic unrest in America. The working class who worked in the factories that made the upper and middle classes rich wanted a share of their wealth. The middle classes were very uneasy about this 'radicalism' and looked back to the more traditional social hierarchy of the past, where gender and class had distinct roles.[84] Furthermore, the growing suffragist movement compounded unease over working-class instability, which itself was seen as a threat to social norms. It was within this environment that the 'revolutionary' role of the female athlete began to be scrutinized.[85]

Up to the 1920s, however, concern was purely with middle-class college girls, reproduction and propriety. Working-class women had limited opportunities for vigorous sport during this period. Once working-class women became involved in sport, the focus shifted from middle-class women and reproductive health to working-class women and sexuality. Donald Mrozek and Pat Griffin both discuss this in their respective works on women, sport and sexuality. Mrozek discusses the concepts of the Amazon and the American, referring to the idea that unbridled displays of physical behaviour could lead to loss of inhibitions and prostitution. Griffin discusses the sportswoman in terms of sexuality and the contemporary belief that masculine sports were linked to the 'mannish lesbian'.[86] Soccer fell into both the categories discussed by Mrozek and Griffin. During the Dick, Kerr tour although nothing derogatory was said about the team, their radical 'new women' image and Amazonian physiques were regularly alluded to. The *Fall River Evening Herald* went as far as providing its readers with the women players' supposedly Amazonian physical statistics:

Fall River Fans will have an opportunity to see an unusual ladies' soccer outfit in action.

Players' Statistics

Walker	22 years	5:8"	132lb
Kell	22 years	5:8"	128lb
Lee	21 years	5:6"	143lb
Pomies	21 years	5:7"	136lb
Woods	20 years	5:8"	151lb
Walmsley	22 years	5:8"	152lb
Haslam	20 years	5: 6"	136lb
Harris	22 years	5:41/2"	112lb
Redford	21 years	5:6"	124lb
Graham	19 years	5:5"	124lb
Parr	17 years	5:7"	132lb
Crozier	23 years	5:81/2"	145lb
Clayton	26 years	5:61/2"	131lb
Ackers	18 years	5:5"	122lb[87]

The *Fall River Evening Herald* went on to comment that 'It is hard to conceive that women folks can play the kicking game with the same aggressiveness as the men folk, but according to all advice this team is as near to perfection in every line.'[88] Although the *Herald* does not make an outright condemnation of the women's 'aggressive' behaviour, this reticence was not representative of the dominant opinion. The women's football tour was a commercial event and a crowd of 8,000 was expected at the next match.[89] In American sport it was not unusual for commerce to overrule popular ethics and the sale of newspapers would override any moral considerations. According to Frederick Allen, commitments to society were put aside in favour of personal gain.[90] However, as Jennifer Hargreaves points out, at the same time even sports' feminists, particularly in North America during the early twentieth century, promoted the idea of separate sports for men and women on moral and ethical grounds.[91] Hargreaves believes this feminist aversion to masculine sports was based on a rejection of aggressive competition, commercialism and over specialization – the very three elements that appear to have characterized this tour.

Commercial interests were the overriding factor in sport during this fast developing period of consumerism. In support of this assertion, D. Waldstein and S. Wagg quote Sam Foulds, an American soccer historian, who was involved in the game as both a player and a coach: 'sports, even soccer, is a business'.[92] Soccer in the US was therefore, 'Primarily a business and second a sport – the reverse of the rest of the world.'[93] Zelickman and Brooks must have been aware of the gate attendance the women's teams had attracted in Britain during and immediately after the war, and were anxious to promote the team commercially.[94] This is reflected in the US$1,000 advance fee for a fixture. However, the organizers must have been rewarded with a good return on their investment as the women's team drew crowds of around 7,000–8,000 a match, whereas the majority of men's soccer football regularly attracted crowds of 4,000–5,000, with the exception of Fall River, who drew up to 12,000.[95] Michael Messner draws attention to the way social changes during the war affected the 'deployment and uses of women's bodies'. In a consumer led society they became marketable and used to sell various products and services. Although this emphasized their social subordination, Messner notes that ironically, this 'commercialisation of women's bodies provided a cultural opening for competitive athletics, as industry and ambitious individuals used women to sell sports'.[96] Zelickman, Frankland and Brooks obviously sought to use this 'cultural opening' to market women's soccer. Media reports of the tour provide further evidence of attempts to make the sport commercially viable. Firstly, the organizers of the Fall River fixture made special arrangements to attract women to the venue with cheap tickets and special seating arrangements. This is important, as there appears to have been an attempt here to give women's soccer the same sense of respectability as baseball, where the whole family would turn out to watch the game.[97] Moreover, the majority of the Dick, Kerr's fixtures took place on Sunday, something that never happened in Britain due to state legislation prohibiting games on the Sabbath. This was to appeal to the more secular and consumer led American society who went to church on Sunday morning and took part in family leisure in the afternoon.[98] Much was also made of the women players' attractive appearance. The *Fall River Globe* stated, 'There were some real beauties among them, but far be it for mere man to go into looks in an article on an athletic competition ...'[99] The objective of all this was to increase gate numbers at an already well subscribed tour. Throughout the tour the team was referred to as Newcastle United F.C. Newsham believes this was due to their striped shirts.[100] However, it is possible that this name was released deliberately as a major British team such as Newcastle United were more likely to attract spectators than an obscure women's outfit. This hypothesis is made all the more convincing by the fact that confusion did not take place in one area, but in all the fixtures of the tour.

The mixed sex games are also interesting because co–ed sport, as it is referred to in America, was a growing phenomenon. Cahn refers to the development of commercial mixed sex leisure from the turn of the century, which was patronized largely by working-class youths. Black working class, mixed sex sport in athletics and basketball preceded the Dick, Kerr tour by several years. According to Cahn this enabled men and women to give expression to 'gender conflict in a light hearted playful manner' during the immediate post-war years. In 1920 the *Chicago Defender* quoted the feminist Madam Caldwell as urging women to attend a 'Bloomer Girls' basketball series against a Chicago boy's club: 'We are equal to the men, so let us prove it to them by demonstrating a real ball game.'[101] However, from media reports, there does not appear to be any public feminist debate regarding the women's soccer tour. This is possibly because it was either too obscure to be worth considering, or because the promoters had gone to considerable lengths to avoid any controversial publicity. Nevertheless, despite the fact that mixed sex leisure, consumerism and the commercialization of sport was growing in America, the women's soccer football tour failed to have any immediate or lasting impact.[102] The tour was of such minor significance that when Jacques M. Henry and Howard P. Comeaux of the University of Southwestern Louisiana, made their study of coed soccer in 1999, they stated 'Coed soccer is a recent and rather uniquely American phenomenon';[103] the latter point being more true than the former. The Dick, Kerr's tour took place in 1922 but it wasn't until 1981 that the oldest American coed soccer organization was established. Had the Dick, Kerr tour had any impact, Henry and Comeaux would surely have noted this. Frankland, Brooks and Zelickman sought to promote soccer commercially as a new sport for 'new women' in America. They had obviously regarded American urban society from the same perspective as the historian of the 1920s, George E. Mowry, who chose for the title of his anthology: *Fords, Flappers and Fanatics.*[104] However, like many of their contemporaries, they had misjudged the depth of conservatism within American society during the 1920s. Rather than seeking to be 'flappers and fanatics', the majority of Americans were retreating further into traditionalism as a defensive backlash to the cultural changes that were taking place. In an age of growing consumerism, had the sport been commercially viable, it would have developed further. However, American popular culture was not yet ready to embrace women's soccer.

By the time the 1922 tour took place, women's soccer was already becoming a minority sub-culture in Britain. This had immediate implications for any prospective development of the game in North America, as there were no formal bases or structures from which an American model could evolve. In January 1921, a local British newspaper in Lancashire, the *Bolton Evening News*, published an article referring to sport being reduced to a debacle by 'recent premature events'; namely women's soccer football and athletics.[105] The article, although heavily biased against women's sport in general, is interesting as it provides a pointer towards establishing why women's soccer failed to maintain its wartime momentum. Within the context of the era women's soccer in Britain was premature and moreover, startlingly successful. Its sudden meteoric rise and swift decline left no time for any form of organizational infrastructure to be established. In December 1921, there was an attempt to form the Ladies' Football Association in Blackburn, Lancashire in order to implement some cohesion for teams spread across the country. However, this initiative was short lived and women's soccer continued on what Sue Lopez described as an 'ad hoc' set of arrangements between the predominantly male managers of a dwindling number of clubs.[106] By the time Dick, Kerr's left for America, the sport was all but finished in Britain. The changes that had been slowly taking place in British society with regard to the physical emancipation of women had gained pace during the war out of necessity and the more conservative dominant culture found these changes disturbingly swift. Women's soccer had been cultivated within munitions factories as a form of rational recreation to boost patriotism and keep the women from drinking and promiscuous behaviour, both of which Lloyd George believed would be a great hindrance to the urgent production of armaments.[107] In the words of Jean-Marie Brohm, 'It is mainly through the repressive sublimation of sexual drives that the practice of competitive sport contributes to the reproduction of the social relations of production.'[108] Soccer had only been intended as a short-term measure related to the war-effort. After the war women were moved to a different mode of production: the regeneration of the male population. Women's physical culture, although given impetus by the war, had not yet reached a stage where it could rationalize and accommodate soccer in the long term. Physical activity for women continued to develop as an enhancement for traditionally prescribed modes of femininity; namely attracting a husband and motherhood. During the 1920s, soccer on both sides of the Atlantic was the antithesis of what women's physical culture was meant to be.

The idea of the body beautiful was already being sold to the consumer culture of American society before the war. In 1912, Marie Montaigne wrote an article on 'How To Reduce Flesh' for *Harpers' Bazaar*, stating, 'the charm of a well proportioned figure is not to be overestimated, and is one which almost any women can possess by the expenditure of systematic effort'.[109] Dudley Sargent, the American advocate of women's physical culture wrote an article for *Ladies' Home Journal* in the same year entitled, 'How can I have a graceful figure?' He stated that a good figure played an important part in the evolutionary process of sexual selection.[110] This philosophy was embraced by the young women of the middle-class collegiate system, who during the 1920s were enjoying mixed sex leisure pursuits related to the traditional gender roles within the new youth culture of 'dating'. Sport, according to G. Lewis, 'was a haven for those fun seekers whose values remained with the traditional'.[111] The 'traditional' role for women within physical culture was exemplified in the work of the educationalist, G. Stanley Hall, who stated in 1903 that 'female emancipation was the freedom from masculine ideals rather than the freedom to share them'. Women, 'had a procreative function in society and should dedicate themselves to the ideal of being the very best of what they were destined to be'. Hall's views on female physicality were from an era that shaped dominant American attitudes towards gender and sport throughout the 1920s and for decades to come.[112] Sport for most young people during the 1920s, represented a 'devotion to the past and not a revolutionary zeal for a new life'. Therefore, women's soccer was unacceptable within American popular culture for the same reasons that it ended so abruptly in Britain. After the First World War both sides of the Atlantic looked to their respective traditional modes of behaviour in order to establish stability in what appeared to be an uncertain social climate. women's soccer had made a premature entrance into a transatlantic sporting culture that was not ready to accommodate it.

Soccer had been such a success in wartime Britain because it was a vehicle of national patriotism. The young woman soccer player bolstered the image of the 'plucky heroine' munitions worker. The fact soccer was the national sport is paramount to the wartime success of the women's game and explains why it never developed in America during the same era. However, during the Second World War, Women's baseball teams were formed in America, showing startling parallels to women's soccer in Britain during the First World War.[113] Mary Pratt stated that in 1943 a 'World War Two phenomenon made history.' This was the All-American Girls' Professional Baseball League. It was the creation of chewing gum magnate Philip K. Wrigley and was supported by President Franklin D. Roosevelt, who was concerned that the national sport would decline whilst the men were being drafted into the forces.[114] Karen H. Weiller and Catriona T. Higgs have stated that during the Second World War, the national sport – baseball – became vital to American morale, in the same way soccer was vital to the British spirit during the First World War. From 1942 to 1946, over 1000 major league players were drafted into the forces and despite measures to keep the game alive with free entrance and substitute players, attendances dropped and much of the 'glamour' was lost.[115] During the First World War in Britain, the FA had abandoned match fixtures by 1915 in order for players to be drafted into the army.

Contemporary football commentators, C.E. Sutcliffe and F. Hargreaves, remarked that 'the season 1915–1916 saw football so transformed as to be unrecognizable. The FA Cup, the Lancashire Cup and other Lancashire competitions dropped' as 4,675 players from the Lancashire Leagues alone were drafted into the forces.[116] The cessation of professional soccer in Britain during the First World War, combined with the need to boost morale, resulted in a similar sanctioning of women entering male sporting domains as the All-American girls' baseball phenomenon of 1943. Although the All-American Girls' Baseball teams were considerably better organized, the management of the women from both sports was very similar in nature. Strictly patriarchal, both sports insisted on a feminine dress code and discouraged 'Tom boyish' behaviour. At the same time, the women were regularly exhibited at gala dinners and charity balls.[117] Although the All-American Girls' Baseball League was not effectively 'outlawed' like women's soccer football in England during 1921, it was marginalized after the war. A full comparison of the two sports belongs to another study. However, for the purposes of this discussion, what is clearly demonstrated is the role of war and national morale in the reconstruction of gender roles within popular sport. Neither of these issues was applicable to the tour of 1922. It was issues of national identity and gender conservatism that were the important factors in determining the long-term significance of the Dick, Kerr's tour.

On the 2 October 1922, the *New York Times* reported the match between Dick, Kerr's Ladies and the Hispanic immigrant team, Centro-Hispano F.C. The first casualty of the game was Nelson, the right full-back of the Hispanos, who 'keeled over as the Amazons charged down the field'.[118] Nelson, like the rest of American society, was obviously not yet ready for the vigour of women's soccer. It would be over sixty years before the vision of Brooks, Frankland and Zelickman was realized. In 1999, Jacques M. Henry and Howard P. Comeaux estimated that over half the 18 million soccer players in America were women; which is probably the highest ratio in the world. Furthermore, there are now 22 co-ed soccer organizations across 14 states in the US.[119] Since the Educational Amendments Act of 1972, women's soccer has developed rapidly in America and on a global scale is one of the fastest growing sports.[120] Ironically, however, the growing popularity of soccer as a sport for American women and girls has sealed its fate with regard to ever becoming a national sport. According to J. Sugden, the ability of women and girls to succeed at soccer supports the American view that it is a game for 'second rate athletes, unable to contend with the masculine rigours of the home grown variety of football'. Sugden notes that issues of anti-foreign sentiment, class and gender roles still persist, stating that as long as soccer is 'viewed as a game for foreigners, rich white kids and women, its chances of becoming established as a mainstream professional sport [in America] are minimal'. [121]

NOTES

The author would like to thank both Gail J. Newsham and Professor J.A. Mangan of the University of Strathclyde for their help with this article.

1. Gail J. Newsham, *In a League of Their Own!* (London: Scarlet, 1997), p.56. Little is known about the role of David Brooks except that he was supposed to be acting as coach. Herbert Stanley, who was the club secretary and acted as linesman throughout this tour, stated that Brooks was an unsavoury character who preyed on emotionally vulnerable women. According to contemporary hearsay he left his wife and family to start afresh in the US. At the time there was a demand for professional players from the Britain and Frankland notes this in a letter home to the *Lancashire Daily Post*, 13 Feb. 1922, stating, 'there [are] plenty of opportunities for good men to earn big money'. This is supported by Waldstein and Wagg in their study of soccer football in North America. D. Waldstein and S. Wagg, 'Un-American Activity? Football in US and Canadian Society', in Stephen Wagg (ed.), *Giving the Game Away: Sport and Politics on Five Continents* (London: Leiscester University Press, 1995). Newsham believes that Brooks was using the tour as an escape route to the US.

2. Joan S. Hult, 'Women's Struggle for Governance in US Amateur Athletics', *International Review for the Sociology of Sport* (hereafter *Int. Rev. Soc. Sport*), 24 (1989), 251.

3. For early developments in women's sport in the US see Roberta Park, '"Embodied Selves": The Rise of Development of Concern for Physical Education, Active Games and Recreation for American Women, 1776–1865', *Journal of the History of Sport* (hereafter *J. Hist Sport*) 5, 2 (1978), 5–41. See also Susan Cahn, *Coming on Strong: Gender and Sexuality in Twentieth Century Women's Sport* (Boston, MA: Harvard University Press, 1995), Ch.1 and 2; Jennifer Hargreaves, *Sporting Females: Critical Issues in the History and Sociology of Women's Sports* (London: Routledge, 1994), Ch.3 and 4.

4. Cahn, *Coming on Strong*, p.287, footnote 49. See also, Pat Griffin, *Strong Women, Deep Closets: Lesbians and Homophobia in Sport* (Champaign: Human Kinetics, 1998), Ch.3.

5. For an initial discussion of these issues in relation to sport see Cahn, *Coming on Strong*, Ch.1, footnote 41, p.287.

6. For notes on conservatism in American society c. 1920's, see Paul A. Carter, *The Twenties in America* (London: Routledge, 1968), and also E.W. Hawley, *The Great War and the Search for a Modern Order: A History of the American People and Their Instituuions, 1917–1933* (New York: St Martin's Press, 1979). For an impression of how contemporary Americans perceived the 1920s see Frederick L. Allen, *Only Yesterday* (New York: Harper and Brothers, 1931).

7. For a discussion of the 'Golden Age' of US soccer see Waldstein and Wagg, 'Un-American Activity?', p.77.

8. For the nature of men's soccer in America *c.*1920s see also Nathan D. Abrams, 'The Strange Fate of Soccer in the United States', *International Journal of the History of Sport*, 12, 3 (1995), 1–17. Also, Andrei S. Markovits, 'The Other "American Exceptionalism": Why is there no Soccer in the United States?', *International Journal of the History of Sport*, 7, 2 (1990), 230–64.

9. See Abrams, 'The Strange Fate of Soccer in the United States', and also, Hawley, *The Great War*, pp.27–30.

10. For leisure and consumerism see Kathy Peiss, 'Cheap Amusements: Working Women and

Leisure in Turn of the Century New York' (Philadelphia: Philadelphia Temple University Press, 1986), p.69 quoted in Cahn, *Coming on Strong*. Also Carter, *The Twenties*, Ch.1; Allen, *Only Yesterday*, pp.159–86.

11. Newsham, *In a League of Their Own!*, pp.52–3.
12. David J. Williamson, *Belles of the Ball* (Devon, R and D, 1991) p.8.
13. Ibid., see also J. Williams and J. Woodhouse, 'Can Play, Will Play? Women and Football in Britain', J. Williams and S. Wagg (eds.), *British Football and Social Change* (Leicester: Leicester University Press, 1991) p.86; Eric Dunning *et al.*, *Football on Trial* (London: Routledge, 1990) p.2; Newsham, *In a League of their Own!*, p.2; N. Tranter, *Sport, Economy and Society in Britain 1850–1914* (Cambridge: Cambridge University Press, 1998) pp.78–9; Jennifer Hargreaves, 'Victorian Familism and the Formative Years of Female Sport', in J.A Mangan and Roberta J. Park (eds.), *From 'Fair Sex' to Feminism* (London: Frank Cass, 1987), pp.130–142; Sheila Fletcher, *Women First: The Female Tradition in English Physical Education 1880–1980* (London: Athlone, 1984), Ch.1.
14. For a full discussion of the development of women's soccer football in British munitions factories see, Alethea Melling, '"Ladies' Football": Gender and the Socialization of Women Football Players in Lancashire 1916–1960' (unpublished University of Central Lancashire Ph.D., 2000), Ch.2.
15. The Imperial War Museum Women's Work Collection (hereafter IWM [WWC]), MUN24/6.
16. Angela Woollacott, *On Her Their Lives Depend* (California, California University Press, 1994), p.158, Woollacott quotes, Margaret Weddell, 'My Friend Sarah', *The Common Cause*, 9 (March 1917), 632, with reference to organizing rational recreation for the munitions girls of the north-east. With regard to the reordering of gender roles necessary for the war effort see also, D. Lloyd George, *The War Memoirs of David Lloyd George*, 1(London: Oldhams, 1936), p.49, for a discussion of wartime expenditure on munitions 'undreamt of before 1914'. Also, Lloyd George on steps to obtain adequate supplies of munitions, p.75, et seq., conference on munitions 5 March 1915, p.102, growing uneasiness over shortage of munitions in 1915, p.132, Lloyd George's analysis of position regarding munitions in July 1915, pp.153–4, setting up of the Central Labour Supply Committee, p.187, foolish attitude of allied generals to supply, p.280, War Office neglect of munitions, p.308. For a further discussion on wartime gender roles see Jenny Gould, in M. Randolph Higonnett *et al.* (eds.), 'Women's Military Services and the First World War in Britain', *Behind the Lines: Gender in the Two World Wars* (London: Yale, 1987), pp.114–25.
17. See Woollacott, *On Her Their Lives Depend*, pp.44, 135, 153–7 and also, IWM (WWC), MUN 24/15, p.66 for an account of the welfare supervisor system at Armstrong Whitworth and Co., in the north-east of Britain, the biggest armaments manufacturer during the First World War.
18. Joanna Bourke, *Dismembering the British Male: Men's Bodies, Britain and the Great War* (London, 1996) pp.33–4, discusses popular outrage at the extent of injuries to soldiers during the First World War.
19. For notes on the ideology of the 'plucky heroine' see S. Ouditt, *Fighting Forces, Writing Women: Identity and Ideology in the First World War* (London: Routledge, 1993).
20. Alethea Melling, 'Cultural Differentiation, Shared Aspiration: The Entente Cordiale of International Ladies' Football, 1920–1945', *The European Sports History Review* (hereafter *Eur.Sports Hist Rev.*), 1 (1999), 27–53; for further details on Alice Milliat see M.H. Leigh, 'The Pioneering Role of Madame Alice Milliat and the FSFI in Establishing International Trade and Field Competition for Women', *J.Sports Hist*, 4, 1 (1977), 72–83.
21. For a good account of the realities of urban life during this period see Carl Chinn, *They Worked All their Lives: Women of the Urban Poor in England 1880–1939* (Manchester: Manchester University Press, 1988). Also Rex Pope, 'Unemployment Between the Wars in North-east Lancashire 1920–1938' (unpublished Lancaster University M. Phil, 1974).
22. Susan Kingsley Kent, 'Gender Reconstruction after the First World War', Harold Smith (ed.), *British Feminism in the Twentieth Century* (London: Routledge, 1990) pp.66–83. Also P. Horn, *Women in the 1920's*, (Gloucester: Alan Sutton, 1995), pp.12–13. See also Sheila Rowbotham, *Hidden From History* (London: Pluto, 1974), Ch.21, and for a detailed discussion on feminist politics in the First World War see Jo Vellacott, 'Feminist Consciousness and the First World War', *History Workshop*, 23, 24 (1987). For a discussion of women and employment after the

First World War see Gail Braybon and Penny Summerfield, *Out of the Cage: Women's Experience in Two World Wars* (London: Pandora, 1987).

23. C. Koos, 'Gender, Anti-Individualism and Nationalism: The Alliance Nationale and the Pronatalist Backlash against the Femme Moderne 1933–1940', *French Historical Studies*, 19, 3 (1996), 669–724.
     See also, Gertrud Pfister *et al.*, 'Women and Football – A Contradiction? The Beginnings of Women's Football in four European Countries', *Eur.Sports Hist Rev.*, 1 (1999), 11.

24. Newsham, *In a League of Their Own!*, p. 49; Melling, 'Ladies' Football', Ch.5.

25. For details on British women's Athletics see Lynne Robinson, 'Tripping Daintily into the Arena: A Social History of English Women's Athletics 1921–1960' (Warwick University unpublished Ph.D., 1997). For general notes on attitudes to sport see Hargreaves, *Sporting Females*, Ch.6 and on the reproductive process see Fletcher, *Women First*, Ch.5.

26. Newsham, *In a League of Their Own!*, p.50.

27. Ibid.

28. Ibid., p.56.

29. *The Fall River Evening Herald*, 13 Oct. 1922, courtesy of Gail Newsham.

30. Newsham, *In a League of Their Own!*, pp.60–1.

31. Ibid.

32. In 1919 the FA took a firm stand against playing Germany. Other countries failed to agree to this resulting in the British withdrawing from FIFA. J. Walvin, *The People's Game* (London, 1968) and Dave Russell, *Football and the English 1863–1995* (Lancashire: Carnegie, 1996). For the wider implications see Stephen Jones, 'Sport Politics and the Labour Movement: The British Workers Sports Federation 1923–1935', *The British Journal of Sports History*, 2 (1985), 154–78.

33. Newsham, *In a League of Their Own*, pp.61–2. The Dominion of Canada FA was formed in 1912, joining FIFA the same year. Waldstein and Wagg, 'Un-American Activity?', p.75

34. Newsham, *In a League of Their Own!* p.62. See also *The Lancashire Daily Post* 18 Nov. 1922, courtesy of G. Newsham.

35. Newsham, *In a League of Their Own!*, p.62. For notes on the US Women's Olympic Team, see Cahn, *Coming on Strong*, Ch.3.

36. Newsham, *In a League of Their Own!*, pp.62–3. For notes on the development of the USSFA see Waldstein and Wagg, 'Un-American Activity?', pp.73–87.

37. Abrams, 'The Strange Fate of Soccer in the US', *International Journal of the History of Sport*, 12, 3 (1995), 1–17.

38. For a discussion on the phenomenon of folk football see Russell, Ch.1.

39. Abrams, 'The Strange Fate of Soccer in the United States'.

40. Ibid.

41. Carter, p.89.

42. Abrams, 'The Strange Fate of Soccer in the United States'.

43. Ibid.

44. Ibid.

45. Ibid.

46. Andrei S. Markovits, 'The Other American Exception: Why is there no Soccer in the United States?', *International Journal of the History of Sport*, 7, 2 (Sept. 1990), 246.

47. Abrams, 'The Strange Fate of Soccer in the United States', refers to Kathleen Neils *et al.*, 'The Invention of Ethnicity: a Perspective from the USA', *Journal of American Ethnic History*, 12 (Fall 1992) 5, for a further discussion on this concept.

48. For example, Abrams quotes, 'the all Jewish Hokoah team, New York in 1926 imbued New York Jewery with a hitherto unknown sense of pride and esteem'. B. Horowitz, 'Hokoah in New York 1926–1932: A New Dimension for American Jewery', *Judaism*, 25 (1977), 375–82.

49. Abrams, 'The Strange Fate of Soccer in the United States'.

50. Ibid.

51. *Fall River Evening Herald*, 2 Oct. 1922, courtesy of G. Newsham.

52. The full list of fixtures is in Newsham, *In a League of Their Own!* pp.62–9.

53. Hawley, *The Great War*, pp.29–31.

54. *New York Times*, 2 Oct. 1922, courtesy of G. Newsham.

55. *Lancashire Daily Post*, 18 Nov. 1922.

56. E. Gerber *et al.*, *The American Woman in Sport* (Philippines: Addison-Wesley, 1974), p.36, uses the term All-American girl to describe middle-class born Americans.

57. Betty Spears and Richard A. Swanson, *History of Sport and Physical Education in the United States* (Boston: McGraw-Hill, 1995).

58. When baseball was introduced to Britain in the 1888–89 tour it failed to catch on due to its 'Americaness'. Another tour in 1920 failed for the same reason and the fact that soccer football had already effectively crowed out any openings for other mass sport in Europe. Markovits, 'The Other "American Exceptionalism"'.

59. *The Fall River Evening Herald*, 13 Oct. 1922, courtesy of Gail Newsham. For details on immigrant women and patriarch control see W.H. Chafe, *American Women in the Twentieth Century* (hereafter *American Women*) (New York: Oxford University Press, 1991), p.73. For a note on religious beliefs and patriarchy see Jeanne Becher (ed.), *Women, Religion and Sexuality: Studies on the Impact of Religious Teachings on Women*, (Geneva: WWC, 1990).

60. Park, '"Embodied Selves"'.

61. Cahn, *Coming on Strong*, p.18.

62. Ibid., p.17.

63. Ibid., p.18. For a good local study of girls clubs in the context of leisure and social control in Britain see Liz Oliver, 'Liberation or Limitation: A Study of Women's Leisure in Bolton *c.* 1919–1939' (Lancaster University unpublished Ph.D., 1997).

64. Cahn, *Coming on Strong*, p.19.

65. In England women over 30 years old were granted the vote in 1918 as a result of their contribution to the war-effort. America followed this in 1920 with the Nineteenth Amendment.

66. Chafe, *American Women*, p.47.

67. Ibid.

68. Ibid.

69. Cahn, *Coming on Strong*, p.18.

70. *The New York Times*, 25 Sept. 1922, courtesy of G. Newsham.

71. *The New York Times*, 2 Oct. 1922.

72. *The Fall River Globe*, 16 Oct. 1922, courtesy of G. Newsham.

73. Allen, *Only Yesterday*, p.105.

74. Ibid., p.88.

75. Ibid., p.89.

76. Ibid.

77. Gerber *et al.*, *The American Women in Sport*, p.36. For further details on Babe Didrikson see Griffin, *Strong Women*, pp.39, 62, 138.

78. Cahn, *Coming on Strong*, p.18.

79. Carter, *The Twenties*, p.13.

80. Ibid., p.12.

81. Ibid., p.14. For further details on the women's movement see Lois Banner, *American Beauty* (Chicago: University of Chicago Press, 1983) and Nancy Cott, *The Grounding of Modern Feminism* (New Haven: Yale University Press, 1987), pp.145–62.

82. See Hargeaves, *Sporting Females*, pp.83–4. See also, Patricia Vertinsky, 'G. Stanley Hall's Totalitarian Views on Female Health and Physical Education', *Int.J. Hist Sport*, 1 (1988), 69–95.

83. Cahn, *Coming on Strong*, p.288, footnote 57, refers to George Engelman, 'The Modern Girl Today: Modern Education and Functional Health', *American Physical Education Review* (March 1901), 29–30. See also, Vertinsky, 'G. Stanley Hall's Totalitarian Views'. For the British perspective see Fletcher, *Women First*, pp.26–29.

84. Cahn, *Coming on Strong*, p.287, footnote 41.

85. See Chafe, *American Women*, p.47–8.

86. Donald Mrozek, 'The Amazon and the American Lady: Sexual Fears of Women as Athletes', in Mangan and Park (eds.), *From 'Fair Sex' to Feminism* (London: Frank Cass, 1987), p.283. Also, Griffin, *Strong Women*, Ch.3, 'Damaged Mothers, Muscle Molls, Mannish Lesbian and Predatory Dykes'.

87. *Fall River Evening Herald*, 13 Oct. 1922, courtesy of G. Newsham.
88. Ibid.
89. Ibid.
90. Frederick L. Allen quoted in G. Lewis, 'Sport, Youth Culture and Conventionality 1920–1970', *J.Hist Sport*, 4, 2 (Summer 1977), 129–50.
91. Jennifer Hargreaves, 'Gender on the Sports Agenda', *Int.Rev.Soc.Sport*, 25 (1990), 291. See also Hult, *Int.Rev.Soc.Sport*, 24 (1989), 251.
92. Waldstein and Wagg, 'Un-American Activity?', p.76.
93. Ibid.
94. See Newsham, *In a League of Their Own!*, pp.47–9.
95. Based on figures from the American Soccer League, 1921. Waldstein and Wagg, 'Un-American Activity?', p.76.
96. Michael A. Messner, 'The Female Athlete as Contested Ideological Terrain', *North American Society for the Sociology of Sport* (Nevada, Oct. 1986).
97. For example, the Leadville Blues baseball team made a special effort to get the ladies out onto the track. Of all the various sporting events in Leadville at the time, only baseball was judged family orientated. Duane A. Smith, 'Baseball Champions of Colorado: The Leadville Blues of 1882', *J.Sports Hist.*, 4, 1 (1977), 51–71.
98. See Carter, *The Twenties*, Ch.1.
99. *The Fall River Globe*, 16 Oct. 1922, courtesy of G. Newsham.
100. Newsham, *In a League of Their Own!*, p.63.
101. *Chicago Defender*, 6 Oct. 1920, quoted in Cahn, *Coming on Strong*, p.293.
102. For further details on the context of middle–class mixed sex sport in the US see Glena Matthews, *The Rise of the Public Woman: Women's Power and Women's Place in the US 1630–1970* (Oxford: Oxford University Press, 1992), p.177.
103. Jaques M. Henry and Howard P. Comeaux, 'Gender Egalitarianism in Coed Sport: a Case Study of American Soccer', *Int.Rev.Soc.Sport*, 34, 3 (1999), 277–90.
104. Carter, *The Twenties*, p.27.
105. *Bolton Evening News BUFF*, 29 Jan. 1921, quoted in Melling, 'Ladies' Football', Ch.5.
106. Sue Lopez, *Women on the Ball* (London: Scarlet, 1997), pp.7–9.
107. Woollacott, *On Her Their Lives Depend*, Ch.5; Braybon and Summerfield, *Out of the Cage*, Ch.1. One of the major concerns was the consumption of alcohol. Lloyd George commented that, 'The sudden onset of unaccustomed danger drove many who were out of the danger zone to the vicarious philosophy of 'let us eat and drink – especially drink – for tomorrow our comrades may die!'. The disorganization of social habit through the war, the reckless excitement that thrilled the air, the feeling that tables of the law had once more been smashed amid the thunder of a grimmer Sinai, led some of both sexes to excesses in all directions – and as war work increased the earnings of the multitudes, those who drank, drank deeply, for they could afford the indulgence as they never did before. The evil was not confined to men – it spread to women'. Lloyd George, *War Memoirs*, 1, p.193.
108. J-M. Brohm, *Sport a Prison of Measured Time* (London: Pluto, 1989), p.56.
109. *Harpers Bazaar*, 46 (March 1912), 144, quoted in Cahn, *Coming on Strong*, p.19.
110. *Ladies Home Journal* (Feb 1912), 15, quoted in Cahn, p.19. For a British perspective see J.J. Matthews, 'They Had Such a Lot of Fun: The Women's League of Health and Beauty', *History Workshop Journal*, 30 (1990), 22–54.
111. Lewis, 'Sport, Youth Culture and Conventionality', 129–50.
112. Vertinsky, 'G. Stanley Hall's Totalitarian Views'.
113. For details of American women's war work in the First World War see Maurine Weiner Greenwald, *Women, War and Work: The Impact of World War One on Women Workers in The United States* (Westport, 1980); and for World War Two see, Allan M. Winkler, *Home Front USA: America During World War Two* (Illinois: Harlan Davidson, 1986), pp.49–56; Maureen Honey, *Creating Rosie the Riveter: Class, Gender and Propaganda during World War Two* (Lincoln, 1984).
114. M. Pratt, 'The All-American Girls' Professional Baseball League', in G.L. Cohen (ed.), *Women in Sport: Issues and Controversies*, (California: Sage, 1993) pp.49–57.
115. 'The All-American Girls' Professional Baseball League, 1943–1954: Gender Conflict in

Sport?' *Sociology of Sport Journal*, 11 (1994), 289–97.

116. *The History of the Lancashire Football Association 1978–1928*, compiled by C.E. Sutcliffe and F. Hargreaves (London: Taulmin, 1928).

117. For comparisons regarding women's soccer football 1922–1954 see Melling, 'Ladies' Football' Ch.5; Newsham, *In a League of Their Own!* and Lopez, *Women on the Ball*.

118. *New York Times*, 2 Oct. 1922, courtesy of G. Newsham.

119. Henry and Comeaux, 'Gender Egalitarianism in Coed Sport', 277–90.

120. Ibid.

121. J. Sugden, 'USA and the World Cup: American Nativism and the Rejection of the People's Game', J. Sugden and A. Tomlinson (eds.), *Hosts and Champions: Soccer Cultures, National Identities and the World Cup* (Aldershot: Arena, 1994) quoted in Henry and Comeaux, 'Gender Egalitarianism in Coed Sport', 279.

The Soviet Protégé: Cuba, Modern Sport and Communist Comrade

ROBERT CHAPPELL

INTRODUCTION

Cuba is the largest and most diverse island in the Caribbean Sea. It is the large island at the western end of the Antilles chain, and is situated 90 miles south of Florida, United States (US). The island is approximately the same size as England; it is 750 miles in length, but it also includes more than 1500 islands. The largest of the islands is the Isla de la Juventad (Isle of Youth) shaped like an apostrophe to the south of Cuba.

The terrain is largely low-lying being a mixture of sugar plantations, forests, swamps and rolling hillsides. The tallest point in the island is Pico Turquire (6,476 feet) in the Sierra Maestra Mountains in the far south-east of Cuba. The highest peak in the Escambray Mountains in the centre of the island is Pico San Juan (3,465 feet). To the west of Cuba is a small range of mountains, the Cordillera de Guaniguanico in the region of Pinar del Rio. This area features the strange mogotes, the large limestone humps that rise dramatically out of the Vinoles valley.[1]

Cuba is divided into 13 provinces, plus the capital city Havana; these provinces are sub-divided into municipios (counties). The population is 11 million, one-fifth of which live in and around Havana. Santiago de Cuba is the second largest city, which has 500,000 inhabitants and is situated in the south-east of Cuba. Guantanama Bay in the south-east, a 45–square mile patch of Cuba is a US navel base and is inaccessible from the rest of the island. Approximately two million Cubans live in exile in the United States.[2]

Cuba lies in the tropics and has two climatic seasons – the rainy season from May to October and the dry season from November to April. The average daily temperature in the hottest months of July and August is 32 degrees centigrade (89 degrees Fahrenheit), and 26 degrees centigrade (79 degrees Fahrenheit) in the coolest months of December to March. Hurricanes are frequent. Hurricane Flora killed 4,000 people in 1963. The humidity is high, averaging 62 per cent, but it increases in the south-east of the island. Even the Cubans find the heat and humidity hard to bear in the summer.

Cuban society exhibits a remarkable ethnic diversity. Official statistics on ethnic groups in Cuba state that the population is 66 per cent white/Hispanic, 12 per cent black, 21.9 per cent mixed Hispanic and black, and 0.1 per cent Asian. In reality, the majority of the Cuban people (70 per cent) are of mixed race. Most of the pure black Cubans, descendants of African slaves, live in Havana and Matanzas province. The Asian community are descendants of Chinese contract labourers, shipped to Cuba in the latter part of the nineteenth century as the slave trade from Africa collapsed.

PRE-REVOLUTION CUBA

Before 1925, there was a series of ineffectual presidents in Cuba prior to General Gerardo Machado taking power. This marked the beginning of a military dictatorship that lasted for eight years. At this time there was a world economic depression, and also a period of unrest in Cuba due to corruption and inequality in the country. In 1933, there was a general strike in Cuba organized by a fledgling communist party who also succeeded to overthrow General Machado.[3]

An army sergeant, Fulgencio Batista, stepped into power and initially enjoyed a certain amount of popularity. He won the presidential election in 1940, but failed to be re-elected in 1944. He went into 'voluntary exile', but returned in 1952 to stage a military coup. Batista developed a cruel and oppressive regime in which he dissolved Congress, abolished the constitution and suppressed any opposition. Cuba and the capital Havana became prosperous mainly due to US influence. Havana became a playground for rich Americans who developed casinos and brothels. The Mafia took control of tourism in Havana.[4]

On 26 July 1953 a guerrilla group led by Fidel Castro and 125 other dissidents who opposed Batista, attacked the army base at Moncada near Santiago de Cuba. Castro had attended Catholic and Jesuit schools, and in 1945 attended Havana University. He graduated in law six years later, but it was politics that became his passion. After the military coup by Batista in 1952, Castro decided that an armed insurrection was the only means to liberate Cuba. Many of the rebels died in the attack in 1953.

Castro was arrested and imprisoned on the Isle of Pines. He was later sent to Mexico where he met the Argentine revolutionary Che Guevara.

In 1956, 82 guerrillas led by Castro, his brother Raul and Che Guevara invaded Cuba on the south-east coast of Cuba. Conflict with the Batista forces reduced this number to 12, but they still managed to establish themselves in the Sierra Maestra Mountains. Assisted by four underground movements in the cities, they won the approval of the Cuban people. The rebellion gained momentum and territory fell easily to the revolutionaries.

Che Guevara was born in 1928 to 'left wing' middle-class parents in Buenos Aires. He originally joined the guerrilla cell as a medic, but subsequently became a fighter. He became an important member of the new government and as head of the Cuban National Bank, arranged for an oil-for-sugar swap with the Soviet Union. However, he became unhappy with the course adopted by Castro and left Cuba in 1965 to fight other causes. He tried to initiate another revolution amongst peasants in Bolivia in October 1967, but was captured and executed. As a result of his activities, he achieved revolutionary martyrdom and became a romantic hero in many parts of the world.[5]

Sport in Cuba before the revolution was almost non-existent. Where it did exist, it reflected the rural economy and Cuba's cultural background. Hence pelota was played, which is a traditional Basque courtyard game for two players using slings and a hard ball. The influence of the US was significant in the establishment of boxing on the island[6] and it became popular in the cities amongst Cuba's poorer classes, most of which were of African decent. In rural areas, both horse-racing and cock-fighting was popular mainly due to the associated betting. Elite sports such as sailing, equestrianism, hunting, tennis and fencing were popular with 'white' Cubans of Spanish decent. Fencing became a particular strength at the turn of the century.

Cuba competed in the 1900 Olympic Games in Paris where Ramon Fonst won the gold medal in the epée event. He won two further gold medals in 1904. In the Olympic Games of 1900 and 1904 the Cubans won 12 medals in fencing including six golds. However, Cuba gained no other Olympic medals prior to 1960.[7]

Before the 1959 Revolution the Cuban government played a relatively minor role in sport. Between 1957 and 1958, only 1.75 million pesos (0.5 per cent) of the total budget was spent on sport. In 1955, the Batista government would not fund the Cuban team to attend the Pan-

American Games. Before 1959, sport in Cuba was characterized by limited facilities and limited access. Most athletic equipment was imported from the US. Physical education and sport were almost unknown in schools; of the few physical education teachers, most were not qualified. Equality of opportunity in terms of participation did not exist and participation tended to reflect the gender, racial and class divisions that characterized Cuban society before 1959. Access to sport was almost exclusively restricted to wealthy, white males.[8]

REVOLUTIONARY CUBA

Fidel Castro came to power in 1959 and had overwhelming public support. The economy was near to collapse, as it had been developed simply to satisfy American tourists, investors and gamblers rather than the Cuban people. Castro's first act was to seize American assets without compensation, which enraged the US and triggered economic retribution. Castro looked around for new allies and the Soviet Union offered support. From the Soviet model of government, Castro adapted a centralized, bureaucratic political system and imposed it upon the Cuban people.[9] Trade with the socialist countries expanded and diminished with capitalist countries. For example, in 1959 trade with Eastern European countries represented 2 per cent of exports, but this increased to 62 per cent by 1962.

The US severed diplomatic links with Cuba on 3 January 1961, and President John F. Kennedy promoted the destabilization of Cuba, being unhappy with a socialist country in his 'back-yard'. The Central Intelligence Agency (CIA) in the US recruited 1400 anti-Castro Cubans who had fled to the US, and gave them military training. On 17 April 1961, they invaded Cuba at the Bay of Pigs (Playa Giron) in the south of the island, aiming to overthrow Castro, but were repulsed. This invasion galvanized the Cuban people's support for Castro. Castro proclaimed Cuba to be a Socialist republic, and communists were included in the ruling political alliances from which the Partido Comunista de Cuba (PCC) emerged in 1965. In some respects Castro's emergence as a communist was a pragmatic response to the need for economic support following the severing of links with its former main trading partner, the US.[10]

On 22 October 1962 President Kennedy announced that the

Pentagon had identified a build-up of military activity in Cuba. Surveillance aircraft had spotted a Soviet convoy heading to Cuba with a cargo of atomic weapons. The US navy was mobilized to stop the missiles reaching Cuba. The outcome of the situation was that Kennedy reached an agreement with Nikita Krushchev, the Soviet Premier, and a confrontation was avoided. Kennedy ordered the CIA to increase its efforts against Castro and Cuba, and as a result there were several attempts to assassinate Castro. The US tightened the economic embargo; trade between the countries is still prohibited. Thirty-five years of economic sanctions have failed to bring about the political liberalization designed by the Americans.

Castro has also had to deal with insurgents within Cuba. A particularly fierce campaign was waged in the Escambray Mountains, with the last rebels not actually defeated until 1965. As part of a campaign to deter rebels neighbourhood Committees for the Defence of the Revolution (Comites de Defensa de la Revolucion) were established and are still visible on every street or block of flats.[11] With the help of the Soviet Union schools were built, clinics opened, and education and health became widely available. Generally, wealth was diverted to rural areas from urban areas and the standard of housing was improved. In comparison with other developing countries poverty, disease and illiteracy were virtually eradicated.[12]

Certainly Castro's brother Raul and Che Guevara were Marxists. Initially Castro was unclear as to the political direction Cuba should take.[13] However, due to an uncooperative United States, which along with its allies, imposed a trade embargo, Castro aligned the country towards the Soviet Union. The Soviet Union was only too willing to have an ally to the south of the US at a time when diplomatic relations were strained. In response, the Soviet Union subsidized the Cuban economy and Cuba established its republic on a socialist model.

John Sugden[14] has argued that in the early years Castro's regime was more 'popularist than orthodox communist'. According to Sugden, this was:

> a model which emphasised collective goals over individual freedoms, the dictatorship of the proletariat over democracy, and a command economy over market forces. It was justified by a Marxist-Leninist ideological principle that true communism had to be dragged from the womb of capitalism and, in its infancy,

nurtured by cadre of committed and informed revolutionaries who would seize the apparatus of the state and use it for the benefit of the people until such a stage that the economic and social foundations for genuine collectivism had been securely laid.

More specifically, 'Cuba's current Socialist government is organised according to notions of Marxist–Leninist democratic centralism, with decision making centralised at the national level. Policy making and funding are centralised in all areas including sport.'[15] Sport was now used as a means of displaying antagonism towards the US, and as a vehicle for confirming solidarity with the Soviet Union.

The new Cuban system of sport was not necessarily a copy of the Soviet system, but the infrastructure of Cuban sports is unmistakably Soviet.[16] Cuba is now a socialist dictatorship and is structured along the lines of the Eastern European countries that collapsed after 1989.[17] Once established in power Castro reformed Cuban society, including the area of sport. From the earliest moment of involvement in Cuba, the Soviet Union had a declared commitment to sport that was reflected through success at international sports competitions between 1952 and 1989.[18] In this respect Cuba was a 'shop window' for the display of superior socialist values.

SPORT IN MARXIST CUBA

The body responsible today for the organization of sport in Cuba is the Instituto Nacional De Deportes, Educacion Fisica y Recreacion (INDER), which was established in February 1961, two years after Castro's military victory. INDER built upon the work began by the Ministry of Education (MINED), the Army (FAR) and the General Sports Council (DGO).[19] In effect, INDER became the Ministry of Sport and was bound up with central government and reflected its views.[20] For John Coghlan the system adopted by INDER represents the key to the development of mass sport, physical education and high-level performance in developing countries, and even in some developed countries. For some this system is too governmental and this may be a valid criticism, but there is no doubt that sport prospers because government backing is forthcoming.[21] In democracies, a centralized system will always be questioned in terms of the balance between collective goals and individual freedom. INDER's work was difficult due to the limited sports tradition in Cuba prior to the Revolution, and subsequently it initially only planned to physically educate the population. Indeed, there was a virtual absence of physical education in schools and as in many countries, at times of crisis, levels of fitness become a priority for governments, Cuba believed that to ensure military survival it was necessary to produce a physically fit nation. Obviously, this was highlighted by the abortive invasion of Cuba at the Bay of Pigs. In 1961, there was the threat of war during the confrontation between the US and the Soviet Union during the 'missile crisis'.[22] It was not surprising therefore that the Cuban government attempted both to demonstrate the superiority of the socialist system compared with the capitalist system of the US and to produce a physically fit nation that was ready to meet any foreign invasion. Cuba has a large standing army and a comprehensive civilian militia. The role of the army has been expanded as Cuba has sought to extend its military influence overseas, especially in Africa. Apart from ideological and military considerations there have also been altruistic considerations. As in other developing countries participation in sport has been linked to its contribution to health education, fitness and the well being of the whole population. For example, Leonard Hampson reported that in 1961, INDER organized two large gymnastic/athletic displays involving 25,000 and 70,000 people respectively, in turn demonstrating the new capacity of the population to show its fitness.[23]

In order to stimulate participation and discover athletic talent, INDER organized physical tests called Listas Para Vencer (LPV, Ready to Win).[24] In 1961, athletic examinations were established, which were similar to the Soviet GTO badge[25] in that they had a fairly high militaristic content. The tests involved gymnastics, standing long jump, rope climbing, endurance running, and swimming. In order to determine the achievement tables 15,000 trials were conducted in 1961. By 1964, nearly one million people participated in these tests. The socialist propaganda machine has no doubt exaggerated the claims of mass participation in the same way that this has been done in the Soviet Union.[26] In order to generate interest in these tests the mass media provided television, radio and press coverage, and the postal service issued a set of stamps illustrating the various tests. No prizes were awarded but successful participants were awarded certificates and badges. In 1965, the LPV tables were revised and more ambitious physical objectives set. This reflected a concern to know the physical efficiency of the population, not only as a reflection of sports participation, but also as a result of better nourishment and public health.

What sport facilities did exist in Cuba before the Revolution were located in the capital Havana. INDER wished to promote sport in both urban and rural areas and consequently devised a plan known as the 'Plan of the Mountains'[27] which offered the rural population an opportunity for participation in sport. In 1963, the Escambray Mountains, north of Trinidad in Las Villas province, were chosen as a pilot study. INDER representatives visited the rural towns and villages to determine the type and nature of the facilities required. The administrators did not impose their ideas, but asked the rural citizens what facilities they would like, and together they devised a plan. The study indicated that there was a large source of untapped sports talent in the mountain region, and therefore 31 installations were built in the Escambray Mountains. All of the installations were attached to farms and were by no means complex sports centres. After all, the Cubans were attempting to resolve a problem that was unique to their situation.[28] The sports centres therefore usually consisted of an outdoor area, or possibly a barn-type covered building. These were simple facilities for football, baseball, basketball, and volleyball which were sports that required little capital expenditure for people to take part.

John Coghlan[29] notes that it is people who make things work and not the facilities, hence sports administration and coaching courses were organized to train volunteers. Two people from each area in which installations had been sited were sent on a course to prepare them to increase participation in that area. They were taught the basic rules of sports, how to develop interest in these sports, fundamental coaching, and how to organize competitions. The success of the schemes was largely due to the time freely given by those who volunteered to attend the courses and return to lead and motivate their population. The success of this scheme was also attributed to returning scholarship students who had been studying in East Germany (GDR) and were required to spend six months on their return working in the mountains.[30] Due to the success in the Escambray Mountains, the scheme was extended to the Sierra Maestra where 22 sports installations were constructed and the first inter-mountain regional games was initiated.

In 1964, in an attempt to provide more qualified physical education teachers the plan INDER-MINED was launched by Castro himself, thus symbolizing the involvement of the state in the organization of sport in socialist Cuba. The aim of the scheme was to provide a qualified physical education teacher for every elementary school. Leonard Hampson describes how in 1964, the INDER-MINED summer school in which basic physical education activities were taught, was attended by 26,000 elementary school teachers. At a later stage, a further 14,500 teachers were re-trained to teach physical education. The organizing of such a plan would be impossible in any country that was not state-controlled. It was a commendable scheme and indicated what advances could be made given the enthusiasm of the state and the political control to encourage teachers to be involved. Although some government claims have been shown to be fictional, the level of physical education teaching was raised.[31]

Another plan to encourage participation was the 'Plan of the Streets' launched in 1966.[32] This plan was aimed at children aged from six to twelve, who were given the opportunity to participate in the streets of towns and villages. Administered by the local voluntary sports workers of the area, every Sunday morning between 8.00 a.m. and 1.00 p.m. the streets were closed to traffic and various activities were offered to children. To promote participation INDER organized the Consejos Voluntarios del INDER (CVIs) who were unpaid men and women who organized street activities. This voluntary service was a distinctive feature of sport for all in Cuba and once again emphasizes that even governments with substantial powers can only do so much – it is people who can make it work.

Castro introduced a strategy both to unite the population behind common sporting goals and to create a shared national identity through sport. Three hundred and ninety-six zones were established and sports activities such as baseball, volleyball, hockey and races were offered to the children.[33] The Plan of the Mountains, INDER-MINED and the Plan of the Streets were aimed at promoting 'sport for all'. However, the government also thought that every person should be given the opportunity to achieve excellence in sport. INDER argued that from this reservoir of participation top international athletes would emerge to the glory of Cuba.

SPORT IN SCHOOLS

Ron Pickering speaks about babies as young as two months old being physically manipulated by their mothers in order to stimulate coordination.[34] Since pre-school education is a right, all Cuban children have access to a pre-school programme, and in which physical education has a high priority. This initiative was adopted with the intention that by the time a child arrives at primary school at the age of five they would be physically literate. As a result of these impressive innovations, Cuban children have a foundation in physical literacy unsurpassed in most developed countries. The training of physical education teachers by the state has ensured that all primary school children are now exposed to a specialist teacher. Curriculum time is spent on elementary forms of rhythmic gymnastics and non-competitive games. In secondary schools physical education became a priority and accordingly it is allocated substantial time.[35] The students are introduced to a wide range of sports that allow for selection into local, regional and national competitions. A pupil's physical development is closely monitored by means of a series of tests, from which potential high-level performers are identified. Running in parallel to the school physical education curriculum is physical activity in the 'Pioneer Movement'.[36] This is a uniformed youth movement which occupies most Cubans in military-type activities and physical activities, including boxing. The overall objectives are fitness for national defence and labour.

Pupils who have been identified as the most promising performers through the school testing programmes, or have performed well in the inter-scholastic competitions, are sent to any of the 30 Escuelas d'Inciacion Deportiva Escolar (EIDE, Schools for the Initiation into Scholastic Sport), located throughout the island. These are boarding schools in which the students are able to train and be physically monitored whilst pursuing in the normal school curriculum. Chess is included as an activity as well as the more familiar activities to enable the children with intellectual rather than physical ability to attend EIDE schools. Children are usually admitted to these schools at the age of twelve, but swimmers and gymnasts may be admitted at ages eight or nine. The schools are primarily concerned with producing a sports elite that will form the basis of Cuba's national teams. They have a general education like any other child and if they do not study then their place at the school may be lost.[37] Leonard Hampson describes in detail the impressive facilities at the sports school at Holguin to the south-east of the island.[38] These include its own hospital and facilities for paediatric, dental, orthopaedic and psychological care. Pupils also receive supplementary food rations to compensate for the expenditure of energy while training. These facilities are indicative of the emphasis that the Socialist government places upon the development of athletes. All pupils attending sports schools must maintain their athletic performances, maintain a high academic level and show a high degree of political commitment.[39] After several years at the EIDE those pupils with the most potential graduate to one of Cuba's Escuelas Superior Perfeccion Atletico (ESPA, High Schools of Athletic Excellence). There are 13 of these sports schools, one in each of the provinces and one in the capital city, Havana.

Most athletes remain at an EIDE until the age of 19. Top athletes can then transfer to the National Training Centre in Havana known as the Cuidad Deportiva, which also serves as the headquarters of INDER. Most athletes have a nominal occupation, but are essentially full-time athletes. Some transfer to the University of Havana to continue their studies, but are able to extend the number of years to complete their degree. Alternatively, an EIDE student can become a specialist physical education teacher at a Escuela Provinciale de Educacion Fisica (EPEF).

There are seven such specialist institutes in Cuba. Courses at an EPEF last for five years, while the entrance requirements are the completion of seventh grade education (minimum age 13), and an interest in sport.[40] The very best EPEF students are able to complete their sports studies course at the specialist physical education college in Havana (Escuela Superior de Educacion Fisica, ESEF). In pre-Revolutionary Cuba, it was called the National Institute of Physical Education. In 1967, the first graduating year, 272 physical education students graduated from the specialist college. Prior to this Cuba sent its best athletes to study in the Soviet Union and the GDR. Between 1963 and 1985, a total of 45 Cubans graduated from sports related programmes from other countries, 35 from the Soviet Union, 6 from the GDR, and 2 each from Bulgaria and Czechoslovakia.[41] A graduate from the ESEF college would be expected to initiate research in sports sciences, biological sciences and teaching technique. Furthermore, they would also be expected to work in the community so that the general level of physical education and sport could be raised.

The headquarters of INDER, the Cuidad Deportiva (Sports City), is situated on the outskirts of Havana. It is a large complex not unlike a national sports centre in England or a sports facility on a US university campus. The complex is dominated by a large indoor stadium capable of holding 12,000 spectators. Murals of Che Cuevara are located everywhere around the stadium and on the walls of blocks of apartments en route to it. It is at the Cuidad Deportivo that the best athletes are given highly specialist sports coaching and the necessary attention in order that they may represent Cuba in international events.[42]

INDER readily acknowledges the past support of other socialist countries such as the Soviet Union, Poland, Czechoslovakia and the German Democratic Republic (GDR). These socialist countries developed a system of exchange whereby expertise was shared between them. In the period 1969 to 1972 more than fifty Soviet coaches helped to train Cuban athletes in preparation for major international sports events.[43] Initially, Cuban athletes did well in boxing and athletics. Their boxers were particularly successful, but it must be remembered that they were competing against young amateur boxers from other countries as the best boxers in other countries were professional.

However, in time Cuba began to be successful in those sports associated with developed countries such as weightlifting, judo and water polo. Pickering noted on a visit to an EIDE on the Isle of Pines in 1976, the priority given to swimming, diving, canoeing, sailing and water polo.[44] Success in water-based activities is surprising, as they are not sports traditionally associated with Cubans. In addition, black women are not usually involved in throwing activities in athletics. Ironically, there is no cycling velodrome in Cuba, but the cyclists are very successful in the Pan-American Games. Performance is as much dependent on determination and commitment as on the availability of expensive facilities.

In Cuba, what is achieved in sport is based on political philosophy. Clearly, 'Cuba's success in the development of sport has to be located in the political and social context in which they occur.'[45] Sport is an integral part of the political culture and it is available to all. Sport in Cuba is deeply integrated with politics and political ideology borrowed from Eastern Europe ideology. To a greater or lesser extent this is the case in most countries, but in Cuba as in Eastern Europe, it is a 'service to the people no more and no less than any other component of the culture'.[46]

COMMUNIST COMRADESHIP

In view of Cuba's population of eleven million people, Cuba has achieved remarkable success in international sport, especially at the International Amateur Athletic Federation (IAAF) World Athletic

Championships, the Olympic Games and the Pan-American Games. The ideology of sports development is based on the former socialist countries of Eastern Europe and on China and North Korea. Sports policies in these countries were and are not identical, but all have, or had, similarities, which distinguish them it from the structure of sport in capitalist countries such as the United States. The structure of sport in the former Soviet Union and Cuba represented a model of sport used to promote health and hygiene, defence, labour productivity, international recognition and prestige.[47] Sport offers developing countries such as Cuba the opportunity for gaining recognition and respect. This is significant for countries that feel they have been subject to domination by more powerful countries. As Castro said of imperialist states with regard to Latin America, 'Imperialism has tried to humiliate Latin American countries, has tried to instil an inferiority complex in them; part of the imperialists' ideology is to present themselves as superior. And they have used sport for that purpose.'[48] In the former Soviet Union and today's Cuba athletes were and are, respectively, perceived by political leaders as ambassadors for a country, who may encourage a sense of pride in their team nationality, country or political system.[49]

As in the former Soviet Union, in Cuba there is a commitment to sporting excellence based on the provision of facilities and organization structures, identification of talent, coach education and the use of sports medicine.[50] This common philosophy in the organization of sport is guided by a Marxist philosophy that stresses the interdependence of the physical and the mental, and that both are necessary for the health of the country.[51] Sport had a particular social and political significance in the development of the Soviet Union. Sport was more central in the social system and was controlled and directed by the state.[52] This is still the case in Cuba. In the Soviet Union responsibility for co-ordinating the development of sport vested in with the Supreme Council of Physical Culture, regional districts and councils.[53] In Cuba this responsibility is vested in INDER. Both the former Soviet Union and Cuba lived under the perceived threat of war or invasion, and subversion, so the defence of the nation was important.[54] Sport was a means of producing a fit and healthy population who could be used to defend the nation, as well as for internal policing against dissidents. The fear of invasion prompted the Soviet government to establish in 1931 a national fitness programme which emphasized military training.[55] It was called Prepared for Labour and Defence (GTO). The scheme was revised in 1972, 1985 and 1987 in order to embrace all aspects of physical and sporting activity in schools.[56] In Cuba, INDER organized similar military tests called Listas Para Vencer (LPV, Ready to Win) in 1961, which also had a fairly high military content.

In both Cuba and the former Soviet Union, central state control motivated by the desire to demonstrate the superiority of their politico-ideological philosophy led to resources being used to pursue sporting excellence.[57] In the Soviet Union, the Communist party utilized sport for political ends to show supremacy over capitalist countries. Similarly, Cuba promoted schemes in the pursuit of the creation of national consciousness and nation building, as well as a device to achieve national recognition and investment.[58] They utilized a system similar to their mentor in order to develop elite athletes. This system is achieved by state sponsorship of all aspects of preparation and competition within a comprehensive sports system.

The Soviet Union initially established 300 out-of-school Sports Schools in 1939, and created 30 Sports Schools in 1945 to train top-class athletes. These were funded by the Ministries of Education and Defence, the Soviet Union Sports Committee and the Trade Unions.[59] These schemes expanded and by 1991 there existed 7,900 elementary level Sport Schools attended by 35 million children and served by 50,000 coaches. Furthermore, 1300 designated Sports Schools were expected to produce a defined number of elite performers in the four-year period between the Olympic Games; 144 Higher Sport Schools were used to prepare top class performers, and 43 Sports Boarding Schools catered for 15,100 students specializing in Olympic sports.[60] In Cuba there is a similar system. Talented athletes are sent to the Escuelas d'Iniciacion Deportiva Escolar (EIDE) of which there are 30 throughout the island. Those showing the most potential graduate to one of Cuba's Escuelas Superior Perfeccion Athletisme (ESPE), of which there are 13, one in each province and one in Havana. Top athletes graduate at the age of 19 to the National Training Centre in Havana, which also serves as the headquarters of INDER, the central controlling body. Similarities between these systems are demonstrably clear. In both countries there is a substantial investment in facilities for elite athletes. Provision includes multi-purpose stadiums, swimming pools, sports halls, and indoor and outdoor training facilities. In order to develop World and Olympic champions, athletes are also supported by professionally qualified coaches, sports medicine and other ancillary systems. The development of a general sports movement in the Soviet Union (Massovost) and in Cuba was closely connected with spartakiade activities. Ken Hardman reported that the 1967 Spartakiade in the Soviet Union attracted eighty million participants.[61] In Cuba, gymnastic/athletic displays involving large numbers of people have been a common feature of sport for all programmes. Other measures to promote mass sport in the Soviet Union included health/sports camps, exercising prior to the commencement of work and physical culture camps. In Cuba similar schemes were adopted and include the 'Plan of the Mountains', and the 'Plan of the Streets'.

In the Soviet Union and Cuba control of the organization of sport, the planned application of resources and the priority given to sport achieved great success. The infrastructures provided conditions that were more conducive to discovering, organizing and developing talent than in more disparate western systems.[62] As both countries have adapted to market forces economics, materially many people are worse off, inflation is higher and the cost of food and clothing has risen. In order to counter the problems of insufficient funding for sport, support may now be sought from local enterprises to provide and refurbish facilities and equipment.

CUBA IN THE 1990s

The Cuban media minimized news of the events in the Soviet bloc between 1989 and 1992, as the authorities were concerned that Cubans would follow the example of the masses of Eastern Europe and rise against state communism. The Soviet Union, GDR and Czechoslovakia had ceased to exist, and due to the radical shift in the balance of world power and the economic chaos in Eastern Europe, material support for Cuba was not economically possible. The economic effect of changes in Europe was devastating to Cuba, as it had become reliant on the Communist bloc for assistance. The US was not inclined to lift the economic boycott and kept pressure on the North Atlantic Treaty Organization (NATO) allies to follow suit. As a result, Cuba began to suffer material shortages. The subsidy of US$5 billion per year from the Kremlin evaporated. In 1990, Castro implemented an austerity package known as the 'Special Period in Peacetime'. Here, the conservation of energy was a top priority; factories and offices were closed down, power cuts became a feature of everyday life, bus services were reduced, oxen and carts took the place of tractors, Chinese bicycles were imported for use, and rationing was introduced.[63]

Washington, DC increased the pressure on Cuba. The Torricelli Bill approved by Congress in 1992 banned overseas subsidies of American corporate companies from trading with Cuba and authorized the US President to cut off trade or introduce economic sanctions to any country that assisted them.[64] At a later stage, Senator Jesse Helms, a republican from North Carolina who described Castro as 'a bloody, murderous dictator, a brutal tyrannical thug' introduced the Helms-Burton Bill. This bill has been described as the toughest legislation ever enacted to bring about the fall of the Castro dictatorship and subsequently, indicates the animosity that was felt by some US citizens towards Castro and Cuba.[65]

There was unrest in Cuba, and Arnaldo Ochoa, a popular figure rumoured to be in favour of a Soviet-style perestroika, was executed. This was perceived to be a warning to those who might think of undermining Castro in a time of economic and political unrest. In 1991, the Communist Party Congress reiterated the message that Cuba had no intention of following the recent example of its former Eastern European bloc allies. There was a spate of small demonstrations in Havana in 1993, with hundreds of Cubans imprisoned. Others tried to flee to the US across the Florida Straits. On 5 August, thirty people were injured in rioting in Havana. The United States could not handle the estimated 30,000 people who attempted to gain entry to the country and subsequently, President Clinton had to reverse the country's long-standing policy of granting automatic political asylum to Cubans.[66]

There does appear to be momentum behind the economic liberalization in Cuba. For example, there has been legalization of private markets and restaurants and this in turn has created more pressure for political change. Cuba is today in a financial mess; there is material deprivation; there are long queues for limited products; and there is rationing. Havana is dilapidated. At night it is shrouded in darkness. Due to the high cost of fuel, power cuts are frequent and most parts of the city are dimly lit, sometimes only for a few hours each night. Old Spanish-style colonial buildings dominate old sections of Havana, while Utilitarian Soviet-style high-rise office blocks are scattered elsewhere across the city. Relics of the 1940s and 1950s in the form of

American limousines pollute the atmosphere. Old Soviet Lada cars, ancient trucks and rickshaws transport citizens around the city. The streets are rutted. People wait patiently at the side of the road for a bus or a lift from a passing motorist. Children play in and out of doorways and in the streets. Adults lounge on the doorstops or in open grilled windows chatting, smoking or gazing into space. Flats and houses are devoid of luxuries. In 1995, Cuba had the highest suicide rate in the Western Hemisphere; there is a feeling of resignation and little time for insurrection. Dissatisfaction with the regime has risen during the Special Period, but few dare express their feelings. Many Cubans believe the revolution has become stagnant because Castro has failed to adapt his political, economic views, despite radical changes in the former Soviet countries.[67]

There is still only one political party in Cuba, the Partido Comunista de Cuba (PCC). It maintains a rigid centralized control that does not allow for any opposition. Castro has survived 35 years of American sanctions, the death of the Soviet Union and the political upheavals of 1994. He is still at the centre-stage of many international events such as the investiture of Nelson Mandela and the fiftieth anniversary of the United Nations.[68] The leadership has had to display increased openness towards the West in order to boost tourism and foreign investment. Cuba is now one of the most popular destinations for British holidaymakers on long haul flights. Cuba is in desperate need of hard currency, particularly dollars. Now Cubans are able to use the US dollar in shops that are usually frequented by tourists. The Cuban peso is worthless on the international currency market and so the government will do almost anything to earn 'hard' currency. The government made it legal to possess dollars in 1993, but as Cubans are paid in pesos, life is a constant scrabble for dollars. Cuba has developed a thriving 'sex-trade' in which Cubans prostitute themselves individually and collectively to foreigners. Petty thieves make a living by robbing tourists. Many thousands of people have been imprisoned since the 1990s, as they are perceived to be a threat to social and political order. The security forces closely watch known dissidents and approximately 300 Cuban prisons contain 5,000 people whose political beliefs are not to the liking of the authorities.

Cuba is the largest and most fertile island in the Caribbean and it ought to have the strongest economy. The break-up of the Soviet Union and Cuba's highly centralized command economy, however, has resulted in a weak economy. The sugar industry, traditionally the mainstay of the economy has been hit by a shortage of fuel and spare parts. Harvests have declined and prices have fluctuated on the world market. Manufacturing industries are running at 50 per cent of full capacity and imports have been reduced by one-half. Since 1989, Cuba has lost most of its Warsaw Pact trading partners, which used to account for over 85 per cent of its trade. Cuba has turned to Latin America to compensate for this. For example, imports from this area rose from 7 per cent in 1990 to 47 per cent in 1993.[69]

In addition to developing a wider range of trading partners, an increase in foreign investment is also necessary. Mexico has been the leading foreign investor along with Colombia, Canada, Spain, Japan and Great Britain. In particular, Spain has given Cuba US$12.5 million in aid and US$100 million in soft loans over a four-year period. Further assistance has been given from Spain in terms of private investment associated with the tourist trade.[70] All the countries noted above have shown an interest in all areas of the economy including biotechnology, pharmaceuticals, oil exploitation and nickel refinement. Tourism has now surpassed sugar as the main currency earner for Cuba. In 1995, it grossed US$1 billion, with the number of workers employed in tourism also having increased from 630,000 in 1994 to 740,000 in 1995. Predictions suggest that there will be over two million tourists by the year 2000. Most of the best tourist facilities have been developed in partnership with mainly Spanish, Canadian or British foreign capital. In return the foreign investor receives 49 per cent of the profit and the Cuban government 51 per cent. This is an attractive proposition for European investors, as they do not have to compete with North American companies to invest in Cuba. The presence of tourists on the island with a 'daily spending capacity in excess of $100 per day, in a country in which a doctor might earn $20 per month, and a manual worker far less presents problems, and therefore tourists are a target for unsolicited attention'.[71] Young men and women patrol tourist quarters, hotels and beaches to seek ways to make money from the tourist industry.

SPORT IN CUBA IN THE 1990s

US$80 million is still invested in sport annually. This represents two per cent of the Gross Domestic Product (GDP).[72] The Cuban government invests a disproportionate amount of its resources to its athletes – educating, feeding and clothing them, and paying for equipment and travel. Being a top class athlete gives the opportunity for foreign travel that is denied to most other Cubans. In 1991, seventy athletes defected from Cuba. This is very irritating, as much money has been spent on their sports development.[73] Baseball players and boxers are most likely to defect due to those sports being professional in the United States. Athletes in Cuba lead a marginally better life than the average Cuban. They are educated, and are provided with an apartment, a car and an allowance for better food and clothing. On retirement they are guaranteed employment within the sports system as either coaches or sports development officers.

With the economy in chaos, sports facilities are deteriorating. Many of the sports facilities now consist of shabby, rusty buildings with gaps in the roof from which rain enters. The author witnessed the Cuban Junior handball team training in the Sala Polivalente Kid Chocolate (named after a famous Cuban boxer), during which there was a power cut. The athletes continued as if it were a common occurrence, undeterred by this 'slight' inconvenience. The weight training room was in disrepair, but the Cubans were quite proud of its dilapidated machines. There are not enough facilities to meet demand[74] – they are now outdated, impoverished and in need of repair. There are no lavish community recreation and leisure centres anymore, few swimming pools, no velodrome or ice rinks. There used to be organized gymnastic classes in clubs and at workplaces, locally organized Public Physical Efficiency classes and groups who met to exercise within a housing commune or block of flats. There is no evidence of this happening now.[75]

Fidel Castro once proclaimed that 'one day when the Yankees accept peaceful coexistence with our own country, we shall beat them at baseball too and then the advantages of revolutionary over capitalist sport will be shown'.[76] At a time when diplomatic links between the US and Cuba have been minimal, sport has occasionally been used as a means of communication. There have been exchanges in basketball, baseball and volleyball in the 1970s and 1980s. The Baltimore Orioles baseball team visit to Cuba on 28 March 1999 was of great significance. It is forty years since a US Major League team has played in Cuba. The Baltimore Orioles beat a Cuban all-star team 3–2 at the Estadio Latinamericano in Havana, a match during which Castro was present.

However, professional baseball was abolished after the revolution and Cuban players are no longer able to play for US teams. The countries now only meet in major international tournaments such as the Olympic Games in which US professional players do not play. Cuban teams therefore tend to dominate such events; for instance, they were the first baseball Olympic champions in 1992. Furthermore, although the game had no political agenda Peter Angelos, the Baltimore owner said, 'if this leads to an improvement in relations between our two countries, and ultimately much greater contact between our two people, millions of Americans would be delighted'.[77] In the return match on 5 May 1999 Castro got his wish. The Cuban national team won 12–6 in Baltimore. It is claimed that this was a huge propaganda coup for Castro.[78]

However, the current political relations between the two countries remain bitter. This is because they have different motives for cultural exchanges. The United States continues to work to undermine Castro's administration, whereas Cuba wants to highlight the injustices of US policy. Even so, perhaps such cultural exchanges offer a vital contribution to overcoming political differences. The solution in the short term might lie with Cuba's attempt to boost tourism and increase foreign investment. It is hoped that this will lead to an increasing openness towards the West. This may occur simply because Cuba is in need of hard currency. Cuba's hard currency earnings increased 15.6 per cent to US$1.3 billion between 1993 and 1996. The tourist industry is designed to earn as much money as possible. Resorts such as Cayo Coco, an offshore island developed exclusively for tourists, and Varedero, are examples of areas developed for the tourist industry. In these resorts, long stretches of Cuba's best beaches are adjoined by luxury hotels in which mainly Canadian and European tourists congregate. The leadership must display increased openness towards the West (including the United States) to boost tourism and foreign investment. But of course the economy should not rely completely on the tourist industry, as tourists will travel to new destinations as they present themselves.

Cuba is essentially an agricultural nation and therefore an economy based on its natural resources and the influx of tourists should be the goal of the government. In the short term, finance generated by the tourist industry should be used to sustain and improve the infrastructure of the country. If US citizens were able to travel to Cuba one suspects that the economy would be greatly improved. The roads and railways in particular need to be improved. This is a requirement as more tourists arrive. Further finance could be used to improve the deteriorating quality of education and physical education teaching. With every new reform expectations of new facilities among the Cuban people rise, thus creating political pressure for yet more change and a re-orientation towards a Western political ideology. As more money becomes available the shabby, rusty and dilapidated sports facilities should improve. An obvious method of improving facilities would be to develop commercial interests. But at the moment sponsorship and commercialism as found in the United States has no place in Cuban ideology.

Despite many social problems in Cuba since 1990, it still remains successful in international sport. At the 1996 Olympic Games in Atlanta, Cuba won 25 medals; at the 2000 Olympic Games in Sydney, Cuba won 29 medals and was one of the leading nations. But it is difficult to imagine that over the next decade communism can enjoy the same levels of social and educational development as in the past. There is evidence to suggest that there has been a halt to social programmes during the Special Period. It seems unlikely that Castro will be able to maintain socialist structures while seeking to move towards a free market economy. Whether there are social and political changes in Cuba during the next ten years might depend on the longevity of Castro.[79] However, it is hoped that the system adopted by Cuba can be fine-tuned rather than radically altered. Those involved in sport must decide how to break with the past and adopt a system based on market conditions. The former Soviet Union is in the process of doing this whereas Cuba has yet to adapt to such a system. In such conditions sport could well end up with the worst of both worlds – communist and capitalist.[80] It is to be hoped that this will not be the case and that a system emerges unique to the situation in Cuba which utilizes the best elements of the old system and merges them with commercial and privatized forms of facilities and programmes in which elite athletes can succeed and sport for all policies can once again be promoted.

NOTES

I would like to express my gratitude to J. Coghlan for his help in the preparation of this paper.

1.   S. Caldwell and E. Hatchwell, *Cuba* (Oxford: Unwin Bros, 1996), p.11.

2. R. Pickering, 'Sport in Cuba', in J. Riordan (ed.), *Sport under Communism* (London: Hurst, 1980) pp.143–74.
3. Calder and Hatchwell, *Cuba*, p.30.
4. Ibid., p.17.
5. Ibid., p.19.
6. For a perceptive account of boxing in Cuba, see J. Sugden, *Boxing in Society: An International Analysis* (Manchester: Manchester University Press, 1996).
   For a description of life in Cuba,see J. Sugden and A. Tomlinson, 'Hustling in Havana', in G. McFee, W. Murphy and G. Whannel (eds.), *Leisure Cultures: Values, Genders, Lifestyles* (Brighton: LSA Publication, 1995).
7. Pickering, 'Sport in Cuba', p.148.
8. P. Pettavino and G. Pye, 'Sport in Cuba', in L. Chalip, A. Johnson and L. Stachura (eds.), *National Sports Policies: An International Handbook* (London: Greenwood Press, 1996).
9. Sugden, *Boxing in Society*, p.137.
10. Ibid., p.136.
11. Calder and Hatchwell, *Cuba*, p.19.
12. For a more detailed analysis of sport in developing countries, see R. Chappell and J. Coghlan (eds.), *Sport for All in Developing Countries* (London: Brunel University, 1996).
13. CBS: *The Last Revolution*, 18 July 1996.
14. Sugden, *Boxing in Society*, p.137.
15. Pettavino and Pye, 'Sport in Cuba', p.117.
16. Ibid.
17. For a more detailed analysis of sport in Eastern European countries, see Riordan (ed.), *Sport under Communism*.
18. Pickering, 'Sport in Cuba', p.150. and Pettavino and Pye, 'Sport in Cuba', p.121.
19. J. Griffiths and P. Griffiths, *Cuba: The Second Decade* (London: Writers and Readers Books, 1979).
20. J. Sugden, A. Tomlinson and E. McCarton, 'The Making and Remaking of White Lightning: Politics, Sport and Physical Education 30 years after the Revolution', *Arena Review*, 14, 1 (1990), 101–9.
21. J. Coghlan, 'The Reduction of Current Disparities between the Developed and Developing Countries in the Field of Sport and Physical Education' (ICSSPE, 1986), p.40.
22. CBS: *The Last Revolution*, 18 July 1996.
23. L. Hampson, 'Socialism and the Aims of Physical Education in Cuba', *Physical Education Review*, 3, 1 (1980), 64–82.
24. Griffiths and Griffiths, *Cuba: The Second Decade*, p.251.
25. Ibid.
26. K. Hardman, 'The Former Soviet Union', in K. Hardman (ed.), *Comparative Studies in Physical Education and Sport* (Manchester: Centre for Physical Education and Leisure Studies, 1996), p.62.
27. Hampson, 'Socialism', p.67.
28. Ibid.
29. Coghlan, *The Reduction*, p.42.
30. Hampson, 'Socialism', p.67.
31. Ibid.
32. Ibid., p.68
33. Ibid.
34. BBC, *Cuba-Sport and the Revolution*, August 1977.
35. Hampson, 'Socialism', p.74.

36. Sugden, *Boxing in Society*, p.149.
37. Hampson, 'Socialism', p.76.
38. Ibid., p.77.
39. Griffiths and Griffiths, *Cuba: The Second Decade*, p.254.
40. Hampson, 'Socialism', p.78.
41. Pettavino and Pye, 'Sport in Cuba', p.121.
42. Sugden, *Boxing in Society*, p.148.
43. Ibid., p.254.
44. BBC, *Cuba: Sport and Revolution*, August 1977.
45. Griffiths and Griffiths, *Cuba: The Second Decade*, p.260.
46. Ibid., p.260.
47. J. Riordan, 'The Impact of Communism in Sport', in J. Riordan and A. Kruger (eds.), *The International Politics of Sport in the 21st Century* (London: Spon, 1999), p.48.
48. J. Riordan, *Sport, Politics and Communism* (Manchester: Manchester University Press, 1991), p.61.
49. Ibid.
50. K. Hardman and C. Fielden, 'The Development of Sporting Excellence-Lessons from the Past' in P. Duffey and L. Dugdale (eds.), *HPER–Moving Towards the 21st Century*, (Champaign, Illinois: Human Kinetics, 1994), p.161.
51. Riordan, 'The Impact of Communism in Sport', p.49.
52. Ibid.
53. Hardman, 'The Former Soviet Union', p.47.
54. Riordan, 'The Impact of Communism in Sport', p.51.
55. Hardman, 'The Former Soviet Union', p.47.
56. Ibid.
57. Ibid., p.57.
58. Ibid.
59. Ibid., p.59.
60. Hardman and Fielden, 'The Development of Sporting Excellence-Lessons from the Past', p.166.
61. Hardman, 'The Former Soviet Union', p.60.
62. Riordan, 'The Impact of Communism in Sport', p.63.
63. Riordan, *Sport, Politics and Communism*, p.62.
64. Calder and Hatchwell, *Cuba*, p.21.
65. CBS: *The Last Revolution*, 18 July 1996.
66. Calder and Hatchwell, Cuba, p.22.
67. Sugden, *Boxing in Society*, p.138.
68. Calder and Hatchwell, *Cuba*, p.22.
69. Ibid., p.26.
70. Sugden, *Boxing in Society*, p.150.
71. Ibid., p.141.
72. *Daily Telegraph*, 26 May 1996.
73. Sugden, *Boxing in Society*, p.145.
74. This paper draws upon information gathered during a visit to Cuba, which entailed visiting sports facilities on the island.
75. Pickering 'Sport in Cuba', p.162.
76. Ibid., p.152.
77. *Daily Telegraph*, 30 May 1999.
78. *Daily Telegraph*, 5 May 1999.

79. Sugden, Tomlinson, and McCarton, 'The Making', p.108.
80. Riordan, 'The Impact of Communism in Sport', p.63.

From East to West: The Way of the Master – Oriental Martial Arts in Modern European Culture

HANS BONDE

APPRENTICESHIP

It is a sad fact that the qualities of a phenomenon often only become manifest when it has been lost. Apprenticeship (in Danish *mesterlæren* or the learning of mastery) has often been regarded in present-day Western society as a relic of feudalism which permitted the master of a craft to exploit young manpower without giving them a proper education, using them as 'gophers' rather than teaching them the trade.[1] Without romanticizing apprenticeship, it can be said however to have been one of the few activities in society where knowledge could be transferred through visual and tactile experiences communicated in the close relationship between master and pupil. Apprenticeship was an island in our intellectualized society where young people without great powers of abstraction could learn directly by imitating and identifying with the master.[2] At the same time pupils with their book learning in order, could in apprenticeships experience non-verbal and intuitive qualities in the human working process. The move away from apprenticeship has been further aggravated by the growth of routine work, which has more and more undermined the master's individual insight and problem solving in unique situations. Instead, an ever-increasing part of the craft is subjected to the standardized routines of mass production. It is suggested here that the growth in popularity of martial arts in Europe is related to the situation outlined above.

One of the few places where learning processes that recall the traditions of apprenticeship may be found, as demonstrated by the psychologist Ejgil Jespersen, is sport. This applies to a special degree, as will be illustrated below, to that part of sport which is inspired by

Oriental, especially Japanese, martial arts (but also the martial arts of many other countries such as Brazilian capoeira and Indonesian *pencak*).

The appeal to modern Europeans of these various forms of martial arts, to no little extent, lies in their evolution over centuries in the East. This is now briefly outlined below.

MONKS AND WARRIORS

The following is not an attempt to offer fresh revelations about Zen Buddhism, which is well described, not least by D.T. Suzuki.[3] A summary of the centuries-long history of Zen-oriented martial arts philosophy shows extraordinary philosophical continuity, with various martial arts schools upholding the same fundamental ideas.[4] Reference to this ideational continuity is not the same, of course, as justifying the bloody practices often characterized among samurais.

While the samurais were primarily responsible for the development of the practical fighting technique, it was the monks who developed the mental dimension of martial arts. It was first and foremost the Zen Buddhist sect that had an influence on the conceptual world of the warriors, and particularly their mental training for battle. From the time when the warrior class established itself as the ruling class in Japan, the Zen monks achieved high status with that class. In the Kamakura period (*c.*1185-1333) under some of the first shoguns, the Zen monks won support from those in power, and subsequently the importance of Zen grew not only among the warriors, but also among broader sections of the Japanese people.[5]

Zen Buddhism was a variant of the traditional Buddhism that had been created in India on the basis of the Buddha's doctrines in the sixth century BC. Later Buddhism came to China, and from there it was passed to the Japanese monks.[6] Central to Buddhism is the idea of not taking life. Furthermore, Buddhism holds to the belief that meditation is the path to the discovery of the deeper essence of life. An element in the path to enlightenment that Buddha prescribed was the realization that men exist as part of a cosmic whole, not as individuals who are independent and freely floating in the universe.[7]

In reality, however, in Japan Buddhism was practised by many orders of monks. One of the largest was the Zen order, which greatly emphasized the importance of being present in the 'now' of things. The Zen Buddhists rejected speculation and instead pointed to the direct path to enlightenment through action. By meditating, painting, writing, drawing, drinking tea, performing drama, archery and training in swordsmanship, one could develop mentally. Fighting, drawing and painting became meditation in motion.[8]

What was it about Zen Buddhism that attracted the Japanese warriors? What counted was action in the immediate present – not long deliberations on the future. The warrior was a man of action and when he stood in direct confrontation with the enemy on the battlefield, there was no time for long analyses of the situation. The warrior, therefore, used Zen meditation to improve his spontaneous action at crucial moments in his military life.[9]

Around the year 1600 the civil wars that had plagued the country for generations subsided. For the newly established Tokugawa regime, the need to maintain a certain combat readiness among its warriors to keep other warrior dynasties and rebellious peasants in check remained a priority. However, at the same time, since war had almost ceased, it was also important for the regime to subdue the bellicosity of Japan's warriors. The Tokugawa regime therefore sought to pacify the martial arts.[10]

The large warrior class continued under the Tokugawa regime, but what were the warriors to use their fighting capabilities for in a society without war? Duels were not everyday events, so daily training in the martial arts was not necessary. On the other hand the martial arts were the only craft the warriors were really trained in, so it was essential to introduce a new ethos into these traditional activities. The warrior's goal subsequently changed, and focused less on killing an external enemy, and more on killing the destructive and inhibiting parts of oneself. From being the arts of war the martial arts now increasingly became a means of personal development.[11]

Training in swordfighting was now often practised with wooden swords – rarely steel ones. The handling of the sword was also governed by unwritten rules. For example, a sword's blade must not be exposed towards the spectator, and a sword was to be drawn slowly from the scabbard and rarely drawn all the way out. Obviously, these rules were symbolic of the fact that strong restraints had now been imposed on violence and aggression.[12]

THE WAY OF THE MASTER

Mountains should be climbed with as little effort as possible and without desire. The reality of your own nature should determine the speed. If you become restless, speed up. If you become winded, slow down. You climb the mountain in an equilibrium between restlessness and exhaustion. Then, when you are no longer thinking ahead, each footstep isn't just a means to an end but a unique event in itself. This leaf has jagged edges. This rock looks loose. From this place the snow is less visible, even though closer. These are things you should notice anyway. To live only for some future goal is shallow. It is the sides of the mountain which sustain life, not the top. Here is where things grow. But of course, without the top you can't have any sides. It's the top that defines the sides.[13]

Below is a brief outline of the philosophy of Japanese martial arts. This forms the background for the exotic and mystical aura that surrounds Japanese martial arts in twentieth-century Western culture. It should, however, be emphasized that many of the martial arts that have been exported to Europe in the process of assimilation have lost their philosophical–religious roots. Judo is probably the best example of a totally 'sportified' Japanese martial art. In international contests all competitors now wear advertising logos, while during the match the two combatants respectively wear a blue and white costume, for the benefit of television viewers.

That an activity ends in *-do* means in Japanese that it is an expression of a *path* to mental development, and so, in the case of judo the full meaning is 'the way of gentleness'. Below *mental development* is the development of both body and mind. The word *do* sums up the great upheaval Japanese martial arts have undergone in the period since 1600. Martial arts such as *kenjutsu* (swordfighting), *kyujutsu* (archery), *iaijutsu* (the art of unsheathing a sword), *sumo* (traditional Japanese wrestling) and *aikijutsu* (the art of defeating an opponent by harmonizing one's movements with his attack) were gradually transformed from warlike arts to 'paths' for maturing mentally. The ending *-jutsu*, which means 'technique' was removed and replaced by the word *do*, 'path'. Thus at the end of the nineteenth century *jiu-jitsu* was renamed *judo,* in the 1940s *aikijutsu* was renamed *aikido,* and in the 1920s *karate* became *karatedo.* All the Japanese martial arts that end in *-do* are summed up in the concept of *budo*, the path of combat or war.

The word *do* is evidence of how great a debt Japanese martial arts owe to Chinese philosophy. The word comes from Chinese Taoist philosophy, in which *do* is called *tao*. The hall in which one trains in Japanese martial arts is called a *dojo*, which means 'the place where one studies the path'. The pioneer behind the development of French judo, the Japanese Kawaishi, expressed the relationship between training exclusively to compete and training for mental development as follows: 'The champion's prime is over in about ten years, but the master's ... will last all his life.'[14]

If Zen Buddhism took such a strong hold of martial arts it was presumably because the fighter faced a life-or-death situation or at least a situation that seemed life-threatening, and the philosophy of immediate action was pragmatic. Today, even in such a relatively regulated and peaceful martial art as judo, strangulations occur which would result in death if they were taken to the extreme. For this reason the absolutely central constant is total concentration in order to act with immediate and complete freedom in any situation. Of what use is perfect analysis in a fight if one freezes and is paralyzed by fear? In combat there is no time to think about where the opponent may strike, how strong he is or if one will be hurt. Such distracting thoughts destroy concentration and spontaneity. In the West success in sport is linked with a certain degree of analytical reflection. When a physical activity is viewed as a *path* (an Eastern one), the perspective is fundamentally changed: the goal is to disengage consciousness. The ego is viewed in Oriental philosophy as almost an obstacle to perfect sportsmanship. Budo is about reacting intuitively. The aim is to throw the opponent without having planned it in advance. It is as if the throw comes out of nothing. There is neither a hair's breadth, nor a thought, between idea and action.

If Japanese martial arts are viewed as a path towards the development of body and mind, the aim is not at first to conquer something external, but to create the development of the inner human being. The result, whether counted in centimetres, grammes, seconds or points, is less an achievement than the *process* that leads to the result. 'It's the sides of the mountain which sustain life, not the top. For that is where things grow.' In short, it is in the judo bout itself that the human being can grow mentally, not by dwelling upon pats on the shoulder, medals, records and championships.

TACIT KNOWLEDGE

> On Lake Sarusawa,
> the moon shines clear,
> but does not think about it,
> nor does the water below,
> which allows the moon
> to look forth.
>> From *Judo* (Tokyo, 1915)

In the discussion of the rehabilitation of apprenticeship, research on 'tacit knowledge'[15] has been emphasized.[16] The transmission of craft skills under the tutelage of the master has usually taken the form of practical demonstrations of action without much verbalization. Within Japanese martial arts an intuitive, concentrated mood called *mushin* – the empty mind – is cultivated. This state can, it is suggested here, clarify elements of the concept of 'tacit knowledge' in the apprenticeship context, for the term illustrates an attempt to achieve what in fact cannot be described verbally. Images provide an impression of what *mushin* involves. *Mushin* can be translated as 'emptiness' or 'purposelessness'. The mind of the swordsman and the *judoka* must be as blank as the sword blade of a samurai; it must be calm and concentrated as the reflection of the moon in a woodland lake. All thoughts of past and present, defeat and victory, must yield to a total immersion in the here-and-now.

All this may sound rather abstract, for how can one use consciousness to stop the stream of consciousness? Everyone, however, has presumably, at certain times in one's life, experienced the feeling of total immersion in an activity – for example, after an initial stiffness and feeling of embarrassment, abandoning oneself to dancing with someone. The true *masters* differ from the rest of us in being able to achieve a state of emptiness, an absence of ego, and fusion with the space, the time, the sound and the light on a regular basis. They also know, more than most other people, the state that they aspire to, and they are better at preparing for it.

When a pupil in the traditionally cultivated Japanese martial arts (*budo*) has acknowledged that the combat is based on the instantaneous merging of the two combatants, the next stage in his development comes. He is now expected to have a better awareness of the unity of the human being with all mankind, with the plants, the earth, the sea, in fact the whole cosmos. The concept of *mushin*, emptiness, should not be understood in the normal Western sense of the word, as a feeling of indifference and meaninglessness. On the contrary, one can experience meaningfulness by stopping the churning flow of thought. Many people from the West are afraid of emptiness and cram their heads with messages and images from newspapers, television, video and comic strips. For many European exponents one of the greatest attractions of martial arts is the pursuit of *mushin*.

In the book *Illustrated Kodokan Judo*, published in 1955 by Tokyo's judo association, the highest level a *judoka* can reach is described as a state in which the self and the universe are one and where we and others merge together.[17] It should not be overlooked, of course, that other cultures have concepts that resemble *mushin* and 'fusion'. In Spanish bullfighting there is a word for the state where the bullfighter, bull and audience in the arena merge into a higher unity. The word is *el duende*, and traditionally the bullfighter will only achieve the highest honour – the bull's ears – when *el duende* has manifested itself in the fight.

It may seem self-contradictory that the highest goal of *budo* is harmony. Fighting is apparently based on a strict separation of two opponents who are determined to defeat each other; but in the heat of combat the feeling of unity with one's opponent can arise. The opponent is a mirror of one's weaknesses. This helps one to develop. When one is thrown, one learns that one's balance in a particular position is inadequate. When one attacks, and the opponent simply yields, turns around and throws one with one's own strength, both competitors merge together for a brief moment. Without an opponent, there is no judo and thus no self-development.

The two partners in martial arts are called *uke* and *tori*. On the face of it, *uke* means a person who loses or gives, while *tori* means a person who wins or takes. But literally, *tori* means 'he who takes' and *uke* 'he who receives'. In other words, both get something out of the process, although one throws and the other is thrown.[18]

The Zen-inspired martial arts are not inimical to the concept of a trade apprenticeship. The goal of budo is to transfer the experiences of the dojo to everyday life. Even such everyday activities as hammering a nail, washing up or commuting to work can take place in an atmosphere where the activity is not just something to be endured, but a moment of vibrant meaningfulness. The hammer and nail are not simply tools, but are an extension of oneself; in calm, rhythmic movements and perfect balance the nail moves, almost by itself, deeper and deeper into the wood. The action produces a state of mind.

THE MASTER AND THE PHILOSOPHER

In the book *Zen in the Art of Archery* the German philosopher Eugen Herrigel offers an atmospheric description of his relationship with the Japanese master of archery, Kenzo Awa. Herrigel's text is somewhat romantic, but still important in its accurate uncovering of the ideals behind martial arts teaching. Furthermore, the book is a rare example of a Westerner's initiation in the more esoteric aspect of Japanese martial arts in Japan during the inter-war years.

Herrigel lived in Japan between 1929 and 1948 and taught at Tohoku University in Sendia. He vividly describes the shock of studying archery (*kyodo*) in 1930s Japan. His initial attitude was that the only thing that mattered was to hit the target with the arrow, and with this goal in mind he experienced one defeat after another. However, he soon came to realize that the most profound aim of Japanese archery was not to hit the target as accurately as possible, but to work towards self-insight and self-forgetting in the activity. If one achieved this immersion, the arrow would also hit the target perfectly. He was not allowed to shoot an arrow before he had penetrated far into the technique of archery. He therefore felt that he was not able to 'measure' his progress, yet his master could gauge his stage of development. Only when he was sufficiently mentally mature was he allowed to practise the next step. He describes his learning process as years of perseverance, training, crises and frustration before being able to glimpse mastery.

As in Western apprenticeship, the traditionally cultivated Eastern martial arts are also concerned with *imitation* and *identification* as the two central didactic mechanisms. Herrigel describes the imitation model as follows: 'At first no more is demanded of the pupil than that he conscientiously imitates what the teacher shows him. Since they are against endless explanations and justifications this is restricted to curt instructions, and the pupil is not expected to ask questions. The teacher kindly observes the fumbling efforts without expecting independence and initiative.'[19] The word 'imitation' is preferable to 'copying'. 'Copy' implies a completely unaware, mechanical reproduction, which is far from the idea of Japanese martial arts. Research is badly lacking on the extraordinary process whereby human beings, through vision, can 'record' others' movements and reproduce them in themselves. It is not a question of copying others' movements but of a whole new manifestation created by a different individual. It is probably important to distinguish between different phases of the imitation. First there is a relatively mechanical copying. Then the movements begin to be 'felt'. In the end they become a completely inevitable part of the actor. Then it is no longer an imitation, but a new, fully valid expression which has only at the outset taken its model from another. In Japanese martial arts one speaks of 'living' and 'dead' movements[20] to indicate the difference between the spiritless copy, where the mind forces the body into patterns of movement, and the process where the distinction between body and mind has been cancelled out, and only the action exists.

The quotation from Herrigel shows a further affinity between apprenticeship and martial arts: far too many explanations and rationalistic justifications shatter the concentration and create an impeding illusion that true mastery can be grasped intellectually. Instead of rationalist arguments the Zen masters use images (and enigmas) as the gateway to sensing the incomprehensible. For example, the master described the purposelessness of the archer by comparing it to a bamboo leaf laden with snow, which suddenly throws off the snow and straightens up.

For a European philosopher like Herrigel, accustomed to ordering the whole world with his head, it was a shocking experience that the goal of archery was in fact to disengage all thoughts and reflections. Does this mean that Japanese martial arts reject *intelligence*? Or is it perhaps our Western concept of intelligence that is too narrow? In Japan the archer can be a philosopher and the philosopher an archer. The sharp distinction between the citadel of intelligence, the university and the rest of society, is sometimes transcended in Japanese martial arts. Archery and other practical activities are thought to be able to open the door to greater philosophical depth than reading books, no matter how many. Interestingly in Europe and America today, alongside the rehabilitation of apprenticeship and with the broad interest in physical culture, there are also efforts to extend the concept of intelligence. Understanding the concept of 'bodily intelligence' may also lead to a deeper understanding of the distinctive character of apprenticeship.[21] *Identification* with the teacher also promotes the development of the pupil. In Herrigel's words: 'The path to mastery is steep. Often there is nothing else to keep the pupil going than trust in the teacher, from whom he now glimpses mastery: he stands for him as a living example of the inner work and appears convincing exclusively because of his mere presence.'[22]

Here, though, is to be found the Achilles Heel of both martial arts and apprenticeship. They require an almost submissive attitude from a pupil who acknowledges the true mastery of his teacher. This can be extremely dangerous if an authoritarian trainer exploits the devotion of his pupils for immoral ends. Martial arts are like dynamite – if used constructively they can be used to 'blast holes' through alienation and connect people; used destructively it can 'blow them up'. Herrigel was lucky. His master understood that after the identification phase *emancipation* occurred. In Herrigel's own words:

> How far the pupil gets does not concern the teacher and master. As soon as he has shown the pupil the right path, he lets him go on alone. There is only one thing he must still do so that the pupil can endure the loneliness: he releases him from himself; from the master, heartily urging him to carry on as himself and to 'rise up on the shoulders of the teacher'.[23]

The pupil must take the tradition upon himself, but in true mastery he must express what he has learned in his own way. In fact, therefore, the Achilles Heel of oriental martial arts may be more theoretical than actual. In reality, it encapsulates the occidental preference for the autonomy of the individual.

The similarity between martial arts and apprenticeship must not be overemphasized. Whereas apprenticeship is organized within production and has a worldly, commercial purpose as its framework, martial arts are cultivated in a far more ideal context. At their highest level they are lifted above the utilitarian thinking of the production sphere, in which the pupil reaches a deeply religious insight into the limitations of the ego and the connection of the self with the All. Herrigel speaks of the master's emphasis on how: 'all true creation only succeeds in a state of complete selflessness, during which the creator can therefore no longer be present "himself". Only the spirit is present, a kind of waking state which precisely no longer has any hint of "self", and which therefore without inhibitions can penetrate space "with eyes that hear and ears that see".'[24]

As expressed in the universe of archery, the archer should become so much part of the process that it feels as if the arrow shoots itself, and that target, arrow, bow and archer merge together. In this case the result of the process will be that of excellence, but this is only a contingent phenomenon and not the goal. One day Herrigel, who could not help constantly asking questions, asked the master if he could hit the target blindfolded. The master replied curtly: 'Come this evening'. That evening, Herrigel experienced something that prompted him to immerse himself in archery. Herrigel says:

> The practice-hall was brightly lit. The master ordered me to stick a mosquito candle, which was as long and thin as a knitting-needle, in the sand in front of the target, but I was not to light the candle there where the targets stood. It was so dark that I could not even make out the outline of the targets, and if the tiny sparks from the mosquito light could have been seen, I would probably have been able to glimpse the place where the target stood, but would have been unable to point it out accurately. The master 'danced' the ceremony. His first arrow was shot from the brightest light into the darkest night. By the thud I understood that it had hit the target. The second arrow hit it too. When I had lit the candle at the target point, I saw to my amazement that the first arrow was stuck in the middle of the black, while the second had splintered the notch of the first and had split the shaft some of the way before piercing the black beside it.[25]

CONCLUSION

This chapter has considered differences and similarities between the master–apprentice custom in traditional Western crafts and Japanese martial arts. It has attempted to show how the concept of martial arts can be used to extend an understanding of the transfer of 'tacit knowledge' in the apprenticeship context. The similarities between oriental martial arts and occidental apprenticeship should not be overemphasized. Apprenticeship today takes place within the utility-oriented framework of mass production; the martial arts today seek personal spiritual development. Another significant difference is that Japanese martial arts have especially been cultivated by the more mature members of the prosperous classes, while apprenticeships catered for the young from the working class.

It is evident that Japanese oriental martial arts have taken a significant hold in Europe and this is probably because of the need for rituals that arose in the wake of the youth revolution as well as the general intellectualization of European society.[26] Martial arts provide close physical contact and ordered rituals in a society typified by poverty of the senses and a lack of social guidelines. The young's fascination with the masters of martial arts can certainly be viewed in relation to the loss of apprenticeship and the general undermining of craft mastery as well as the need for leadership. What cannot be achieved in the workplace can perhaps be achieved during one's leisure time in the judo club. Whatever the reasons for the popularity of ancient oriental martial arts in modern European culture, it is clear that the East is making its contribution to shaping global societies currently embracing the heritage of cultures across the globe. Europe has given modern sport to Asia, but Asia is giving ancient sport to Europe.

NOTES

I should point out that I have an intimate association with martial arts, especially judo, in which I have been Danish champion (in Danish, the word used is *mester*, 'master') several times. Although I have tried to maintain as high a degree of objectivity as possible, my commitment to the sport could hardly avoid colouring my analysis. I should like to express my appreciative thanks to Professor J.A. Mangan for helpful editorial assistance with this chapter.

1. E. Herrigel, *Bueskydning og Zen* (Hasle v: Munksgård, 1971).
2. E. Jespersen 'Fra krop til krop – Gensyn med idrætsmesterlæren', *Dansk pædagogisk tidsskrift*, 1/1993 (Slagelse, 1992), pp.26–30.
3. D.T. Suzuki, *Zen and Japanese Culture* (New York: Pantheon Books, 1958).
4. L. Ratti and A. Westbrook, *Secrets of the Samurai* (A Survey of the Martial Arts of Feudal Japan) (Tokyo: Charles E. Tuttle Company, 1973), p.376.
5. H. Dumoulin, *A History of Zen Buddhism* (New York: Pantheon Books, 1963), p.143 and Suzuki, *Zen and Japanese Culture*, p.29.
6. Suzuki, *Zen and Japanese Culture*, p.3.
7. Ratti and Westbrook, *Secrets of the Samurai*, p.376.
8. Suzuki, *Zen and Japanese Culture*, p.1.
9. Ibid., p.60.
10. Ratti and Westbrook, *Secrets of the Samurai*, pp.22 and 62.
11. Ibid.
12. Ibid., p.254.
13. Robert M. Pirsig, *Zen and the Art of Motorcycle Maintenance* (Danish ed., Copenhagen: Munksgård, 1978).
14. K. Kawaishi, *Standing Judo* (London: W. Foulsham, 1963), p.10.
15. H. Dreyfus and S. Dreyfus, *Intuitiv ekspertise* (Copenhagen: Munksgård, 1991); M. Polyani, 'Tacit Knowing', in *The Tacit Dimension* (London: Routledge & Kegan Paul, 1967), pp.1–25.
16. S. Kvale, 'En pædagogisk rehabilitering af mesterlæren' (unpublished manuscript, Aarhus University, Aarhus, 1992), 2. See also J. Lave and E. Wenger, *Situated Learning – Legitimate Peripheral Participation* (Cambridge: Cambridge University Press, 1991); P. Fibæk Laursen, 'En ny ydmyghed overfor praksis', in *Dansk pædagogisk Tidsskrift*, 1 (1993).
17. *Illustrated Kodokau Judo* (Tokyo, 1955), p.23.
18. These Japanese words were translated for the author by the Japanese interpreter, Eiki Ishizaki.
19. Herrigel, *Bueskydning og Zen*, p.47.
20. T. Leggett, *A First Zen Reader* (Tokyo: Charles E. Tuttle Company, 1960), *passim*. T. Leggett, *Zen and the Ways* (London: Routledge & Kegan Paul, 1978), *passim*.
21. H. Gardner, 'Bodily-kinesthetic Intelligence', in *Frames of Mind, The Theory of Multiple Intelligences* (New York: Fontana, 1985), pp.205–36.
22. Herrigel, *Bueskydning og Zen*, p.53.
23. Ibid.
24. Ibid., p.51.
25. Ibid., p.66.
26. H. Bonde, 'Ritualets genkomst, orientalsk kampkunst og vestlig ungdom', *Social Kritik* (Copenhagen, 1990), pp.77–91.

The New Scramble for Africa:
African Football Labour Migration to Europe

PAUL DARBY

INTRODUCTION

In much the same way that the general process of sports labour migration is accelerating,[1] the global flow of football players between and within nations and continents is gathering momentum. The reasons for this are manifold and multifaceted. In the broadest sense, the transnational and transcontinental stream of football labour can be interpreted as part of the same processes of globalization which have led to the 'crystallisation of the entire world as a single place'.[2] Indeed, the current trend to locate sports related developments within an analytical framework cognisant of globalization is partly in recognition of the fact that a global sports culture has emerged over the last century.[3] The diffusion, development and almost universal popularity of football can be viewed as part of this homogenizing trend and one that has contributed to the shrinking of time and space in international sport.[4] As a consequence of this and other related globalization processes such as developments in technology, communications, transport and finance, the transfer and movement of football migrants have become much more prominent features of modern sport. Athletic talent migration has also become a major area of investigation amongst sport sociologists, historians and geographers.[5] This chapter not only contributes to the growing body of knowledge in this emerging field of enquiry but also adds a new dimension by responding to calls to assess the impact of sports migration on 'donor' nations and more specifically, by examining the nuances, nature and consequences of football labour migration from Africa.[6] Before assessing the specifics of football migration patterns between Africa and Europe, it is necessary briefly to chart the introduction and early dissemination of football to Africa. This will allow the relationship between Africa and Europe as mediated through football labour migration to be set in its proper historical context.

FOOTBALL'S DIFFUSION TO AFRICA

It cannot be denied that football in Africa is a legacy of European colonialism. The advent and development of European colonial endeavour has been the most significant factor in the socio-cultural transformation of African society. As part of this change forms of European sport supplanted the traditional culture of games, sports and dance in Africa and it was not long before football captured the imagination of indigenous populations resulting in rapid and mass popularization. Although it is difficult to generalize about the spread of the game in an area that is as geographically vast and ethnically diverse as Africa, it is possible to identity a number of central features of the game's development throughout the continent. Industrialization and associated population transfers and the creation of urban environments had already proved conducive to the diffusion of football throughout many of the other European colonies during the late nineteenth and early twentieth centuries. In Africa, the destruction of traditional agricultural communities and the resultant massive migration into wage labour in the new cities and mining regions that developed during the first four decades of the twentieth century, also proved to be fertile ground for the game's growth. The European education system that was invariably transported to the formal colonies throughout the world was also a feature of late nineteenth- and early twentieth-century African society and it was also instrumental in introducing the game to Africans. Schools were specifically established for the African elite who, in their eagerness for the higher status afforded for cultural imitation of their colonial masters,[7] began to take up soccer. Thus, participation in football in the early part of the twentieth century was largely dependent upon privileged contacts with Europeans and hence, the game developed as a somewhat elitist enterprise.[8]

Opportunities for participation soon became widespread with the game's downward diffusion to local populations. Whilst contact with European settlers, traders and soldiers was important in this respect, the work of the missions was also crucial to the broader dissemination of football and its mass popularization. The self-stated aim of the missionaries in Africa during the colonial period was to civilize indigenous populations by imbuing them with Christian values and beliefs and they viewed European, predominantly British, games as invaluable tools in this respect. This was critical for football's continued diffusion for as long as it was viewed by educators and churchmen as possessing a civilizing and educational function, as well as being a potential recruitment mechanism for the mission schools, then the game would remain central to the missionary impulse in Africa.[9] The view that the provision of constructive, rational leisure opportunities would benefit indigenous African populations was also shared by various colonial administrations and governmental agencies but their motives for promoting the game differed from those of the missionaries. Alongside the belief that it could instil positive character traits in individuals, football had been identified by European, particularly British, social reformers as having a cathartic function and within the context of colonial Africa's crowded, industrialized cities, the game was used for the purpose of minimizing any tendencies towards social disorder. As a consequence, in parts of French Equatorial Africa, the Belgian Congo and Colonial Zimbabwe, for example, the colonial authorities took a more pro-active role in the game's diffusion in the belief that it would help ensure the maintenance of the colonial order.[10]

Although football developed in a relatively unplanned, haphazard fashion in some of the more remote towns and villages, there can be little doubt that within the larger industrial centres, European colonialists utilized their hegemonic position to impose western cultural forms and sports for their own ends. Consequently, Africa's strong cultural heritage, which included deep-rooted sporting traditions, was seriously undermined and in many cases completely destroyed.[11] The subsequent promotion of the game, particularly through the education system, was intimately tied up with the broader imperialist drive to socialize the African population into accepting colonial rule as the norm, thereby facilitating continued economic penetration.[12] However, what is fascinating about the role of football in colonial African society is, although participation in a western sporting form may have imbued sections of the indigenous elite with an appetite for all things European, when the game was gradually diffused downwards to the labouring classes it came to represent a site for opposition and protest against colonial exploitation. Furthermore, during the final two decades of European rule the indigenous elite and intellectuals, disenchanted and frustrated by western imperialism, recognized the potential of football as an instrument for generating resistance to colonialism and promoting nationalist aspirations.[13] However, whilst football served as a key locus for resistance to European imperialism, exploitation and inequality continued to manifest themselves through the game in other ways, not least of which was the expropriation of Africa's most talented football players.

A GENEALOGY OF AFRICAN PLAYER MIGRATION TO EUROPE

As part of the broader acceleration of global flows that have characterized social, political and economic life in the latter part of twentieth century, the transcontinental migration of African footballers to elite European leagues has undergone a period of dramatic expansion. A trawl through the team rosters of those nations competing in the African Nations Cup 2000, co-hosted by Ghana and Nigeria, reveals that of the 352 players who represented their countries in African football's most prestigious international competition, 178, over 50 per cent, ply their trade in Europe.[14] However, this export of African football labour is not a recent phenomenon but rather has a long history that can be traced back to the colonial period. It is not surprising that those European nations whose football leagues currently possess relatively large numbers of African migrant players, such as France, Belgium, Portugal, Germany and increasingly, England, also had a significant imperial presence in Africa (see Figure 1 below).

FIGURE 1
DESTINATION OF AFRICAN MIGRANT FOOTBALLERS (SEASON 1999/2000)[15]

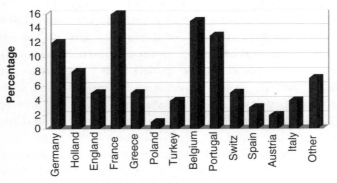

Destination of African Migrant Footballers

The fact that France is currently the most popular destination of African migrant footballers says much about the strength of the link between football migration from Africa to Europe and broader socio-economic processes associated with colonialism. The expropriation of African players to play their domestic and international football in France during the first half of the twentieth century can clearly be interpreted as an extension of France's colonial policy of Gallicization or the assimilation of the local population into the citizenship of the motherland.[16] The proactive encouragement of Africans to compete for the French national football team clearly allowed France to accrue important symbolic capital in the wider international world. For example, by pursuing the naturalization of indigenous football talent in their African colonies, the French were able to maximize the potential for acquiring the sort of national cohesion and prestige that success in international competition is believed to confer upon a nation.

The Moroccan born Larbi Ben Barek started the long tradition of African players representing the French national team and provides the most famous example of this phenomenon in the inter-war period. Ben Barek, widely recognized as the best African player of his generation, hailed from Casablanca and following outstanding performances for his home town club and for Morocco in a friendly game against a French 'B' team, was transferred to Marseille. Distinguished performances for his new club soon propelled him into the French national squad and during the late 1930s and 1940s he was capped 17 times.[17] Ben Barek ended his career with Marseille following four years with the Paris club, Stade Français, and two seasons with Atletico Madrid with whom he won two Spanish league titles.[18] In the post-war period, the goal-scoring feats of Ben Barek's compatriot, Just Fontaine, for France during the 1958 World Cup where he scored a record 13 times, continued the trend of Africans making a significant contribution to the global standing of their colonial 'masters' in the international sporting arena.[19] More recently, the French national team of the mid-1980s, which was renowned for playing its particular brand of 'Champagne football', also owed much to the talents of Africans.[20] The success of the French squad during the 1998 World Cup, which included a number of key players who have national roots in Africa,[21] indicates that France continues to benefit in sporting terms from its former African colonies.

The most obvious example of the tradition of Africans winning for their European 'masters' significant acclaim and status in world football is exemplified in the career of Eusebio da Silva Ferreira. Eusebio, as he came to be known globally, was born in 1942 in Mozambique, which at that time was still under Portuguese colonial rule. Mozambique was recognized by Portugal as a region rich in natural resources and cheap labour not just in the economic sense but also in relation to football. A number of the more prestigious and successful clubs in Portugal viewed the African colonies as a fertile source of football talent and as a result teams such as Sporting Lisbon, Benfica and Porto invested in training facilities and coaching provision in Mozambique and neighbouring Angola. In addition to this, a few nursery teams were established and once indigenous African talent had been identified and nurtured, it was transported into Portuguese league football and also the national side. Bela Guttmann, the veteran Hungarian coach of Benfica, was a strong proponent of this rich vein of talent migration and indeed, the nucleus of the Benfica team he guided to the club's first European Cup success in 1961, was African.[22] It was with Benfica of course that Eusebio first came to global prominence and during his thirteen seasons with the club he helped them win the European Cup on two occasions. His contribution to the Portuguese national team mirrored his efforts on behalf of Benfica and during the 1966 World Cup he inspired Portugal to third place, their highest ever position in the game's premier international tournament.

The naturalization of Africans has continued into the new millennium and at present, there are 70 players who, despite their eligibility to represent an African country have chosen to pursue an international career with a European national team.[23] With the idea of a 'metropolitan France' persisting beyond the colonial era, it is hardly surprising that the French international set-up is currently, and indeed historically, the main beneficiary of this Europeanization, in the strictest sense, of elite African football talent (see Figure 2 below).

In addition to Africans being co-opted to play for the national sides of European countries, there has also been a long tradition of players being drafted into domestic European football. During the colonial era, for example, north Africans were recruited to bolster the strength of French domestic leagues and competitions and by 1938, a total of 147 African footballers were participating in France's first and second divisions.[25] Colonial connections were also exploited by British talent

FIGURE 2
PERCENTAGE OF AFRICANS WHO HAVE CHOSEN TO PURSUE INTERNATIONAL
HONOURS IN EUROPE (SEASON 1999/2000)[24]

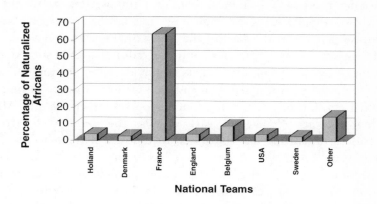

scouts and as early as the inter-war period Egyptian players, such as
Tewfik Abdallah, who played in the English, Scottish and Welsh
leagues, were signed by British clubs. South Africans were also
prominent in British football in the inter-war period and at one time,
Liverpool held the registrations of six such players.[26] African players
continued to settle in Europe in the immediate aftermath of
colonialism and by the mid-1970s there was a steady flow of football
talent to leagues in France and Belgium.[27] For instance, migrant players
from the former French colonies such as the Malian, Salif Keita, Jules
Bocande from Senegal, the Algerian Rabah Madjer and the
Cameroonian duo, Roger Milla and Joseph Antoine Bell, became
particularly prominent in France whereas the Belgian club,
Anderlecht, began its tradition of actively recruiting African talent
during the 1960s and 1970s. The successes and profile of these players
paved the way for further waves of talent migration between the mid-
to late 1970s. However, although there are other instances of Africans
playing their club football in Europe in the twenty years following the
end of imperial activity, it was not until the early 1980s that African
talent began to cross European borders in relatively large numbers.[28]
This trend accelerated significantly during the 1990s and by the

midpoint of the decade the transcontinental migration of African footballers to first and second division European leagues was estimated at more than 350.[29] At the start of the new millennium this figure had reached 770, an increase of over 100 per cent in five years.[30] A further 145 Africans were also playing in the lower reaches of European leagues at the start of the 1999/2000 season.[31]

Processes of naturalization and the administration of African territories by European imperialists largely accounts for the numbers of Africans representing national and club teams in Europe during the colonial era. Despite the collapse of European imperialism in Africa during the late 1950s and early 1960s, the exodus of African footballers to Europe has continued to follow a pattern which, at a superficial level, appears to have its roots in the imperialist connections between the key European powers and their former African colonies. For example, of the 118 Africans currently playing their club football in Portugal, almost 69 per cent hail from the former Portuguese colonies of Angola, Mozambique, Cape Verde and Guinea-Bissau (formerly Portuguese Guinea). A similar pattern emerges from an analysis of the countries of origin of the 162 Africans playing in French leagues with 59 per cent being nationals from the former French territories of Senegal, Cameroon, the Ivory Coast, Algeria and Mali. Africans from those regions of the Congo that were once under Belgian control also constitute the largest grouping of African migrants, currently 31 per cent, within Belgian football. In addition, Nigerians and South Africans make of 62 per cent of African players in England.[32]

These simple correlations reveal that historical and colonial links are still a significant factor in the migrations of African footballers inasmuch as they play a role in determining the destination of many of these players.[33] Indeed, the opportunity of playing in leagues where there are likely to be fewer linguistic and cultural barriers is undoubtedly an important determinant in football migration patterns. However, neo-colonial bonds offer only a partial explanation of a complex process. Hence, in order to more adequately understand the explosive and increasingly diffuse nature of the exodus of African footballers to Europe since the 1980s it is necessary to set this phenomenon within a broader analytical framework.

AFRICAN PLAYER MIGRATION IN THE MODERN ERA:
FIFA POLITICS, IMPROVING STANDARDS AND TALENT
SPECULATORS

The growing profile and status of African national teams in the international arena has undoubtedly been one of the most significant factors in the increasingly rapid flow of football talent from Africa to Europe.[34] The improving levels of performance which have brought individual African players to the attention of European club sides did not occur in an *ad hoc* fashion. Rather they were closely linked to radical political and economic transformation within the Fédération Internationale de Football Association (FIFA). Until the emergence of the Brazilian businessman and former double Olympian, João Havelange, FIFA was a largely European oriented institution with only a passing interest in the development of football in Africa.[35] As part of the election manifesto, which brought him the FIFA presidency in 1974, Havelange promised the Third World that he would take steps to improve their profile within world football's institutional and competition structures. After initiating a series of development programmes aimed at improving the standard of the game in Africa at grassroots level, Havelange took steps to provide a platform upon which the fruits of this work could be displayed. Thus, Africa's representation at the World Cup Finals increased dramatically from one place in 1974 to five places for the most recent edition of the tournament in 1998. In addition, within three years of coming to power Havelange introduced the first of the International Federation's two youth tournaments, the World Youth Championship (under-20) which provided Africans with further opportunities for showcasing their talents on the world stage. The inauguration of an under-17 World Championship in 1985 did likewise and within five years of this tournament's inception the profile of young African football talent had been raised immeasurably.

These developments were augmented by the fact that Havelange had set FIFA's competitions on a course leading them to becoming global media and marketing spectacles which penetrated almost every corner of the globe.[36] Thus, African players playing in any of FIFA's competitions or indeed, high profile African tournaments, could demonstrate their playing prowess to a global audience and thereby increase the likelihood that they would attract the attention of European teams. A curious and unintended by-product of Havelange's efforts to work towards levelling international football standards and developing the game in Africa was the fact that European club sides were awakened to the massive potential which this largely untapped pool of talented players offered. Thus, the World Cup, the World Youth tournaments and even national competitions within Africa, such as the African Nations Cup, were increasingly viewed by European scouts as an opportunity to judge the potential of and purchase recruits from a cheap marketplace.

The success of African teams at world senior level has clearly been a factor in generating the current upsurge in interest in the continent's most talented performers. In each of the last four World Cup competitions, for example, a representative from Africa has reached the later stages[37]. In 1996, Nigeria were crowned Olympic Champions, a feat repeated by Cameroon at the Sydney Games in 2000. The performances of European-based Africans who have not had the opportunity to parade their abilities on the game's most visible international stages has also increased the extent to which the continent is viewed as a rich source of talent. The on-field achievements of the Liberian, George Weah, which brought him the titles of African, European and World footballer of the year in 1995, have been particularly pertinent in this respect. African success at world youth level has also been significant in raising the profile and status of the African game,[38] which in turn has had a huge impact on the rush to secure the services of the continent's most talented young players. For example, in the aftermath of Ghana's triumph in the 1991 FIFA/JVC World U-17 Championship, African Football Management, a recruiting agency run by the Italian Dominic Ricci, succeeded in luring eight members of the squad to Europe. Ricci's involvement in the transfer of three Ghanaian's to the Italian club Torino for a combined fee of US$840,000 led Antonio Matarese, the president of the Italian Football Federation at that time, to declare: 'we will not allow a slave market. Torino has concluded a 'deceitful' transaction. It would be a shame for Italy to give away kids to speculators. We must not plunder in Africa'.[39]

The loss of African football's human resources has worsened during the 1990s due to what can be clearly interpreted as exploitative practices of the increasing numbers of scouts, agents and speculators who, unfettered by the types of regulatory systems operating in Europe, have recognized the trade of African talent as an opportunity for personal financial gain. M. Broere and R. van der Drift comment critically on the activities of the systematic network of agents, particularly from former colonial powers such as Belgium, Portugal and France, who currently work in Africa:

> Africa is the stamping ground for dozens of scouts and player agents. They hope to make a good living out of the trade in African talent and boys as young as 15 or 16 are lured to European clubs. They sign contracts which specify that their agent receives a percentage of their salary and that if they go on to another club he also gets part of the transfer fee. In short, it is a modern form of slavery.[40]

Broere and van der Drift's qualitative research goes on to provide accounts of the experiences of African players who have been financially exploited by unscrupulous emissaries or have suffered in other ways through their involvement with the European recruiting system. For example, an interview with the Nigerian, William Osundu, reveals that he signed a contract with a Dutch agent who claimed 50 per cent of the player's earnings. Jan van Tuijl, the Dutch adviser to the Football Association of Guinea and a representative of Guinean players in Europe, is particularly critical of the contracts drawn up to secure the services of African players. Indeed, his inspection of Guinean players' contracts revealed that half of them were being exploited by both their clubs and agents.[41] Broere and van der Drift's findings as well as the views of van Tuijl are supported by other accounts of contracts which do not give African players their market value and which also appear to be vehicles for maximizing agents' profits. The African journalist, Osasu Obayiuwana, for instance, has provided a detailed account of the exploitation suffered by the Nigerians, Rashidi Rakini and Tijana Babangida, during their time in Portugal and Holland, respectively, as well as the Zimbabwean, Peter Ndlovu, who discovered that the initial financial package he signed with Coventry City placed him amongst the club's worst-paid players.[42]

Despite the evidence provided above, it would be overly deterministic to suggest that African football labour migration is a process initiated and driven solely by European interests or is one in which African players have been duped into signing exploitative contracts. The lure of European football is extremely enticing for African players. Not only is it seen as an opportunity for maximizing earning potential and hence escaping the harsh economic realities of life in many parts of Africa, but it is also seen as a means of supporting the families they leave behind.[43] Consequently, many Africans, particularly those signing their first contract with a European club, are often aware of and are prepared to overlook blatantly irregular financial arrangements in their agreements with agents and clubs. The fact that 'it is almost every aspiring African footballer's dream: to catch the eye of a foreign scout and be called to the riches and glories of the European, professional game' means that many willingly sign exploitative contracts.[44] After all, such contracts are perceived to be stepping stones to more lucrative deals once the players have become established. This is a view articulated by Tijana Babangida, who eventually extricated himself from an indecorous contract with his 'business managers', when playing for the Dutch club, VV Venlo: 'At the start you are always cheated. You don't as yet have an idea what a contract actually implies. You are only too happy that you can make the move to Europe.'[45] This undisguised eagerness to gain a foothold in Europe clearly contributes to the cycle of exploitation faced by African players who aspire to the fame and fortune that success in European football can undoubtedly bring. Until such players acquire more shrewd business advice or acumen, and in the continued absence of a regulatory system, then it is likely that Africa will remain an attractive proposition for European clubs seeking to add cheap recruits to their playing resources.

THE IMPACT OF AFRICAN PLAYER MIGRATION: DEVELOPMENT OR UNDERDEVELOPMENT?

The migration of elite African players is often perceived, predominantly by Europeans, as having a positive impact or contributing to the development of football in Africa. Although it is difficult to define and quantify 'athletic' or 'football' development, superficial indicators can be employed to suggest that African football has benefited from the export of its skilled talent. In terms of playing standards, the popular contention is that the African diaspora in Europe have enhanced their technique, improved their team play and acquired a more disciplined outlook. This in turn is viewed as being beneficial for Africa in international competition because the more efficient, organized and professional approach these players experience in Europe is then passed on to their home-based compatriots and it is this which has helped African nations to progress on the world stage. Nelson Rashava, the South African football journalist, alludes to this view when he suggests that: 'Africa's footballers are scattered across the globe; many regret the diaspora, but most agree that the experience brought back by the overseas-based professionals has been a key element in raising the continent's game.'[46] This hypothesis is also supported by the testimonies of European coaches and European-based Africans as well as the general correlation between the numbers of migrant players signing for clubs in Europe and improved performances at the World Cup. In addition to the impact of migration on playing standards, it can also be posited that the successes and international reputations gained by the most prominent European-based Africans has contributed to football's huge popularity in Africa and subsequently, has had a beneficial impact on the playing resources available to its individual clubs and national teams. At the level of individual migrant players, 'development' cannot only be evidenced in improving playing standards but also in increased wealth and more comfortable lifestyles.

This view of the impact of labour migration on African football is strongly contested within Africa. In general terms, the view of those who have responsibility for safeguarding the interests of the game on the African continent is that, rather than contributing to the development of football, the processes involved in the export of the continent's elite talent serve to underdevelop the game. This occurs on the domestic front by reducing standards of play and hence, attendance, gate receipts and media interest, whilst international teams are often weakened by the difficulties involved in procuring player releases from European clubs.[47] Prominent figures within the Confédération Africaine de Football (CAF) have long regarded the de-skilling of domestic African football by elite European leagues as a phenomenon which has seriously undermined the development of the African game. Ydnekatchew Tessema, the former president of the African confederation (1972–87), was a particularly vociferous critic of the trade in African footballers, spelling out in stark terms the implications of the development of European club football at the expense or impoverishment of the domestic African game, particularly in the last decade:

> African football must make a choice! Either we keep our players in Africa with the will power of reaching one day the top of the international competitions and restore to African people a dignity that they long for; or we let our best elements leave their countries, thus remaining the eternal suppliers of raw material to the

premium countries, and renounce, in this way, to any ambition. When the rich countries take away from us, also by naturalisation, our best elements, we should not expect any chivalrous behaviour on their part to help African football.[48]

Tessema's sentiments have been echoed by the sports historian, Bill Murray, who has argued that the greatest problem currently afflicting the African game is the loss of its best players to countries (predominantly European) where they are better paid.[49] Further support for viewing football migration as a form of underdevelopment has also been provided by African journalists and historians. For example, Issac Olu Akindutire, a Nigerian historian, cites the drift of Nigerian players to foreign countries as a major debilitating factor for Nigerian football[50] whereas the Ghanaian sports journalist, Joe Aggrey, contends that: 'The exodus of players from Ghana to seek greener pastures has meant that it is nearly impossible to build any meaningful national team from the home-based stars.'[51]

As a result of these and other long-standing concerns, CAF has attempted to implement regulations and systems aimed at restricting the player exodus. For example, in 1965, the African confederation introduced a rule preventing African national teams from playing more than two overseas-based players. This idea, originally introduced to encourage the development of the African game and persuade players to remain in domestic leagues rather than move to Europe, resulted in much controversy and did little to prevent players from migrating to Europe. It thus appeared that African players were prepared to forgo the opportunity of representing their countries in prestigious tournaments such as the African Cup of Nations in order to pursue more financially rewarding careers in Europe. However, as African teams then had to pick from a weakened pool of players for international competition, the rule was eventually rescinded in 1982.[52]

The most recent attempt to limit the talent drain was the inception of the African Champions League in 1997. The Champions League, modelled on its European equivalent, is aimed at not only providing top-level club competition but also creating the administrative structures and economic incentives necessary to encourage players to remain with African clubs.[53] Mustapha Fahmy, CAF's general secretary, elaborates on the rationale underpinning the Champions League by stating that the competition is intended, in part, to 'reinforce the clubs of Africa in order to allow them to put an end to the exodus of our best football talents and allow them to play under better circumstances on African soil'.[54] A number of African national associations have gone a stage further in their attempts to limit the talent drain or at least minimize its more exploitative features. Recently, the football federations of both South Africa and Nigeria, viewed in Europe as a rich source of raw talent, introduced measures which now require clubs to put up a US$250,000 bond if they wish to sign native players. The rationale behind this move is to make it less attractive for European clubs to speculate on the potential of young players who are relatively unproven. These players will instead be able to continue their football development in Africa and contribute to the domestic game.[55]

Despite strong political rhetoric and the imposition of measures aimed at checking talent migration, CAF has been relatively powerless to prevent individuals from accepting approaches from speculators and club officials. However, the concerns of African football's most influential administrators have recently been echoed in the higher echelons of the world governing body. For example, in an editorial in *African Soccer*, the FIFA president, Sepp Blatter, wrote of the need to regulate the export of Africa's young football talent and encouraged those nations which benefited most from the trade in African players to display a sense of solidarity towards their Third World counterparts. Blatter elaborated on this: 'Solidarity means giving the weak the opportunity to grow and develop, rather than exploiting them and plundering their limited resources.'[56]

Blatter's intervention in African football's struggle to regulate talent migration has recently moved beyond political advocacy. During a visit to Ghana in late January 2000, Blatter revealed his determination to introduce measures aimed at eradicating the exploitative export of young players from Third World countries. At a press conference which he shared with Issa Hayatou, the current CAF president, Blatter intimated that FIFA recognizes the extent of the problem and its negative consequences for the African game and suggested the introduction of an age limit for the transfer of young players which would help alleviate the most damaging aspects of the talent drain. He said, 'It is time to fight against the exodus of young players from Africa. We have studied this problem and are working on a solution. It [the solution] is about creating an age before which a player cannot be transferred.'[57] Crucially, the FIFA president also addressed the question of compensation for African clubs which had invested in the nurturing of young African players only to see them being sold on for hugely inflated fees by European clubs. He therefore concluded that FIFA intended to introduce a system that would allow a player's original club to receive a percentage of future transfers.[58]

It remains to be seen whether FIFA's proposed intervention in and plans for the regulation of African player migration will be effective. CAF has welcomed Blatter's comments and believes that if the systems that have been advocated are implemented, then the extent to which European football de-skills the domestic African game will be restricted. However, despite the FIFA president's commitment to regulate the export of elite football talent from African clubs, a number of European sides have begun to establish a system of recruitment which will circumvent any imposed statutory regulation. In recent years, a range of academies and training schools have been established by European clubs in Africa and although the continent's emerging talent has undoubtedly benefited from European technical expertise and materials, there are growing concerns that the motivations underpinning these 'nurseries' are less than altruistic. Indeed, during his press conference in Ghana, Blatter voiced serious concerns over this relatively new dimension of football labour migration. His worry, like that of CAF and the individual national associations, was that European clubs would simply use their academies as vehicles for talent identification and recruitment. At the same time as calling for the provision of opportunities for all African players to, at least, start their career in domestic leagues, Blatter argued that those clubs that have formed training schools should 'not just show up, take the best players, not let anyone have them and take them off to Europe'.[59]

The trend of establishing systems for nurturing young talent in Africa has been taken a stage further by the Dutch club, Ajax Amsterdam, which has a long tradition of recruiting African players. During 1999, they were involved in negotiations which gave them a 51 per cent controlling stake in the South African club, Cape Town Spurs, subsequently renamed Ajax Cape Town. Similar to the establishment of academies there are real concerns that arrangements such as these will soon multiply and function as nothing more than a front for the systematic de-skilling of the domestic African game. Issa Hayatou expressed his reservations about mergers between African and European clubs in the following terms:

> It is a terrible thing, but once again, CAF cannot do anything. It is

the responsibility of the national federations to come up with some kind of legislation to regulate this process. CAF cannot intervene in this matter, but we could advise them to avoid the exploitation of African talents to enrich the football of the countries above our continent.[60]

It is possible to interpret football labour migration from Africa to Europe as a process contributing to both the development and underdevelopment of the African game. The 'development thesis' is promulgated primarily by those who have a vested interest in the preservation of the current flow of football talent between the two continents whilst the latter view is put forward by those who wish to see an end to the trade in African talent. However, the two conditions should not be viewed as mutually exclusive or oppositional.[61] By drawing on the work of the dependency theorist, Andre Gunder Frank, development and underdevelopment can certainly be viewed as 'two sides of the same coin'.[62] The debate surrounding the impact of football labour migration on Africa reveals that the football world can be represented systematically as a contested brokerage within which clusters of clubs, national federations and intercontinental confederations are interdependent and compete for the game's natural resources or raw materials. This idea has drawn the author to economic models of globalization and development as a basis for constructing a theoretical framework within which to locate African football labour migration to Europe.

THEORIZING AFRICAN PLAYER MIGRATION

It was suggested earlier that sports labour migration is intimately linked to the broader globalization of social life. Consequently, drawing upon explanations of globalization and global societal development can enrich any analysis of the processes at work in the migration of football talent between Africa and Europe. In particular, the author is drawn to three perspectives: imperialism and neo-imperialism; dependency; and world system theory. Immanuel Wallerstein's world system theory is one of the most prominent and perhaps most insightful attempts to theorize the functioning and dynamics of the global system. According to Wallerstein, a world system of commerce and communication has developed from the sixteenth century, resulting in a plethora of political, economic and social networks and connections across the globe and in turn, the development of a world economy. He argues that the world coheres around four interdependent sectors whose position vis-à-vis the global capitalist economy have all been determined through combinations of colonial history and economic power. These sectors include: the core (north-west Europe, North America and Japan); the semi-periphery (southern Europe and the Mediterranean region); the periphery (Eastern Europe, North Africa and parts of Asia); and the external arena (most of Africa, parts of Asia and the Indian sub-continent) which, given the advance of colonialism and transnational corporate activity, can now be classified as being peripheral.[63]

The conceptual language drawn upon within Wallerstein's analyses can be used as a general framework within which to locate the dynamics of football labour migration and situate the relationship between the donor and recipient countries. In keeping with Wallerstein's thinking, a 'world-system' in respect of international football has been developing since the late nineteenth and early twentieth centuries. This system has emerged from the rapid increase in global playing contacts, institutional and political relationships, the growing economic significance of world football as well as the dynamic movement of players around the globe.[64] In order to understand the way in which nations or regions within this system relate to one another politically, economically, culturally and in terms of sports labour migration flows, it is useful to draw upon the core-periphery thrust of world system theory. Based on an insightful study commissioned by FIFA in 1996, and carried out by the Zürich based consultancy firm, LSSFB (Lamprecht and Stamm, Sozialforschung und Beratung), it is possible, using the indicators of football tradition and economic strength, to classify Europe as a core region within football's 'world system' whereas Africa can generally be categorized as peripheral.[65] The fact that Africa is currently one of the main donors of football labour whilst Europe has become the main destination for migrant players lends further support to this notion of UEFA as core and CAF as peripheral.[66]

In terms of the nature of interaction or links between sectors of the world system, Wallerstein argues that peripheral regions are enmeshed in a dependency relationship with the core countries. He also postulates that the core areas, given their dominance of the world economy, are able to exploit and impoverish the underdeveloped periphery by organizing world trade to favour their own interests. The flow of skilled sports talent from Africa to Europe correlates with this idea of hierarchical dependency and exploitation within the world system. As demonstrated in this chapter, the machinations that occur within the football world in respect of the migration of players from peripheral regions can clearly be seen to favour the interests of core nations whilst at the same time acting to exploit the game's less developed constituents. Furthermore, European football is also able to dictate the economic terms of this trade because of the desire on the part of players to sign for clubs in Europe.

African football may be closing the gap between itself and Europe in terms of international performances and in relation to its political profile and influence within FIFA. Nevertheless, the core–periphery thrust of Wallerstein's work and its application to Afro-European relations within world football clearly retain analytical utility. Despite the significant advances of African football, it is difficult to avoid the conclusion that the relationship between the first world and Third World soccer nations is lopsided and nowhere is this more apparent than in patterns of football migration. World system theory, therefore, represents an appropriate starting point for understanding African football labour migration and some of the analytical concepts and terms utilized within this framework including core–periphery exploitation, dependency and dominance provide clues as to the location of a more penetrating theorization.

It has been shown in this chapter that the diffusion of football to Africa reflects aspects of imperialism. FIFA's subsequent brokerage of an African constituency for the world game can also be explained by drawing upon notions of imperialism.[67] Likewise, the relationship between Africa and Europe as mediated through the flow of football migrants also bears broad similarities to the type of imperialism described by Lenin and subsequent theorists of neo-imperialism such as B. Warren. The expropriation of Africans by wealthy European clubs can be interpreted as an extension of the economic imperialism of the post-colonial period during which first world development has been sustained by exploitation of other parts of the world.[68] This chapter has discussed how European football concerns drew upon colonial links to source raw materials and cheap labour. It has also been shown that this trend of hegemonic nations utilizing their privileged position to exploit underdeveloped football regions has continued unabated in the post-colonial era and is in many ways akin to broader neo-colonial exploitation. This is certainly the view of Hayatou who has articulated

his concerns over the impact of player migration on African football in
the statement:

> After the flight of brains Africa is confronted with the muscle
> exodus. The rich countries import the raw material – talent – and
> they often send to the continent their less valuable technicians.
> The inequality of the exchange terms is indisputable. It creates a
> situation of dependence ... The elite of African football is out of
> the continent [*sic*], hence the pauperisation of some clubs and
> whose evil effect is the net decrease of the game quality and of the
> level of most of the national championships. Prestigious clubs are
> regularly deprived of their best elements and even the juniors
> cannot escape the voracity of the recruiting agents, who profit from
> the venality of their leaders.[69]

Whereas notions of imperialism and neo–imperialism can be used to
provide insights into the exploitative nature of the trade in football
labour between Europe and Africa, the idea of dependency, alluded to
above by Hayatou, represents a more dynamic and detailed framework
for interpreting the consequences of this labour exchange. Indeed the
dependency paradigm, most definitely, is one of the most influential
approaches employed by those who have sought to explain sport
migration.[70] Developing from the work of a group of Latin American
economists, dependency theorists set out specifically to analyse the
nature and causes of the developmental gap between rich and poor
countries and to determine the forms of dependency between these
regions. Although there is a general consensus within the tradition that
global societal development has been uneven and the main core of the
industrialized world has assumed a dominant role with the Third World
dependent upon it,[71] there are a number of strands which differ with
regard to how the causes, nature and manifestations of dependency are
explained. These have been termed: dependent underdevelopment;
dependent development; and dependency reversal.

The notions of dependent development and dependency reversal are
the most recent perspectives to be promoted within this tradition and
they emerged as a response to pockets of development in selected
regions of the Third World. The former approach acknowledges
economic and social growth, albeit limited, in some Third World
countries but argues that this development is based almost entirely upon
its linkages with the first world. The latter approach goes a step further

and suggests that certain Third World countries or regions could actually escape from the confines of the dependency relationship and reverse their position in relation to sectors of the developed world. It can be argued that football development in Africa has occurred as a result of its dependent relationship with Europe, on the other hand it is difficult to see how the dependency reversal approach could realistically be employed to analyse football labour migration between the two continents.

A more fruitful path to follow when drawing upon the dependency paradigm as a way of explaining football migration would be to utilize the work of the economist, Andre Gunder Frank.[72] Frank was largely responsible for the dependent underdevelopment thesis, which argues that the global capitalist system, dominated by the core industrialized states, is the prime mover in the underdevelopment of the Third World. Furthermore, as long as this system of exploitation remains, sustained development within the Third World is unrealistic. The central thread of this version of dependency, that the first world develops and prospers through the underdevelopment of the Third World, in many ways encapsulates the nature of the processes at work during the course of sports migration from Africa to Europe. Core nations of the West are clearly in a position to dominate the global football industry and actively underdevelop the sports industry of the periphery. FIFA's political history, specifically the attempts of the world games' established European constituency to exclude the Third World from the centre of political and economic decision making, is particularly revealing in this respect.[73] However, as this study reveals, it is the context of the de-skilling of African football on terms and conditions set by recruiting European clubs, that one of the clearest examples of dependent underdevelopment in the international sporting arena is observed.[74]

The employment of the dependent underdevelopment thesis allows African football labour migration to be understood as part of the broader economic and political relationship between the donor and recipient countries. However, it should be recognized that explanations of sports migration also need to take into consideration internal factors of the exporting countries which may contribute to the exodus of its sporting talent. It has been highlighted earlier that human agency and the 'pull' of economic reward are significant factors in the migration of African players. Whilst the commodification of football in Europe during the last two decades has generated a pool of wealth capable of satisfying Africans' financial aspirations, the stunted financial development of football in Africa has acted as a motivational factor to 'push' players from its domestic game. Indeed, the ability of African clubs, officials and administrators to hold on to elite talent is seriously hampered by the atrocious financial state of the African game. Sir Bobby Charlton, an ex-England international, has been involved in a number of development programmes in the Third World and has highlighted the impact of the weak African economy in relation to player migration: 'The only problem with African football is money. Just that one word. It is their downfall because they don't have enough of it. And because of that, their best players leave home to play in Europe.'[75]

Extreme poverty is the most serious obstacle to the development of football in Africa, but the extent to which this contributes to player migration is augmented by the almost endemic presence of corruption and maladministration within the game on that continent.[76] Given the fact that dependency relations are often strengthened by internal phenomena inherent within the periphery,[77] it seems certain that for as long as this situation continues and in the absence of an international regulatory system for football migration, Africa will continue to lose its most talented footballers to Europe.

CONCLUSION

African football has entered a crucial phase in its development. It has acquired credibility and status within the game's administrative structures and competitions. However, if the dramatic advances made in the international arena are to be reflected in the domestic African game, then that continent's regional administrators and national federations must take steps to regulate, if not work towards a cessation of, the export of its most talented players to Europe. In order to achieve this, a self-sustaining development dynamic must be initiated within the African game. The sizeable financial subsidies currently being invested in all national associations by FIFA will certainly help in this respect, provided, of course, that unscrupulous administrators or officials do not siphon off the money. The creation of the type of professional and commercial culture surrounding, for example, European football is also crucial. The formation of the CAF Champions League is a step in this direction and may make the harsh economic climate within which

African football functions, less problematic. However, it remains to be seen whether an improved financial infrastructure would allow football in Africa to float free of the wider socio-economic and political context in which it is situated. For as long as the continent continues to reside in the periphery of the world capitalist economy it looks certain that it will remain enmeshed in a dependency relationship not only in economic terms but also within the global football industry.

NOTES

1. J. Maguire and J. Bale, 'Introduction: Sports Labour Migration in the Global Arena', in J. Bale and J. Maguire (eds.), *The Global Sports Arena: Athletic Talent Migration in an Interdependent World* (London and Portland, OR: Frank Cass, 1994), p.5.
2. R. Robertson, 'Globalisation and Societal Modernisation: A Note on Japan and Japanese Religion', *Sociological Analysis*, 47, 5 (1987), 38.
3. B. Houlihan, *Sport and International Politics* (Hemel Hempstead: Harvester Wheatsheaf, 1994), p.173.
4. This is borrowed from Giddens's work on what he describes as 'time-space distantation'. See A. Giddens, *Sociology* (Oxford: Polity Press, 1989), and A. Giddens, *The Consequences of Modernity* (Oxford: Polity Press, 1990). See also G. Jarvie and J. Maguire, *Sport and Leisure in Social Thought* (London: Routledge, 1994), p.231.
5. See for example the seminal collection by Bale and Maguire, *The Global Sports Arena*.
6. See J. Maguire and J. Bale 'Postscript: An Agenda for Research on Sports Labour Migration', in Bale and Maguire (eds.), *The Global Sports Arena*, pp.281–4. See also J. Maguire, *Global Sport: Identities, Societies, Civilisations* (Oxford: Polity, 1999), p.101. Here Maguire makes reference to the dearth of research on the migration of African footballers and stresses the need to explore this neglected area. It should also be noted that the author is following up on the issues raised in this chapter and is currently undertaking qualitative research in collaboration with Dr Jonathan Magee (University of Wales Institute, Cardiff) on the experiences and labour rights of African migrant players in the English Premier league. Again, this is an area of sports labour migration that has not yet been explored in any detail (this point is made explicitly by J. Maguire and B. Pearton, 'Global Sport and the Migration Patterns of France '98 World Cup Finals Players: Some Preliminary Observations', in J. Garland, D. Malcolm and M. Rowe (eds.), *The Future of Football: Challenges for the Twenty-First Century* (London and Portland, OR: Frank Cass, 2000), pp.175–89. Collaborative research with Dr Peter Alegi (Harvard University) exploring the impact of migraation on African styles of play is also being undertaken.
7. For an account of the cultural dependence created by the colonial education system, see A. Mazrui and M. Tidy, *Nationalism and New States in Africa* (Oxford: Clio Press, 1982), pp.40–3.
8. O. Stuart, 'The Lions Stir: Football in African Society', in S. Wagg (ed), *Giving the Game Away: Football, Politics and Culture on Five Continents* (London and New York: Leicester University Press, 1995), pp.27–8.
9. See Stuart, 'The Lions Stir' for a general discussion of the role of the missionaries in the spread of football. For a specific example of the importance attached to football by missionaries see J.A. Mangan, *The Games Ethic and Imperialism: Aspects of the Diffusion of an Ideal* (London: Frank Cass, 1998), pp.176–7. Here Mangan illustrates the centrality of football to the missionary work of A.G. Fraser who viewed the game as fundamental to the spread of the

Christian message in King's School, Budo in Uganda and later Achimota College in the Gold Coast.

10. P. Darby, 'Football, Colonial Doctrine and Indigenous Resistance: Mapping the Political Persona of FIFA's African Constituency', *Culture, Sport, Society*, 3, 1 (2000), 61–87.

11. For specific examples of Africa's pre-colonial sporting traditions and the role of sport in Africa prior to European intervention, see W. Baker and J.A. Mangan, *Sport in Africa: Essays in Social History* (New York and London: Africana Publishing Company, 1987). Also K. Heinemann, 'Sport in Developing Countries', in E.D. Dunning, J. Maguire, and R.E Pearton (eds.), *The Sports Process* (Champaign IL: Human Kinetics, 1993), p.144, asserts that the traditional culture of games, sports and dance in many developing countries was forcefully suppressed by the missionaries and colonial administration which regarded aspects of this culture as immoral. He goes on to argue that the spread of European sport further advanced the destruction of traditional cultural forms. H.N. Ndee, 'Sport, Culture and Society from an African Perspective: A Study in Historical Revisionism', *International Journal of the History of Sport*, 13, 2 (1996), 199, supports this view by providing empirical evidence relating to the encouragement of 'civilized' games at the expense of indigenous physical activities, particularly local dance. Further support for this position is lent by R.C. Uweche, 'Nation Building and Sport in Africa', in B. Lowe, D. Kanin and A. Strenk (eds.), *Sport and International Relations* (Champaign IL: Stipes Publishing Company), p.540, who highlights the case of the Suk, Masai and Turkana tribes in East Africa which had elements of their traditional sporting culture proscribed because it was perceived to be disruptive of colonial administration.

12. T. Monnington, 'The Politics of Black African Sport', in L. Allison (ed.), *The Politics of Sport* (Manchester: Manchester University Press, 1986), p.153. See also Uweche, 'Nation Building and Sport in Africa', p.540.

13. Darby, 'Colonial Doctrine and Indigenous Resistance'.

14. Figures obtained from official team lists released by CAF.

15. Raw Data obtained from F.M. Ricci (ed), *African Football: Yearbook 2000*, 3rd ed. (Rome: ProSports, 2000). It should be noted that the dynamic nature of the football transfer market is such that these figures are likely to have altered for the 2000/2001 season.

16. For a discussion of the policy of Gallicization see R.V. Albertini, *European Colonial Rule, 1880–1940: The Impact of the West on India, Southeast Asia and Africa* (Oxford: Clio Press, 1982).

17. A. Versi, *Football in Africa* (London: Collins, 1986), p.41.

18. African Soccer Obituary, 'Death of a Star: Larbi Ben Barek', *African Soccer*, 1 (Dec-Feb. 1992/93), 22.

19. K. Radnege, *The Complete Encyclopaedia of Football* (London: Colour Library Direct, 1998), p.433. Fontaine also played for Nice in the French first division and had a brief spell as national manager. His record of 13 goals in a single edition of the World Cup Finals still stands.

20. As the French ethnologist, Christian Bromberger, points out, the French team which played Yugoslavia in December 1985 contained the Algerian born, Ayache and the Malian immigrants, Tigana and Touré. C. Bromberger, 'Foreign Footballers, Cultural Dreams and Community Identity in some North-western Mediterranean Cities', in Bale and Maguire, *The Global Sports Arena*, p.173.

21. For example, Marcel Desailly, France's most consistent defender during the tournament, was born in Ghana whilst Zinedine Zidane, scorer of two goals in the 3–0 victory over Brazil in the final, is of Algerian descent.

22. The African players in the victorious Benfica side of 1961 were as follows: goalkeeper Costa Pereira; centre forward and captain Jose Aguas; and inside forwards Joaquim Santana and Mario Coluna. Most of these players also played in Benfica's three other European Cup Final appearances between the 1960/61 and 1964/65 seasons.

23. Data obtained from Ricci, *African Football: Yearbook 2000*, p.303.

24. Raw data from Ricci, *African Football: Yearbook 2000*.

25. B. Murray, *Football: A History of the World Game* (Aldershot: Scolar Press, 1995).

26. M. Taylor, 'Through the Net', *When Saturday Comes* (Feb. 2000), 27–8. It is also worth noting that during the 1950s Charlton Athletic F.C. from London also recruited a relatively large number of South Africans whilst the English national team benefited from the talents of Bill Perry, Brian Stein and Colin Viljoen, all of whom were African born. Amateur clubs in Britain also benefited from the acquisition of African players during the 1950s. For example, a number of players who represented a Nigerian team that toured Britain in 1949 were signed by English clubs. Tesilimi Balogoun signed for the Midlands league club, Peterborough United whilst his teammate and captain of the touring side, Etim Henshaw signed for Cardiff Corinthians. P. Vasili, 'Colonialism and Football: The First Nigerian Tour to Britain', *Race and Class*, 36, 4 (1995), 55–70.

27. See M. Broere and R. van der Drift, *Football Africa!* (Oxford: Worldview Publishing, 1997), pp.83–5.

28. This contention is evidenced by the fact that it was not until the 1982 World Cup in Spain that Africa's representative(s) in the tournament possessed players who played their club football in Europe. The Egyptian (1934), Moroccan (1970), Zairian (1974) and Tunisian (1978) national teams did not include any European-based players. This is contrasted sharply with what happened at subsequent World Cups: 1982, Algeria – 7 players, Cameroon – 4 players; 1986, Algeria – 10 players, Morocco – 4 players; 1990, Cameroon – 9 players, Egypt – 3 players; 1994, Cameroon – 9 players, Morocco – 9 players, Nigeria – 17 players; 1998, Cameroon – 16 players, Morocco – 15 players, Nigeria – 20 players, South Africa – 14 players, Tunisia – 4 players. Statistics gleaned from Ricci, *African Football: Yearbook 2000*.

29. M. Gleeson, 'The African Invasion', *Kick-Off: African Cup of Nations 1996 Fans Guide* (January 1996), p.106.

30. Ricci, *African Football: Yearbook 2000*.

31. Ibid.

32. It should be noted here that although South Africans and Nigerians constitute the main groupings of African migrant players in the British leagues, Britain appears to be the exception in terms of African migrant patterns in Europe. Although the number of Africans playing their club football in Britain has dramatically increased during the last two seasons, British leagues still have a relatively small number of Africans in comparison with French, Belgian, Portuguese and even German domestic football. This is predominantly because of the regulations surrounding applications for work permits that are required for non-European Union nationals wishing to play in Britain. To qualify for a work permit, African footballers must be current internationals that have appeared in at least 75 per cent of their countries competitive matches in the last two seasons. There is also the possibility of future restrictions on African talent migration to British clubs given the current debate on limiting the numbers of foreign players. For example, UEFA is, at present, looking at proposals to limit the numbers of foreign players in the starting 11 to five. It has also been suggested that stereotypical attitudes regarding the abilities of African footballers, particularly the belief that Africans are not suited to the physical rigours of the British game place further restrictions on their movement into Britain. See A.S. Duncan, 'Hope and Glory: Africans in England', *African Soccer*, 38 (Dec. 1998), 6–9.

33. The impact of historical and colonial links in determining the destinations of migrant footballers is also cited as a contributory factor by Maguire and Pearton, 'Global Sport and Migration Patterns of France '98, pp.175–89.

34. Performance in international competition has been recognized by other academics as a crucial factor in determining the extent to which a particular country or region becomes a donor of football labour. For example, R.L. Jones and R. Chappell, 'The Continued Rise of the Global Sport-Media Complex as Reflected in Elite Soccer Migration Patterns' (unpublished paper, Brunel University College), have argued that the prominence of players from Ireland,

Denmark, Sweden and Norway in top flight British football during the 1980s and 1990s can be partially explained through the attainments of these nations in senior international competition.

35. See P. Darby, *Africa, Football and FIFA: Politics, Colonialism and Resistance* (London and Portland, OR: Frank Cass, forthcoming).

36. For a detailed analysis of Havelange's role in establishing FIFA's contemporary political economy see J. Sugden and A. Tomlinson, *FIFA and the Contest for World Football: Who Rules the Peoples' Game?* (Cambridge: Polity Press, 1998).

37. Morocco reached the last 16 in 1986, Nigeria did likewise in 1994 and 1998 whereas Cameroon were narrowly defeated by England 3–2 in the quarter-finals of the competition in 1990.

38. Africa's record in the World Youth Cup (under-20) is as follows: USSR 1985 – Bronze medal for Nigeria; Saudi Arabia 1989 – Silver medal for Nigeria; Australia 1993 – Silver medal for Ghana; Nigeria 1999 – Bronze medal for Mali. African performances in the under 17 World Youth Championships reads: China 1985 – Gold Medal for Nigeria; Canada 1987 – Silver medal for Nigeria; Italy 1991 – Gold medal for Ghana; Japan 1993 – Gold medal for Nigeria, Silver for Ghana; Ecuador 1995 – Gold medal for Ghana; Egypt 1997; Ghana – Silver medal; New Zealand 1999 – Bronze medal for Ghana.

39. Cited in F. Mahjoub, 'The Exodus: A Savage Market', in F. Mahjoub (ed.), *Confédération Africaine de Football: 1957–1997* (Cairo: Nubar Printing House, 1997), p.133.

40. Broere and van der Drift, *Football Africa!, p.*79.

41. Ibid., pp.79–91.

42. O. Obayiuwana, 'Passport to Success?', *When Saturday Comes*, 109 (March 1996), 37–8.

43. Broere and van der Drift, *Football Africa!*, pp.117–24, provide evidence which illustrates that the tightly knit nature of the family unit in many African countries is such that most expatriate African footballers conscientiously fulfil what they perceive to be their obligation to contribute financially to the upkeep of their family.

44. M. Gleeson, 'The Professionals: Africans in Europe', *African Soccer* (Sept/Oct. 1995), 28.

45. Cited in Broere and van der Drift, *Football Africa!*, pp.84–5. Babangida's general point is reinforced by Emmanuel Maradas who has argued that players willingly accept poor contracts in the first instance, hoping that once proven in a European league they will increase their earning power.

46. N. Rashava, 'Foreign Legion on the March', *African Soccer*, 8 (Oct/Dec. 1994), 36.

47. FIFA had attempted to ensure that the interests of a player's national team are given precedence over clubs by introducing a rule whereby players must be released for international duty. However, very often clubs place pressure on players to remain with them rather than travel vast distances to play for their countries in what are perceived in some European circles as 'meaningless' matches and tournaments. The African Nations Cup is a case in point. The timing of the tournament has long been an issue with European clubs because it is played in early February when most European leagues have just passed the midway stage. This has caused problems for African players and their respective national sides in terms of preparation for the tournament. The dispute between the British side, Arsenal and the Nigerian F.A. over the release of Nwanko Kanu is particularly revealing in this respect. See Agence France-Press, *African Nations Cup: No Shuttles to Arsenal for Kanu* (Agence-France Press, 17 January 2000).

48. Cited in F. Mahjoub, 'Ydnekatchew Tessema: The Match of His Life', in Mahjoub, *Confédération Africaine de Football*, p.155.

49. Murray, *Football: A History of the World Game,* p.235.

50. I.O. Akindutire, 'The Historical Development of Soccer in Nigeria: An Appraisal of its Emerging Prospects', *Canadian Journal of the History of Sport*, XXII, 1 (1991), 20–31.

51. J. Aggrey, 'Ghana', *Kick-Off: African Nations Cup Fan's Guide* (Jan. 1996).

52. Radnege, *The Complete Encyclopaedia of Football*, p.109.

53. F. Ahlstrom, 'Interview with Issa Hayatou – President of CAF', *The Meridian Cup Report*

(Nyon: UEFA Press Department, 1997), pp.5–8.

54. M. Fahmy, 'Editorial', *CAF News*, 60 (Jan. 1997), 1.

55. Al-Ahram Weekly, 'The Flight of Africa's Best', *Al-Ahram Weekly*, 467, 3–9 (Feb. 2000).

56. S. Blatter, 'Message from the FIFA President', *African Soccer*, 51 (Jan. 2000), 5.

57. Blatter cited in B. Homewood, 'FIFA President Wants Minimum Transfer Age', *Reuters News Service*, 25 Jan. 2000.

58. Panafrican News Agency, 'FIFA to Set Age Limit for Player Transfer' 22 Jan. 2000.

59. Blatter cited in Homewood, 'FIFA President Wants Minimum Transfer Age'.

60. Interview with Issa Hayatou, *Soccer Africa* (Oct. 1999).

61. See also J. Bale and J. Sang, *Kenyan Running: Movement Culture, Geography and Global Change* (London and Portland, OR: Frank Cass, 1996), pp.163–75. Here, Bale and Sang interpret the prominence of athletics and the performances of Kenyan runners as a process involving both the development and underdevelopment of the Kenyan movement culture. J.L. Arbena, 'Dimensions of International Talent Migration in Latin American Sports', in Bale and Maguire, *The Global Sports Arena*, pp.103–5, provides evidence to demonstrate that discourses around the issue of football labour migration from Latin America to Europe explain this process in terms of both development and underdevelopment.

62. A.G. Frank, *Capitalism and Under-Development in Latin America* (New York: Monthly Review Press, 1969), p.4.

63. I. Wallerstein, *The Modern World System* (New York: Academic Press, 1974); I. Wallerstein, *The Capitalist World Economy* (Cambridge: Cambridge University Press, 1979). Wallerstein argues that this has been achieved through the core nations' capacity to organize world trade to favour their economic interests.

64. P. Darby, 'Theorising World Football Politics: FIFA, Dependency and World System Theory, *Scottish Centre Research Papers in Sport, Leisure and Society*, 1, 2 (1997), 103.

65. M. Schneider, 'Factors Governing Success in International Football: Tradition, Wealth and Size – Or is There More To it?', *FIFA Magazine* (Aug. 1996), 7–11. See also P. Darby, 'Africa's Place in FIFA's Global Order: A Theoretical Frame', *Soccer and Society*, 1, 2 (2000), 36–61. This article expands on Lamprecht and Stamm's research and also highlights some of the challenges involved in attempting to locate a football nation or region within Wallerstein's economic typology.

66. Research undertaken by Maguire and Pearton on the global migration patterns of those players who took part in in the 1998 World Cup lends further support to this idea of Europe as constituting the apex of a football world system and Africa as being rooted in its margins. Their data reveals that UEFA attracted most players from other countries' playing in the World Cup (122 in total) whilst Africa not only attracted no players from other football regions but was one of the main exporters of talent. See Maguire and Pearton, 'Global Sport and the Migration Patterns of France '98 World Cup Finals Players'.

67. Darby, *Africa, Football and FIFA*. See also Darby, *Football, Colonial Doctrine and Indigenous Resistance.*

68. This point is supported in general terms by the work of Jarvie and Maguire who have argued that the de-skilling of periphery states by the western core is conducted in an exploitative fashion which results in the creation of a position of dependent trading for peripheral regions. G. Jarvie and J. Maguire, *Sport and Leisure in Social Thought* (London and New York: Routledge, 1994), p.249.

69. Cited in CAF, 'The Importance of Football for the African Countries', *CAF News*, 64 (April 1998), 37. Hayatou was speaking at a symposium in March 1998, organized by the Institute of International and Strategic Relations on the theme of 'Football and International Relations'.

70. See the articles by Arbena, Klein, Bale and Maguire and Bale and Sang in Bale and Maguire (eds.), *The Global Sports Arena*. See also P. McGovern, '"Across the Water": The Initial Recruitment of Irish Soccer Players by English Clubs' (paper presented to the British

Sociological Association Conference 1996, Worlds of the Future: Ethnicity, Nationalism and Globalisation, 1–4 April 1996, University of Reading).

71. See the reviews of dependency literature in Jarvie and Maguire, *Sport and Leisure in Social Thought*, Bale and Maguire, *The Global Sports Arena*, and L. Sklair, *The Sociology of the Global System* (Hemel Hempstead: Harvester Wheatsheaf, 1991).

72. Frank, *Capitalism and Under-development in Latin America.*

73. Darby, *Africa, Football and FIFA.*

74. For further evidence of the extent of African dependency on Europe specifically in terms of global migration patterns see Maguire and Pearton, 'Global Sport and Migration Patterns of France '98', pp.184–5. Here the authors present data revealing the destination of those overseas-based Africans playing in the 1998 World Cup was overwhelmingly to European countries. Indeed, only four per cent of the migrant African players played outside Europe.

75. Cited in the *Independent*, 11 Jan. 1992, 46.

76. For a fuller discussion see, Darby, *Africa's Place in FIFA's Global Order*; Sugden and Tomlinson, *FIFA and the Contest for World Football.*

77. R. Prebisch, 'Dependence, Development and Interdependence', in G. Ranis and T., P. Schultz (eds.), *The State of Development Economics: Progress and Perspectives* (London: Basil Blackwell, 1998), p.31.

For World Footballing Honours:
England versus Italy, 1933, 1934 and 1939

PETER J. BECK

Journalistic hyperbole ensures that every decade, even every year, has its own 'match of the century'. During the 1930s, the three matches played by England and Italy attracted this descriptor, or a variant thereof, by journalists previewing what were perceived as major tests of global footballing strength or looking back on what had proved distinctive sporting experiences. Indeed, in many respects they came to be presented as a kind of world series, given England's status as 'masters of the game' and Italy's World Cup and Olympic successes. Nor did the games remain of mere sporting significance, since the great power standing of Britain and Italy and their resulting prominence in international affairs, gave their encounters an added international political dimension.

Today, the Fédération Internationale de Football Association's (FIFA) national ranking lists, updated monthly on the basis of clearly defined criteria, offer an accessible guide to relative footballing strengths, even if results highlight our continued inability to employ rankings to predict the likely outcome of any specific match or tournament.[1] In any case, unpredictability remains one of the game's enduring attractions, given the manner in which a range of imponderables – these include form, team selection, home advantage, refereeing standards and the weather – ensures that results constantly confound the experts. For example, the FIFA ranking list published immediately prior to the 1998 World Cup Finals failed to include France, the eventual winners, in the top 16. In fact, France was ranked only joint seventeenth, with Egypt![2]

However, FIFA's ranking list was started only in 1993 and looking back to the period covered by this article, that is, the 1930s, contemporary rankings, like the often used descriptor of British footballers as 'masters of the game', proved far more problematic.

Admittedly, the World Cup, introduced on a four-year cycle in 1930, offered some sort of guide, at least respecting the year (that is, 1930, 1934 and 1938) in which the event was held, but the three tournaments held during the 1930s suffered from a distinct lack of universality. British teams were notable non-entrants throughout the decade, while the relative lack of European participation in 1930 was paralleled by limited Latin American representation in the next two tournaments. Nor should the Olympic Games football tournament, held at four-yearly intervals midway between World Cup Finals, be overlooked at a time when Italy, like many other countries, had yet to follow the British lead in formally adopting professionalism.

One contemporary assessment inspired by the regular annual ranking lists drawn up by the Ring Café in Vienna, appeared in *Pesti Napló*, a Hungarian newspaper, in January 1933.[3] England and Scotland, together with Austria and Italy, were placed in the 'super class' category.[4] *Pesti Napló*'s listing, though less systematic than its modern-day FIFA counterpart, proves of historical interest in acknowledging a demand for rankings at a time when rising continental European standards were challenging traditional perceptions of British footballing supremacy. Certainly, the top spot assigned to Austria's 'wunderteam' showed that Britain's primacy could no longer be taken for granted, especially as the eurocentric character of *Pesti Napló*'s listing rendered it easy to overlook the success of Latin American sides in the 1924 and 1928 Olympic and the 1930 World Cup tournaments.

POLITICAL FOOTBALL IN THE 1930s

Regardless of such controversies, *Pesti Napló*'s listing was undoubtedly correct in presenting England and Italy as two of the leading footballing powers. Inevitably, their matches came to be interpreted as possessing significant implications in terms of pitting the self-styled inventors and 'masters of the game' against a country whose national teams emerged as the most successful in the major football tournaments held in the 1930s. Thus, Olympic gold in 1936 complemented Italy's victories in the 1934 and 1938 World Cup Finals.[5] Moreover, the prominent role played by the two states in international politics and the 'European Civil War' – this term described the conflict of ideologies between liberal democracy, fascism and communism – ensured that any England–Italy fixture was imbued with an extra-sporting significance, most notably in terms of impacting either positively or adversely upon national prestige and power. By contrast, this identification proved less significant in terms of internationals played by Scotland, given the common tendency of both Britons and foreigners to use 'England' and 'Britain' as interchangeable descriptors.

Italy, though increasingly overshadowed as an international problem by Hitler's Germany, remained an enduring preoccupation for British policymakers, since Mussolini's intervention in Ethiopia (1935–36), the Spanish Civil War (1936–39) and Albania (1939) threatened British interests in key strategic areas, like the Mediterranean and East Africa.[6] In particular, his restless foreign policy exacerbated Britain's fundamental problem, that is, over-stretch resulting from the simultaneous threat posed to national interests by three potential aggressors (that is, Germany, Italy and Japan) increasingly active in different parts of the world.[7] Subsequently, the Axis link (October 1936), drawing together Italian Fascism and German Nazism, reaffirmed the ideological challenge to Britain and other liberal democracies, while reinvigorating the British government's search for an Anglo–Italian agreement as part of its efforts to help contain German power.

Sport became another battleground in this conflict, especially as – to quote A. Teja – 'sport in Italy was a creature of Fascism, and strictly dependent on it'.[8] Italian sport, operating within a context defined by Mussolini's totalitarian aspirations, was 'increasingly propagandized by the fascist regime', whose instrumental, even Darwinian, approach was typified by Mussolini on 28 October 1934, when addressing athletes after a mass parade celebrating the twelfth anniversary of his march on Rome:

> Remember that when you take part in contests beyond our borders, there is then entrusted to your muscles, and above all to your spirit, the honour and the prestige of national sport. You must hence make use of all your energy and of your willpower in order to obtain primacy in all struggles on the earth, on the sea and in the sky.[9]

Their role, he asserted, was to epitomise 'the new race which Fascism, in its virile way, is forging and is tempering for all competitors'. Just as Mussolini's Italy was generally credited with making the trains run on time so his regime was only too willing to acquire any kudos arising from the performance of the nation's teams on the sports field.

Unsurprisingly, football's propaganda potential was fully exploited, given the manner in which the national side's World Cup and Olympic honours provided the regime with an opportunity to reach a large and receptive audience both within and beyond Italy. Likewise, club successes, most notably Bologna's victory over Chelsea in the 1937 Paris Exhibition tournament, were presented 'before the crowds of the whole world in the image of their nation' as a 'crystalline victory' for Fascist Italy.[10] Thus, Bologna's success, ascribed in part to Chelsea's 'outdated' style of play, was exploited also to highlight the opposition's shortcomings and hence to challenge British footballing primacy.[11] Moreover, the use of language (for example, '*calcio*' replaced 'football') and the adoption of a distinctive style of play (*il metodo*), based on an attacking centre half, sought deliberately to distance the Italian game from lingering British and other external influences.[12]

THE BRITISH FOREIGN OFFICE TAKES INTERNATIONAL SPORT SERIOUSLY

In December 1932, the Football Association (FA) accepted invitations from Italy and Switzerland for its 1933 close season tour, thereby setting up the first ever full international between England and Italy.[13] The FA's procedure, that is, making fixtures unilaterally without any reference to the British government, illuminated what was presented as the distinctive separation of politics and sport in Britain as compared to Italy and a growing number of other continental countries. Even so, the FA's decision soon provided the British government with a difficult dilemma; indeed, the resulting official exchanges about the forthcoming game suggested that even British sport was not as apolitical as Britons liked to think.

British governmental involvement did not really commence until March 1933, when Sir Harry Luke, the lieutenant governor of Malta, informed the Colonial Office about the importance for British prestige of a good England performance against Italy. Malta neither belonged to FIFA nor played football internationals, but the game's rapid growth in popularity meant that the performance of British teams, particularly *vis-à-vis* those from Italy, influenced islanders' images of Britain. Luke, identifying the propaganda value of a British victory, pressed the Colonial Office to leave 'no stone unturned' in ensuring the FA's selection of the best possible team.[14] The Colonial Office, interpreting the matter as involving 'higher diplomacy', forwarded his communication to the Foreign Office. The fact that the Foreign Office only learned of the forthcoming fixture for the first time at a relatively late stage and in a somewhat fortuitous manner, reflected the *apparent separation* of politics and sport in Britain, at least in terms of respecting the relative freedom of operation of non-governmental bodies like the FA. By contrast, the Italian government would have been involved in the fixture from an early stage; indeed, as Teja observed, opponents were chosen increasingly carefully as the decade progressed.[15]

Orme Sargent, the head of the Foreign Office's central department, said 'our attention has frequently been drawn to the importance attached to sport in Italy and to the necessity for winning matches etc.',[16] thereby conceding that more was at stake than a mere football match, especially given the politicization of Italian sport. He also admitted previous official interference: 'We have on several occasions in the past ... done our best to encourage our people to send a first rate team to meet the Italian footballers.' But he struck a note of caution:

> You will realize, I am sure, the hubbub there would be in the press if it should leak out that the Foreign Office, 'for reasons of British prestige abroad', was bringing pressure to bear upon those responsible for the government of football! If this should ever become publicly known (*we very nearly had a case once*) and should then be telegraphed abroad, our position would be rather ridiculous.[16]

For him, the key risk arose from a FA-inspired press leak, which might undermine the government's carefully cultivated image respecting sport: 'Unfortunately, the Football Association here is not quite as intelligent in these matters as we should like them to be.' Despite conceding official interference in the past, Sargent's angst reflected the usual reluctance to undermine traditional perceptions about the autonomy of British sport, particularly during a period when the British authorities were seeking to present this to the wider world as a distinctive British liberal value as compared to the overt politicization characteristic of sport in Fascist Italy.

Sargent's retrospective references, including his fears about a press leak, reflected the Foreign Office's eagerness to avoid another media controversy *à la* 1928–29. This episode began when Thomas Preston, the British consul in Turin, submitted a report about Italian football in the light of media speculation about a forthcoming England–Italy fixture. Preston, having identified the 'different mental angle' adopted towards the game by continental countries, warned Whitehall that any match would be far more than a mere game. Rather, it would represent 'an event of international importance' possessing significant political consequences: 'It might be argued that sport is sport and that it does not matter so much who wins; this is all very well with matches with our colonial teams, but not so with continental teams.'[17] The need for a good result led Preston to urge the Foreign Office to advise the FA that only 'the strongest and best professional combination' should be fielded against Italy's 'amateurs', who had been placed third in the 1928 Olympic football tournament.[18] Reportedly, they often earned far more than their British *professional* counterparts!

Despite articulating the government's usual laissez-faire preferences, the Foreign Office agreed with Preston about the prudence of informing the FA about the merits of sending 'a really strong side' because of the strength of Italian football.[19] As a result, on 7 December 1928, the Foreign Office dispatched a 'semi-official' letter warning the FA about the improving quality of continental European football in general and Italian football in particular. Action was suggested, not demanded: 'Do you think that it would be possible to get a hint passed to the right quarter – the organizers of the England team – that it is worth their while to send a really strong side?'[20] In addition, the Foreign Office, taking up Preston's point about the 'different mental angle' adopted towards international matches in continental countries, quoted from his report to draw the FA's attention to extra-sporting aspects, including the impact of results and fair play upon national prestige.[21] In the event, the press soon picked up the Foreign Office's behind-the-scenes moves, most probably, it was assumed, as the result of a leak via the FA. Even worse, on 31 December 1928, the *Daily Express* headlined the story in sensational terms: 'Football by order of the F.O.: English teams must win abroad.'[22] The *Daily Express* championed the traditional autonomy of British sport before moving on to attack 'absurd' government attempts to link international football matches to 'abstract considerations' of 'British prowess'. Other newspapers, including *The Times* and *The Scotsman*, joined the resulting press flurry, which also drew in the *Berliner Tageblatt* and the *New York Times*. Naturally, such extensive media interest proved extremely unwelcome to a somewhat embarrassed

Foreign Office, which sought to defuse the issue by publishing a formal statement acknowledging that 'there seems to be some misunderstanding as to the nature of the interest which the Foreign Office takes in football matches'.[23]

In the event, the press soon moved on to other topics, and, viewed from the long-term perspective, this episode failed to seriously dent traditional images about politics and sport in Britain. Even so, memories of unwelcome press comment strengthened official sensitivity about intervention in sport, or rather of being discovered in doing so. As a result, in 1933 Sargent, when considering Luke's proposal, ruled out the dispatch of a letter of the type sent to the FA in 1928 on the grounds that such action seemed likely to cause as many, if not more, problems than an Italian victory. Charles Duff summed up the department's preferred position:

> Imagine the damage to our prestige, if it leaked out, that we had interested ourselves in this – in other words, if we had attempted to make politics of sport – and if afterwards our footballers were thoroughly beaten (which might easily happen as football is more seriously taken by foreigners than by English people). We shall lose far more in such circumstances than we are ever likely to gain by any representations we might make.[24]

For him, 'the less we do to put diplomatic pressure on football, the better'. Readers might question Duff's claim that foreigners took the game 'more seriously', even if he was using the word 'seriously' in political rather than in footballing terms. The archives offer little or no documentary evidence about what actually took place, if anything, but at one point Sargent implied the exertion of behind-the-scenes pressure, perhaps through Howard Marshall (1900–73), a sports journalist who worked for the *Westminster Gazette* and the *Daily Telegraph*, among other newspapers, during this period.[25] Nevertheless, inaction failed to prevent the expression of an official opinion in private about international football. Indeed, *political reasons* led the Foreign Office to hope not only for a win by England but also that players 'comport themselves properly off the football field as well as on', since 'anything to the discredit of the British team will be enormously magnified by the Italian propagandists' throughout and beyond the Mediterranean region.[26]

In this manner, important football internationals repeatedly apprised the Foreign Office about sport's relevance to British interests in the wider world and hence further eroded the case for the traditional non-interventionist attitude. No longer was it possible for the government to feign indifference to, or display an unawareness of, the political implications of any fixture, particularly one pitching a British national team against another representing a country where sport represented a major part of its propaganda apparatus. Regardless of the British government's position, its Italian counterpart was bound to exploit any match for propagandist reasons, possibly as part of the Darwinian-type analyses feared by J. Perowne: 'a defeat wd. enable their propagandists to point triumphantly to the effeteness of the British race as compared with the Italians of today and give an enormous fillip to the Italianising influences in the colony [i.e. Malta]'.[27]

In the meantime, the British government awaited the outcome of what was likely to be a close match, especially as Scotland, which lost 0–3 to Italy in 1931, boasted a recent 2–1 win over England (April 1933). Moreover, the game promised to be a highly visible encounter attracting above average media attention and hyperbole within and outside Britain, including the usual stories that Italy's 'amateur' footballers were being promised substantial monetary and other inducements to win.[28] Football's relative lack of impact in the United States (US) failed to prevent the *New York Times* acknowledging the match's broader significance, most notably the Italian desire to 'prove that the Continental pupils have reached the level of the masters ... No other contest in the history of modern Italian sport has caused so much interest as the forthcoming match.'[29] Some 50,000 spectators, including Mussolini and Sir Ronald Graham, the British ambassador in Italy, watched the match, played at Rome on 13 May 1933.[30] A draw of 1–1 enabled both parties to gather some comfort from the result. For Walter Bensemann, 'the Football Association has proved once more that there is life in the old dog yet, and Italy has shown that the great teams of the Continent, led by Connaisseurs [*sic*] like Hugo [i.e. Meisl in Austria] or Vittorio Pozzo, are on their way to assume supremacy'.[31] By implication, England remained a leading force in world football, but had to be alert in the face of the strong challenge from continental European and other teams.

By contrast, minimal official attention was devoted to the other tour game, since the government's attention focused selectively upon the more politically sensitive fixtures. Even so, England's decisive 4–0 victory over Switzerland at Berne, witnessed by Jules Rimet (FIFA president), among other dignitaries, was deemed extremely good sporting propaganda in terms of offering foreigners – to quote one informed spectator – an 'object lesson in heading, dribbling, passing, shooting and position play'.[32]

'THE BATTLE OF HIGHBURY', NOVEMBER 1934

On 14 November 1934, Arsenal's ground provided the setting for the return match, which even today is still depicted as one of the most controversial internationals played on British soil. In fact, at that time one reporter headed his match report, 'The Battle of Highbury: From our War Correspondent, Highbury, Wednesday.'[33]

By this time, an even sharper focus was being placed upon Anglo-Italian relations in both the international political and international sporting spheres. Moreover, debates about footballing primacy, left unresolved one year earlier, had acquired an added edge in the wake of Italy's recently acquired status of World Cup champions.[34] Was Italy really the best team in the world, as implied by both its 1934 World Cup triumph and excellent record (seven wins, one draw, and one loss) since playing England in 1933? Or was England, a notable absentee from the 1934 World Cup competition hosted by Italy, still the game's leading force, despite a rather mixed record (five wins, three defeats) following its visit to Rome? Indeed, England's close season tour, undertaken just prior to the 1934 World Cup Finals, brought 1–2 defeats to two teams, Czechoslovakia and Hungary, scheduled to participate in the World Cup a few days later. Whereas Hungary departed at the quarterfinal stage, Czechoslovakia reached the final, where it lost to Italy in extra time.

Reportedly, Mussolini was relatively unenthusiastic about football *per se*, but this failed to prevent him employing the international stage furnished by the 1934 World Cup Finals to impress domestic and external audiences with the qualities of Fascist Italy as reflected through, say, the high standard of Italian football and the regime's ability to organize a home victory. Inevitably, Italian propaganda, glossing over the absence of British teams and Uruguay (the 1930 World Cup winners), the usual inducements offered to Italian players and the contribution of foreign players based in Italy who had represented Argentina in the 1930 World Cup final, exploited victory by presenting it as a function of the dynamic qualities of the Fascist regime in general and the personal influence of *Il Duce* in particular. Significantly, Mussolini, normally sporting a yachting cap, attended most of Italy's games and often received the team afterwards.[35] Obviously, the politico-sporting impact of World Cup success in a competition hosted and organized by the Italian authorities would be considerably boosted if England could be beaten for the first time on British soil a few months later. Once again, the Foreign Office was presented with a fixture made by the FA as a *fait accompli*, and only became involved following the receipt of a FA invitation for ministerial representation at the game. The resulting departmental exchanges guided by the known attendance of the Italian ambassador in London, led to the decision that Sir John Simon, the foreign secretary, would attend the match.[36]

Italy, having gone 0–3 down, fought back with two second-half goals, but failed to get an equalizer. As a result, England, watched by a 50,000 crowd including an estimated 5,000 visiting Italians, became the first team to beat the 1934 World Cup champions.[37] However, the victory was tarnished to some extent by the game's unsavoury features. Unsurprisingly, these featured prominently and picturesquely in players' memoirs. Typically, Eddie Hapgood, who suffered a broken nose, wrote that good football and fair play proved difficult 'when somebody closely resembling an enthusiastic member of the Mafia is wiping his studs down your leg, or kicking you up in the air from behind'![38] For Stanley Matthews, the Italian players 'meant to win – at any price'.[39] However, Mussolini, when personally welcoming players back to Rome, blamed defeat on the injuries – this resulted in the loss of one Italian player (no substitutes were allowed) – and, by implication, the tactics employed by England. Whether or not the episode seriously disturbed bilateral political relations, most notably ongoing efforts to form an Anglo-French-Italian front to contain Hitler's Germany, remains questionable at a time when Mussolini's eyes were turning greedily towards Ethiopia.

BRITAIN'S SPORTING AMBASSADORS TAKE ON ITALY AGAIN
IN 1939

The final fixture played between the two countries during the decade took place in 1939, by which date Italy had added two more titles to its footballing honours, that is, the 1936 Olympic and 1938 World Cup crowns. Nor was success confined to the national team, as highlighted by Bologna's victory over Chelsea in the 1937 Paris Exhibition tournament.

Meanwhile, England retained a high footballing reputation in spite of a somewhat variable recent record and continued absence from the World Cup. England's 3–0 win over FIFA's 'Rest of Europe' team – this fixture was arranged as part of the FA's 75th anniversary celebrations – certainly reinforced impressions of primacy, especially as commentators glossed over the problems facing scratch teams, even one including seven Italians. Admittedly, a 'Great Britain' team participated in the 1936 Berlin Olympics – the team lost to Poland in the quarter finals – but the fact that, unlike Italy, it was composed of players satisfying a strict definition of amateurism rules out any meaningful comparison. Once again, the footballing significance of an Italy–England international – to quote one British journalist, L.V. Manning, 'the world's championship is the prize' – was accentuated by extra-sporting considerations.[40] Even the FA was forced to acknowledge that 'in view of the political situation, this match had assumed, in the eyes of the Press and the Public, a greater significance than it otherwise would have'.[41] Indeed, the worsening international situation, in conjunction with Italy's recent footballing successes, gave it even greater perceived importance than the two previous fixtures.

Neville Chamberlain (Prime Minister, 1937–40) visited Rome in January 1939, and his government's continuing search for Anglo–Italian détente provided the political context within which the FA finalized arrangements for England's 1939 close season tour to Italy, Romania and Yugoslavia.[42] However, within days, the rapid deterioration in the international situation consequent upon Germany's occupation of Prague (15 March), the emerging German threat to Poland, and Italy's advance into Albania (7 April), prompted a radical review of British foreign policy.[43] Following hurried consultations with the Foreign Office, the FA imposed footballing sanctions on Italy's Axis partner by withdrawing approval for close season matches arranged against German clubs, but surprisingly allowed England's tour to go ahead as planned.[44]

Memories of the two previous encounters imparted added interest to a game viewed in both countries as possessing an obvious propaganda value due to widespread media and public interest within and outside Italy.[45] Significantly, the Italian government, seeking to use football yet again to bolster its position in Malta, planned to transport 400 Maltese people to the game to 'watch a real football team lick the English'![46] According to Percy Loraine, the British ambassador, 'the Italians

regarded the event as a test in which the prowess of the new Italy would
be matched against the skills of the country where football has its
home'.[47] Likewise, the British media, glossing over the 1938 World Cup's
global significance, presented the match as the 'real battle for world
honours' testing 'the masters of the game' versus the world champions.[48]
Memories of the 'Battle of Highbury' gave significance to reports by the
British embassy at Rome that Italian players were lectured about the
need for both a win and good behaviour, even if recent history suggested
that, in the event of any conflict, the former objective would take
precedence.[49] By way of response, FA officials accompanying the tour
party warned players to expect trouble, given Italy's history of rough
play and use of fiscal inducements, but urged them to avoid retaliation
regardless of provocation.[50] Nor were players allowed to forget the
game's broader propagandist dimension; thus, Stanley Matthews
acknowledged that 'we were fighting for English prestige'.[51]

More significantly, FA officials, overlooking the Nazi salute
controversy occasioned one year earlier by the Germany–England match
at Berlin, decided that players should give the Fascist salute during the
playing of the Italian national anthem.[52] Despite media reports that
players executed the instruction in a somewhat half-hearted manner, the
FA claimed that the gesture was 'greatly appreciated' by the large crowd
and helped ensure the success of the fixture.[53] Even so, it failed to
prevent England's opening goal being greeted by virtual silence! The
American embassy in Rome echoed the FA's positive assessment:

> A gesture which was warmly applauded by the Italian spectators
> was provided by the British team which gave the Fascist salute
> when the Italian national anthem was played and there was little
> doubt, according to Embassy information, that the appearance of
> the British side was greeted with considerable enthusiasm.[54]

Reportedly, the England players also saluted the crowd after the game.
However, unlike the 1938 Nazi salute episode, their action failed to
either prompt much controversy in Britain or feature prominently in
players' memoirs.

The game, played at Milan's San Siro stadium on 13 May, ended as
a 2–2 draw. England, helped by an early goal, dominated the first half,
but proved less impressive after the break and only a late equalizer
cancelled out Italy's 2–1 lead. Generally speaking, British journalists,
albeit questioning Italy's second goal on the grounds of handball,

focused on the broader picture. For the *Daily Sketch*'s L.V. Manning, the game won high praise as 'the greatest international match I have seen'; in fact, he headlined his match report: 'It *was* the match of the century'.[55] John Macadam, writing for the *Daily Express*, echoed this line:

> How does a fellow start to write about this Italy v. England match in Milan? ... Italy had gone and leveled terms with England, the acknowledged masters of the game, and Italy had the honour of staging what will probably go on records as the greatest game of football ever played. I doubt whether we of this generation shall ever see its like again for sheer football glamour ... Both sides played to the uttermost limit of their class, this must be the greatest game ever.[56]

Mussolini himself missed the game – he was engaged in a high-profile tour of Piedmont – but his sons, like members of the Italian government, watched the game seated in the same enclosure as Loraine and British embassy staff. Significantly, at the post-match banquet, Loraine employed his speech to praise the way in which the match reflected and strengthened the friendly state of Anglo–Italian relations.[57] Likewise his report informed by a subsequent exchange of views with King Victor Emmanuel III about the game's broader implications, pointed to the visibility given to British footballing skills and sportsmanship alongside the event's 'valuable contribution to friendship between the two nations'.[58] For the British ambassador, the match offered a useful instrument for fulfilling his hope that no bridges, 'which one day the Italians might wish to re-cross', were burned.[59] In this vein, the fixture, complementing other bilateral contacts, might be interpreted as helping to patch up the increasingly rickety 'bridge' joining London and Rome, even if for the Italian government the Axis link with Germany remained the crucial relationship, as demonstrated soon afterwards by their conclusion of the Pact of Steel on 22 May 1939.

Loraine was impressed by the enthusiastic welcome given by large 'soccer-mad' crowds to England players upon their arrival at Milan railway station as well as outside the team's hotel; indeed, for him, the whole episode offered '*an interesting insight into the attitude of the Italian masses to Anglo–Italian relations*'.[60] A high profile football international, providing a meaningful point of contact with all levels of Italian society, gave the Italians – to quote Andrew Noble – 'an opportunity for showing that they still like us'.[61] Italian newspapers, albeit dominated by reports of Mussolini's northern tour, gave considerable space to the match, which therefore offered the British government an effective method of national projection throughout the country with the active compliance of both the Fascist authorities and media.[62] Normally, British propaganda directed towards Italy faced strict censorship and counter-measures. The Foreign Office, which was only too aware of international football's unpredictability and ability to project the wrong sort of national image, welcomed the match's seemingly beneficial extra-sporting consequences. England had not only avoided defeat – this was adjudged possible given the recent records of the two sides – but also displayed, it was believed, the appropriate blend of skill and sportsmanship to maintain, even enhance, Italian perceptions of British sporting prowess and values. Nevertheless, the episode failed to prevent the usual departmental jibe to the effect that this positive outcome proved 'an all too infrequent result of international contests of this kind'.[63]

'England experienced mixed fortunes on the remaining tour games. A 1–2 defeat to Yugoslavia in Belgrade followed by a 2–0 win over Romania in Bucharest meant that England returned home with a relatively modest tour record (one win, one draw, one defeat), including a defeat by a 'second class soccer power' whose failure to qualify for the 1938 World Cup Finals was compounded by recent losses to both Germany and Romania.[64] However, as had happened in 1938, contemporary observers focused on the Italian game as being the crucial benchmark in both footballing and political terms. Certainly, England's 1939 close season tour, though conducted against the background of an increasingly unstable international situation, was adjudged politically successful in terms of supporting the Chamberlain government's ongoing efforts to improve relations with Italy as well as to enhance Britain's world image.[65] Nor could the FA overlook the underlying political dimension and the way in which football was – to quote the *Daily Express* – 'pulled into the quagmire of politics'.[66] Looking back as the FA member-in-charge, B.A. Glanvill recalled initial doubts about the wisdom of undertaking the tour at such a sensitive political time, but felt that the effort and risk proved worthwhile: 'the remarkable reception accorded to us from the time we reached Milan until we left Bucarest [*sic*] proved conclusively from a football point of view that the friendship which has existed for many years has not diminished one iota'.[67] Similarly, the FA's official tour report, though indulging in a certain amount of retrospective justification, concluded that 'the main object of the visit was achieved – to show that International matches can be played between teams of England and continental countries before big crowds in a vigorous yet friendly spirit'.[68]

Significantly, the extra-sporting dimension figured prominently in media coverage, as evidenced by the *Daily Express*: 'It was a political gamble and it came off. Thanks not to the politicians, but to the twenty-two players who took part in it.'[69] Frequently, players were depicted as 'sports ambassadors' engaged on a 'great peace-through-football role'.[70] For Manning (*Daily Sketch*), England's 'football ambassadors' performed a task of 'national importance', most notably reaffirming British values to the man in the street in the countries visited.[71] Similarly, the *Daily Dispatch*'s Ivan Sharpe praised football's 'powerful' contribution 'at a ticklish time': 'The reward has been a splendid and opportune fillip for British prestige.'[72] Moreover, Manning pointed out that these benefits were secured by the players 'for their country' at minimal cost to the government:

> My view is that if ever there arose the danger of the F.A. dropping the European tour Whitehall should step in and make it compulsory. The sixteen players who stepped off the train at Victoria ... have done a grand job of work for their country. Sixteen professional footballers, paid £24 for the job ... They have blazed a lasting trail of friendships, and in every legation, every consulate in the countries visited there is, I know, an appreciation of the national importance of their achievement.

As Manning noted, players received the princely sum of £8 per international, although positive official and media feedback about the tour led the FA to award players an extra gift in recognition of their 'splendid sportsmanship'.[73]

CONCLUSION: BRITAIN AND THE 'WORLD GAME'

Despite its professed apolitical approach to sport, the British Foreign Office conceded the inevitable blurring of the line between politics and sport in any Anglo-Italian footballing encounter:

> Then to take the Italian case, if they happen to win a game (and they work, almost fight, to do so) it merely proves to a vast assembly of people, including perhaps Il Duce and his supermen,

that the Fascist system produces a finer type of homo sapiens than the decaying system of Parlty Govt. Football becomes a sub-section of the creed.[74]

In this context, the 1930s saw frequent foreign references to British decline in not only the political and economic, but also sporting spheres. Of course, 'decline' is a relative term, and it might have been more accurate to acknowledge that, as happened in the world of football, it was perhaps more a case of constant readjustment to the game's advance elsewhere rather than of absolute British decay. British footballers were required perpetually to prove themselves on the field as the 'masters of the game' against an ever-wider range of opponents, especially as Czechoslovakia (1934), Hungary (1934) and Yugoslavia (1939) vividly demonstrated to Britons the growing strength of teams categorized as merely 'second' or 'third class' by *Pesti Napló* in 1933.

Nevertheless, in 1939 most Britons continued to believe, like Ivan Sharpe, a leading football correspondent, that British football 'still stands at the top of the list'.[75] Stanley Rous, who acted as linesman at the 1934 game and accompanied the England team to Milan five years later, applied such thinking to the England–Italy encounters: 'Mussolini's offer of huge bonuses to his team for the Highbury game in 1934 was only a reflection of the immense prestige which accrued to any country beating England. Italy at least clearly regarded this as just as important as winning the World Cup!'[76] These perceptions, alongside non-participation in the World Cup, the British media's disinterest therein and the British withdrawal from FIFA in 1928, symbolized strong isolationist tendencies rooted in the initial ascendancy of the British game.[77] As James Walvin observed: 'Throughout the inter-war years football in the British Isles never questioned the belief in inherited superiority; an attitude compounded by administrative isolationism and shored up by domestic buoyancy. It was to be many years before the reality of football abroad and the relative decline of the domestic game were fully appreciated.'[78]

Prior to the Second World War, British football showed a greater willingness to arrange fixtures against continental European teams as well as to dispatch representative teams to the empire, but gave little or no thought to the strength of the game in the wider world other than to assume its inferiority.[79] However, this arrogant complacency resulted also from the fact that, notwithstanding their complete absence from lists of Olympic and World Cup footballing honours between the wars, England and Scotland had good, even outstanding, results in high profile games against foreign sides, especially Italy. Impressive performances (one win, two draws, no defeats) against the 1934 and 1938 World Cup champions and 1936 Olympic football gold medallists, as well as a 3–0 victory over FIFA's 'Rest of Europe' team in 1938, consolidated England's reputation during a decade when Scotland displayed less overall consistency, but finished with a strong run of results (1936–38: five wins, one draw, no losses) against leading continental sides, including Austria and Germany.[80] As one Hungarian writer observed, 'in those days, and for a long time to come, no team was ashamed to being beaten by the England eleven; it was the rule'.[81] Of course, neither England nor Scotland, though unbeaten at home by non-British teams, went undefeated by foreign sides, although losses like that to Yugoslavia in 1939 often seemed capable of rationalization in terms of, say, injuries to key players, poor foreign referees, varying interpretations of the laws of the game, uneven pitches, adverse climatic conditions, excessive travelling, and tiredness after a long league season – factors preventing British players from displaying their assumed innate superiority. In turn, it proved easy for the British footballing authorities, media and people to interpret Britain as having nothing to prove in the World Cup and to still see the real test as the home international tournament. For Britons, the latter, alongside the domestic league and cup competitions, remained the pinnacle of world football.

Therefore, as the 1930s came to a close, the relatively healthy state of the domestic game was paralleled by a general acceptance by Britons that they continued to rule the game that was made in their country, exported to the world, and played to laws decided by a body, the International Football Association Board, dominated by the four British football associations.[82] Inevitably, three high profile England-Italy matches played between 1933 and 1939 performed a crucial role in reaffirming such perceptions, given England's excellent record in a series depicted both within and outside Britain as contests for world footballing primacy. The international political context, in conjunction with the overt politicization of Italian sport during a period when – to quote Richard Butler, Minister of State at the Foreign Office (1938–40) – 'the world is full of propaganda today on a scale as great, if not greater, than at the time of war', merely reinforced this tendency to interpret any England–Italy encounter as far more than an event of merely European significance.[83] British footballers were projected variously as playing and scoring for their country, with a premium being placed upon success as the best form of sports propaganda. Likewise, the FA and the Scottish Football Association (SFA), though still preferring, as non-governmental organizations, to do their own thing and believing 'that politics should be kept out of sport', were forced increasingly to recognize that international football did not take place in a political vacuum. As acknowledged by Stanley Rous (the FA secretary): 'the FA were always conscious of the political implications of tours by our national team and we kept in close touch with the Foreign Office over arrangements'.[84]

The Second World War proved instrumental in the diplomatic eclipse of Britain by the two superpowers, the US and Soviet Union. Moreover, war ushered in a period when the traditional smug and blinkered vision of British football was exposed repeatedly, often cruelly, by foreign teams, including Moscow Dynamo (1945), Eire (1949), the US (1950), FIFA's 'Rest of the World' XI (1953), Hungary (1953, 1954) as well as Uruguay (1953, 1954) from the hitherto ignored Latin American continent. During the inter-war years football, despite being strongly established only in Europe and Latin America, was acknowledged increasingly as the 'world game'. For Britons, this descriptor was interpreted to mean a game invented, developed and *dominated* by Britain, whereas, like many good teachers, they found that many pupils were launching an increasingly serious challenge to their footballing primacy. The England–Italy games, played between 1933 and 1939, enabled the fiction to be preserved a little longer, even if hindsight suggests that England's performance flattered to deceive and distracted attention from both the fundamental weaknesses of the British game and the rapidly growing strength of the game around the world.

NOTES

1. FIFA's list, updated monthly, is available on its website: http://www.fifa.com.
2. The relevant ranking list, dated 20 May 1998, is available on the FIFA website. The next list, issued on 15 July after the World Cup Finals, ranked France second.
3. *Pesti Napló*, 28 Dec. 1932, 1 Jan. 1933; W. Capel-Kirby and Frederick W. Carter, *The Mighty Kick: Romance, History and Humour of Football* (London: Jarrolds, 1933), p.81; Peter J. Beck,

Scoring for Britain: International Football and International Politics, 1900–1939 (London and Portland, OR: Frank Cass, 1999), p.131.

4. Northern Ireland and Wales were not listed, but, prior to this date, neither had played a non-British team.
5. There was no Olympic football tournament at Los Angeles in 1932.
6. On Anglo-Italian relations, see Richard Lamb, *Mussolini and the British* (London: John Murray, 1997).
7. David Reynolds, *Britannia Overruled: British policy and World Power in the 20th Century* (Harlow: Longman, 1991), pp.126–33.
8. Angela Teja, 'Italian Sport and International Relations under Fascism', in Pierre Arnaud and James Riordan (eds.), *Sport and International Politics: the Impact of Fascism and Communism on Sport* (London: E & FN Spon, 1998), p.158.
9. Public Record Office, London (PRO), Foreign Office Correspondence (FO), Sir E. Drummond, Rome, to Sir J. Simon, 9 Nov. 1934, FO371/18427/R6327; Victoria de Grazia, *The Culture of Consent: Mass Organisation of Leisure in Fascist Italy* (Cambridge: Cambridge University Press, 1981), p.170; Ivan Sharpe, *Forty Years in Football* (London: Hutchinson, 1952), pp.68–9; Teja, pp.147–67; Arnd Krüger, 'Strength through Joy: the Culture of Consent under Fascism, Nazism and Francoism', in Jim Riordan and Arnd Krüger (eds.), *The International Politics of Sport in the 20th Century* (London: E & FN Spon, 1999), pp.76–81.
10. Quoted Pierre Lanfranchi, 'Bologna: the Team that Shook the World', *International Journal of the History of Sport*, 8 (1991), 336; Pierre Lanfranchi, 'Frankreich und Italien', C. Eisenberg (ed.), *Fussball, soccer, calcio: ein englischer Sport auf seinem Weg um die Welt* (Munich: DTV, 1997), pp.56–9.
11. Lanfranchi, 'Bologna', 336–7.
12. Ibid., 338–9.
13. Football Association, London (FA), International Selection Committee (ISC), 28 Dec. 1932, minute 6, 1932–33.
14. PRO, H. Luke, Lt.-Governor, Malta, to Colonial Office, 9 March 1933, encl. A.J. Dawe, Colonial Office, to Orme Sargent, 15 March 1933, minutes by C. Duff, R. Lindsay, J.V. Perowne, A. Willert, March–April 1933, FO395/492/P673.
15. Teja, p.163.
16. PRO, Orme Sargent to Dawe, 5 April 1933, FO395/492/P673.
17. PRO, T. Preston to Consular Department, 30 Nov. 1928, FO370/289/L7516.
18. Ibid.
19. PRO, S. Gaselee to F. Wall, FA, 7 Dec. 1928, FO370/289/L7516.
20. Ibid.
21. PRO, minute, C.J. Norton, 2 Jan. 1929, FO395/434/P4; minute, G. Thompson, 24 Dec. 1928, FO395/434/P1900.
22. *Daily Express*, 31 Dec. 1928, Beck, *Scoring for Britain*, pp.117–24.
23. PRO, Foreign Office Statement, 31 Dec. 1928, FO395/434/P4.
24. PRO, minute, Duff, 18 March 1933, FO395/492/P673.
25. PRO, Orme Sargent to Dawe, 5 April 1933, FO395/492/P673. Nor have the author's searches at the PRO and the British Library's Newspaper Library revealed such an article.
26. PRO, minute, J. Perowne, 20 March 1933, FO395/492/P673.
27. Ibid.
28. PRO, minute, A. Noble, 22 May 1939, FO371/23785/R4193; Frederick Wall, *Fifty Years of Football* (London: Cassell, 1935), p.11.
29. *New York Times*, 14 May 1933. See also P.J. Bauwens, 'England-Italien', *World's Football*, 44 (15 Jan. 1935), 10–11. Note that Bauwens refereed the 1939 Italy-England match.
30. *The Times*, 15 May 1933; *New York Times*, 14 May 1933.
31. Walter Bensemann, 'Missionaries of Sport', *World's Football*, 37 (1933), 153–4. Vittorio Pozzo

was the Italian team coach/manager.

32. Bensemann, 'Missionaries of sport', 152.

33. Quoted Roy Peskett (ed.), *Tom Whittaker's Arsenal Story* (London: Sporting Handbooks, 1957), p.112; Brian Glanville, *Soccer Nemesis* (London: Secker & Warburg, 1955), p.88; John Cottrell, *A Century of Great Soccer Drama* (London: Hart-Davis, 1970), p.76.

34. FA, ISC, minute 3, 5 March 1934, 1933–34.

35. Cottrell, pp.76–7.

36. PRO, minute, Orme Sargent, 1 Nov. 1934, P. Mason to Rous, 3 Nov. 1934, minute by Mason, 7 Nov. 1934, FO371/18439/R6262. Subsequently, parliamentary commitments made Sir John Simon, the Foreign Secretary, unavailable, thereby resulting in his replacement by a member of the Foreign Office.

37. See, for example, Glanville, p.88; Jim Munro, 'An old rivalry with passion aplenty', *Sunday Times*, 5 Oct. 1997; Eddie Hapgood, *Football Ambassador* (London: Sporting Handbooks, 1945), pp.36–8; Stanley Matthews, *Feet First* (London: Ewen & Dale, 1948), pp.23–4. Stanley Rous, who was soon to succeed Wall as FA secretary, was linesman for this match, and arrived late due to the crowds and traffic: Stanley Rous, *Football Worlds: a Lifetime in Sport* (London: Faber and Faber, 1978), p.29.

38. Hapgood, *Football Ambassador*, p.37. Compare Cliff Bastin (with B. Glanville), *Cliff Bastin Remembers. An Autobiography* (London: Ettrick Press, 1950), pp.113–14.

39. Matthews, *Feet First*, p.24; Stanley Matthews, *The Way it Was: My Autobiography* (London: Headline, 2000), pp.46–9; Rous, *Football Worlds*, pp.28–9.

40. *Daily Sketch*, 13 May 1939; Bill Murray, *The World's Game: A History of Soccer* (Urbana, USA: University of Illinois Press, 1998), p.80.

41. FA, Report on Continental Tour 1939, encl. ISC, 5 June 1939, 1938–39.

42. FA, ISC, 11 March 1939, 1938–39.

43. R.A.C. Parker, *Chamberlain and Appeasement: British policy and the coming of the Second World War* (London: Macmillan, 1993), pp.200–20.

44. *The Times*, 4, 17 April 1939; George F. Allison, *Allison Calling: a Galaxy of Football and other Memories* (London: Staples, 1948), pp.148–51; author's interview with Sir Stanley Rous, 28 March 1980; *Daily Sketch*, 9 May 1939; Hapgood, *Football Ambassador*, pp.41–2; Tommy Lawton (with Roy Peskett), *Football is my Business* (London: Sporting Handbooks, 1946), pp.77–8; Rous, p.104.

45. *Daily Sketch*, 11 May 1939.

46. PRO, report, n.d., encl. Major J.H. Dodds, Consul-General in Nice, to P. Nichols, 16 May 1939, FO371/23785/R4205; Matthews, *Feet First*, pp.92–3.

47. PRO, Percy Loraine, Rome, to Halifax, 16 May 1939, FO371/23785/R4193.

48. *Daily Dispatch*, 15, 30 May 1939; *Daily Sketch*, 12, 13 May 1939.

49. PRO, minute, A. Noble, Southern dept., 22 May 1939, FO371/23785/R4193.

50. In 1937, Italy's rough play led to the abandonment of an international versus Austria: *The Times*, 22 March 1937; FIFA, Circular 1937/16. Reportedly, Italian players, though still nominally amateur, had been promised the equivalent of a £50 bonus to beat England: *Daily Sketch*, 11 May 1939; Guy Oliver, *The Guinness Book of World Soccer: the History of the Game in over 150 Countries* (Enfield: Guinness Publishing, 1992), p.360.

51. *Daily Sketch*, 12 May 1939; Matthews, *Feet First*, p.92.

52. Author's interview with Rous, 28 March 1980; *Daily Express*, 13 May 1939; *Daily Sketch*, 13 May 1939; *Daily Dispatch*, 15 May 1939; Glanville, p.97. In May 1938 England players were 'instructed' to give the Nazi salute during the playing of the national anthem prior to their game versus Germany. The gesture prompted substantial comment and controversy: Beck, *Scoring for Britain*, pp.6–7.

53. PRO, Report, n.d., enclosed in Dodds, Nice, to Nichols, 16 May 1939, FO371/23785/R4205; *Daily Express*, 13, 22 May 1939; *Daily Dispatch*, 29 May 1939. Gate receipts were £12,000:

Daily Sketch, 13, 18 May 1939.

54. Archives II, College Park, Maryland, USA (hereafter USA), State Department files (RG59), W. Phillips, US ambassador, Rome, to State Dept., 19 May 1939, RG59, Box 6870, 865.00/1821.

55. *Daily Sketch*, 15 May 1939; *New York Times*, 14 May 1939; *Daily Express*, 15 May, 22 May 1939; *Daily Dispatch*, 15 May 1939; FA, Report on Continental Tour, 1939, encl. ISC, 5 June 1939, minute 3, 1938–39.

56. *Daily Express*, 22 May 1939.

57. Hapgood, *Football Ambassador*, p.46.

58. PRO, Loraine to Halifax, 16 May 1939, FO371/23785/R4193.

59. Gordon Waterfield, *Professional Diplomat: Sir Percy Loraine of Kirkharle, 1880–1961* (London: John Murray, 1973), p.228.

60. Ibid.; Matthews, *Feet First*, pp.92, 97; Matthews, *The Way it Was*, pp.105–6; *Daily Sketch*, 11 May 1939. For a picture of the welcome, see *Daily Sketch*, 12 May 1939.

61. PRO, minute, Noble, 22 May 1939, FO371/23785/R4193. Agreed by Sargent, 25 May 1939.

62. USA, Phillips, US ambassador, Rome, to State Dept., 19 May 1939, RG59, Box 6870, 865.00/1821; PRO, Foreign Office to M. Lampson, 23 April 1939, FO371/23785/R3104; PRO, Lord Perth to Foreign Office, 15 April 1939, FO371/23785/R2899. Generally speaking, the British government decided that any attempt to counter hostile Italian propaganda would do more harm than good.

63. PRO, minutes, Broad, 22 May, Ingram, 23 May, Sargent, 25 May 1939, FO371/23785/R4193. Throughout the late 1920s and 1930s the Foreign Office received complaints from abroad about the poor performance and/or player misconduct of British teams, especially club sides engaged on close season tours: see Beck, *Scoring for Britain*, pp.113–17, p.125, pp.225–6.

64. *Daily Sketch*, 18, 19 May 1939; *Daily Dispatch*, 29 May 1939.

65. Donald Cameron Watt, *How War Came: the immediate origins of the Second World War, 1938–1939* (London: Heinemann, 1989), pp.292–6.

66. *Daily Express*, 22 May 1939.

67. Quoted, Ivan Sharpe, 'Tell England', *Daily Dispatch*, 30 May 1939.

68. FA, Report of Continental Tour, 1939, encl. ISC, 5 June 1939, minute 3, 1938–39; FIFA, Rous quoted, Schricker to G. Vaccaro, 6 June 1939, Italy correspondence 1939–58.

69. *Daily Express*, 22 May 1939.

70. *Daily Sketch*, 10 May 1939; *Daily Express*, 23 May 1939; Sharpe, p.76.

71. L.V. Manning, 'Sixteen men do a fine job of work', *Daily Sketch*, 29 May 1939; *Daily Dispatch*, 24 May 1939.

72. Ivan Sharpe, 'Tell England', *Daily Dispatch*, 30 May 1939.

73. FA, ISC, 5 June 1939, minute 3, 1938–39.

74. PRO, minute, Duff, 19 Jan. 1934, FO395/515/P165. Agreed by M. Huxley and Leeper, 22, 23 Jan. 1934.

75. *Daily Dispatch*, 18 May 1939; Matthews, *Feet First*, p.106; George G. Graham, *Scottish Football Through the Years* (Scottish Daily Record and Evening News, Glasgow, 1947), p.21; James Walvin, *The People's Game: A Social History of British Football* (London: Allen Lane, 1994 revised edition.), p.143; Willy Meisl, *Soccer Revolution* (London: Phoenix, 1955), p.62. By contrast, Brian Glanville felt that British football reached its zenith in 1914: Glanville, p.11.

76. Rous, *Football Worlds*, pp.62, 90.

77. On British football and FIFA, see Peter J. Beck, 'Going to War, Peaceful co-existence or Virtual Membership?: British football and FIFA, 1928–46', *International Journal of the History of Sport*, 17 (2000), 113–34.

78. Walvin, *The People's Game*, p.14; Murray, *The World's Game*, pp.80–2.

79. See Beck, *Scoring for Britain*, pp.106–7, on imperial tours to Australasia, Canada and elsewhere.

80. Wales played only two foreign internationals in the 1930s (one draw, one defeat), while

Northern Ireland played none.

81. József Vetö, *Sport in Hungary* (Budapest: Corvina Press, 1965), p.52.
82. The four British associations accounted for 4/5ths of the votes (FIFA had the rest) on a body requiring a 4/5ths majority for any change!
83. PRO, minutes, Duff, 29 Jan. 1934, Leeper, 30 Jan. 1934, Leeper to McClure, 2 Feb. 1934, FO395/515/P165; Trinity College Library, University of Cambridge, Lord Butler Papers (RAB), R. Butler, 23 May 1938, RAB K4/8.
84. Rous, *Football Worlds*, pp.63, 104; author's interview with Rous, 28 March 1980.

Epilogue:
Post-imperialism, Sport, Globalization

Postmodernism, Roy Porter suggests, in his dazzling *Enlightenment: Britain and the Creation of the Modern World* 'has one virtue at least – it has reopened inquiries into modernity and its origins'.[1] Porter is of the firm opinion that the eighteenth century was crucial to the creation of modern mentalities; the claim is made here with equal firmness that the nineteenth century was crucial to the creation of modern sports – both developments, if not perhaps of the same magnitude, are of immense contemporary global significance. If Porter is of the contentious view that British thinkers were prominent in the eighteenth-century intellectual revolution, the uncontentious argument is advanced here that British sportsmen were pre-eminent in the nineteenth-century modern sports revolution. They comprised a cadre of international cultural brokers.[2]

In Britain in the eighteenth century 'New [middle-class] personae for the modern thinker were being forged ... an urban sociable sort in the vanguard of humanity.'[3] In the nineteenth century, a new, mostly middle-class, persona[4] emerged, also urban, sociable and in its way – 'in the vanguard of humanity'.[5] Those who possessed it created and populated new playing fields and arenas across the world. In the Era of Enlightenment if many of its secular thinkers saw themselves as teachers, so too did the religious sportsmen of the later Age of Recreational Revolution.[6] They, too, coined new moralistic terms and phrases that have passed into the English language. It is not claimed here that Britain's sportsmen in this Recreational Revolution were unique, any more than Porter claimed that British thinkers of the Enlightenment were unique, but they were *prominent*, and as in the Enlightenment, did it 'their' insular way. A small island off the mainland of Europe led the way and most of the world followed, but not to any Promised Paradise of Play. The Recreational Revolution much as in the earlier Enlightenment was 'no tale of 'progress', but rather one of *Kulturkampf*, 'racked with contradictions, struggles and ironies, and leaving in its wake multiple [cultural] casualties and victims'.[7] This fact, incidentally, has been barely explored! Modernity with its swirling eddies, fast rip tides and swift currents of cultural change has witnessed old customs which have sunk beneath cultural waves as well as new ones which have floated on them.

In the modern world globalization has occurred certainly in politics, economics and culture.[8] At the same time, it is wise to recognize, that national sentiment has become a widespread collective reaction of societies facing the unification of the world.[9] Nevertheless, in the modern world, as mentioned in the Prologue, nineteenth-century imperialism was an early impetus to modern cultural universalization. On the back of imperialism, direct or indirect, capitalism under hegemonic sponsorship, 'was carried to many parts of the world'.[10] Capitalism stimulated in turn rival political ideologies – fascism, communism and socialism. In their different ways all these powerful ideologies in the twentieth century adopted sport, used sport and promoted sport within their representative cultures often dressing it in the most florid doctrinal rhetoric. It has been a cultural component of them all, and in some instances, of enormous ideological importance – a manifestation of the health of a political ideology. It is still viewed in this way.[11]

Marc Ferro narrowly discerns dance as the most widespread manifestation of cultural unification leading to cultural standardization.[12] Arguably, more shrewdly, he should have selected sport. Sport has become a standardized global symbol of ideological commitment, if differently preached and practised. Of course, ideologically to maintain difference, to demonstrate difference, to enhance difference – a difference that exudes superiority, there has had to be, to use a now fashionable and, in this instance, appropriate metaphor, 'a level playing field'. To abandon metaphor and state the matter simply; there has to be common sports at which to compete. Only then is ideological superiority visibly flaunted.

The common sports of modern political, economic and cultural systems, whatever the accidental or deliberate variations, now ensure the existence of societies which are as much *global* as insular. As yet there is no such thing as a Global Society, but societies *are* increasingly global! In the shaping of the sport of these global societies Europe has played the pre-eminent part – for the simple reason that the nineteenth century, when the globalization of sport began in earnest, was the European century. Within Europe, the extraordinary espousal of sport for practical and philosophical reasons by the English middle-class educational institutions of the then richest nation of the world with, at the time, the largest empire, ensured in turn the transmission of much of modern sport played in the modern way to many parts of the globe where it was mostly assimilated, frequently adapted, and only infrequently rejected.

The outcome has been a contemporary cultural revolution of gargantuan size. The world, at one level, is now a vast common playground but its play has become far more than play. The political, economic, cultural and emotional resonances of 'the common playground' – the global playground – are stupifyingly deafening. Self-evidently in significant and substantial ways sport is now part of politics, economics and culture – within nations and across nations. Modern sport played globally, organized globally, commercialized globally, politicized globally and, last but not least, *enjoyed* globally – whatever the local variations, interpretations and nuances – resulted in twentieth-century sport-obsessed global societies with common 'play' pleasures and purposes. It is an obsession that will only grow in the twenty-first century. And it all began in Europe!

NOTES

1. R. Porter, *Enlightenment: Britain and the Creation of the Modern World* (London: Allen Lane, 2000), p.477.
2. Ibid.
3. Ibid., p.479.
4. See J.A Mangan (ed.), *Sport, Europe, Society: Middle-Class Revolutionaries* (London and Portland, OR: Frank Cass, forthcoming).
5. Porter, *Enlightenment*, p.479.
6. See J.A. Mangan, *The Games Ethic and Imperialism: Aspects of the Diffusion of an Ideal* (London and Portland, OR: Frank Cass, 1998), *passim*.
7. Porter, *Enlightenment*, p.489.
8. M. Waters, *Globalization* (London: Routledge, 1996), p.159.
9. M. Ferro, *Colonialization: A Global History* (London: Routledge, 1997), p.350.
10. Waters, *Globalization*, p.160.
11. By way of an excellent illustration, see Dong Jinxia, 'Holding up *More* than Half the Sky: Elite Sport, Women and Society in New China' (unpublished Ph.D. thesis, International Research Centre for Sport, Socialisation and Society, Strathclyde University, 2001). The thesis will be published by Frank Cass in the series: Sport in the Global Society under the title: *Sport, Women and Society in New China: Holding up More than Half the Sky!*
12. Ferro, *Colonization*, p.354.

Notes on Contributors

Peter Beck is Professor of International History at Kingston University, Kingston upon Thames, England. He works on a range of international history topics, including the politics of British sport. His publications include *Scoring for Britain: International Football and International Politics, 1900–1939* (London and Portland, OR: Frank Cass, 1999) and 'Going to War, Peaceful Co-existence or Virtual Membership?: British Football and FIFA, 1928–46', *International Journal of the History of Sport*, 17 (2000).

Hans Bonde is Associate Professor at the University of Southern Denmark. He is currently writing a biography of the internationally renowned Danish youth leader Niels Bukh.

Robert 'Bob' Chappell is a lecturer in the Department of Sport Sciences at Brunel University, London. He has a particular interest in sport in developing countries. He has contributed to various journals and international conferences. Most recently he presented a paper at the 2000 International Society for Comparative Physical Education and Sport in Brisbane, Australia. His passion is basketball, in which he is manager of the Great Britain team for the World University Games.

Paul Darby is a Lecturer in the sociology of sport at Liverpool Hope University College. He has written broadly on the relationship between Europe and Africa as mediated by football. His book exploring the institutional and political development of African football within the Fédération Internationale de Football Association (FIFA), *Africa, Football and FIFA: Politics, Colonialism and Resistance*, will be published by Frank Cass in 2001. He is currently undertaking research on identity, Gaelic sport and the Irish migrant community in Boston and is also Senior Academic Editor of the international journal *Soccer and Society*. He received his doctorate from the University of Ulster in 1997.

Allen Guttmann is the author of a number of books on sports history, the best known of which is *From Ritual to Record* (1978). His most recent books are *Games and Empires* (1994) and *The Erotic in Sports* (1996).

Colm Hickey studied at the former Borough Road College and is a graduate of the University of London. He completed his MA at the University of London, Institute of Education. He is currently Deputy Headteacher of St Bernard's Catholic School, High Wycombe.

Peter Horton is a Lecturer in the School of Education at James Cook University, Townsville. He has previously worked in schools and universities in Singapore, Australia and England. This article is the product of several years' research into the nature and role of sport in Singapore. He has published widely in the area of sport studies, particularly on the nature of sport in post-colonial territories and on Olympic issues.

J.A. Mangan is Director of the International Research Centre for Sport, Socialisation and Society at the University of Strathclyde, Glasgow, and author and editor of many books. He is founder and General Editor of the Cass series Sport in the Global Society and founding and executive academic editor of the Cass journals *The International Journal of the History of Sport, Culture, Sport, Society, Soccer and Society* and *The European Sports History Review*. His internationally acclaimed *Athleticism in the Victorian and Edwardian Public School* and *The Games Ethic and Imperialism* have recently been reprinted by Frank Cass.

Alethea Melling works in widening participation at the University of Central Lancashire and is currently developing girls' football as part of out-of-school hours learning initiatives.

Ha Nam-gil is a professor in the College of Education, Department of Physical Education, Gyeongsang National University, Korea.

Amir Ben-Porat has a Ph.D. from Strathclyde University, Glasgow. He is Associate Professor in the Department of Behavioural Sciences in Ben Gurion University and in the College for Management in Tel Aviv, Israel. His research interests are sport (mainly football), class and state.

Artur Blasio Rambo and Leoman Tesche are Brazilian educationalists with a strong interest in the history of German immigrants to southern Brazil, and have written widely on this subject.

Lee Thompson, author of a number of essays on Japanese sport, is co-author, with Allen Guttmann, of *Japanese Sports: A History* (forthcoming).

Abstracts

Reconstructing the Fatherland: German *Turnen* in Southern Brazil in the Nineteenth and Twentieth Centuries
Leoman Tesche and Artur Blasio Rambo

This chapter deals with the local adaptation of the German *Turnen* Movement in southern Brazil from the mid-nineteenth century until the Second World War. The cultural migration of *Turnen* is prefaced a short description of German immigration into southern Brazil – one of the most important land movements in nineteenth century South America – and involves a detailed analysis of documents associated with sample institutions of the period.

Educators, Imitators, Modernizers: The Arrival and Spread of Modern Sport in Japan
Allen Guttmann and Lee Thompson

When Westerners arrived in late nineteenth-century Japan, they found a rich and varied ludic culture with more or less familiar sports (like archery) and exotically unfamiliar ones (like sumo wrestling). Westerners brought with them their own sports, which were added to the mix of indigenous pastimes. Diffusion of Western sports like athletics and baseball took two major forms. There was direct transmission from British and American educators to their students and from French and German military personnel to the men whom they trained. In this fashion, ballgames spread through private universities like Keiô, Waseda, and Doshisha while fencing and skiing became popular among army officers. There was also indirect transmission as Japan's modernizing elites began to emulate Westerners whom they observed at play.

Confucianism, Imperialism, Nationalism: Modern Sport, Ideology and Korean Culture
J.A. Mangan and Ha Nam-gil

All countries have sports which they have inherited. Korea is no exception. With the expansion of Western imperialism in the second half of the nineteenth century Western sport spread to several continents.

This chapter considers how Western sport was introduced to and spread throughout Korea during the period 1876 to 1945. It explores the influences that ideologies, which emerged in the difficult social and political circumstances of the period, had on the development and diffusion of modern sport. By approaching the history of Korean sport from the perspective of dominant ideologies this chapter offers an original analysis of Korean sport, embracing Confucianism, Imperialism and Nationalism.

Complex Creolization: The Evolution of Modern Sport in Singapore
Peter A. Horton

As an ex-British Imperial territory Singapore still exhibits many features resulting from British influence. Sport, one of the most pervasive cultural exports of the British, played an important part in the new colony. This chapter examines the emergence and development of modern sport in Singapore, and particularly the role of the dominant racial group, the Chinese, in this process. Chinese cultural imperialism ran parallel to the apparently dominant British version. The sport of modern Singapore is thus a complex creolized form of the residual culture left by the British.

Globalization, the Games Ethic and Imperialism: Further Aspects of the Diffusion of an Ideal
J.A. Mangan and Colm Hickey

This chapter adds additional colour to an already variegated historical canvas. It sketches in fresh details of a fundamentally English moral crusade in the guise of the promotion of educational principle and practice, which directly and indirectly had an extraordinary global influence in the late nineteenth and early twentieth centuries, and a later extensive, if sometimes serendipitous, impact on all the inhabited continents during the age of modern global sport. The dissemination of 'Anglo-Saxon' sport can be considered retrospectively, of course, from a number of perspectives, but many period proselytizers saw themselves as moral crusaders. It scarcely needs to be repeated that the participants of the games-playing educational revolution that occurred initially in British public schools (private schools for the privileged) were directly and indirectly responsible, far from exclusively of course, but to a remarkable degree, for a twentieth-century 'global sports culture' of exceptional enthusiasm, commitment and importance involving countless millions across the world. This is both the measure and significance of the cultural diorama in which during this chapter yet another small part of the canvas is painted in for the first time – this being athleticism and the imperial teacher training college.

'Linesmen, Referees and Arbitrators': Politics, Modernization and Soccer in Palestine
Amir Ben-Porat

This chapter deals with the contribution of the British Mandate to the modernization of football in Palestine in the years 1920 to 1948. It is suggested that the policy in Palestine involved non-intervention as long as British interests were not jeopardized. Three non-exclusive modalities are suggested to specify the colonialist (British) and natives' (Jews and Arabs) relationship in football: Linesman, Referee and Arbitrator. Although football was played in Palestine before the British, the latter had a specific effect on the modernization of the game in this part of the world. British teams, mostly related to the army, played football in various cup competitions, while a few individuals played in the 'natives' teams. The British also assisted in organizing the Football Association in Palestine. Furthermore, the British sometimes acted as referee, and in other times as arbiter. The actual modality was determined their general policy and the specific political atmosphere in Palestine at any particular period.

Charging Amazons and Fair Invaders: The 1922 Dick, Kerr's Ladies' Soccer Tour of North America – Sowing Seed
Alethea Melling

In 1999, Jacques M. Henry and Howard P. Comeaux estimated that over half of the 18 million soccer players in America were women; which is probably the highest ratio in the world. Furthermore, there are now 22 coed soccer organizations across 14 states in the United States. Since the Educational Amendments Act of 1972, women's soccer has developed rapidly in America and on a global scale is one of the fastest growing sports. This article examines the beginnings of women's soccer in Britain, the attempts to introduce it to America in 1922, and why initially the sport failed to arouse the interest of American women.

The Soviet Protégé:
Cuba, Modern Sport and Communist Comrades
Bob Chappell

At the 2000 Olympic Games in Sydney, Russia finished second in the medal table with 88 medals, and Cuba ninth with 29 medals. In view of Cuba's population of 11 million people it has achieved remarkable success in international sport, especially at the Olympic Games, the Pan-American Games and the IAAF World Athletics Championships. The ideology of sports development in Cuba is based on former socialist countries and in particular the former Soviet Union. This paper examines the development of sport in Cuba from Pre-revolution Cuba to Revolutionary Cuba, and finally to sport in Cuba in the 1990s and beyond. It also compares the similarity in the organization of sport between the former Soviet Union and Cuba, notably the fact that the ideology of sports development was underpinned by Soviet Marxist philosophy in which sport was of great social and political significance.

From East to West: The Way of the Master – Oriental Martial Arts and Modern European Culture
Hans Bonde

The Chapter deals with to and fro diffusion. It outlines differences and similarities between the master tradition in traditional European crafts and in Japanese martial arts. It argues that the concepts of Zen-inspired martial arts can be used to enhance Western understanding of the transfer of 'tacit knowledge' in the context of the master-apprentice relationship. The popularity of Oriental martial arts is related to the need to cultivate the idea of personalized leadership and ordered rituals at a time when these appear to be declining in modern life due to the increasing mass production of the new post-millennium, increasingly technological, society.

The New Scramble for Africa: The African Football Labour Migration to Europe
Paul Darby

During the last decade top flight European football has witnessed a huge influx of African players. Furthermore, the vast proportion of Africa's elite talent currently play their club football in Europe. For example, of the best ten African players of 1999, as selected the Technical

Development and Press committees of the Confédération Africaine de Football (CAF), eight play in the top level leagues of England, Germany and France. This article sets out to present some preliminary findings on the dynamics of African football labour migration to Europe. In order to set the context, attention is accorded to sketching the European driven diffusion of football to Africa. This is followed by an account of African player migration to a selection of elite European leagues. In particular, the article focuses on the impact the exodus of football talent has had on domestic, national and international football in Africa. The empirical evidence presented within this study is located in a theoretical frame that is rooted in current debates on sport labour migration and globalization. In particular, the study assesses the extent to which African player migration can be informed by theories of imperialism and dependency as well as by Immanuel Wallerstein's explanations of global economic inequality.

More than 'Matches of the Century' for World Footballing Honours: England versus Italy, 1933, 1934 and 1939

Peter J. Beck

The three England–Italy matches played between 1933 and 1939 were viewed and presented within and outside Britain as possessing both a footballing and international political significance, given the fact that the two countries were not only leading footballing nations but also great powers in international affairs. England's good record against Italy, the 1934 and 1938 World Cup winners and 1936 Olympic football gold medallists, reinforced British football's reputation 'masters of the game', even if in reality continuing British claims to dominate the 'world game' were being undermined by a range of factors, most notably British isolationism and the rapid improvement in the game in the wider world.

Select Bibliography

Reconstructing the Fatherland: German *Turnen* in Southern Brazil in the Nineteenth and Twentieth Centuries
Leoman Tesche and Artur Blasio Rambo

F. Altmann, *A Roda. Memoria de um professor* (São Leopoldo, 1991).

M.R. Cantarino, 'A Educacao Fisica no Brasil', in H. Ueberhorst (Hrsg), *Geschichte der Leibesübungen* (Berlin, 1989).

E.N. Coceicao, *Maconaria. Raizes Historicas e Filosoficas* (São Paulo, 1998)

E.L. Colussi, *A Maconaria Gaucha no Seculo XIX* (Passo Fundo, 1998).

L.P. DaCosta, 'Bodies from Brazil: Fascist Aesthetics in a South American Setting', in J.A. Mangan (ed.), *Superman Supreme: Fascist Body as Political Icon – Global Fascism* (London and Portland, OR: Frank Cass, 2000).

L. Telles, *Do Deutscher Hilfsverein ao Colégio Farroupilha- 1858/1974* (Porto Alegre, 1974).

Educators, Imitators, Modernizers: The Arrival and Spread of Modern Sport in Japan
Allen Guttmann and Lee Thompson

S.N. Eisenstadt, *Japanese Civilization* (Chicago: University of Chicago Press, 1996).

A. Guttmann, *Games and Empires* (New York: Columbia University Press, 1994).

E. Hobsbawm and T. Ranger, *The Invention of Tradition* (Cambridge: Cambridge University Press, 1983).

D.H. Shively (ed.), *Tradition and Modernization in Japanese Culture* (Princeton: Princeton University Press, 1971).

H.P. Varley, *Japanese Culture*, 3rd edition (Honolulu: University of Hawaii Press, 1984).

Confucianism, Imperialism, Nationalism: Modern Sport, Ideology and Korean Culture
J.A. Mangan and Ha Nam-gil

Ch'on-sok Oh, *Hanguk-ui sinkyoyuksa* (A History of Korea's New Education) (Seoul: Hyunda Kyoukchongsu Co., 1964).

G. Cubitt (ed.), *Imagining Nations* (Manchester: Manchester University Press, 1998).

Hyon-song Na, *Hanguk undongkyonggisa* (The History of Athletic Competition in Korea) (Seoul: Pomun, 1985).

P. McIntosh, *Sport in Society* (London: West London Press, 1987).

Maeng-ryol Cho and Hui-dok No, *Cheyuksa* (History of Physical Education) (Seoul: Hyong-sol Publishing, 1998).

J.A. Mangan, *The Cultural Bond: Sport, Empire, Society* (London: Frank Cass, 1992).

J. Richards (ed.), *Imperialism and Juvenile Literature* (Manchester: Manchester University Press, 1989).

Complex Creolization: The Evolution of Modern Sport in Singapore
Peter A. Horton

J.N. Brownfoot, 'Emancipation, Exercise and Imperialism: Girls and the Games Ethic in Colonial Malaya', *International Journal of the History of Sport*, 7, 1 (1990).

J.Cleverly, *The Schooling of China: Tradition and Modernity in Chinese Education* (Sydney: Allen & Unwin, 1991).

Fan Hong, *Footbinding, Feminism and Freedom: The Liberation of Women's Bodies in Modern China* (London and Portland, OR: Frank Cass, 1997).

P.A. Horton, '"Padang or Paddock"? A Comparative View of Colonial Sport in Two Imperial Territories', *International Journal of the History of Sport*, 14, 1 (April 1997).

W.E. Makepeace, R. St. J. Braddell and G.S. Brookes (eds.), *One Hundred Years of Singapore* (London: Murray, 1921).

J.A. Mangan, *Athleticism in the Victorian and Edwardian Public Schools: The Emergence and Consolidation of an Educational Ideology* (Cambridge: Cambridge University Press, 1981 and London and

Portland, OR: Frank Cass, 2000).

J.A. Mangan, *The Games Ethic and Imperialism Aspects of the Diffusion of an Ideal* (Harmondsworth: Penguin/Viking, 1986; and London and Portland, OR: Frank Cass, 1999).

Song, Ong Siang, *A Hundred Years of the Chinese in Singapore* (Singapore: Oxford University Press, 1923).

C.M. Turnbull, *A History of Singapore 1819-1988*, 2nd edition (Singapore: Oxford University Press, 1988).

E. Wijeysingha, *The Story of Raffles Institution, 1823-1985* (Singapore: Pioneer Books, 1989).

C.H. Yen, *A Social History of the Chinese in Singapore and Malaya, 1800-1911* (Singapore: Oxford University Press, 1986).

Globalization, the Games Ethic and Imperialism: Further Aspects of the Diffusion of an Ideal
J.A. Mangan and Colm Hickey

C. Hickey, 'Athleticism and the London Training Colleges' (unpublished Ph.D. thesis, University of Strathclyde, forthcoming).

J.A. Mangan, *Athleticism in the Victorian and Edwardian Public School: The Emergence and Consolidation of an Educational Ideology* (Cambridge: Cambridge University Press, 1981).

J.A. Mangan, 'Imitating their Betters and Disassociating from their Inferiors: Grammar Schools and the Games Ethic in the Late 19th and Early 20th Centuries', *The Fitness of the Nation: Physical and Health Education in the 19th and 20th Centuries*, Proceedings of the 1982 Annual Conference of the History of Education Society of Great Britain, History of Education Society, Leicester, 1983.

J.A. Mangan, '"Oars and the Man": Pleasure and Purpose in Victorian and Edwardian Cambridge', *British Journal of Sports History*, 1, 1 (1984).

J.A. Mangan, '"Lamentable Barbarians and Pitiful Sheep": Rhetoric of protest and pleasure in late Victorian and Edwardian Oxbridge', in T. Winnifrith and C. Barnet (eds.), *Leisure in Art and Literature* (London: Macmillan, 1992).

J.A. Mangan and Colm Hickey, 'English Elementary Education Revisited and Revised: Drill and Athleticism in Tandem', in J.A.

Mangan (ed.), *Sport in Europe: Politics, Class, Gender. The European Sports History Review*, Vol.1 (London and Portland, OR: Frank Cass, 1999).

J.A. Mangan, *The Games Ethic and Imperialism: Aspects of the Diffusion of an Ideal* (London and Portland, OR: Frank Cass, 1999).

J.A. Mangan and C. Hickey, 'Athleticism in the Service of the Proletariat: Preparation for the English Elementary School and the Extension of Middle-Class Manliness', *Making European Masculinities, The European Sports History Review*, Vol.2 (London and Portland, OR: Frank Cass, 2000).

'Linesmen, Referees and Arbitrators': Politics, Modernization and Soccer in Palestine
Amir Ben-Porat

R. Giulianotti and J. Williams (eds.), *Games Without Frontiers* (Aldershot: Arena, 1994).

A. Guttmann, *From Ritual to Record* (New York: Columbia, 1978).

J.A. Mangan, *The Games Ethic and Imperialism* (London and Portland, OR: Frank Cass, 1999)

J.A. Mangan (ed.), *The Cultural Bond: Sport Empire Society* (London: Frank Cass, 1992).

T. Mason, *Passion of the People?* (London: Routledge, 1998).

A. Ben-Porat, 'The Commodification of Football in Israel', *International Review of Sociology*, 33, 3 (1998).

A.J. Sherman, *Mandate Days* (London: Thames and Hudson, 1995).

C. Sykes, *Crossroad to Israel* (Indiana: Bloomington, 1973).

Charging Amazons and Fair Invaders: The 1922 Dick, Kerr's Ladies' Soccer Tour of North America – Sowing Seed
Alethea Melling

S. Cahn, *Coming on Strong: Gender and Sexuality in Twentieth Century Women's Sport* (Massachusetts: Harvard University Press, 1994).

J. Hargreaves, *Sporting Females* (London: Routledge, 1994).

S. Lopez, *Women on the Ball* (London: Scarlet, 1997).

G. J. Newsham, *In a League of Their Own!* (London: Scarlet, 1997).

The Soviet Protégé: Cuba, Modern Sport and Communist Comrades
Bob Chappell

S. Caldwell and E. Hatchwell, *Cuba* (Oxford: Unwin Bros, 1996).

R. Chappell and J. Coghlan (eds.), *Sport for All in Developing Countries* (London: Brunel University, 1996).

P. Pettavino and G. Pye, 'Sport in Cuba', in L. Chalip, A. Johnson and L. Stachura (eds.), *National Sports Policies: An International Handbook* (London: Greenwood Press, 1996).

R. Pickering, 'Sport in Cuba', in J. Riordan (ed.), *Sport under Communism* (London: Hurst, 1980).

J. Sugden, *Boxing in Society: An International Analysis* (Manchester: Manchester University Press, 1996).

J. Sugden and A. Tomlinson, 'Hustling in Havana', in G. McFee, W. Murphy and G. Whannel (eds.), *Leisure Cultures: Values, Genders, Lifestyles* (Brighton: LSA Publication, 1995).

From East to West: The Way of the Master – Oriental Martial Arts and Modern European Culture
Hans Bonde

H. Dreyfus and S. Dreyfus, *Intuitiv ekspertise* (Copenhagen: Munksgård, 1991).

E. Herrigel, *Bueskydning og Zen* (Haslev: Gyldendal, 1971).

J. Lave, and E. Wenger, *Situated Learning – Legitimate Peripheral Participation* (Cambridge: Cambridge University Press, 1991).

T. Leggett, *A First Zen Reader* (Tokyo: Charles E. Tuttle Company, 1960).

T. Leggett, *Zen and the Ways* (London: Routledge & Kegan Paul, 1978).

M. Polyani, *The Tacit Dimension* (London: Routledge & Kegan Paul, 1967).

L. Ratti and A. Westbrook, *Secrets of the Samurai (A Survey of the Martial Arts of Feudal Japan)* (Tokyo: Charles E. Tuttle Company, 1973).

The New Scramble for Africa: The African Football Labour Migration to Europe
Paul Darby

J. Bale and J. Maguire, *The Global Sports Arena: Athletic Talent Migration in an Interdependent World* (London and Portland, OR: Frank Cass, 1994).

J. Bale, and J. Sang, *Kenyan Running: Movement Culture, Geography and Global Change* (London and Portland, OR: Frank Cass, 1996).

M. Broere and R. van der Drift, *Football Afrique!* (Oxford: Worldview Publishing, 1997).

P. Darby, 'Football, Colonial Doctrine and Indigenous Resistance: Mapping the Political Persona of FIFA's African Constituency', *Culture, Sport, Society*, 3, 1 (2000).

P. Darby, *Africa, Football and FIFA: Politics, Colonialism and Resistance* (London and Portland, OR: Frank Cass, forthcoming).

A.G. Frank, *Capitalism and Underdevelopment in Latin America* (New York: Monthly Review Press, 1969).

J. Maguire and B. Pearton, 'Global Sport and Migration Patterns of France '98 World Cup Finals Players: Some Preliminary Observations', in J. Garland, D. Malcolm and M. Rowe (eds.), *The Future of Football: Challenges for the Twenty-First Century* (London and Portland, OR: Frank Cass, 2000).

A. Ricci (ed.), *African Football: Yearbook 2000*, 3rd edition (Rome: Prosports, 2000).

A. Versi, *Football in Africa* (London: Collins, 1986).

I. Wallerstein, *The Capitalist World Economy* (Cambridge: Cambridge University Press, 1979).

For World Footballing Honours: England versus Italy, 1933, 1934 and 1939
Peter J. Beck

P.J. Beck, *Scoring for Britain: International Football and International Politics, 1900–1939* (London and Portland, OR: Frank Cass, 1999).

A. Krüger, 'Strength through joy: the culture of consent under fascism, Nazism and Francoism', in J. Riordan and A. Krüger (eds.), *The International Politics of Sport in the 20th. Century* (London: E & FN

Spon, 1999).

R. Lamb, *Mussolini and the British* (London: John Murray, 1997).

P. Lanfranchi, 'Bologna: the Team that Shook the World', *International Journal of the History of Sport*, 8 (1991).

P. Lanfranchi, 'Frankreich und Italien', C. Eisenberg (ed.), *Fussball, soccer, calcio: ein englischer Sport auf seinem Weg um die Welt* (Munich: DTV, 1997).

B. Murray, *The World's Game: A History of Soccer* (Urbana, IL: University of Illinois Press, 1998).

D. Reynolds, *Britannia Overruled: British Policy and World Power in the 20th Century* (Harlow: Longman, 1991).

S. Rous, *Football Worlds: A Lifetime in Sport* (London: Faber and Faber, 1978).

A. Teja, 'Italian Sport and International Relations under Fascism', in P. Arnaud and J. Riordan (eds.), *Sport and International Politics: The Impact of Fascism and Communism on Sport* (London: E & FN Spon, 1998), pp.147–70.

J. Walvin, *The People's Game: A Social History of British Football* (London: Allen Lane, 1994 revised edition).

Index

Titles of Related Interest

Making European Masculinities:
Sport, Europe, Gender
The European Sports History Review, Volume 2
J A Mangan, *University of Strathclyde* (Ed)

This collection of original studies on the making of modern masculinity discusses the relationship between sport and the development of European male identity from the nineteenth to the twentieth century.

224 pages   2000
0 7146 5089 7   cloth
0 7146 8130 X   paper

Sport in Europe: Politics, Class, Gender
The European Sports History Review, Volume 1
J A Mangan, *University of Strathclyde* (Ed)

As sport has grown, progressively replacing religion, in its power to excite passion, provide emotional escape, offer fraternal (and increasingly sororital) bonding, it has come to loom larger and larger in the lives of Europeans and others, and become an inescapable reality linking public environment with intimate experience. This collection considers the evolution of modern sport in Europe and examines its relationship with politics, gender and class.

280 pages   1999
0 7146 4946 5   cloth
0 7146 8005 2   paper

FRANK CASS PUBLISHERS
Crown House, 47 Chase Side, Southgate, London N14 5BP
Tel: +44 (0)20 8920 2100 Fax: +44 (0)20 8447 8548 E-mail: info@frankcass.com
NORTH AMERICA
5824 NE Hassalo Street, Portland, OR 97213 3644, USA
Tel: 800 944 6190 Fax: 503 280 8832 E-mail: cass@isbs.com
Website: www.frankcass.com

Making Men
Rugby and Masculine Identity

John Nauright, *University of Queensland*, and
Timothy J L Chandler, *Kent State University, Ohio* (Eds)

> *'This book is a "must" read for students of rugby, as well as those with interests in gender and the politics of identity, and it will lead the way in future discussions of sport and invented traditions.'*
> **Sporting Traditions**

> *'Highly recommended not only to all those who fashion rugby but also to all those interested in the role of sport in the sociocultural process.'*
> **CHOICE**

272 pages 6 illus 1996 repr. 1999
0 7146 4637 7 cloth
0 7146 4156 1 paper

European Heroes
Myth, Identity, Sport

J A Mangan, *University of Strathclyde* **Richard Holt**, *University of Leuven, Belgium* and **Pierre Lanfranchi**, *De Montfort University* (Eds)

The contributors to this collection of essays explore the symbolic meanings that have been attached to sport in Europe by considering some of the mythic heroes who have dominated the sporting landscapes of their own countries, including W G Grace, Jean Borotra, Max Schmeling, Raymond Kopa and Gina Bartoli. The ambition is to understand what these icons stood for in the eyes of those who watched or read about them.

192 pages 1996
0 7146 4578 8 cloth
0 7146 4125 1 paper

FRANK CASS PUBLISHERS
Crown House, 47 Chase Side, Southgate, London N14 5BP
Tel: +44 (0)20 8920 2100 Fax: +44 (0)20 8447 8548 E-mail: info@frankcass.com
NORTH AMERICA
5824 NE Hassalo Street, Portland, OR 97213 3644, USA
Tel: 800 944 6190 Fax: 503 280 8832 E-mail: cass@isbs.com
Website: www.frankcass.com

Tribal Identities

Nationalism, Europe, Sport

J A Mangan, *University of Strathclyde* (Ed)

> *'This volume represents an important and welcome contribution to the
> literature on the creation and reproduction of national identity and
> nationalism. The book can be read with interest by specialists and
> nonspecialists, including upper level undergraduates and graduate
> students.'*
>
> **Nationalism & Ethnic Politics**

> *'A fascinating insight into the links between sport and nationalism in
> Europe and beyond. An important and valuable text.'*
>
> **Contemporary British History**

248 pages   1996
0 7146 4666 0 cloth
0 7146 4201 0 paper

The Nordic World

Sport in Society

Henrik Meinander, *University of Helsinki* and
J A Mangan, *University of Strathclyde* (Eds)

This volume explores the political, social and aesthetic impact of modern sport
on Northern Europe, and the relationship between the Nordic nations and
Nordic cultures, attitudes to the body and the evolution of specific Nordic
visions of sport. *The Nordic World* shows why sport has played such an
important part in both twentieth-century Nordic society and contemporary
European culture.

200 pages   1998
0 7146 4825 6 cloth
0 7146 4391 2 paper

FRANK CASS PUBLISHERS
Crown House, 47 Chase Side, Southgate, London N14 5BP
Tel: +44 (0)20 8920 2100 Fax: +44 (0)20 8447 8548 E-mail: info@frankcass.com
NORTH AMERICA
5824 NE Hassalo Street, Portland, OR 97213 3644, USA
Tel: 800 944 6190 Fax: 503 280 8832 E-mail: cass@isbs.com
Website: www.frankcass.com

Athleticism in the Victorian and Edwardian Public School

New in Paperback

The Emergence and Consolidation of an Educational Ideology

J A Mangan, *University of Strathclyde*

Foreword by **Sheldon Rothblatt** with an introduction by **Jeffrey Richards** and a new introduction by the author

Games obsessed the Victorian and Edwardian public schools. This obsession has become widely known as athleticism. When it appeared in 1981, this book was the first major study of the games ethos which dominated the lives of many Victorian and Edwardian public school boys. Written with Professor Mangan's customary panache, it has become a classic, the seminal work on the social and cultural history of modern sport.

380 pages 2nd revised edition 2000
0 7146 8043 5 paper

The Games Ethic and Imperialism

Aspects of the Diffusion of an Ideal

J A Mangan, *University of Strathclyde*

This book is far more than a description of the imperial spread of public school games: it is a consideration of hegemony and patronage, ideals and idealism, educational values and aspirations, cultural assimilation and adaptation and, perhaps most fascinating of all, the dissemination throughout the empire of the hugely influential moralistic ideology athleticism.

240 pages   1985; 2nd revised edition   1998
0 7146 4399 8 paper

FRANK CASS PUBLISHERS
Crown House, 47 Chase Side, Southgate, London N14 5BP
Tel: +44 (0)20 8920 2100 Fax: +44 (0)20 8447 8548 E-mail: info@frankcass.com
NORTH AMERICA
5824 NE Hassalo Street, Portland, OR 97213 3644, USA
Tel: 800 944 6190 Fax: 503 280 8832 E-mail: cass@isbs.com
Website: www.frankcass.com